Theodor Mundt, Thérèse J Radford

Count Mirabeau

A Historical Novel

Theodor Mundt, Thérèse J Radford

Count Mirabeau
A Historical Novel

ISBN/EAN: 9783337027773

Printed in Europe, USA, Canada, Australia, Japan

Cover: Foto ©Thomas Meinert / pixelio.de

More available books at **www.hansebooks.com**

BY

THEODOR MUNDT,

AUTHOR OF "ROBESPIERRE," "THE MATADOR," "NO DIVORCE," "CARMOLA; OR, THE REBAPTIZED,"
ETC., ETC.

TRANSLATED FROM THE GERMAN, BY

THÉRÈSE J. RADFORD.

COMPLETE IN ONE VOLUME.

With Illustrations.

NEW YORK:
D. APPLETON AND COMPANY,
443 & 445 BROADWAY.
1868.

CONTENTS.

COUNT MIRABEAU.

THE FRIENDS AT AUTEUIL.

CHAPTER I.

THE COUNTRY-SEAT OF MADAME HELVETIUS.

At the entrance of the Bois de Boulogne, scarcely a mile from Paris, is the village of Auteuil, containing the celebrated country-seat formerly owned by the poet Boileau, and in which the later proprietors received the most celebrated men of France. For thirteen years it was occupied by Madame Helvetius, one of the most amiable women of her country, who had bought the property after the death of her husband, the famous freethinker and philosopher. She had made the villa a social rendezvous for her more immediate friends, and also for those who were influential or distinguished in Paris. In this unpretending and peaceful residence had been established a learned and very interesting society, but which the government of France considered very dangerous, though controlled by the gentle influence of a woman, who displayed her authority only by promoting the happiness of her guests, and rendering them more intimate.

Since the days of Madame Geoffrin, who, for nearly half a century, fostered all native and foreign genius in Paris, there was no social circle to be compared with that of Madame Helvetius at Auteuil. Its members entertained the ideas disseminated by Claude Adrien Helvetius in his celebrated work "Of the Mind"—a production violently attacked by the clergy and the Parliament, and at last burned by the public executioner. Helvetius's friends, who, like Diderot and Baron d'Holbach, had aided in the composition of this work, remained faithful to the philosophy of its reputed author, and his widow truly and lovingly revered his memory. Younger men had associated themselves with them, as the Marquis de Condorcet, the amiable and witty Chamfort, the physician Cabanis, who for some time had made Auteuil his home, and, latterly, Count Gabriel Riquetti de Mirabeau, introduced by Chamfort, and from whom great things were expected.

The rural drawing-room of Madame Helvetius, in which, as we have intimated, affairs were often discussed that at Versailles seemed very suspicious, was consecrated by the apparent innocence of its proprietor; for she united cheerfulness, grace, and intellect, with childlike goodness of heart, which made itself felt at every opportunity, and exerted on all about her a mild and happy influence. The extraordinary beauty of her youth had not yet disappeared. Her expressive eyes fascinated those on whom their glances fell; and if Elise Helvetius, in the exciting conversations of her company, appeared as the guiding spirit who revealed that soon something new and great must occur to save the French nation from degeneracy and ruin, she presently assumed a bantering and merry tone, and, by her quick repartees and charming fancies, banished the political anxiety and gravity of her friends. Her person was tall, and her presence imposing. In her outward bearing she never permitted that her aristocratic origin should be forgotten—that she was the daughter of the Count de Ligneville, while a certain idyllic naturalness of manner manifested her preference for country life and occupation.

This remarkable woman had added, as if by contrast, a sort of background to her polished and philosophic drawing-room; for she cultivated a farm, to which she herself industriously attended. It was, however, her poultry-yard upon which she bestowed especial care, daily spending several hours with her chickens, ducks, and geese. Her goldfinches received extraordinary favor, and their training was greatly admired. Singing birds hung in decorated cages on the outer walls of the house, often interrupting the conversation within by their warbling songs. There was also no lack of cats and dogs in this country-seat; and, next to her birds, Madame Helvetius loved her cats, making great pets of them. She surrounded herself also with rare varieties of other animals, and the complete harmony that reigned in her family was regarded with wonder by her friends, who ascribed it to some magic charm which she exerted over all around her.

On this first day of our narrative, Madame Helvetius withdrew sooner than usual from her favorite employment, which occupied so considerable a portion of her mornings, as preparation had to be made for the reception of guests whom she expected at dinner. Two motives had induced her to send invitations for this particular day. The celebrated Dr. Benjamin Franklin, for many years one of her particular admirers, was to dine at the villa, which more especially delighted her other friends, because the public demonstrations and attentions with which Franklin had been overwhelmed during his second sojourn in Paris, had made private social intercourse with him somewhat difficult.

The preliminaries for the acknowledgment of the independence of the United States of America had been signed by the plenipotentiaries of Great Britain as well as by Franklin, representing his native country, the preceding year (1783); and now the full and formal recognition of those States produced much excitement among the Parisians. In every quarter the effect of this national admission of the right of a people to change or modify their government was deeply felt, and it was the fashion of the time to load the venerable Franklin with distinguished honors. By reason of his popularity, Madame Helvetius had therefore to make great efforts to secure his presence for this day, which for a particular reason her good-natured and amiable coquetry had chosen. She was to celebrate her sixty-fifth birthday, and she wished thus to remind Franklin of her age; for his friendship for her had increased until he had made her an offer of his hand. She desired him, therefore, to join in a celebration which delicately declared her reluctance to a new marriage.

Dr. Franklin, who was already entering his seventy-eighth year, had wooed the amiable widow of Helvetius, when, eight years before, he visited Paris for the first time. Elise had then assured him, with her natural frankness, that she would on no account marry him. This declaration she firmly repeated when he renewed his offer, although their friendship remained uninterrupted. Franklin had had a rival in Turgot, the former minister of Louis XVI.; but death had removed this noble competitor, and the cheerful old man, on his return to Paris, reappeared in the lists of love.

Although Madame Helvetius intended thus to give prominence to the fact of her advanced age, she could not resist a very interesting temptation in reference to her toilet, with which she began gravely to occupy herself. At the moment when she considered it her duty to discourage her old lover, she yielded to the fancy of rendering herself as attractive as possible by appropriating the style of head-dress which had lately been made fashionable by the young Queen Marie Antoinette. Until now Elise had been faithful in imitating the toilets of the regency, and as she had always appeared well in them, she did not hesitate to retain them even in her old age. The gold powder on her beautiful blond hair had always made an irresistible impression, and the hoop she by no means despised, as well as the patches, sprinkled with diamond dust, that were worn on the face. Now, however, in a merry humor, she arranged her coiffure differently, which, of course, required an entire revolution in the rest of her dress. This was the "coiffure à la jardinière," which M. Leonard, the celebrated hair-dresser of the queen, had invented. It consisted of a cloth raised very high, artistically folded and twisted, and surrounded with vegetables of various kinds, such as small artichokes, cabbages, carrots, and turnips. With the assistance of her maid, she completed her toilet, and stood laughingly before the mirror, to criticise her appearance, but found no reason to be dissatisfied with it. The new mode seemed to please her so well that she was about attempting some ingenious improvements, when the footman announced the arrival of two of her expected guests.

Cabanis and Chamfort were the friends first in the drawing-room of Madame Helvetius, and they were both most cordially received.

"We are taking advantage of the rights of good neighbors, in being impertinently punctual!" began Chamfort, approaching and respectfully kissing the small white hand held out to him.

"Quite the contrary, gentlemen," replied Madame Helvetius, with her charming smile, "I really do not find that you act as good neighbors and faithful friends. I always imagined that you had taken up your residence here at Auteuil, that I might enjoy your society. But when I invite you to a solemn dinner, is that any reason why you absent yourselves from our usual friendly and sociable breakfast? Is that right? Our good Dr. Cabanis may perhaps be excused, for he practises in the village, and is overrun with patients. But yet he ought to remember that I belong to the number, having appointed him my physician in ordinary. Why did you pay me no visit this morning, Dr. Cabanis?" She approached the young man, who was standing dreamily at the other end of the room, and, taking his hand and drawing him toward an easy-chair, she seated herself opposite, and motioned Chamfort to take a chair beside her.

Cabanis was a man of scarcely twenty-seven years, appearing even younger on account of his slender figure, and of a fair, transparent complexion. At the same time his whole manner expressed suffering, owing partly to the fatiguing studies to which he devoted himself, and partly to a nature prone to lose itself in subtle speculations. His friend Chamfort presented a peculiar contrast. He had passed his forty-second year. In person he was firm and powerful; his countenance, surprisingly handsome; his regular features indicated as much intellect as amiability, the principal expression being that of an attractive gentleness; yet they easily changed, indicating a biting sarcasm, wit, and quickness of apprehension. In his dress, Chamfort was, as usual, negligent, and even his linen was rather soiled. The invitation he had received, expressly announced for a festive occasion, had not induced him to correct his carelessness in that respect, which he ascribed to absence of vanity and indifference to general society. On the other hand, Cabanis, who was always most carefully attired, seemed to have made it a point to honor the dinner of his friend Madame Helvetius by a most elegant toilet. "In fact," said Dr. Cabanis, with his somewhat melancholy smile, "during the whole morning I was engaged with a patient. A beginner like myself, who commences to practise in a small place, considers it quite an event when a poor woman has an inflammation, and he can attend to her, and at the same time procure bread for her hungry children."

"Yes, it is true, our friend Cabanis begins his

practice with all kinds of poor, fevered people," Chamfort interrupted, in his sarcastic manner. "He is a real child of the times, for that will soon be the principal occupation of the world, and especially in this hungry France."

"Tell me, dear Chamfort, where were you this morning?" replied Madame Helvetius, contemplating him with friendly pleasure. "For if you cannot give a satisfactory excuse, I take it that you have broken an earnest compact with me. You came to Auteuil to be my guest, nay, to consider yourself as my boarder, only I could not find quarters for you in my small villa; but you ought to consider that an advantage, otherwise you would have been my prisoner, and I should have grudged every hour you passed elsewhere."

A glance of profound gratitude beamed in Chamfort's eyes, and for a moment his features assumed their mild yet fervent expression. But suddenly recovering himself, he said, lightly: "I could not come this morning because I was busy with court interests. Not the court I wish always to pay you, my dearest lady, but that of Versailles —of their most Christian majesties King Louis XVI. and Queen Marie Antoinette. As friend Cabanis has been working for the poor sick people, so I have been at work for their superiors. Etienne Montgolfier was with me, and I assisted him in the preparations for his balloon, the new and wonderful invention. Their majesties have ordered him to let it ascend at Auteuil. The whole court is to be here this afternoon to witness the magnificent spectacle for the third time. They cannot enough admire an object that rises by its own weight. At Versailles no one can ascend unless with great difficulty, but Montgolfier's machine demonstrates quite simply that it is very easy for any one, even without influence or intrigue, to rise to the clouds. The curious court have no presentiment that the 'Montgolfière' is only the precursor of something that will move by-and-by in its own strength, and make good its pretensions to overlook the earth—I mean the 'people.' Do they not resemble the balloon beginning to tremble with its own power of motion, ready to take flight at the first signal? These

were the thoughts that occupied me while assisting my friend Montgolfier. It is also said that the Duke de Chartres will graciously take an air-voyage to-day. Is not my excuse sufficient, dear friend? Montgolfier intends paying his respects to you, and offering seats to yourself and all your company, to view the ascension?"

"Is it possible?" cried Madame Helvetius, in astonishment, naïvely clasping her hands. "What news you announce to me in one breath! And all this without my knowledge happens in this small lantern-like Auteuil? Truly, I almost fancy myself a hermit in a forest hut, and feel quite solitary—as if, in fact, abandoned by all."

"I had imagined the contrary, noticing that new head-dress," said Chamfort, pointing with a light motion of his hands to the ornaments on the lady's head, and bowing as if paying her homage. "I thought our amiable friend had made her arrangements, festively to represent our Auteuil at the royal visit; for the toilet worn to-day by the fair widow of our great Helvetius is nothing more nor less than an acknowledgment of the prevailing fashions. But I must compliment you, madame, and remark that it becomes you exceedingly, and aids in symbolizing most gracefully all your charms. You may wear cabbages and carrots in your beautiful hair, for you are the representative of pure and noble nature, and your husband wrote 'Of the Mind'—now mind must always be the support of nature. But at court there is at present neither the one nor the other, and the vegetables crowning proud heads have a bad effect and trouble the people."

"You are altogether too wicked, Chamfort," replied Madame Helvetius, rather excitedly. "How can you drag every thing into politics, even the innocent toilet of the ladies? In this instance I prefer my gentle Cabanis. He has never scolded me on account of my coiffure, and, I have no doubt, thinks it quite suitable that a country lady, such as I have become, should rather adorn herself with fresh vegetables from her garden than with enormous powdered curls."

"I am inclined to acknowledge the new style of our friend in its highest signification," cried

Cabanis, whose pale face was momentarily enlivened by a smile. "I see the symbol of better times—of liberty and equality—if the fashions at Auteuil and Versailles begin to assimilate. The very fact of the royal party coming to this village shows that extraordinary changes are at hand. Did you ever before hear of the king and queen visiting a place ignorant of court etiquette?—especially Auteuil, that has so bad a reputation with our rulers since we, people of enlightened views, have made our residence here? And, as if to confirm some new bond of friendship, our lady-president has adopted the modes of Queen Marie Antoinette. This suggests decidedly some secret occurrences; and, if I did not see Madame Helvetius's truthful eyes, I could almost fancy that treachery was at work, and that 'la Société libre des Égoïstes,' * as our circle of friends is called, is to be betrayed into the hands of our enemies."

Madame Helvetius, whose natural cheerfulness easily interpreted and patronized such pleasantry, interrupted it by hearty laughter, in which both the gentlemen joined. It was difficult to resist the contagion of her merriment. She seemed to possess all the unrestrained charm of youth.

"That is really a good idea," she said, still laughing. "The profound melancholy that possessed M. Cabanis on his first arrival at Auteuil seems already to have vanished, thanks to our pure atmosphere, and he has become quite a jocose character. But I must own," she continued, more gravely, "that from day to day I feel my respect for Queen Marie Antoinette increasing. I am attracted by the naturalness that shows itself in all we hear of her. She is certainly a noble woman, aiming at that which is best and highest; and, if her influence alone governed the king, she would guide him in the path of right, and finally lead him back to his people. And is she not herself an advance champion of the new times, in her fight with the old dragon Etiquette? By her blooming youth and loveliness she has destroyed this monster. Has she not thus given the

first blow to the aristocracy of France, who were always the origin of what was most hurtful to society? That the king and queen with their suite come to such a place as Auteuil must be considered as a new victory the queen has gained over the old court party. She wishes all around her to have more liberty—to have less constraint forced upon them—she desires gradually to loosen the prejudices that weighed them down, and entirely separated them from the people and all national life. She is benevolent and kind to all, and likes to assist in every new attempt to benefit and even to amuse the people. For the pension M. Etienne Montgolfier receives for his new invention he is indebted to her."

"I am another instance of the queen's condescension to struggling genius of the present day," said Chamfort, with a curious expression of countenance. "My tragedy, 'Mustapha and Zeangir,' was acted before the court at Fontainebleau a few weeks ago, and Marie Antoinette was so much delighted with it that she ordered the author an annuity of twelve hundred francs. I had demanded nothing, but could not very well refuse the bounty of the beautiful young queen. I only heard of my unexpected fortune this morning, but at Paris it was known yesterday, and proved my misfortune, as the sequel will show. I concealed from you the fact that my tragedy was to be played yesterday, for the first time in public, at the Théâtre Français. If you had known it, you would have had no rest, and permitted me none, until I took you to Paris; but you must acknowledge the correctness of my misgiving when I tell you that my production completely failed. At the conclusion, the audience drummed and hissed as if the last day had come for the poor author. The sad news I received this morning by express. The critics think that the play would not have been so harshly treated but for its extraordinary success at court. The author was punished at Paris for the queen's favor. The voice of opposition against the higher grades of society, and especially against Marie Antoinette, is becoming louder, and the public consider it a duty to condemn what she applauds. Here I sit, with my

* The Free Society of Egotists.

twelve hundred francs in my pocket, on the ruins of my first and last tragedy. Yet it is better than my comedies, particularly 'L'Indienne' and 'Le Marchand de Smyrne,' which, notwithstanding their want of merit, seem to sustain themselves on the stage. In my 'Mustapha and Zeangir' I intended to give a sublime creation in the style of Racine, and that was a hypocritical frivolity on my part, so that the condemnation of the piece is after all nothing but justice. No one has a right to assume what he cannot sincerely defend. The court rewarded me because they nursed the agreeable deception that the days of pathetic court tragedy had not yet passed, and that the national poets would again begin to warble with as much art, learning, and adulation, as during the despotic reign of Louis XIV. But the people, who are becoming almost too acute, tore away my disguise, threw it into my face, and left me but the poor satisfaction of jingling my pension in my pocket. Have I not received my deserts?"

At this moment the conversation was interrupted by the noise of an approaching carriage. Madame Helvetius hastened to a window to see which of her guests were coming.

"There is my old Franklin!" she exclaimed. "The one sitting at his side is the Marquis Condorcet—our 'snow-covered Vulcan,' as D'Alembert always called him. Opposite is Count Mirabeau. The latter is springing from the carriage to aid, with filial tenderness, Dr. Franklin; but the old man refuses all assistance to descend, and is proud of the youth of his seventy-seven years. How he is stamping on the ground after his ride, almost making it shake! See how straight and firm my old Benjamin still walks!" She could no longer restrain her impatience, but hurried to the entrance-hall, followed by Chamfort and Cabanis.

Franklin, immediately on entering the house, beheld his old friend, and uttered a cry of joy. He clasped her tenderly to his heart; but the embrace was so prolonged that Madame Helvetius withdrew herself half indignantly, pushing him somewhat forcibly away, that she might also greet Condorcet and Mirabeau.

"It seems I am not so welcome as formerly to my friend Elise," said Franklin, laughingly, as they entered the drawing-room. "I am not permitted to retain her two minutes in my arms, even after so long an absence! Perhaps I am also expected to apologize for appearing at her dinner in my plain dress, just as I am received at Versailles. A dress which is, so to say, a part of myself, will I hope be equally tolerated at Auteuil." Franklin pointed somewhat complaisantly to the garments he was accustomed to wear. His brown cloth coat, already often recognized in Paris society, and his smooth silver hair and broad-brimmed hat, added to the peculiarity of his appearance. His whole costume was that of an American farmer, and when it suddenly presented itself in the drawing-rooms of Paris and Versailles it contrasted forcibly with the embroidered and glittering vestments, and the powdered and highly-perfumed hair, demanded by the fashion of the times. His style was a novelty, and as such had great success, extending its charms particularly to the ladies, who, at the brilliant festivals given in his honor, tried the most extraordinary and coquettish arts to attract the attention of the transatlantic philosopher and apostle of liberty.

Madame Helvetius looked at him so long and with such undisguised pleasure, that Franklin was obliged to acknowledge that he retained his old place in her heart. She herself took his hat, and placed on his head his little leather cap, repeatedly expressing her delight at seeing him again. Then she led him to a magnificent easy-chair near the hearth, which seemed to be placed there especially for him, the back being decorated with wreaths of roses and laurels.

Franklin was a very handsome old man. Purity and regularity of feature, such as are rarely seen, were combined with wonderfully-preserved freshness and cheerfulness in his countenance. His simplicity was sublime. The classic outline of his head was slightly disturbed by the spectacles that he never removed, yet they tended to increase the expression of deep thought which was his principal characteristic.

"Nowhere else in the world do I feel so well

as at your house, my dear Elise," said Franklin, looking pleasantly around. "Here dwell peace, cheerfulness, and freedom; and if I were not obliged to return to Philadelphia, where new-born state affairs need me, I would like to remain in Auteuil and take a share in Madame Helvetius's pastoral life, if only as chicken-boy or goldfinch-overseer. What do you say, my friend, would you be willing to trust me with such work, and thus retain me here?"

All present laughed at the drollery with which Franklin made this proposition to the dignified lady of the house, as he seized her hand at the same time and pressed it to his breast.

"Oh, you would soon be weary here," replied Madame Helvetius, blushing. "You are a great deal too young for the retired life I lead. You would wish to return to the scenes of your great deeds, where there is still much for you to do. And my society could not compensate you for your sacrifices; for I have grown an old woman, who to-day celebrates her sixty-fifth year."

"To-day!" exclaimed Franklin, rising with youthful alacrity, and intending to embrace Elise again; but her other friends pressed around her with congratulations, which she received with bewitching affability. She appeared to listen with peculiar favor to the obliging expressions of Count Mirabeau, who had but lately been received into this circle, but nevertheless reproached himself for his negligence in not having noticed the date of such a festive day, saying that the birthday of an amiable woman ought to be as well known to her friends as the saints' days are to Christians, and that the short time during which he had' been intimate at her house was no excuse.

"You are a true Frenchman, and know how to make good use of your tongue," said Franklin, approaching Mirabeau, and patting the young man's thick locks with a familiarity which the philosopher sometimes condescended to. Count Mirabeau looked a little surprised, but recovered himself quickly. His face, inclined to express a gloomy satire, changed to the most considerate urbanity toward Franklin.

"It is more especially my fault that the birthday of our friend was not known," said the Marquis de Condorcet, a man of about forty years, from whose eyes beamed a decided kindliness of heart, while his high-arched brow and strongly-defined Roman nose, as well as slightly-compressed lips, announced the mathematician. "I think," he continued, in his good-natured self-accusation, "as I am the accountant and mathematician *par excellence* of this society, and am day and night engaged in all kinds of calculations, I ought not to have failed in that of the heart, and all my other computations ought to have ceased of their own accord on this day, which expresses the formula of happiness for us all. Well, do not on that account receive the congratulations of your friend Condorcet less kindly."

"It was exceedingly gallant of you all that you kept no reckoning with me!" said Madame Helvetius. "How happy I ought to be that you wish me so well! Even Condorcet, who, in his sublime repose, generally appears like an ice-palace, has wafted toward me a warm breath from his concealed but loving heart. But now let us speak of something else. Dr. Franklin owes me a report of his last triumphs in Paris. It is due to nothing but the delightful personality of Benjamin Franklin that the Parisians are, as it were, intoxicated with American liberty, and behave in such a different manner."

"I have again been received very kindly in this wonderful Paris," replied Franklin, stretching himself comfortably and smilingly in his chair. "The ladies gave me yesterday, at the Hotel de Ville, the most brilliant reception that I have ever been honored with. After I had found myself as one of the blessed in Mohammed's paradise, the most beautiful among three hundred was chosen to show the sympathy of the French ladies for the liberty won by America. The choice fell upon the Countess Diana de Polignac, one of the highly-intellectual members of the court. She approached me with a laurel-wreath, and did not content herself with placing it on my white locks, but added two kisses, one on each of my cheeks. This was according to the programme of the festival. You may fancy with what pleasure, as ambassador of independent America, I received those salutes, which were more than mere dispatches to be forwarded from Paris across the ocean." *

"And how did the court like this demonstration?" asked Chamfort, with that sarcastic tincture characteristic of all his remarks. "It is said that the Countess Diana received a strange sort of reprimand from the king, if the story be true."

"It is said to be quite true," replied Franklin, laughing, and rubbing his hands, as was his custom, when particularly pleased, and ending his sentence with the words "*Ça ira!*"

"You mean then to sanction the king's conduct," said Chamfort, "but his object was not so much to reprimand the countess, or to bring yourself into contempt, for he could not very well do that in reference to one of whom D'Alembert had written the splendid line: '*Eripuit cœlo fulmen sceptrumque tyrannis.*' † And doubtless the king remembered also that he who could defend himself from the thunderbolt would not probably be overcome by a lady's kisses."

"Had we not better change the subject?" suggested Madame Helvetius, with some signs of impatience.

"In alluding to the story at all," replied Chamfort, "I merely meant to indicate the tone of court society, as well as the opposition of the king to such institutions as those represented by Franklin, whom of course he could not openly insult. The queen is much more frank. As she allows free scope to her amiable levity, even when contrary to etiquette, so she more promptly shows her vexation at the sympathy felt for American liberty."

"You cannot deny," said Franklin, rather solemnly, "that we Americans are beginning to infuse a little confidence into you Frenchmen. By our victorious struggle we have alarmed tyranny in all countries and among all peoples.

We owe it to God through our magnanimous Washington that we have been able to throw off the slavery which the British had imposed on a freeborn people, and that we are again men. But, next, we are indebted to the French. In the commencement of our revolution you gave us a helping hand, and, excitable as you are, you won us favor among the nations of Europe, which very considerably weakened the determination and courage of England. You were the first power that, after our successful resistance, entered into a defensive and commercial alliance with the new republic. Your best and noblest sons were among our warriors. Did you not send us Rochambeau, and that heroic youth Lafayette, to assist us in gaining the palm of freedom? Now it is our turn to be grateful to you. And how can we better show our gratitude than that we disseminate our ideas of national liberty, so that you may feel the desire to be and remain free? Yes, Frenchmen, you are beginning to be Americanized, and the whole world will at last follow our example. Mind what old Franklin says, 'a new era is dawning.' '*Ça ira!*'"

"Yes," exclaimed Count Mirabeau, rising impetuously, and standing before Franklin with an excited gesture. "'It will go,' for it will come! America has said to us, '*Ça ira!*' and this, your favorite expression, noble Franklin, which we receive from you as a significant invitation, will at a future time be one of the cries of French liberty, arousing the masses of our people. We know what we owe you, but also what France will have to owe to herself. In America the bells of freedom have already rung; and France, awakened, needs but remember herself, to rise from the sleep of slavery. It has been a long sleep; but oppression is the natural school of liberty, and Paris is the principal seat of this learning for the modern world. In America, a nation with a great future relies on the strength of its citizens, and so far we regard it with envy and admiration. In France, however, philosophy has long been the teacher of liberty, first arming the mind to strike. Oh, I remember the profound impression made on me in my dark prison,

---

* "Mémoires de Madame Campan," vol. i., p. 233.
† "He snatched from heaven the lightning, and from tyrants the sceptre."—Vide Condorcet, "Mémoires," vol. i., p. 166.

on hearing the story of your struggles for independence! It seemed to me as if the whole tower of Vincennes, in which I was then incarcerated, opened to a flood of celestial light. Think of a man—for years imprisoned by the tyranny of a father who treated his children and subordinates as slaves—hearing for the first time, in his dark and lonely cell, of a whole people that had made itself free! You can imagine the joy and the misery that alternately agitated me. Patience could not tolerate my unhappy destiny, and to behold my prison walls was to render me a maniac. I thought what happiness it must be to become a soldier to aid the New World in throwing off the yoke of the Old, and I wrote to the Count de Maurepas for permission to go to America and enter the service. I promised to die there, and begged, in the name of society, to place the reconciling breadth of the ocean between an unnaturally angry father and his son. But my complaints and prayers were unheard, as those of so many besides, and I remained in solitary confinement. During those fearful nights I made resolutions that will extend over my whole life, and I swore to fight for France as I had desired to do for America. I thought of Montesquieu, Voltaire, Mably, Rousseau, and I vowed to give the impulse in reducing to practice the work of those great minds." *

Franklin rose and stood leaning on his walking-stick, which he seldom laid aside, in an attentively listening attitude. After Mirabeau had ended, Franklin gazed at him for a long time gravely and searchingly, seeming to review his body and soul. The powerful brow of Mirabeau was still glowing with the thoughts he had passionately expressed, and the hair, which crowned his head like a lion's mane, almost seemed to sparkle with electricity. Franklin moved his small black cap a little, as if in token of an esteem which he could not repress, and then said in a heart-felt voice: "Young man, you please me, and I shall

have to make you a declaration of friendship. If I am not greatly deceived, you are the practical man for the ideas of our century, and by your means liberty will blossom in France. It is no idle vanity on our part, when we believe that our young American independence will have a powerful influence upon the future of all nations. Americans shed their blood for liberty and independence, and blood sanctifies sincerity, as well as strengthens the soul to great deeds. My share in my country's honor and success was insignificant. I have no other merit than that of having thought the best foundation of society to be love, fraternity, and industry, and that there lies the harmony of human action, with the certainty of the highest possible human welfare. If my fellow-citizens recognize such sentiments, and reward so richly the poor printer with the most important ministries in the state, I am indebted to the respect which every one is entitled to who thoroughly understands his epoch. But when I see so many and highly-gifted men as those I meet in this company, I fancy that France, when her hour has come, will give a brilliant festival for all mankind!"

"Hear him!" exclaimed Chamfort, in his clear voice. "The great American entices us most enchantingly. Really the inventor of the lightning-rod must be decidedly qualified to manage the political electricity of France. Lately we have ourselves made attempts of various kinds in philosophic discovery. When people, in fact, essay to renew the spirit of a nation, they first open the book of Nature, and try to fathom its laws—how each individual is created for itself—how it exists, lives, and enjoys. But when we heard of your discoveries, Father Franklin, we were rejoiced, thinking we saw symbolized the means of our national welfare. As you sent up your kite to draw from the clouds the magnetic influence, so we have discovered that the French people possess something similar in their own inherent strength, which will presently ascend into high and uninvestigated regions. You see we freely admit that you are our teacher; and my friend Mirabeau, although he thinks it incumbent

* Montigny, "Mémoires sur Mirabeau," vol. ii., p. 267. Peuchet, "Mémoires sur Mirabeau," vol. ii., p. 295. Cadet de Gassicourt, "Essai sur la Vie de Mirabeau." (Works of Mirabeau, vol. vi., ch. xxii.)

on him to represent the proud Frenchman, was one of the first to send up such a kite in France, in the shape of his work 'On Despotism.' Has he not intimated that a terrible storm will soon break over our devoted heads?"

At this moment the servant announced M. Etienne Montgolfier. The mention of this name made quite a sensation in the company, and they remembered the news of the day, which was confirmed by those who had last arrived from Paris. Etienne Montgolfier entered. He was known to most of those present, and Madame Helvetius received him with polite kindness. He was still rather a young man of some thirty years, whose pale, interesting countenance showed traces of the great exertions and struggles he had passed through, in reaching results now crowned with such wonderful success. His unassuming manners made an impression of the most amiable modesty and timidity, which were especially indicated by his disclaiming to be the inventor of the air-balloon, endeavoring to ascribe all the honor to his brother Joseph, with whom he consulted and labored. But it was well known that the idea first originated with Etienne, who had received orders to explain the new invention at Paris and Versailles, and to make the trial excursions. All regarded Montgolfier with visible interest. They surrounded him, and, in answer to their questions, he corroborated the fact that he was to make a new ascension at Auteuil, in presence of the whole court. He invited all the company to witness the spectacle, saying that he would reserve a platform for them, and that he considered their patronage of great importance, as he had undertaken to make some improvements, which he would like to have examined by such renowned and experienced men.

"It is not yet dinner-time," said Madame Helvetius, hesitatingly, "and I cannot refuse to let you have my guests for an hour, but, with their own consent, and provided that your exhibition does not last longer, otherwise I would protest against it, for my dinner would be completely spoiled. I have several novelties on my table to-day, particularly an American ham, a present from General Lafayette, which he has received direct from the plantation of General Washington. You may suppose that such a dish ought to be eaten at the proper time. Besides, our dear friend the Marquis de Lafayette will be here, as well as Diderot. The latter has been ill for several days, but he has nevertheless promised to be here. I must therefore remain at home until they arrive, that they may not find my house quite tenantless."

Montgolfier seemed to be satisfied with this excuse for the lady's absence, yet he seemed to have something on his mind which he hesitated to express. At last he found courage to say what it was: he wished to accompany him in his balloon a few birds and domestic animals, and so he begged Madame Helvetius to allow him to take a few of the inhabitants of her farm-yard for this purpose. He promised that no harm should befall them—he had already experimented in a similar manner in his former voyage, and the effect had not been in the least injurious to his fellow-travellers. The Duke de Chartres, who was to ascend with him on this day, had expressed a wish to observe the effect of the rarer atmosphere on different species and forms of life. Montgolfier added that he would like to have some very fine specimens, such as he could find nowhere but at Madame Helvetius's.

The lady smilingly shook her head, and said: "No, my dear Montgolfier, I can let you have none of my animals—they are too near my heart. I should never pardon either you or myself if the meanest of my pets were hurt. My birds are all away at this time, so that I could not even give you a lame titmouse. I never close my aviary during the day, and all that choose may fly into the fields and gardens; they always return regularly at nightfall. They are my family, and I know and love each one of them. I really could not accede to your request, though to oblige even the Duke de Chartres. See, the aviary is quite empty." And she opened a window looking into the yard, in the centre of which stood the large aviary with its wire doors wide open.

Montgolfier blushed, and, bowing, indicated

that he renounced his wish. But Count Mira- beau approached, and, clapping him on the shoul- der, said with the air of a patron: "Perhaps I can help you a little in your perplexity, M. Mont- golfier. Our friend, Madame Helvetius, has of course a very tender heart for her pets, and prob-' ably she fears a moral as well as physical injury to them if they are even a few minutes in the society of the Duke de Chartres. I have, how- ever, a dog, called 'Miss Sarah,' to which I am certainly much attached, but which has recently acquired several disagreeable tricks. I have for some time been thinking of devising an extraor- dinary punishment, and I have found it at last: I sentence her to be the companion of a royal personage such as the duke. I am curious to ob- serve the effects on the dog-nature of my favor- ite, not of the higher atmosphere, but of the im- mediate proximity of such a privileged gentle- man. My dog is in the yard, and at your service. Miss Sarah is a creature of rare beauty, and, if you wish to take her, I will bring her to you."

These words seemed to be received with much favor by the rest of the company, who manifested it first in whispers, and then in loud laughter. Montgolfier thankfully accepted the offer.

"I should like to intercede for M. Montgolfier," said Chamfort, with a humorous expression. "Do you not think it would be suitable to make a little addition, from the philosophic country-seat at Auteuil, to the society of the Duke de Char- tres? I propose for this purpose 'Tamtam,' the old black cat, that has so often vexed us by her malignant disposition, and who recently scratched the hands of our fair friend. I know you inherit this cat from your husband, the great Helvetius, who was very fond of her, and under whose table she used to sit while he was composing his works. The hero of materialism often placed his feet on the back of this cat while he was writing; and his powerful precept, declaring the whole being of man to be physical sensibility, may be said to have been founded on this electric catskin. Tamtam must, therefore, be a portion of history. It is probably on that account she considers it right to scratch and bite her old friends, but we

shall punish her a little for this. Besides, it will be gratifying to send up into the air this signifi- cant favorite of Helvetius (in which, I am sure, dwells one of the archdemons), and especially so in company with the amiable Duke de Chartres. The cat that was present at, and perhaps aided in the composition of, the new system of the cen- tury, would be a most interesting *vis-à-vis* for a prince who represents to us the height of all that was sinful in a past and reprobate age."

"Very cunning and paradoxical as usual, but not wicked as usual," replied Madame Helvetius. "Well, you may have Tamtam, M. Montgolfier. I will order your black *compagnon de voyage* to be immediately brought."

At this moment a slight rattling was heard at one of the folding-doors of the drawing-room lead- ing to the yard and garden. It was not latched, and opened as if of itself, giving ingress to a large black cat. Every one was taken by sur- prise at her unexpected appearance at that mo- ment, and her mistress allowed her to cross the room unrebuked. She came purring at the feet of Madame Helvetius, as if instinctively suspect- ing some danger, and asking for protection.

"Away, old Tamtam!" cried Madame Helve- tius, angrily. "You are very importunate, be- cause of your antecedents."

But other animals had entered by the open door, and even a goat stood at the entrance, shak- ing his beard, and seemingly making an inquiry with a motion of his head. Several of the birds had returned from their excursions sooner than usual, and seemed to seek their mistress with strange anxiety, as she had not received them, as her practice was, with food and endearing words. She looked in great astonishment at the inex- plicable actions of her favorites, who seated them- selves on her neck and shoulders, flapping their little wings incessantly, opening their bills, appar- ently expecting the kisses they generally re- ceived. Two goldfinches had even perched them- selves upon her new head-dress, and pecked at the leaves and vegetables that adorned it.

"Something extraordinary must have hap- pened, since you return so early," said Madame

Helvetius, frightening off the impudent goldfinches. "Your habit is to flit around until sunset, you rovers, before you even think of bringing me your evening greeting. And to-day you disturb me in the drawing-room among my guests. What in the world is the matter? Have you been alarmed, or chased away by something very unusual?"

The answer to this question was given by a distant rolling sound, but coming rapidly nearer.

"The equipages of the court are arriving!" said Chamfort, laughing, and hastening to a window. "The animal paradise of our fair friend, which she rules so angelically, must have felt the approach of the court serpent, and the wanderers are home earlier. But, really, that is an awful noise—the whole royal family and suite—ten-twelve carriages, and a host of cavaliers with their no less brilliant servants! In this quiet village the court has never before appeared; how can we then be surprised if all these creatures in their fear have fled from the fields and roadsides to their accustomed refuge?"

M. Montgolfier took his leave. The punctual arrival of the court urged him to finish his preparations. He was assured that the two extra companions to ascend with him should be safely conveyed to the appointed place. The rest of the company also began to leave, previously making the arrangement that Madame Helvetius should follow with her other expected guests.

CHAPTER II.

MIRABEAU'S DOG AND HELVETIUS'S CAT.

In the large open space lying in the centre of Auteuil, accommodations had been made for those who wished to witness this third ascent of the balloon. Even before the arrival of the royal party, the platforms intended for the general public were filled to overflowing with spectators of all ranks from Paris and its environs. The motley crowd expressed the most impatient expectation, enlivened by many sarcastic and inconsiderate jests in reference to the Duke de Chartres, whose intention of accompanying Montgolfier was already well known.* The company from the villa of Madame Helvetius took reserved seats, after the court had entered the royal compartments, gorgeously lined with velvet and gold. In the central one were the king and queen. Beside the latter the Princess de Lamballe, who had lately been nominated superintendent of the queen's household. This position was secured to her through the extraordinary and tender friendship of Marie Antoinette. In the *loges* to the right and left, the king's brothers, the Count de Provence and the Count d'Artois, with their consorts and suite, had taken their places. In another was Duke Louis Philippe d'Orleans, the father of the Duke de Chartres, with beautiful Madame de Montesson, whom he had but a short time before secretly married. Among the dignitaries of the court was the new minister of finance, M. de Calonne, who in the preceding year had been called to this post, whose business became every day more complicated and difficult.

When the royal family with their suite appeared, they were received in profound silence by the people. This had not so much the character of indifference as of painful depression. The time was past when the young king would be received in public with noisy exultation by his subjects, as at his accession ten years before. At that time, after the death of the vicious and criminal Louis XV., France could breathe for a moment, and the surname "*Le Desiré*" was bestowed on Louis XVI. The king of nineteen years did not, however, relish that designation, though he wished by his deeds to deserve the title of "Benefactor of the People." Since then the nation seemed to be silent, moody, and full of distrust toward him wherever he showed himself.

The public temper, which thus silently expressed opposition to the court, became more suspicious when contrasted with the enthusiastic reception extended to Franklin, who had scarcely

* Vide Soulavie, "Mémoires du Règne de Louis XVI.," vol. ii., p. 109.

appeared than all arose, and continued *vivats* resounded on all sides, accompanied by the waving of the ladies' handkerchiefs. Franklin contented himself, in acknowledging this honor, with his characteristic smile and the raising of his small cap. Then he seated himself between Mirabeau and Condorcet, with whom he had entered, crossed his hands on his walking-cane, and cast a curiously anxious glance at the royal seats opposite. Chamfort and Cabanis took their places behind him in the second tier, while the public seemed to observe the group with great interest. Next to Franklin, Mirabeau and Condorcet received the greatest attention. All knew that these men had participated more or less in the deliberations held in Paris concerning the constitution of independent America. The ideas of liberty, equality, and the rights of man, had been circulated in connection with the names of Franklin, Condorcet, and Mirabeau. *

The countenance of the king darkened at these new demonstrations of homage with which the French nation received Franklin. The noble features of Louis XVI., expressing his honesty and conscientiousness, became melancholy. At times, when he was out of humor, a certain unfortunate demeanor was obvious, making prominent his personal negligence, especially the disorder of his hair. While he seemed to be lost in unpleasant reflection, the queen raised her beautiful head only the more haughtily and triumphantly. She glanced around on the spectators with a decidedly ironical expression, leaning back in her chair and contemplating them with an air half of pity and half of contempt. The enthusiasm of the French for Franklin was not only personally offensive to Marie Antoinette, but she recognized, with much greater penetration than the king, the intention of the people to insult the monarchy by this honor done to the venerable American, as representative of a republic. She was too proud and too honest to conceal her opinion, or, in presence of the masses, to disguise it even for an instant with an appearance of toleration or compromise. She had thus augmented the number of her enemies, and the ill-feeling against herself daily increased, on account of her petulance and irony, her free contradiction of what she disliked, and her prompt rejection of what she disbelieved. It was, however, evident that Marie Antoinette did not consider herself as having a really serious misunderstanding with her people. This was evident in her cheerfulness of countenance and sense of security, adding to the expression of her natural beauty, and forbidding a shadow of real fear. On her regular features could be perceived a complacent assurance in herself and her sovereignty, believing that she could win the affection of all, whenever she condescended to do so. But at this moment it was plain that the public had no inclination to admire the queen, or do justice to her truly enchanting appearance. She was only in her twenty-ninth year, but gave an impression of being much younger. This was in consequence of her exceedingly white and delicate complexion, the bright color of her cheeks, and her fair hair. The opposition that had early arisen against Marie Antoinette seemed as blind to the charms of her rare beauty as ungrateful to her exertions in alleviating the sufferings of the people by benefits of all kinds. They had accustomed themselves to regard her as an enemy of the nation, whatever she did or intended—every action was followed by numerous slanders, often taking form in ribald songs, obscuring or perverting all perception of the truth.

As the queen continued to regard the assembly in so haughty a manner, in a certain sense challenging them, a whispering and murmuring soon pervaded the space occupied by them. She seemed immediately to perceive this feeling of resistance; but jested and laughed about it. Against all the rules of etiquette, she raised herself, and, bending over to the Princess de Lamballe, whispered apparently mocking and contemptuous words.

"We are again in a characteristic situation!" said Chamfort, who sat behind Mirabeau, touching the latter's shoulder to attract his attention. "The queen is again amusing herself at her own

* "Mémoires de Madame Campan," vol. 1., p. 236.

expense. The nightly promenades on the terrace do not occur any more. An inundation of hateful couplets made her recede from this innocent amusement. Now the sportiveness of the ingenious queen finds entertainment in the public itself, and makes merry at the grimaces of the good French people. Look, how the Roman nose of the fair lady, which is almost too sharply defined, expresses her sarcasm, and the thick Austrian underlip is just making a new *bon-mot*, and, I wager, a cutting one."

"You may ridicule every thing except the queen's beauty!" replied Mirabeau, losing himself in the contemplation of Marie Antoinette. "I think I am somewhat of a connoisseur, and I sincerely say I have never seen any thing to equal the charming contour of her countenance; it has an indescribable grace. Her figure is faultless, or, at least, very seldom does such a form come from the hands of Nature. All her movements are those of unrestrained and innocent youth, knowing nothing of kingdoms and the privileges of rank! I should think, Chamfort, that that angelic countenance ought to belong to our new era!"

"For Heaven's sake, what are we to think of your principles, Count Mirabeau?" laughed Chamfort. "You are in a fair way to fall in love with the queen, and then where is your new era, that is awaiting you as its leader? And how is it that you have no longer any interest in the companion of the queen, the Princess de Lamballe? Is she not also a charming blonde? It is not so very long since you were proud of being her secretly-favored lover, and justified in boasting of tender interviews with this princess of the blood royal."

"You know my ideas of woman, Chamfort," replied Mirabeau, casting an ardent glance on the princess; "I know we shall never agree on that subject. You may be the greatest satirist the time has produced, but you look on woman as a higher revelation of genius, and think it possible to make a compact for life and death with her. My views are much more cheerful. A woman's early life is as a flowery day of spring that passes

away so soon. We must appreciate it while we can, for its sweet blossoms may to-morrow be withered by the sun, or scattered by the storm. We must not delay the acceptance of charming promises, though for us they may not be fulfilled; and this language interprets the history of my acquaintance with the Princess de Lamballe."

"I fancy it must have lasted a little longer than a day," remarked Chamfort. "She was your friend when you were imprisoned in the tower of Vincennes, and you were indebted to her for many a trip to Paris.* Really she is fascinating, not only on account of her mildly-beaming countenance, but her misfortune enhances her beauty, for it has imparted to her whole being a certain depth of tenderness and affecting melancholy. For I consider it as the most terrible calamity that can befall a pure and noble woman, to have been married to a prince of the house of Bourbon."

"She was chained to this prince only for fifteen months," said Mirabeau. "She had but one sentiment in reference to this marriage—disgust; and, by this means, she has preserved her naturally good temper. Her husband, though but twenty years old, was addicted to all depraved propensities. She confessed to me that, when she stood at the death-bed of this miserable prince, she often wished she had been a simple daughter of the people, so that she might never have inhaled the pestilential air of the French court."

"Ah," replied Chamfort, laughing, "you wish me to understand how well you can make even princesses democratic, and that we may safely trust you for the future. France relies on your talents, Count Mirabeau!—But see, the noble Duke de Chartres appears in the vacant space below, and speaks to Master Montgolfier. Probably he is asking about the security of the balloon, which I hope will soon ascend. Indeed, it is no small matter to forward to the heavens a prince of the royal house; and even if he has courage, all danger must be provided against for

* Cadet de Gassicourt, "Essai sur la Vie de Mirabeau" (Œuvres de Mirabeau, vol. vi., p. 18).

this precious head. But Montgolfier seems to be late. The perspiration falls from his brow while filling his machine, and he seems to hesitate. Our duke impatiently turns his back on the poor man, and returns to his place with a light step."

"What an interesting monster is the duke!" said Mirabeau. "If he were not such a fool, he might pass for a hardened criminal. But his infamous actions are so mingled with his fopperies, that he has made on me the impression of a comic character."

"Perhaps he will soon be a tragic character in our hands," said Chamfort, in a lower voice. "He has shown some talent for that in the fatal part he played as brother-in-law of the unfortunate Prince de Lamballe, contriving an infamous scheme to seduce him to a licentious life, that finally ruined him—poisoning him, soul and body, with intoxicating drinks, and thus exposing him to unutterable vice. Had the prince not been the only son and heir of the rich Duke de Penthièvre, the Duke de Chartres would not have selected De Lamballe as the victim of that satanic strategy. De Chartres wished to have a share of the large fortune the prince would have inherited. Do you call this a comic or tragic role, friend Mirabeau?"

"I do not alter my opinion," replied Mirabeau, "my impression is still that of a comedy. For if M. de Chartres, that duke of orgies, had not seduced the Prince de Lamballe, the princess would perhaps have loved her young husband, and they might still be living in the idyllic union of two turtle-doves. Then I would not, perhaps, have met the beautiful princess during my hours of recreation on the fortifications at Vincennes, where she was accidentally. I would not have been introduced to her by her companion, the Count d'Entraigues, an old friend of mine, and she would not have transferred to my person the interest she took in my destiny. This 'perhaps,' Chamfort, is the true comedy of life, and you see, M. Philosopher, that I owe much gratitude to the wickedness of the Duke de Chartres."

"Well, then, you owe him gratitude!" replied Chamfort, with ironic cheerfulness.—"But see, he

has again appeared, and is hurrying poor Montgolfier. The impatience to make himself prominent on this occasion is irritating him. He has dressed himself in English style. He is the leader of the English imitators in Paris, and thus contrasts a little with the rest of the court. What is your opinion of the duke's dress, Count Mirabeau? How picturesque this individual of the blood-royal looks in his scarlet swallow-tail coat, with gilt buttons, muslin vest, black silk pants, and blue-and-white stockings! He plays with his switch very gracefully, continually swinging it, and reminding me of my boot-black beating the dust out of my clothes."

"I am really glad to see that our duke has any dress at all," observed Mirabeau. "It is but a short time ago, that, in one of his mad pranks, he rode from Versailles to his palais-royal in a decided undress. As to his Anglomania, the court seem to be quite reconciled on that point. It is well known that he dislikes every thing on the other side of the channel except this costume and his race-horses. He will never fancy the English Parliament; this he has shown by his childish hatred of our innocent French Parliaments. I wish he would soon ascend high into the air, that we may at last go to dinner."

At this moment attention was drawn to a *loge* that had hitherto remained vacant, at the side of Chamfort and Mirabeau, and in an oblique direction from the compartment occupied by the royal party. All eyes were turned on those that were entering, and the public again broke out in loud cries of joy, accompanied with clapping of hands. It was young General de Lafayette who shared with Franklin the enthusiastic regards of the people. The brave general, since his return from America, the declared favorite of the day, received this homage with a slight and almost reluctant bow. On his arm was Madame Helvetius, who took her seat at his side in a cheerful and pleasant manner. On the other side of Lafayette was the Count d'Estaing, the renowned and courageous admiral of France, who had commanded the French fleet that aided the Americans during their struggle for independence. He had taken up his residence in Paris since the conclusion of peace. Both he and his friend Lafayette wore on their breast the eagle of the order of Cincinnatus, a new decoration, commemorative of the revolution, and which indicated the members of a select society in the United States. Marquis de Lafayette, a young man of twenty-seven, made an impression rather by the romantic and adventurous military renown he had so brilliantly gained, than by his outward appearance, which was wanting in a certain freedom and grace. In all his movements there was something awkward, and this was heightened by an uncommonly short waist. His appearance was, however, redeemed by a natural gentleness and heart-felt goodness, which showed itself winningly and irresistibly in his whole manner. A mixture of childlike mildness and manly decision gave him that popular charm which has always been associated with his person. His very red hair did not detract from the courteous expression of his features, but seemed rather to render them more acute and interesting. After Lafayette had thanked the people somewhat reservedly, he perceived Franklin, and recognized him most cordially. The latter returned the greeting not less ardently, rising with youthful vivacity, and, at the same time, with the dignity he considered necessary as representative of the American people. When the assembly beheld these men saluting each other with such fervency, they again applauded with cheers and clapping of hands. Lafayette, who was of an excitable nature, could not resist the influence of this moment. To show that he understood the intention of the audience, he put his hand on the costly sword at his side, and, drawing it quickly from the scabbard, held it aloft with both hands. This was the golden-sheathed sword which the Congress of the United States had sent to Lafayette, and which had been delivered to him by Franklin in the name of American independence, and at the same time as a symbol of the friendship existing between France and America.* On beholding it, the people renewed their plaudits.

For a moment there was a motionless silence among the members of the court. The countenance of the king expressed more perplexity than anger at this respect offered in disregard of his presence. The queen, on the contrary, more passionate and frank, could scarcely preserve an outwardly calm demeanor. She hastily whispered a few words to the king, probably asking him to order the instant departure of the court, but the ruler of France gravely and decidedly refused to accept her advice.

In the places occupied by the brothers of the king and their young consorts, a noisy cheerfulness seemed to reign. At least it was intended that the public should imagine that the scene just enacted was the cause of the merriment. The eyes of the witty Count de Provence, who seldom appeared in public, really flashed in their contempt and satire. He had lately placed himself in opposition to the people by both public and secret resistance to the reëstablishment of the old Parliaments, and his political principles had been a prominent subject of conversation. This circumstance was too well known not to interpret his present behavior in the most unfavorable manner. Nor did his brother, the Count d'Artois, who sat near him, restrain the levity and wantonness of his character, making gesticulations which the spectators doubtless understood.

"Lafayette is right in his recent remark, that an American era is dawning in France," observed the Marquis de Condorcet, turning again to Franklin, with whom he had been holding an uninterrupted conversation about the construction and possible utility of the balloon.

Franklin smilingly played with his ruffle, the extreme whiteness of which was one of the few vanities in his costume that the representative of a free democracy permitted himself.

"American independence is beautiful, and full of promise for our future," observed Cabanis, behind them, who according to his custom had been silent, apparently occupied with thoughts far distant from the present. "But," he continued, with a touch of irony, "that independence ought not

---

* Condorcet, "Mémoires," vol. ii., p. 53.

to adorn itself with the glittering insignia of the Old World!"

"You mean the insignia of the order of Cincinnatus?" replied Franklin, pushing up his large spectacles, and turning with a searching glance to Cabanis. "Why, I think the gold medal looks quite well on the breasts of young General Lafayette and Count d'Estaing. Worn by such worthy and brave men, it shows that Frenchmen have deserved well in the cause of liberty, and that they intend to devote themselves to it. And the white-edged blue ribbon speaks of the new alliance between France and America."

"Permit me to join in this conversation, but with my most fervent and bitter hatred against your new decoration!" said Count Mirabeau. "Is it not plainly ridiculous that the first sign of life a young republic gives is the institution of an order? But there are dangers in connection with it which you, worthy Franklin, will be the last to mistake or despise. It is decidedly a great weakness in Lafayette that he has become a commissioner for your eagle badges here in France, not only distributing them to his heart's content to every French officer who fought in any one of your battles, but displaying them on every occasion. However, I long ago said that he is nothing but a most amiable amateur of liberty, and will never be any thing more. He will always remain weak, the slave of his own vanity, which will make of him any thing it pleases."

"I will gladly abandon to you our order of Cincinnatus," replied Franklin, gently, "but not your Lafayette, whom we may in some measure also call ours. You may be right that such an order might, though unreasonably, lead to dangerous consequences for our young republic, but I am ready at some future time to discuss the subject with you. It is possible that the most patriotic and virtuous societies may be perverted as precedents for those that are ignoble and narrow-minded. But, tell me what objection you have to the heroic Lafayette?"

Mirabeau cast a glance of hatred toward the place where Lafayette was seated, and, after having searchingly contemplated him for some time, said to Franklin: "If on some idle afternoon I had read a novel having Lafayette for its hero, perhaps I might have been very well entertained; but, as a politician, I think I could not honor him with my confidence. I shall never forget that he did not fail to play the actor in every one of those theatrical mummeries patronized and participated in by the princes, who thus permitted themselves to ridicule the reëstablishment of the old parliamentary sessions. He is said to have discovered a peculiar talent for parody, in conjunction with the Duke de Chartres, who acted the president, while Lafayette represented the procurator-general as a very jolly person. He so indulged in such jests, in face of the good-will of the king, who would gladly meet the requirements of the nation, that I consider the marquis unfit for any earnest political movement." *

"You forget to take into consideration his extreme youth, Count Mirabeau!" said Cabanis. "No one can doubt his honest sentiment for the future freedom of the people, although the souls of Cato and Alcibiades seem to mingle in his nature. It is evident that nothing but his great enthusiasm for liberty drove him to the battle-fields of America. Did not the king cause the young warrior's arrest on his return, and was he not incarcerated for twenty-four hours, because he left France to fight the battles of the new republic without the royal permission? I have before tried to reconcile the antagonism existing between Mirabeau and Lafayette, and I shall not give up until I succeed." The usually pale cheeks of the young man were deeply flushed, and his eyes beamed with a friendly and noble resolution.

"You are always amiable, Cabanis!" replied Mirabeau. "And let us leave the Marquis de Lafayette in the enjoyment of popular favor and the glory of his transatlantic decoration. But I wish to make a proposition, which I especially recommend to the favorable consideration of our honored Dr. Franklin. I intend to issue a paper against the order of Cincinnatus, and you must

---

* Ségur, "Mémoires," vol. 1., p. 43.

all assist me with your ideas on the subject. Franklin, Condorcet, Chamfort, and Cabanis, must contribute. We shall send it into the world as a manifesto, showing how surprised the true friends of liberty are, that the first act of the newly-risen republic is not that of setting a pure example to other nations, but instituting a new sign of inequality—a new recognition of the follies of the Old World. And what a triumph for my undertaking, to have a contribution from Franklin himself, the strong defender of American and European liberty! Am I too bold in my supposition, Father Franklin, or am I mistaken that your great heart beats for the welfare of the people?"

"You really seem to understand me," replied the American. "I confess that it would do no harm, if a pamphlet appeared explaining that an order might possibly be destructive of the principles of real democracy; but this should be written kindly, and without losing sight of our new constitution. If you desire my true opinion, I must say that I opposed the institution of this society for many considerations. I thought it my duty especially to declare against making any honorable distinction hereditary, and my magnanimous friend, General Washington, shared my scruples." *

"Well, then, give me your hand," exclaimed Mirabeau, in his impulsive zeal; "you will all assist in composing a work in which we shall fight against an institution that already begins to disappoint the new-born expectations of liberty in Europe. Such societies would soon create a patrician rank and a military aristocracy. That was the origin of our aristocracy—the innumerable counts, dukes, and marquises, who have despoiled Europe. They first assumed military titles and honors, which were afterward declared hereditary in certain families. † Your order is said to be an association of officers, who, having

fought for American liberty, wish to derive thence particular rights. Therefore, I offer you my hand here, in front of the court of France, surrounded by nobles, who begin to perceive that the popular opposition to the old feudal spirit will make the titles to which they were born of little value."

"Here is my hand, Count Mirabeau!" replied Franklin. "I have heard that your family belongs to the oldest nobility in Provence, and I consider it an honor to fight in company with such a man against the unborn aristocracy of our republic.—But see! at last friend Montgolfier is ready, as well as the prince; and Mirabeau's dog and Helvetius's cat are just brought in."

The public had become very impatient, and were glad when the time had arrived for the balloon to ascend. The suspense was increased by a report that had gained currency everywhere, that the Duke de Chartres intended to decline at the last moment, having declared the machine to be unsafe in all its arrangements and construction. In truth, this was the cause of the delay. The prince, on approaching the frail and as yet untried structure, seemed to be perplexed, and made all kinds of suggestions affecting his personal safety. The balloon, which Etienne had made for the first voyage of himself and his brother, was made of strong linen, lined with paper, one hundred and ten feet in circumference, and intended to weigh five hundred pounds. He had raised it by rarefying the interior air, and former trials bore witness to its safety and easy management. So much the greater was Montgolfier's astonishment when the Duke de Chartres suddenly told him that he had no confidence in his work, and that he would have an aërostatic vessel made for his own use, of about half the size, and in the form of a cylinder. It was known that the duke occupied himself with attempts of that kind, but Montgolfier would not permit him to cast obloquy on his invention, particularly at that time. Besides, it was evident that the prince had scruples, not from better knowledge, but because at the last moment he failed in the necessary courage. His pale face and trembling limbs too plainly declared this.

---

* At the special instance of Washington, the members of the order of Cincinnatus, at a later period, adopted his suggestions.—Vide "Mémoires du Général Lafayette," vol. ii., p. 88.

† Mirabeau, "On the Order of Cincinnatus."

Montgolfier begged him only to have confidence, and not to make the voyage ridiculous in presence of the whole court and the numerous assembly, after he had voluntarily offered himself. Still, the prince hesitated to enter the air gondola, although no more excuses for delay could be found. "He is afraid!" the audience whispered, and the satiric humor of the Parisians began to manifest itself. Old and new *bon-mots* passed from mouth to mouth, and among court-people dubious faces were seen. At last the bell sounded, giving the signal to start, and the murmurs of the public suddenly changed to a joyful "Ah!" as the duke entered for his voyage.

"The spectacle has really commenced!" cried the merry Chamfort. "The Duke de Chartres ascends in all his glory! It seems he is able to muster more courage for a flight into the air than at the sea-fight at Ouessant of honorable memory, where he was deaf, dumb, and blind, to every signal directing the ship he commanded into the battle. And history relates that this prince of the royal blood of France at last crept into a near and peaceful harbor, when the storm of the ocean battle threatened to engulf him. His portrait appeared, at that time, in the costume of a sailor, with this inscription: 'He saw the sea, and fled!'* And now, rising into the purest regions of the atmosphere, he does not think of running away, although such a duke, one would think, must be on ill terms with all the natural elements!"

"Perhaps Helvetius's cat gave him courage by her truly heroic aspect!" exclaimed Mirabeau, laughing. "See how she displays her dignity as the balloon rises, standing by the duke's side as if she considered herself the principal personage, and to my mind she really appears more imposing than his royal highness! Or is it imagination on my part, that the cat is casting humorous glances upon us from her glowing eyes? Perhaps, as she floats above us, she will make discoveries, and disclose to us some of the secrets of the philosopher Helvetius. Was it not said of this great

* "Souvenirs de la Marquise de Créquy," vol. v., p. 123.

man that he made so many enemies because he revealed the most hidden thoughts, and disclosed the concealed actions and motives of our race? And I have no doubt that he made many discoveries of which we have never heard, and which he only whispered into the ear of his loved Tamtam. Tell us now the last secret of thy master; tell us through the air the meaning of Helvetius's doctrine, representing the human organization as one inseparable and perfect whole, deriving its life and happiness from the perception of the senses! Announce it up there, that this is the mystery of the liberation of man! Purr it into the conviction of thy pale neighbor (that he may repeat it to his companions at dinner), that there should exist none but free nations, because Helvetius teaches that man's nature contains in itself all law; and that he needs but ask his own pleasure, to decide his rights!" This half-pathetic, half-ludicrous speech, which Mirabeau declaimed with his passionate zeal, made such an impression on his friends, that they all burst into laughter.

"But Helvetius's cat must not make us forget Mirabeau's dog!" Chamfort rejoined. "See how Miss Sarah ascends in calm intrepidity, looking with contempt on the Duke de Chartres, of whose airy courage I am even inclined to doubt. Tamtam is the symbol of the new knowledge arisen above our heads; Miss Sarah, of new deeds as the consequence. I think I hear your bull-dog bark, Count Mirabeau, and consider it an announcement of the near approach of an active future, in which all must work for the liberty of France. What a Noah's ark is that, where we find knowledge in the shape of Tamtam; deeds, in that of your dog, and the royal prince, the best representative of an infamous past! It is the ark of the future! How uneasily it swings for the ascent!—a moment more, and it spontaneously passes through the clouds, and, in the serene light of heaven, looks down upon them!"

While the company were entertaining themselves in this way, there seemed to be some trouble in the balloon above them; for violent gesticulations, both of the duke and M. Montgolfier, could be perceived. The public were the

first to notice it, pointing upward, with loud exclamations, at a scene becoming more and more
remarkable. The rumor was, that the prince had
again lost courage; having embarked with the
utmost reluctance, he could no longer bear the
motion, and insisted on being at once landed on
terra firma. This was confirmed by what followed. A terribly-ridiculing laughter resounded
on all sides, with derisive songs and the freest
witticisms; and many anecdotes were related
concerning the life of the Duke de Chartres. In
the mean time, Montgolfier exerted himself in
causing the balloon to descend. He was forced
to do so, not only by the continual urging of the
prince, which could no longer be refused (as he
affirmed that the balloon was not safe for more
than one person), but by his truly pitiable appearance, indicating that he was quite ill, although only at the commencement of the
voyage.

"Positively," exclaimed Chamfort, when he
saw the balloon approach the place it had left but
a few minutes before, "the man does look un-
well, and air seems to agree no better with him
than did the salt-water at Ouessant. The inscription might now be: 'He saw the air, and fled!'
Well, there are two elements in which one is
safe from a prince of France! Only earth and
fire remain, and, according to Jean Jacques Rousseau, the earth belongs to the people, therefore it
is quite possible that soon a place in the fire will
be the portion of our dynastic lord."

"Silence, Chamfort!" said Mirabeau, placing
his hand on his friend's mouth. "Your tongue
is as the signal-bell of the future, as I have
often told you; but has the hour come to sound
it? In the mean time, let us admire the heroic
youth who has graciously considered the upper
regions hardly worthy of himself; and who
shows, by his prompt return, how little he cares
for public opinion. The 'Montgolfière' touches
the earth, and the assistants are fastening the
ropes. My brave Miss Sarah is the first to alight,
and makes known her displeasure at the unsuccessful voyage by barking with all her might.
Tamtam follows, and seems to indicate that she

has her own ideas on the subject. And now
our dear duke descends!"

The prince seemed to be suffering so much that
Montgolfier was obliged to lift him out, and lead
him slowly away. The audience, however, did
not receive his return in the manner his condition
ought perhaps to have demanded. They declared
their disapprobation by hissing and whistling, as
well as by execrations of all kinds. Montgolfier
protected the duke by immediately carrying him
behind the curtain. The places occupied by the
court were quickly vacated; for as soon as the
king and the queen perceived the unfortunate
turn of affairs, and the renewed anger of the public against the Duke de Chartres, they arose,
followed by the princes and the whole court,
and went toward their conveyance in the greatest
haste. Fortunately, they reached them before the
assembly broke up, in a very tumultuous manner.

When the guests of Madame Helvetius were
departing, they were in the merriest frame of
mind. The strange scenes they had witnessed
heightened their good-humor, and even Count
Mirabeau and the Marquis de Lafayette, whose
social relations were usually not very cordial,
greeted one another with smiles and considerable
heartiness. Madame Helvetius took the arm of
Franklin, and both walked rapidly, in advance of
the rest, toward the villa.

"It is a bad sign," remarked Franklin, "that
the public have so little consideration for a prince
who loses his courage. If an equestrian performer had been seized with giddiness, they would
have expressed the greatest sympathy for him,
and endeavored to compensate him for his misfortune by words of approbation. The reason
why the spectators were so enraged to-day
is, that you French people still have the notion
that a prince must always declare himself unagi-
tated by any occurrence—that he must be indifferent and even sublime in the most trying
circumstances. You imagine that a nobleman so
recognized is in himself a superior being to a
common performer, or to any other mortal; and
that convinces me how far behind us Americans
you are in reference to ideas of liberty."

Young General de Lafayette heard these words, and, approaching Franklin, said: "So you would have wished, honored friend and compatriot, that we had made his cowardice less painful to the Duke de Chartres by a sort of general sympathy and applause. Well, in a certain sense you may be right. But France, in her views and actions, can only slowly follow the great impulse our America has given to the whole world!"

"It is flattering to my ears as the song of the sirens, to hear General Lafayette, even when in France, call himself the compatriot of Americans. Would that I had the same right to say 'our France,' as you have to say 'our America!' You have gained yours by the bravery with which you fought for the liberty of my country!"

"I consider myself still in the service of the United States, my dear friend!" replied Lafayette, with his hearty cheerfulness. "And my friendship ought to be renewed from time to time; thus you find me making preparations for another transatlantic voyage. Something seems to be impelling me from my native toward my adopted country. You may perceive that I also hold the opinion that the time for France has not come. I wish to present myself before your senate as one who again greets the American cause, always ready to sacrifice every thing for it. It gave me unspeakable pleasure to know that I should meet you at dinner at the house of our friend. I dare say you have many messages to intrust me with for Washington." *

"Yes," said Franklin, quickly, "tell him that we would like him to leave the shade of his 'vine and fig-tree,' and again appear in the tumult of public life. He is the greatest, and, so far as it is possible, the only perfect man of his time; and it is certainly one of the highest traits of his character, that, like Cincinnatus, he withdrew to the quiet of country-life as soon as he had finished his task as leader of our revolution. All Europe admires the patriot who, having reached so grand a result as the deliverance of his country, unas-

suminglly becomes a mere planter on the banks of one of its peaceful streams. But the world has need of Washington. He ought not to surrender his glory to an obscure life, or expend his talents in stock-raising."

"I believe," interrupted Chamfort, who was walking behind them, "that Father Franklin is angry at our retarded dinner. He speaks slightingly of Washington's occupation, although we were especially told by our amiable hostess that, among other delicacies, we were to have a ham sent from his plantation. Please do not depreciate the source whence General Lafayette's generosity to Madame Helvetius originates. For if the great Washington discovers that we have no respect for his genial rural life, his lady, of course, cannot send any more hams to Madame de Lafayette, and the guests of Madame Helvetius will not have gained much by their comments on agricultural pursuits.—I have, by the way, usually a very hearty appetite, and especially to-day, so that I am longing to taste that Virginia dish, in which we may fancy we see the blessings of a free and peaceful future. And I hope we shall also have a glass of that famous peach-brandy, which can only be procured by our Lafayette from the same fountain—we shall then have some things in American style. Do you not consider these reasons sufficient to prevent any of us from interfering in Washington's retirement from state affairs?" All laughed heartily at this sally.

"In fact," remarked Madame Helvetius, "such a style ought to reign supreme in our little dinner of to-day, because it possesses simplicity. You comprehend that I have not forgotten the favorite dish of Franklin—eggs and mustard—which he introduced into Paris, and which has long ceased to be considered a barbarism, but, on the contrary, has become quite fashionable."

Franklin knocked with his cane on the ground, and said, smilingly: "You more than fill the measure of your goodness toward me; although, on the other hand, it renews my sorrow, that I cannot always remain with you, and end my life under the blessing of such a guardian angel!" They were standing before the pleasant villa,

---

* Lafayette made another voyage to America in the spring of 1784.—"Mémoires du Général Lafayette," vol. ii., pp. 81, 87.

while a servant was opening the gate for their entrance. Madame Helvetius had not answered the last remark of Franklin. He stood for some time, with his arms folded, looking above the door of the house, where, from all appearance, a marble slab had been inserted. "I only now observe, dear friend," said he, with rather a vexed expression, "that you have had the marble taken down that formerly adorned the front of your villa. It contained an inscription which I much liked; it praised Boileau and Gendron, and was composed by the witty Voltaire. I really must blame you; nothing of Voltaire's should be lost—at least, in political matters—not even the most insignificant expression in defence of liberty! It is to his mind that we owe much that has been done for human equality. He is, in fact, the originator of this new era, and Benjamin Franklin will never cease to admire his political genius!"

"The inscription had become damaged," replied Madame Helvetius, "and, as I fancied the slab was not fastened securely, I had it taken down and placed in the grove in my garden. I think that place much more suitable for it, as the inscription was intended for the previous proprietors of my little home,* and we have to fight now under our own flag. Is it not so, Count Mirabeau?"

"Yes," cried Mirabeau, excitedly, "and on this standard Madame Helvetius's fair hand will embroider the word Liberty!—But the name of Voltaire will always be the most powerful, under whose auspices the minds of France will unite. My friend, in his adoration of Voltaire, certainly sees the present condition of mankind in its proper light. I can never think unmoved of that scene where Franklin brought his four-year-old grandson to Voltaire, asking the latter to impart his blessing to the child."

"That is an unforgotten moment!" said Franklin, folding his hands. "With a truly sincere

expression of countenance, Voltaire placed both hands on the head of the boy, uttering, in a ringing voice that deeply affected me: 'Liberty, tolerance, and honesty!'*—But let us go into the garden," added Franklin, with a countenance of gentle melancholy, "I should like to see again the words which always made on me an agreeable and heart-awakening impression."

"And I make the perverse proposition to defer this ceremony until after dinner," said Chamfort, with comic urgency. "If it cannot be unanimously acceded to, I make another, that our hungry stomachs shall hold a council in the open air, and take a vote, as formerly the red-haired Germans did."

"If my words have any influence," replied Madame Helvetius, "I give them in favor of this idea, but I beg to make an amendment. Our council should not be held in the open air, but in my dining-room; otherwise, you will find your dinner cold and unpalatable." This invitation could not be resisted, and the guests followed their hostess into the house. In the room a letter was handed to Madame Helvetius, which she opened quickly and eagerly; having read it she laid it on the table with an expression of profound sorrow. After a pause she said, while tears came to her eyes: "Diderot has sent me a refusal. He cannot come, and who knows whether we shall ever see him again? I have an evil presentiment. His health is very bad, and the Marquis d'Holbach in his anxiety would not permit Diderot to take the short trip to Auteuil. How sad that a man of such genius should be taken from those who delight in him!"

"I saw Diderot yesterday in Paris," said Lafayette, "and advised him to confide himself to the German doctor Mesmer, whose extraordinary cures are producing a great excitement in Paris. But he laughed at me, saying that he could not make up his mind to believe in magnetism, after seeing how little consideration intellect has in the world."

"That was a good lesson for General Lafayette,

---

* "C'est ici le vrai Parnasse des vrais enfans d'Apollon. Sous le nom de Boileau ces lieux virent Horace: Esculape y paraît sous celui de Gendron." (This is the true Parnassus of the true children of Apollo. Under the name of Boileau this place beheld Horace: Esculapius appeared under that of Gendron.)

* "Souvenirs de la Marquise de Créquy," vol. v., p. 3.

who has become the pupil of Mesmer!" exclaimed Mirabeau, ironically. "Every man that wills it carries magnetism within himself. Then where is the need of a German charlatan? The only question is, how much strength of will a person possesses. If my will is powerful enough, I can at any time take the hand of the most beautiful girl in the world, and say to her: 'Follow me! I am he!' And by the mysterious influence I have on her, she will obey without looking to the right or to the left, not thinking even of father, mother, or other relatives!" This declaration was received with laughter.

"If that is the case, Mirabeau is the master of magnetic cures!" exclaimed Chamfort.

"I pray you, gentlemen, to end your philosophic disputes for the present!" said Madame Helvetius, in an urgent voice, at the same time inviting her guests to take their places at the table.

CHAPTER III.

HENRIETTE VAN HAREN.

In a convent near the old church of St. Germain des Prés in Paris, a young maiden had been living as a boarder for several years. The few who had any opportunity of seeing her were captivated by her uncommon beauty and gracefulness. She was of Dutch birth, and called Henriette Amélie van Haren, a name she bore as an illegitimate daughter of the Dutch poet Ouno Zwier van Haren. The latter was renowned as the author of the Netherland song of liberty, "Les Gueux," * as well as a statesman and active partisan of the Prince of Orange. At the death of the poet, which occurred in 1779, Henriette was fourteen years old. She was sent to the convent at Paris to finish her education, and to reside there until her future destiny was decided. Her only means of subsistence was a small annuity settled on her by her father. Thus,

* "The Beggars."

in obscurity and almost unknown, she attained her nineteenth year. Her physical beauty and mental power were extraordinary, while the loneliness and retirement of her life must have produced in her romantic thoughts. Henriette not having friends or relatives in Paris, no one was specially interested in the great progress her mind had made, or in the extreme loveliness of her person. The nuns and other boarders, the only companions she knew, treated her like one of themselves, and, having become accustomed to the routine of her duty, the activity of her mind and the cheerfulness of her temper seemed not to have suffered. Her only recreation consisted in visiting the convent garden, and participating in the little parties of pleasure, arranged during the summer, at neighboring places such as Auteuil, for all the residents of the convent, under the supervision of the worthy prioress, a Countess de Montessuy.

The last expedition of this kind seemed to have left many memories in Henriette's mind. While taking a walk with some of her companions in a field near Auteuil, she was greatly annoyed by the importunities of a gentleman, who, after the first glance at her face, turned and followed them, wherever they went. He was near when she entered the carriage to return. At that moment his large commanding eyes, which arrested and held her in a certain sense in bondage, made an impression on her she had never felt before. It was too plain that Henriette was the object of his intrusive attentions; and she was forced to listen to the biting sarcasm of her partly-jealous companions, and the grave exhortation of the prioress. The next day the stranger appeared at the back-gate of the convent; and what was most remarkable, she happened to pass just at that time. His greeting frightened her, and she hurried away to the darker walks of the garden. But, during the whole night, in her lonely cell, she thought of this man; she could not direct her mind to any other object, while this haunting idea of the heroic figure of her admirer was associated with resistance and fear, filling her heart with restless foreboding. This was heightened still more, when, on the following evening, at a later hour, she suddenly saw him before her in her favorite retreat behind the linden-trees. He dared to address her, and, as by some irresistible impulse, she was compelled to answer him. Never had she heard any one speak as he did. While he was addressing her a halo seemed to play about his head, shedding a magic light upon the shadowy paths of the garden. At the same time, she felt the danger of finding herself entirely alone with him, for all her companions had already entered the convent. She had, however, sufficient resolution to snatch her hand away, murmuring some scarcely intelligible syllables, and ran toward her home before the stranger could overtake her, although he was inconsiderate enough to follow her. At the same hour on the succeeding day Henriette sat in her small chamber, absorbed in dreamy meditation and anxiety. Leaning her beautiful blond head on her hand, she thought very seriously of all that had lately occurred to her, believing, in the honesty of her heart, that perhaps she ought to reproach herself. The image of the mysterious stranger forced itself upon her, notwithstanding all her efforts; she renewed her revolting sensations when first she saw him, as if in her soul to gain assistance against him. She acknowledged that her first impression was very fearful; and when she remembered the powerful form that had so strangely met her, she almost fancied that she had to do with a demon enticing her to ruin. As she recalled his face, it seemed to her it was shockingly wild, hard, and repulsive. Yet, while the evening before he was explaining to her the motives of his presence, his countenance seemed flooded with radiant beauty, and then she would rather have likened him to a god. But Henriette resolved henceforth to banish his memory, and not for a moment allow her thoughts to revert to him. To accomplish this purpose, she intended not to enter the garden for some time, pretending illness, so that she might be obliged to remain in her room for several weeks. The pious child was so earnest that she knelt, praying to the pictured Virgin looking down on her pillow.

Some one knocked gently at the door of her cell, and Henriette sprang up with an exclamation. She breathed freely only when she saw Sister Angelica, one of the most religious nuns in the convent, instead of the masculine unknown whom the excited fancy of the girl had led her to expect. This sister had lately been particularly attentive to Henriette; but there was something so acute and lurking in the manner of the old woman that her attention could not but be received with anxiety. Sister Angelica approached with an assumed lightness of step, and kissed Henriette's forehead, at the same time piercing her with such a searching side-glance, that the maiden trembled involuntarily, stepping back as if expecting bad news.

"I sought you in the garden, Sister Henriette," began the nun, "and thought that I would certainly find you under the linden-trees, because you were there yesterday about this time, and seemed to be very well entertained. Why are you not there to-day, my innocent child?"

"Why am I not there?" repeated Henriette, with trembling haste, her manner plainly betraying her.

"Well, I will not torment you; you are a dear, good girl, but you are in great danger!" said the sister, very solemnly. She seized Henriette's arm and drew the confused girl to the sofa, without any resistance. "It is charming this evening under the trees, with their sweet fragrance, but your knight has awaited you there in vain," added Angelica, in a mysterious whisper.

"You know all!" replied Henriette, her tears flowing upon her cheeks; "then you must know also how innocent I am—that the meeting yesterday was accidental, and that I abhor the persecutions of the stranger, whom I wish never to see again. I have vowed not to leave this room until all memory of that man is lost to me!"

"The Holy Virgin bless you now, my daughter!" replied the nun, folding her hands, and, turning to the picture of the Madonna, she whispered a prayer. Then she continued, with her winning smile: "And I have vowed to assist you faithfully in withstanding your temptations. I was near yesterday when the tempter approached you. I prayed for you all night in my cell; and, this afternoon, went punctually to the same hiding-place to reconnoitre the movements of Satan against you. But the world-renowned seducer did not find his victim. It gave me great delight to contemplate at my leisure him before whom all women in France tremble—to whom no house, no convent, no temple is sacred!"

"Of whom are you talking, Sister Angelica, for Heaven's sake!" asked Henriette, seizing the hands of the nun, and clinging to her.

"And is it possible that you do not know his name?" asked the nun, smiling significantly. "You really do not know that the man who pursues you, who is stretching his destructive hands after you—that ensnarer of innocence, who has entered your own retreat and privacy—is no other than Count Mirabeau?"

"No, indeed, I neither knew nor imagined it!" exclaimed Henriette, shuddering. She blushed deeply, and, with her head inclined, fell into a dreamy meditation, seeming to forget the presence of the pious sister.

"Yes, Count Mirabeau!" repeated Angelica, making the sign of the cross, and looking half solemn, half apprehensive. "I recognized him immediately when he met us in Auteuil; and, yesterday evening, when a ray of the moon fell on his face, I was confirmed in my discovery. Poor child, it is Count Gabriel Riquetti de Mirabeau, whose eyes Satan himself must have turned toward you, and who purposes to inveigle you by his infernal arts. His power is great, and I fear you will not be able to resist it!"

"Have no apprehension, Sister Angelica!" replied Henriette, starting from her reverie. The expression of her face had suddenly changed, and a thoughtful smile played on her lips. "And how did you know it was Count Mirabeau?" she timidly asked.

"Oh," replied the old nun, "did I not see him in the convent of St. Clarisse, at Gien, whence he twice attempted to carry off the noble and beautiful Sophie de Monnier? You know I was at Gien before I came here. An unhappy dispute I

had with the abbess made it desirable for me to make a change. My cell was next to that of Sophie, and I can boast that I was her confidante. Alas! she permitted me to read her tortured soul; and, having been a witness of her sufferings, I know something of what it is to be seduced by Mirabeau."

The attention of Henriette was aroused by this recital. "What!" she exclaimed, with a flashing glance, "were you the friend of that unfortunate Sophie, whose sufferings and adventures are known to all France? Every feeling heart has associated the names of Sophie and Mirabeau in a sort of poetic union of the tenderness and the agony of love! Oh, tell me all you know about them, for my heart thirsts after the narrative—nothing ever interested me so much as the fate of those two lovers."

"That is a very dangerous curiosity, my child," observed Angelica, with an austere gesture. "The works of Satan may be recognized by the interest they have in our minds.—We nuns at the convent of St. Clarisse feared every day that Count Mirabeau would attack us! We all thought of being carried off by him and plunged into the sad destiny of our tempted Sophie."

Henriette, who, even in the most serious moments, could not sometimes resist the expression of her natural cheerfulness, suddenly broke out into hearty laughter. "But he never attempted to drag away any of you dignified heads of the convent?" she asked, banteringly.

"Yes!" answered Angelica, hastily and significantly. "Count Mirabeau came twice most criminally to disturb the peace of the St. Clarisse, and subvert as an invader our holy regulations. He came to trouble Sophie's rest—to make her fall out with her own heart, and to urge her, who was still subject to his influence, to flee with him. Those attempts of the Wicked One touched me deeply, as I was Sophie's constant companion, and the ailment in my chest, which will shortly cause my death, takes its date precisely from that period!"

"And how did Sophie behave? Her beauty, heroic courage, and desire of martyrdom, are cel-

ebrated in all the stories related of her," said
Henriette, with a glowing flash from her beautiful
eyes.

"I will tell you all, my child!" replied the
nun. "You know that Sophie de Monnier, the
wife of the governor of Castle Joux, committed
the awful sin of permitting Count Mirabeau to
carry her away from her husband. By my patron
saint, it was a great sin! but Sophie was only
nineteen years old, and the Marquis de Monnier,
whom her mother forced her to marry, was in his
eightieth year. That was exciting the temptations
of the flesh, and the Evil One employed one of
his most successful favorites, in the person of
Count Mirabeau, who was sent as a prisoner to
Castle Joux, near Pontarlier."

"Every child in France knows that, good Sister
Angelica!" exclaimed Henriette, interrupting her,
impatiently. "Who has not heard the wonderful
story, how Sophie and Mirabeau met and loved
each other; and how the latter, whom the law
had delivered into the hands of a despotic father,
won her as the angel that was to compensate him
for his long and cruel sufferings in prison? He
carried her off, as I have read, freeing both from
their chains. He lived with her a life of love in
Amsterdam, until the officers of justice overtook
them, taking Mirabeau to the dungeons of Vincennes, and burying Sophie in the convent at
Gien, at the instigation of her revengeful husband!"

"How well you are acquainted with all the
circumstances, my poor daughter!" sighed Angelica. "And, believe me, it is very dangerous
to pay so much attention to such things. But
Count Mirabeau, in numerous pamphlets, did all
he could to make every thing relating to the affair public, trumpeting to all the world his arts of
seduction."

"Pardon me, I believe you do him an injustice," replied Henriette, quickly. "He only published his memoirs after he had been set free
from Vincennes, his father's anger having at
length cooled. He gave himself up again as prisoner at Pontarlier, to have his lawsuit reëxamined,
and, if possible, the first verdict reversed. That

was why he published his defence. Our physician lately gave his memoirs to me, and they are
well written—they are like sweet melodies at-
tuned by the hand of a master. And did not the
judges themselves become sensible of the injustice of the sentence condemning him to death for
the seduction of Sophie, declaring the decision
void? And was it not Mirabeau's intention, in
justifying himself, also to justify her, and thereby
gain her freedom?"

"No," replied Sister Angelica, impetuously,
"that was only a pretence; his object, in representing his intimacy with Sophie as innocent,
was for the liberation of his own person. Mirabeau desired this, because then he hoped to induce his wife Emilie de Marignane to reunite herself with him. She would not live with him, on
account of his notorious infidelities. He wished
to repossess himself of her, or rather her fortune,
in order to enter a new career. But his calculations failed, and, although he gained his process
in Pontarlier, he did not profit by it. Last year
his wife obtained an absolute divorce."

"It is true," said Henriette, timidly, "I had
forgotten that Count Mirabeau had been married,
and disputed with his wife about her property. It
is also a proof," she added, after a pause, "that
he turned from his Sophie, and that their friendship was not enduring, as she supposed.—But
you were about to tell me of her, and the visits
Count Mirabeau paid you in your convent at
Gien?"

"Yes, I shall never forget those fearful visits!"
sighed the nun, glancing imploringly at the image
of the Virgin, as if to gain courage and consolation. "Mirabeau and Sophie kept up a loving
correspondence during their imprisonment. I
read many of those letters, having Sophie's unconditional confidence. By my hand her epistles
were forwarded to the prisoner at Vincennes.
Count Mirabeau was suddenly set free. The correspondence, formerly so passionate, was no
longer the same. He wrote her rude letters, full
of anger and jealousy, and Madame de Malleroye
(the name Sophie bore in the convent, because
she hated that of her husband) replied no less

bitterly. Mirabeau reproached her with infidelity to him. At one time he accused her of criminal intimacy with her confessor Le Tellier, then with other individuals, whose visits she received in her cell. The most distinguished persons of the town of Gien, attracted by her amiability and gentleness, visited her daily, paying her every attention; but there was not one, I declare it solemnly, who could in the least give cause of jealousy to Mirabeau. Sophie said that he played the part of a jealous lover in order to forsake her. The physician of our convent, Dr. Ysabeau, was a friend of both, and endeavored to effect a reconciliation. He wished to induce a meeting, and Sophie consented, although I dared to make the gravest representations against it. But the doctor carried his point. He himself travelled to Nogent-sur-Vernisson, where the count then was; procured for him the disguise and pack of a pedler, and under this mask led him to Sophie's cell. I was to be the only witness of this interview, that at a future time she might not be accused of having been the cause of any impropriety in the convent. The two lovers greeted each other with monosyllables, and immediately commenced a very stormy interview. Mirabeau maintained his charges against her, but could bring no proof. At first she defended herself with her usual gentleness; gradually she became more excited, and finally she recriminated the accusation, but, unlike him, produced proof of his unfaithfulness. Even while writing the most ardent letters to her from Vincennes, Mirabeau had amorous intrigues with two other women, whom he had fascinated. One was the wife of the governor of the castle where he was imprisoned, and the other a princess of France, whose name I dare not mention. This princess obtained many privileges for him. It was through her friendship that he was sometimes permitted to visit Paris, and it is ascribed to her influence that he was afterward liberated. With these facts, of which every one was talking, Sophie openly reproached him. Mirabeau foamed with rage, his voice sounded like the roar of a lion, and the whole convent was startled by his loud and angry words. The nuns knelt in their cells, praying, and thinking that the arch-tempter himself had broken into the fold, and none had courage to meet him. The Count and Sophie separated, both highly exasperated, and far from regaining the concord of their hearts." *

"Oh, how sad!" exclaimed Henriette, her bosom heaving with a sigh of sympathy. "And did they never again meet in love?" she added, softly, her voice trembling with expectation.

"In our convent at Gien we feared his return every day!" replied Sister Angelica. "Some time, however, passed before the marchioness heard any thing more of him. But suddenly he seemed to repent. He proposed a reconciliation and abduction, in a letter to Sophie, and she was weak and loving enough to agree to his plans. When she saw that I opposed this intention, on account of the future good of her soul, she withdrew her confidence from me and maintained an obstinate silence. I redoubled my watchfulness. Soon I discovered all their arrangements. Mirabeau had by some means procured a wax impression of the keys of the large gate, and gave Sophie the keys he had obtained, so that she could depart. The hour of flight was appointed. He was standing near the gate to receive the beautiful fugitive; but I had betrayed every thing to our abbess, after strengthening myself by prayer. At the moment Sophie put the key into the lock, the arm of the abbess prevented her exit. The count scarcely had time to escape the men-servants of the convent, who had been summoned. I secretly enjoyed the triumph of the just in having saved Sophie from this soul-destroying reunion." †

"And Count Mirabeau has since given up all attempts to regain possession of his Sophie?" asked Henriette, dreamily.

"They have parted forever," replied the nun, with pathetic gravity. "She recovered her liberty some months ago, but he has not troubled himself in the least about her."

---

* Montigny, "Mémoires de Mirabeau," vol. iii., p. 298.
† Cadet de Gassicourt, "Essai sur la Vie de Mirabeau."

"What! the Marchioness de Monnier is no longer in the convent at Gien?" asked Henriette, with an expression of restlessness and sadness.

"The death of her husband freed her from all restraint," said Sister Angelica. "She had been obliged to sign a declaration never to leave the convent during her husband's lifetime, when Mirabeau gained his lawsuit in Pontarlier. After the marquis died she hired a small house in Gien, near the convent, and in fact connected with the place where she had found consolation and refuge. She boarded with the pious sisters of St. Clarisse, without whose companionship she could not live, feeling a reluctance to return to her family, from whom she had suffered so much. She has found peace and a home near the friendly banks of the Loire, and may God bless her, although she is my enemy since the event I have related to you." Sister Angelica prayed softly, and Henriette felt herself called upon to join in the devotion by the severe glances of the nun.—"Now I have prayed for you also, that Heaven may protect you against Count Mirabeau!" said Angelica, rising. "You are sought by the most dangerous and profligate of men, and I considered it my duty to warn and assist you."

"I thank you," replied Henriette, her countenance again crimsoned with a blush. "Your intention is good, and I appreciate it, although I am not in such great danger as you imagine."

"You fancy yourself safe; because Count Mirabeau is an ugly-looking man," replied the old nun, eagerly. "That is just the beginning of the mischief, where he is concerned. When first seen, his savage face, deeply pitted with small-pox, makes a fearful impression, and his broad-shouldered and powerful frame forces you almost to sink down before him. But this is the charm Satan has given him to destroy all he approaches. For, after I had seen him several times, I felt in my heart that his repulsiveness began to change. But now good-night, sister! It is quite late!"

She hastened away, leaving her young friend a prey to the utmost excitement.

CHAPTER IV.

MIRABEAU AND HENRIETTE.

HENRIETTE was still in the same position, musing on the events of Sister Angelica's story. Night and silence surrounded the maiden as she sat absorbed in her own thoughts. The foliage of the convent-garden was rustling in the evening air, that with its perfume came laden to her with many sad and yet pleasing memories. Suddenly she awoke from her dreamy meditation, and became attentive and anxious without apparent cause. A sound as of one whispering seemed to proceed from the hedges. She sprang up, and hurrying to the window carefully closed it. Lighting a candle, she searched around her, though convinced that the noise which so alarmed her in her cell was but the suggestion of her own imagination. Standing at the window she had again opened, nothing was heard but the night-wind sighing among the dark trees and along the flowery paths. Suppressing her fear, she took up a book she had commenced to read some time before, but could not fasten her attention upon it. Placing it aside, she again went to the window, and now plainly heard a voice in the garden. At the same moment she was also attracted by a slight noise at her door, which made her tremble, and a cry of alarm escaped her. She was on the point of locking herself in, but some undefined feeling agitating her mind prevented her. The door opened, and in the dark background of the chamber appeared the figure of a man, whom Henriette immediately recognized. She almost lost control of her senses. "It is he! Count Mirabeau!" she whispered, stretching out her hand, as if to forbid his approach.

"You know my name, Henriette!" he exclaimed, triumphantly, quickly advancing and seizing her hands.

Henriette stood as if petrified, letting him press her hands to his lips and breast. The consciousness that in her surprise she had revealed the knowledge of his name had greatly heightened her confusion, and she felt as if all her power of resistance had departed.

"Henriette," said the count, passionately gazing at her, "I am the happiest of mankind, for you were occupied with me since our last meeting, but I will not ask who has betrayed my name to you. What is there in a name associated with nothing but persecution and suffering, and that can only regain its glory in a new life? This life for Mirabeau can only dawn but through your favor, Henriette! You have probably been told, what is known to all France, how tormented I have been; and now my destiny is placed in your hands, that you may pacify the storms which have hitherto beaten around me, and command for me the peace of love with your gracious lips."

Henriette did not reply, standing with her head inclined on her bosom, motionless as a statue. She seemed to fear that action on her part would increase the power he had over her. But, although she made no outward movement, she could not repress the violent beating of her heart and her involuntary confusion, that betrayed her mind more eloquently than words.

"Repeat the expression with which you greeted me at my entrance, Henriette!" exclaimed Mirabeau, drawing her into his arms. "Say again, 'It is he!' and I will read therein the blessed confession, that you will receive and follow me, never to leave me again, but remain in a union of love and truth. Will you come now, at this moment?"

Henriette slowly shook her head, without withdrawing herself from his arms or uttering a word. A perplexed smile passed over her face, expressing more of anticipated happiness than a reluctance to accompany him.

"You will not speak to me?" recommenced Mirabeau, with the most insinuating tone of his full, deep voice. "But your heart lies open before me; and, if your lips refuse the words I ask, your heart will reply. Yes, 'it is he' who, after having once seen, could not forget, and dared to penetrate even within these sacred walls to call you! 'It is he' who, inspired by your youth and beauty, has knocked at your door to win you to a happier existence, to which, with all your charms, you properly belong. 'It is he' who will carry you in his strong and safe arms out of this prison, and open for you the gates of a brighter life. Then come, and follow your friend who loves you. Every thing is prepared; I have conquered your jailers, and no human hand shall stay our flight."

Henriette looked searchingly into his face, to read more surely his intentions, and she thought she saw some truth and love, confirming all her secret wishes. The wildness of his look, that formerly repulsed her, had changed to tenderness; and if he still had the appearance of a lion in his physical strength, there seemed to be also a submission to her own gentle influences, with which she might subdue him.

Mirabeau, looking steadfastly into her eyes, said: "Come, Henriette, it is time to leave this place. Beyond these walls you will find liberty, air, and a brighter future! Consider me as your servant, who will guide you safely to reach that happiness of which until now you were unjustly deprived. But a few hours, and the night will do homage to the day. By the first beams of to-morrow's sun, you will enjoy a freedom that you have never known. You will breathe, think, and feel differently, and you will confess to me that I have conquered for you the right of a true and youthful life."

Henriette hesitated still, or rather she dared not come to a decision, feeling that she scarcely had control of her mind.

"Take your shawl and cloak, and wrap yourself up carefully, for the night is cool!" said Mirabeau, enjoining obedience by his looks, which she was unable to resist. Almost mechanically she followed his glances, that fell upon a closet containing her clothing. She went to it, walking like a somnambulist, who follows some mysterious impulse. She took out her garments, holding them up for a moment, as if trying to remember something. But Mirabeau approached quickly, and threw her cloak around her, again enfolding her in his arms. She stood motionless, with closed eyes.

3

"And now take your hat and veil, my beloved child, so as to protect your beautiful locks from the rough night."

Henriette obeyed, drawing the veil down over her face. She stood before him, as if awaiting his next command. Mirabeau beheld her with a passionate look, and she seemed as if she felt its piercing fire, for her whole frame trembled, as if touched by an electric shock.

"But do not forget, Henriette, to take with you whatever may be dear to you among your few possessions."

The girl sighed aloud, as she went to a bureau, ornamented with antique carvings, and drew out several drawers, in which she searched for something. Taking out a gold miniature, set with pearls, of her celebrated father, and kissing it, she put it in her bosom. Appearing now to have more confidence, her cheeks regained their color, and, for the first time, she raised her eyes and turned them full and bright on Mirabeau. She seemed to have awakened as from a deep sleep, looking at him in astonishment, and gently nodding, as if glad to find that the reality had not disappointed her dream. With the light step of a gazelle, she returned to her bureau, taking thence a casket, which she opened and regarded smilingly for a moment. Locking it again, she approached Mirabeau with an almost cheerful motion, contrasting with her previous apparent indifference. He looked at her in pleasant surprise. Placing the casket in his hands, she intimated by a gesture that she wished him to take care of the contents. Her expression had something so touching and humble that Mirabeau fell at her feet, covering her hands with kisses. But Henriette had not spoken a word since the exclamation she had uttered at his entrance. And yet she felt that a great event, having power over her whole life, had taken place; that she had said all that was necessary; that there was nothing to add, and that before him there was a sort of rapture in her silence. But Mirabeau wished to hear the words again for which he had pleaded in vain. He took her in his arms, and, pressing his face to hers, he asked gently: "Are you indeed ready to

follow me, to confide yourself to me, so that we live for each other, existing as by the same breath, never to part again?"

Henriette was still silent, but tears were gathering in her eyes.

"And am I he who first discovered the treasure of your heart?" he continued, with sensitive urgency. "Is it Mirabeau to whom you have betrothed and united yourself? Is it he with whom you will go forth into the world; and can he be certain of your pardon, love, and kindness?"

"It is he!" whispered Henriette, so low as hardly to be heard, and again turned tremblingly away.

"You have uttered that expression!" cried Mirabeau, in his impulsive manner, "and our sweet union is sure. Now we must go! May all prisons in France open as easily to love and liberty as yours, to which you shall never return to incarcerate body and soul!"

Thus speaking, he opened the door, letting her go before him. To assure her of his protection, he held his hand over her, as if by a magnetic gesture, so that the points of his fingers almost touched the crown of her head. She seemed to feel encouraged by the proximity of his hand, going unhesitatingly and fearlessly through the halls of the convent to the principal staircase. No footfall along the hushed and sacred corridors was heard by the sleepers in the cells, and without interruption they approached the convent gate. It stood open, and the old portress was invisible. Hastening into the street, and down into an obscure alley, they reached the carriage ready to receive them. The count's servant opening the door, Mirabeau lifted Henriette into it, and the fugitives quickly passed away in the darkness of the night.

CHAPTER V.

THE MYSTERIOUS CHILD.

THE carriage stopped in the Rue de la Roquette, near the square of the Bastile, where

Count Mirabeau was at present living. The sun was just rising when Henriette, leaning on Mirabeau's arm, hesitatingly entered his insignificant abode. Her excited fancy had involuntarily led her to expect a palace, and for a moment she felt wounded when she saw this dark and poverty-stricken house. But one look at Mirabeau, who was carefully leading her up the smooth stone steps of the narrow staircase, transformed every thing around into beauty and splendor. With a beating heart she stepped into the apartments on the first floor, which were opened by the servant. The two communicating rooms were large, but being almost entirely empty, had a very uncomfortable effect. The most necessary furniture was wanting, or indigently represented. It could hardly be supposed that there was disorder in a place so empty, and yet such was nevertheless the case. The few tables and chairs were loaded with books, papers, and all manner of objects. Even the floor was covered with writings and wearing apparel, indicating that negligence reigned supreme. Since Count Mirabeau had exchanged his unfortunate wanderings for a residence in Paris, he had not been able to acquire accommodations suitable to his rank. He was only beginning to lay the foundation of a better future; but all was uncertainty. His finances were in a most deplorable condition; and the descendant of one of the oldest and most renowned noble families in Provence was leading a kind of bivouac-life, altogether unworthy of him. Yet, in his very moderate circumstances, he had managed to retain a shadow of aristocratic fashion. He not only had a footman, but provided him with so rich a livery that the poverty of the master certainly could not be indicated by the appearance of the servant. He also had a secretary, who would be useful to him in the aspiring literary labors he had lately undertaken. The latter lived in a small back-room, opening into Mirabeau's dwelling. At this moment the side-door opened, and the head of a young man, surmounted by a red, turban-like cloth, looked curiously and smilingly at them.

"You are not wanted, M. Hardy," exclaimed Mirabeau, dismissing his secretary by a motion of his hand.

Henriette looked so pale and exhausted, that Mirabeau begged her to step into an adjoining cabinet, where she would find every thing necessary for her refreshment; but she begged not to be left alone. She sat on a sofa, one of the few conveniences in the room, and regarded him with her gentle yet brilliant eyes, while an expression akin to adoration passed over her lovely countenance, which had suddenly changed from a deathly pallor to a rosy glow. Mirabeau sat in the middle of the room at breakfast, which the footman had just served. Henriette had refused repeated invitations to share with him in this repast, and sat at some distance opposite, not once turning from him, but watching all his motions as if in pleasurable surprise. After he had finished his breakfast, with his natural *laissez-aller*, he again seated himself beside her, tenderly seizing her hand and looking searchingly into her eyes.

"I have followed you," she began to say, in a scarcely audible voice; "and I do not ask what is to become of me, for it was my free choice to place my destiny in your hands. I feel that all I am and ever will be really depends on you. I do not wish it otherwise, for I have found myself driven by an unconquerable influence. Will you never despise me for it, Count Mirabeau? Will you never secretly think less of me, because, forgetting all my duties, thinking only of your words that so strangely overcame me, I went as if a part of you?" It was the first time that she spoke to him in a consecutive manner. Until that moment she had only ventured to signify by broken expressions what was passing in her mind, and the feeling that had become stronger than her former conscientiousness.

"Ah," exclaimed Mirabeau, passionately, "Henriette, you bless me by this doubt, which is only another confession of your love. By following me so confidingly, you have forever made me your debtor—your slave—and my gratitude will never cease. I shall be at your feet in whatever condition the changes of life may find us. What is esteem? A poisoned instrument of social superstition! Despots and the privileged classes desire esteem, on account of their positions, because in their vanity they cannot base them on love and liberty. What I am forced to esteem, I can despise. But we, my dearest friend—if we love truly and honorably, according to the laws of God and Nature, we are worthy of each other's respect, and far below us lie both the veneration and contempt of·the crowd."

Henriette was listening happily and dreamily to sophistries designed to excuse both her and him, and when he ceased was about to reply. She was prevented by the loud cries of a child. Alarmed, she sprang up, regarding the count with such perplexity that he burst into loud laughter.

"That is my little Lucas crying," said Mirabeau. "If it ▓▓▓es you, Henriette, let us pay him a visit, for I have a great desire to introduce this little member of my family to you. The boy must have a strong voice to be heard at such a distance." He arose and led Henriette quickly to the door, through a short passage, and into another apartment belonging to the same suite of rooms. There stood a cradle, in which lay a boy of about two years of age. He seemed to be in a violent passion with his nurse, but yet no one could behold him without admiring his extraordinary beauty. Henriette entered hesitatingly, approaching the child with smiling astonishment, while a deep blush overspread her cheeks. She then looked around at Mirabeau, who was following her, and whose countenance expressed a tenderness such as one could scarcely have expected from his usually repulsive features.

The nurse was a country-girl, dressed in the Provence costume. On a sign from the count she raised the child and held it toward him for his greeting, which was accompanied with such lively and playful caresses that the boy was soon quieted, and even began to crow merrily.

"I have the honor to present to you my little darling 'Coco,'" said Mirabeau to Henriette, with difficulty loosening the hands of the boy from his hair. "I have adopted him, although I have not given him my name," he continued, kissing and patting the child. "His name is Lucas Montigny.

He is a lively and honest little fellow. It is a pleasure to see him in his tantrums; and then again he listens with a grave face when told that he must become a sensible man, who is to be the avenger of poor France, so ill used by her tyrants."[1] Mirabeau's playfulness threw such a charm over his whole manner that Henriette could not refrain from seizing his hand,/ and pressing it tenderly, when it happened to touch hers, as she took the child from him. Then she contemplated the little Lucas with a sympathy momentarily heightened by comparing him with the count. Apparently pleased with the boy, she pressed him again and again tenderly to her bosom, then suddenly replaced him in his cradle, while a profound sadness seemed to take possession of her. With her head bowed down, she remained for some minutes in silent thoughtfulness. Mirabeau recalled her from her dream, raising his forefinger in a sportively threatening manner, and exhorting her to bring back her thoughts to him and the present. Henriette sighed as she accepted his offered arm.

"Lucas Montigny will go to sleep again," he said, in that good-natured tone which to Henriette seemed to add a new charm to his usually impassioned utterance. "We shall now leave him and return to ourselves. I have a presentiment that we three—Mirabeau, Henriette, and Coco—are destined to be a happy family. Will you not be as a guardian angel to the young rogue I love so much, under whose wings he may be fostered, and become a true, honest, and great man? For are not you and I bound together indissolubly? And, as a cupid, you must take this lovely little boy into the bargain of our union. Is it not so, my friend?"

Henriette nodded, but when they had returned to the sitting-room, overwhelmed by her feelings, she fell into his arms, and held him long in her embrace. "He is your son, Mirabeau, is he not?" she asked, looking up to him timidly and bashfully.

"The little fellow is an enigma, as I have told you, Henriette!" replied Mirabeau, evasively.

"Is he the son of Sophie de Monnier or of the

Countess de Mirabeau?" she asked again, almost entreatingly. Her heart was tormented by a painful uncertainty, and, for the sake of her own peace of mind, she thought it necessary to discover more about this child.

"Ah, my innocent Henriette," replied Mirabeau, smiling, "I see that the stories of my life have penetrated even into your convent. But where are they not known? You are aware, then, how Sophie and I once loved each other. We were martyrs to society—at least, to some of its unreasonable demands. Abandoned, as on a tempestuous sea, we sought each other's safety. The tyranny of her family had forced upon her a husband old and disagreeable; and I was delivered over to a despotic father, by an unnatural and execrable law, which, for years, dragged me from prison to prison. At Pontarlier, where I was confined last, I saw Sophie. Each loved in the other freedom, happiness, lost youth; and, at that calamitous moment, our destinies were united. How could it be otherwise? We fled separately, and met as lovers on the boundaries of Switzerland; but, as might be expected, our relationship, believe me, was the source of the most bitter persecution and suffering! We lived a love-life in Holland; but who can tell our mental agony? The voice of conscience intruded upon our pleasures, and our iniquitous dream of love was only another adversity. In the midst of our mingled happiness and sorrow, the arm of justice overtook us. I was carried to Vincennes, she to the convent at Gien, where, soon after her arrival, she gave birth to a daughter, the only offspring of our wicked love, and who died in a few months. Soon nothing remained of this melancholy romance but its memory, woven into a web of poetic thought by the exchange of letters from prison to cloister. These, perhaps, will take a classic place among compositions of a tender nature! But, Henriette, my inmost heart, after all, was not touched. It remained for another and truer love—for you—to renew my life! The noisy little Lucas Montigny shall not disturb us in it."

Henriette listened to her lover with profound attention. All he said was to her so important that she accepted it, as it were, with her eyes, and hid it in her heart. Her countenance manifested a certain devotion and indeed veneration. She folded her hands on her bosom, and stood smiling before him, to follow his decision, and hear his judgment of herself.

Mirabeau had passed his youth, being thirty-five years of age; but his appearance expressed youthful feeling, united with great physical strength, and a supple gracefulness, all successful in removing the first impression of his extraordinary ugliness of feature. At this moment, Henriette was subject more than ever to the magic charm of his personality, and clung to him as a child that can make no resistance; but her doubts were not entirely dissolved. For a few moments she relapsed into thought; then she regarded him with her questioning and entreating eye, gently asking: "And the Countess de Mirabeau?"

"The Countess de Mirabeau!" he repeated, with a convulsive gesture. "This fair lady bears no relation whatever to me or to little Lucas. Emilie de Marigny never loved me. At the time I most needed the consoling hand of woman she manifested a cruel indifference, and turned from me. My marriage with her was one of the follies of my age. I was only in my twenty-first year when I committed it. It originated from my roving, adventurous life, resisting my father's wishes, who desired to see me a country gentleman in Provence, a pious cultivator of the earth on our hereditary estates. I might have become a good soldier, for, in my seventeenth year, I was a lieutenant, and participated in the campaign against Corsica. But my parent's avarice and dislike prevented him from buying a higher commission for me. So I thought I would try a country-life in companionship with a rich and beautiful lady, and Emilie de Marigny became my wife. The peace of this new life, however, was a deception as well as the riches of my consort, which belonged to the future, and at that time only amounted to a yearly income of six thousand francs. But this miserable existence with her lasted two years, during which, by the talent I have for making debts, I drew after me a multitude of creditors, who demanded of me more than one hundred thousand francs. My unfeeling father made this a new cause to subject me again to that terrible scourge, the *lettres de cachet*, killing personal liberty, even in the bosom of families. He again incarcerated me, driving me from prison to prison, as one or the other appeared safer or more intolerable. From this moment Emilie withdrew herself from me, refusing to be in any way associated with my destiny. I have never seen her since. The boy she bore me after the first year of our union died, and in him the pledge also of reconciliation with her and my family, on which I had counted. We became and remain forever separated. You have doubtless heard that, after my liberation from Vincennes, I endeavored to effect a reunion with her. I did this because I earnestly desired to reëstablish all my personal relations. I wished to renounce all the extravagances of my youth, and occupy before the world a good social position, working with all my might to gain a higher and worthier name. I must own that the great fortune of which Emilie had become mistress did have some influence on me. I hoped to obtain those advantages from society which can only be snatched, as it were, with difficulty, when we appear with empty pockets. I knew I could more easily rise to those high places my country will one day acknowledge as my right, and I would have raised Emilie with me; but, blinded by the evil counsel of her father, she refused to return, and we entered into a violent and passionate dispute, not only before the courts of justice, but before all France. She had a memoir printed against me that destroyed the last consideration of a reunion. When the divorce was finally pronounced, my only emotion was that of joy at this release from bondage!—But the sweetest compensation for my sufferings I have now received. I saw you, Henriette, and your divine gentleness, goodness, and beauty, made me a prisoner at the first glance. We now enter into a new and enduring bond, that promises me new happiness, and a new life from this day!"

· Henriette regarded him with grateful eyes, clinging tenderly to his side. Her countenance beamed with innocence, mingled with a joyful courage and confidence. She seemed to strengthen herself in the resolutions she was making for Mirabeau. He took her hand and again led her to the sofa, where they both seated themselves. "Is it not so, Henriette, that we have entered into a perpetual bond of love?" he asked, laying his hand on her shoulder. "Let us be faithful companions through life! You will not leave me? You will hold my destiny under the protection of your beautiful eyes. Your hand will soften the rough traits in my character, which I inherited from my unnatural father, and you will change them into grace and virtue? I feel that your presence will make amends to me for the crimes of a paternal despotism as unparalleled as it was unmerited.

"And how, such as I see you here, could your father hate and persecute you?" asked Henriette, naïvely.

"Oh," replied Mirabeau, with bitter recollection, "this hatred was born with me; it darkened the earliest years of my childhood! My father, the Marquis de Mirabeau, disliked me at first, because I was uglier than my brothers and sisters. · He became my bitterest enemy, and is so even to the present day, because I once said, in the proud consciousness of my strength and youth, that he ought to indulge me in my preferences, if he possessed any self-love, for the renown I intended to gain would partly be ascribed to him.* My haughty and obstinate father could never forgive me for this, and he resolved to destroy me. He, the '*Ami des Hommes*' (the title he gave to one of his most famous works, with which he intended to serve the interests especially of the nation and generally of mankind), became the wolf of his own family, whom he attacked and pursued, whenever and wherever he could. He succeeded, through the court friendship he maintained with the ministers of the king, in procuring, one after another, fifty-

---

* Montigny, "Mémoires sur Mirabeau," vol. i., pp. 234, 241.

four warrants against different members of his family. Not only myself and my brothers and sisters, but his wife, my own dear mother, became his victims. This paternal friend of humanity not only imprisoned us, he wearied out the courts of justice in France by the scandalous processes he was continually instituting! And yet a man could do all this who certainly entertained good and excellent thoughts, and possessed a superior mind—nay, who had taken a high position among the leaders of the new school! He wished to conduct society back to patriarchal life, and make the realization of land the measure of all rights and duties in the state. That such advocates of reform were nothing but philanthropic charlatans, was proved by the Marquis de Mirabeau. If his views had been founded on correct ideas and real humanity, one of the principal professors of this agricultural system could not have borne in his heart so much hatred against his own kindred. My father taught me thoroughly what a despot is. This bitter knowledge, although I paid for it with the better part of my youth, may bear good fruit, not only for me, but for France! For it has been infused into all my veins that resistance to unjust authority is the true battle of life in our day. All will soon have to rise against oppressive power, however sanctified—all who do not consider individual right, society, honor, liberty, and happiness, as mere chimeras! By means of my quarrels with my father, I have caught a glimpse of the inner corruption of this French monarchy—of the iniquitous tribunals, where court influence and bribery may make a mockery of right and justice! To such authorities I was long exposed! Mournfully I passed my youth in prisons and fortresses; but in them I learned to worship freedom. In my loss the nation shall find her youth!" He sprang up at these words, and stood in the middle of the room, as if absorbed in his thoughts. The sun had risen, and, shining through the windows, its beams played as a halo about Mirabeau's brow. Henriette looked at him for some time in astonishment, and then arose and softly approached him, wishing to recall him from his vision of the future

to the present. As she came near him, she felt his overpowering influence over her, and lost courage; for, raising her hand to touch him, she dropped it again. He was engaged in a soliloquy, in a low voice, fighting the air with his arms. At last he noticed her, as she stood with folded hands and in smiling expectation.

"Is it you, my fair, good child?" he said, caressing her hand. "Pardon me for withdrawing my thoughts from you for a moment. I was endeavoring to discover what despotism really is, and how this vampire could steal into the freeborn soul of man. What is it? Why, that is despotism when one man binds the fetters of his egotism on another—when one regards his fellow only as unthinking substance to work upon for his own purposes, making it take whatever form he pleases. But despotism is not the creative genius that loves the very material on which it labors, inseparably uniting the thoughts of the worker with that material, and in his enthusiasm aiding him in his ideas of harmony and beauty of execution. Despotism is that destructive hatred always finding cause to assert itself, and attracting its object as the serpent does the innocent bird, until it approaches of its own accord and irresistibly perishes. Thus my father endeavored to destroy me, in order to demonstrate his own will and superiority, forgetting that I belong to myself—to my own will—to my own mind, in all its faculties—capable of directing and moulding the life given me. Such as my unhappy father, is that ruler whose throne rests on the heads of slaves, because he thinks it dangerous to recognize a free people, with whom he would have to enter into a relationship of love and right!

"This reminds me of an anecdote of my youth, that made the gulf between my father and myself wider. He surprised me once while declaiming passionately in my room. In his usual sarcastic manner he said: 'Ah, you are practising to become the future Demosthenes of France!' 'And why not, my father?' I answered, with the inconsiderate courage of a boy. 'Perhaps the Estates of France may be convoked some day, and then I will speak!' My father turned pale and left me. For several days he avoided addressing me a single word. Not long afterward he obtained his first warrant against me, incarcerating me in the fortress on the Island Rhé, ostensibly on account of a love-intrigue that was making quite a sensation, and in which I acted with the levity of a lieutenant of seventeen. He even intended to send me to one of the Dutch colonies in India, where the climate kills many a European immigrant who doubts and dares its unhealthiness. I was saved only by the most pressing representations of his friends. But he thought himself justified in using all means of slower torture, and, on the slightest occasion, depriving me of my newly-acquired liberty. Even recently, when I thought myself past all these sufferings, his reconciliation with me is false—it is the soft covering of the tiger's claw. He not only withholds the yearly allowance he had promised me to reëstablish myself respectably, and through want of which I am exposed to distressing embarrassments, but he immediately laid a judicial interdict on me, publishing the statement that he and the fortune of his family would not be responsible for my debts. In this way he still revenges himself on the boy who dared dream of the freedom of France and the future convocation of the Estates."

At this moment a loud knocking was heard, which seemed to have a terrifying effect on Mirabeau. He stopped and looked around in perplexity. The knocking continued and was accompanied with voices, demanding an entrance to impatient men. Henriette at first considered this interruption as something quite natural, and intended to open the door, but was restrained by the urgent signs Mirabeau made her. With a sort of despairing gesture, contrasting with the heroic character he had just been delineating, he laid his finger on his lips, intimating a necessity for silence. Henriette felt very uneasy, remembering that it might be a search for her own person, and her pale face expressed solicitude and fear. In her rash but confiding surrender of herself to Mirabeau, she had not thought of this probability. One of the doors opened, admitting the footman, hastily followed by Hardy, the secretary. They approached and whispered something to the count, who suspiciously shook his head.

"I thought it might be some of my hungry creditors, who have latterly disturbed at times my morning rest," said Mirabeau, deliberating a moment. "But you have ascertained that two police-officers are outside, and that surprises me. Let one of you glide down the back-stairs, and, going to the front, accidentally begin a conversation with those gentlemen; perhaps you may extract from them their object. It is possible that my dear father has again sent after me, for *lettres de cachet* are to be had for the asking in France."

The secretary undertook this commission and left. When Mirabeau looked again at Henriette, and saw how frightened and trembling she was, seated on the sofa, another thought occurred to him.

"I must also take care of you, my lovely Henriette!" he said, approaching her quickly, and drawing her away by her hand. He led her to a closet, opening it hastily. Inside this was another door, which he opened by a spring. "This is the entrance to a small cabinet, that no one can find!" he whispered. "You must hide here for a short time, my love, until we know what those policemen want. Go in fearlessly, Henriette, for since you have become Mirabeau's companion you have entered the region of adventure! But all good angels will protect your soul and body."

Hardy returned with the intelligence that the officers were in pursuit of a young lady, who had disappeared from a convent in Paris during the night, and who was suspected of being concealed in Count Mirabeau's dwelling. The doors were ordered to be at once thrown open. The police sergeants made, as they thought, a very thorough search of the house, and, politely bowing, departed.

CHAPTER VI.

MADAME DE NEHRA.

THE investigations of the police concerning Henriette were continued from day to day with increased zeal, and Mirabeau noticed that his dwelling was constantly watched. The prioress of the convent, the Countess de Montessuy, expressed everywhere her suspicions of Mirabeau, and exerted herself, with all her influential connections in Paris, to regain possession of her fugitive *protégée*. According to Sister Angelica's information, she considered Henriette exposed to all that could destroy her happiness, both for the present and the future. She raised such an alarm about the affair, that public attention was drawn toward it, and Mirabeau did not see any security either for himself or his new friend. It was the more necessary to come to a decision, as for some days past poor Henriette lived like a prisoner, being obliged to remain concealed in the secret cabinet, which on several occasions had demonstrated its security.

"We must flee from this painful situation!" said Mirabeau one morning to Henriette, who was looking at him in surprise, and with a happy smile. "I know," he continued, "you have not missed your freedom, on account of your previous life, my child! Your eyes are more brilliant, although obliged to hide behind these dark walls. But wait, my pretty prisoned bird, your hour of freedom will soon come, and I will carry you farther away, and make you happy."

"Am I not happy?" asked Henriette, mirthfully. "And do you call being with you imprisonment? I think my cloistered cell was much smaller; I find plenty of room here to dance with joy. The air of the convent-garden, with all its perfumes, never gave me such a sense of freedom as I have in this little cabinet, my friend; the warbling birds in the trees that once flung their shadows upon my window were never so delightful to me as your little, laughing Lucas."

"Your amiable heart is happy," replied Mirabeau, "but I am not happy! I am weary of playing jailer for you, who, instead of being thus caged, should be out in the sweet breezes of the spring. We must go to London. In the mean time all will be forgotten, and when we return you will be a different person, bearing another name. Let us call you a native of Albion—you are as fair and rosy as any of her daughters, my love. If we can procure a passport for you as being of that country, we are safe from all molestation here. Should we continue longer in this undignified situation, besieged by the police, your noble prioress will overwhelm us with her attentions before we are aware of them, and we may have the pleasure of being escorted into some prison, which is rather worse than your peaceful convent."

"And will they separate us?" asked Henri-

ette, anxiously clasping his arm. "Yes, Mirabeau, let us go to London to-day—this very
hour! But we take little Lucas with us, do we
not?"

"Certainly," replied Mirabeau, smiling, "we cannot leave without him. I took an oath never to
separate from the merry boy. But, alas! we are
not ready to think of immediate departure, and
that has put me out of humor. To tell you frankly the truth, I have no money. And I do not see
quite clearly how I am to secure your exit. I am
expecting my friend Chamfort this morning. He
has suddenly announced to me his arrival in
Paris, and intends to pay me a visit. I will take
counsel with him, as he knows all my circumstances. I hope my wily Auvergnat will be able
to point out the best means for me to overcome
every difficulty."

"Why not take counsel with me, my friend?"
exclaimed Henriette, leaning fondly against him.
"Am I not also your friend? Perhaps I may
have some good idea, although I was not born in
Auvergne as your friend Chamfort was. Let us
begin about money. Is it possible that all is
gone, since—"

"Since," interrupted Mirabeau, laughing aloud,
"we had so much of it a few days ago. Yes,
my child, the treasures you brought, and so generously placed at my disposal, have disappeared.
As you would not have it otherwise, and at your
express bidding, I laid my sacrilegious hands
upon the casket, and sold the rings, bracelets,
and the rest of the jewelry. They were no doubt
gifts of friendship. The gold you also gave me,
by no means insignificant, and which you doubtless saved from your pocket-money, my poor
child, has gone the same road that all Mirabeau's
possessions are destined to go. Is it not terrible?"

Henriette sighed, and looked gravely into his
eyes; then she burst into laughter.

"It is true," continued Mirabeau, with a tragi-
comic gesture, "money cannot remain with me;
and I have suffered from this weakness all my
life. As soon as I touch money, it acquires a
faculty of flight to all the points of the compass.

I should never have any, even though I stood on
mountains of gold. I am in that respect really
unfortunate. A state of society, in which there
exists a class of men called 'creditors,' will not
do for me. By their action, all that is valuable in
a community becomes annihilated, and the purse
of the cavalier is a delusion. The three thousand francs I was to receive yearly from my
family, according to our last agreement, are kept
back by my father on account of my improvi-
dence. He deducts this allowance as part-pay-
ment for his former outlay in satisfying my creditors. I am in the condition of the frog under the
air-pump—soon I shall not even know where to
find material for breath."

It was the habit of Count Mirabeau continually to complain of his financial affairs, not spar-
ing any of his friends. But the profound and
real depression showing itself in his whole manner was mingled with so much that was ludicrous,
that his friends easily forgot the painfulness of
the subject, and gladly submitted to the more
cheerful transition of loaning him small amounts.
Even Henriette felt at this moment that she must
do something more to alleviate the embarrassment in which her friend found himself, for it was
unworthy of his usual dignity and greatness.
The poor child had already thrown into the abyss
of her affection every thing she possessed of any
worth; but her desire to assist was so great, that
she thought of a means which until now she had
considered out of the question. She drew from
her bosom the locket set with pearls containing
the likeness of her father, and handed it to her
lover, without even looking at it.

Mirabeau was generally ready to accept any
thing at the hands of his friends, and without
seeming to place any value on important sacrifices made by them; but he took the locket from
her only to replace it around her neck, reproaching her with her imprudence. Then kissing her
he said: "Blessed is he that can keep the memory of his father in his heart. On no account
would I deprive you of this locket. The renowned Van Haren was a man of unimpeachable
honor, let us celebrate his memory in our union!"

"Something else has just occurred to me!" exclaimed Henriette, joyfully clapping her hands. "I have a legacy to receive in Brussels, and how foolish of me not to think of it sooner! It was left me by one of my father's relatives, who resided in that city. The amount is only four thousand francs, Mirabeau, and we must be satisfied with that. I received, only a few days ago, the judicial decree to take possession of the money. You can comprehend how I forgot all about it in the momentous events that have recently taken place in my life. But the paper was in the casket containing the rest of my few possessions."

"Then it is quite possible that, in my carelessness, I have thrown it away," said Mirabeau, hastening to his writing-table to seek the case, which he had retained. The paper was there, and he opened it quickly, while Henriette leaned over his shoulder, awaiting his look of gratification. "This is all right," said he, coolly, "the money is certainly yours, and can be realized at a moment's notice. When we arrive in Brussels we shall attend to it; for we must pass through that city on our way to London. This will prevent us from arriving at our destination as quickly as perhaps we ought to do, on your account, fair fugitive. But this business shall, nevertheless, be settled, I assure you. We must now think of means wherewith to reach Brussels, and that is a trifle. As soon as Chamfort comes we shall see how we can raise a sufficient sum for that purpose. Through him I am speculating on the purse of Madame Helvetius, who gladly applies her superabundant means for the benefit of her friends."

Henriette did not seem pleased with the manner in which Mirabeau received the intelligence of her good fortune; her sweet mouth quivered slightly; but, almost immediately after, she was again the good-tempered, confiding child, having no desire but that of subjection to him, and an agreement in his decisions as sincere as though they were her own.

Some one slightly knocked twice at the door; and Mirabeau, recognizing the manner of his friend, exclaimed: "Come in, Chamfort! Welcome, Chamfort!" His friend entered quickly, and they greeted each other with much heartiness.

"And shall we be together again in Paris, my friend and master?" asked Mirabeau, seizing his hand in a more tender manner than he ever manifested to his other friends. "I thought as much; with your restlessness and love of change, you could never stay long in the philosophic pastoral life of Auteuil."

Chamfort became aware of Henriette's presence, as she was blushingly intending to leave the room; but Mirabeau introduced her to his friend.

"This is Henriette," said the count, solemnly, "who has the courage to become my companion in life, and the sharer of my destiny! You behold her now with your own eyes, and you find that my description of her in my letters to you have been far below the truth. Her beauty alone might have won her a throne; but she prefers to journey through life with the unstable Mirabeau. She is goodness and gentleness themselves—one of those conscientious, elevated souls, in whose society you feel safe and at home. I swear to you that I do not deserve her, but hope one day to be worthy of her love." *

Henriette hastened to him, placing her hand on his mouth, and entreated him anxiously to cease praising her. Then she quickly passed into the adjoining room, after greeting Chamfort, who addressed her many flattering words.

"You are enviable, on account of your talent to create your own happiness, and arrange your affairs to your satisfaction!" said Chamfort, looking for some time at the door by which Henriette had disappeared. "My life, on the contrary, is composed of nothing but contradictions," he continued, a melancholy and almost bitter emotion shadowing his usually cheerful and handsome countenance. "I am again driven to Paris and into new circumstances, for which I am really not fitted; but, as usual, they were forced upon

---

* The words of Mirabeau in reference to Henriette.— "Lettres de Mirabeau à Chamfort," pp. 76, 87, 92.

me by the eccentric irony of my fate. You see me here in the city because the Marquis de Vaudreuil has invited me to live in his house, where he has offered me a brilliant refuge, free from any conditions. He has done this only from his well-known magnanimity and love for art and literature."

"So my master Chamfort will henceforth be at home in the Rue de Bourbon, in the magnificent Palace Vaudreuil?" said Mirabeau, smiling. "Well, you have again entered the most eminent and brilliant society; you will scarcely be able to avoid association with the court and its adherents. For the good marquis is not only a protector of the fine arts, he belongs to the more intimate friends of the queen. He is the most familiar friend of the Countesses Diana and Julie de Polignac, and through them has become one of the favorite few beginning to form a special set around Marie Antoinette. You will have an opportunity of making new court studies, and the events you witness will be made useful to our epoch. I am glad of it, for you know I regard myself particularly as your pupil, Chamfort, always learning from your wise levity and ever-sparkling wit."

"But it renders me petulant to think that my life should be made up of such direct contradiction to my principles!" replied Chamfort, looking really irritable. "I have no love for high and noble persons, and yet I am continually brought into relationship with them. The religion for which I could have the most enthusiasm is that of liberty; and yet my destiny is ever associating me, in one way or another, with princes, princesses, and aristocrats, in whose atmosphere my republican soul must suffer hunger and thirst. I also love voluntary poverty, and yet I suffer the rich to seduce and use me for the purpose of making mind an article of luxury. I was weak enough to yield to the urgency of the Marquis de Vaudreuil. At all events, I shall find myself better situated with him than at the palace of the Prince de Condé, who actually conferred on me the position of secretary. However, I broke this chain as soon as I felt it chafe."

"There was another motive that decided you to throw up your place, my noble friend," said Mirabeau, fervently offering his hand to Chamfort. "You pitied the young man who fulfilled your duties for a small salary, and who had a mother to support. You conjured the prince to accept your resignation, and to bestow the situation, with its title and income, on him who performed the labor while almost starving. Such traits ought to be written in metal and marble, demonstrating to those who would throw suspicions on our morality, because we are striving after liberty, that we are the true minds and the pure hearts of this epoch!"

"Let us not think too highly of ourselves, Mirabeau!" replied Chamfort, all his satire showing itself in his features. "It is generally our egotism that hides itself behind our so-called generous motives, of which we make, as it were, a grand festive costume. How do you know whether I would have given up my position in favor of a poor man, if my otherwise profitable connection with the Prince de Condé had really not been disagreeable to me? What drove me away was the desire to live poor, but contented, in solitude. I became the benefactor of the young man because I wished to do myself a favor. Great happiness seemed within my reach. My friend Lydia had become free by the sudden death of her husband, and she consented to begin a new life with me in utter obscurity. She was no longer young. Of her once matchless beauty nothing remained but the charming expression of her countenance and the brilliancy of her eyes; but her heart and mind were adorably young, and her eloquence captivated me, so that I felt no other desire than to unite myself with her. I had loved many women in my life, but until then had possessed none. Now, Lydia was mine. I felt her to be my own, tenderly as a mother, firmly and confidingly as my friend. I could have never believed that, only three miles from Paris, in a little retired village, one could live as in a paradise. My evil genius, however, sought me even there in a most unexpected manner. Lydia died in my arms, and my Eden became a wilderness. I could not bear solitude any longer. Even the quiet at Auteuil, with our friend Madame Helvetius, who received me so hospitably and consolingly, began to pain me deep in my heart. I left the Prince de Condé to bury myself in obscurity, which to me was more desirable, for love was beckoning me. Now I reënter the fantastic whirl of Paris life, accepting a home in the splendid house of Vaudreuil, only because I cannot now be at rest unless in the tumult of the world. Herein consists the paradox of my existence, loving solitude, and yet seeking society to heal my heart's wounds. Now, tell me, friend Mirabeau, whether all in this miserable world to which we belong is not masquerade and egotism ?" Chamfort laughed aloud, walking hastily up and down the room, and repeatedly altering his merriment to different keys. Mirabeau expressed his sympathy at the misfortune of his friend, in the eloquent, ardent words that were always at his command. "I had almost forgotten to deliver a message to you from the Marquis de Vaudreuil," Chamfort continued. "He sends you this card of invitation. The 'Wedding of Figaro,' by Beaumarchais, is to be given at the marquis's palace to-morrow night, and he lays great stress upon it that you should not fail to appear among the invited guests. Many persons from court circles will be present; it is intended to gain the approbation of the king and queen for the novel and wonderful comedy that has had such a curious history even while still in manuscript. The friends of the author, one of whom the marquis is, hope to carry their point of having the piece acted in public, by a *coup de main* they have in view to-morrow."

Mirabeau took the card, looking at it silently for some time, as if meditating. At length he said : "I accept the invitation of M. de Vaudreuil, although, as you know, I have not the least interest in the comedy of the speculator Beaumarchais. According to all I have heard of it, I am not curious to know even the plot. This Beaumarchais may have a keen ear; he may, while at a distance, hear the cries of the ill-omened birds announcing the death of the present time, and, making good use of his faculty, compose a sort of prophetic-satiric comedy, such as this 'Wedding of Figaro' is said to be—but he does all only for money. I have no sympathy with a man, nor can I count him as one of us, who makes a trade of liberty and the emotions. He calls himself Beaumarchais the American, yet what did he do for American liberty ? Nothing, except that, in his commercial activity, which aims to turn every thing to a mercenary account, he delivered arms to the new republicans for their first campaigns. He made enormous profits by this transaction, not only demanding the highest prices, but giving in return useless guns, and damaged hats and shoes. Besides filling his pockets, he had the satisfaction of being accused of secretly providing foreigners with arms—thus triumphing in the estimation of the world as a martyr to liberty. Oh, I know the creature; and such a mere traffic is this piece. How does it happen that a man like Beaumarchais takes as the subject for an amusing comedy, the sad condition of the age—the falsehood of modern society ? When, at some future time, we fight our battles for freedom, this man will be the Figaro of our revolution—the knavish jester who made fun of the most sacred aspirations, but who took care to profit by his humor !"

"I know that you do not like Beaumarchais," replied Chamfort, "but if you do not come on account of the comedy itself, you might for the entertainment I assure you you will find at the residence of M. de Vaudreuil to-morrow night. A kind of art conspiracy has been formed against the court, of which the most influential courtiers are members. They intend to make the king believe, after the representation, that Beaumarchais has materially altered the play, and that nothing remains in it of that which, at its rehearsal, excited the anger of the king in the highest degree. The good Marquis de Vaudreuil, wishing to sacrifice himself in every way for the fine arts, has offered his connivance and assistance in this dangerous intrigue, which, in fact, he partly arranged. Whatever demon is whispering into the ear of these people, it is certain that he is impelling them to mischief. This excitement will cheer and amuse you, Mirabeau. The king is said to have exclaimed, when hearing Figaro's monologue, levelled as it is at the French administration: ' This man derides and disturbs all that ought to be honored in a government, and I will never permit his comedy to be acted anywhere in France!' The appointed representation in the Hotel des Menus Plaisirs was forbidden by a special order from his majesty, and the audience departed, venting their displeasure in violent exclamations. Some of the court society (particularly the Count de Provence, the patron of Beaumarchais) have misgivings on account of this incident; and, say what you will, it is in some respects a serious affair. Were not such flattering expressions as ' tyranny ' and ' oppression ' heard even in the street ? * The courtiers consider it much less dangerous to have the piece acted than to deprive the public of it; but as Beaumarchais, obstinate and cunning as he is, would not change a syllable, the intrigue to be executed to-morrow night at Vaudreuil's was thought of. It gives me pleasure, for I scent considerable trouble. What do you think of it, Mirabeau ? "

" The nose is the most essential instrument of a good politician," replied Mirabeau, " and you know I have always done justice to yours. But if I go to the house of M. de Vaudreuil to-morrow I do it for an intrigue on my own account, and I desire your assistance, Chamfort. You have just seen my lovely gazelle, who has taken refuge in yonder cabinet, not only from your eager glances, but from the police, that at any moment may pounce upon her. In my last letter I gave you a circumstantial account of Henriette's adventure. Since then I have become convinced that I must remove her from Paris for some time, in order afterward to be enabled to live in safety and comfort. I wish to take her to London, and then bring her back as a naturalized Englishwoman. But I see no possibility of effecting her exit from this house. Secret agents are continually lounging in the street, watching my dwell-

ing; they would rob me of my dear girl. I have a plan, that occurred to me when I received your invitation from Vaudreuil. I dare say the marquis has placed one of his carriages at your disposal. I know this protector of the muses gladly indulges men of genius, considering it an honor to receive them."

" Certainly," replied Chamfort, " he lets the poet ride in the grand equipage of the marquis, and then believes that the marquis has become something of a poet."

" Very well," said Mirabeau, " this carriage may do a service to my young love. Listen to my plan. I will go early to-morrow evening to the house of M. de Vaudreuil, after having made all my arrangements for our departure. Then you must sacrifice yourself so far for me as to lose perhaps an act of the representation of the comedy. You must take one of the marquis's coaches and come to my dwelling at a later hour. Henriette will await you in such a disguise that the police cannot recognize her. She will dress herself in the clothes of the country-girl who is the nurse of my little Coco; carrying the boy in her arms (I intend to take him with me to London), she will quickly enter the carriage with you. The police will observe all this, but will either have no suspicion of the truth, or, seeing an equipage with the livery and crest of the Marquis de Vaudreuil, will not dare to attempt any intrusion. On your arrival at the palace you will leave my friend and the child in the carriage, which you will safely lodge in the coach-house. As soon as I have an opportunity I will leave the company, and you must, by your influence, procure me the further use of this vehicle as far as the foot of Montmartre. There my people will await me with a travelling-coach, and I think I can reach the road to Brussels (to which city I intend to go first), without any further danger."

Chamfort mused for a moment, and, nodding to his friend, said: " You can rely on me as usual, Mirabeau ! Arrange every thing, and I will obey all your instructions. Oh, I am really glad again to have a hand in a secret plot; and, above all, in one that is played at the expense of

---

* "Mémoires de Madame Campan," vol. 1., p. 279.

this unpopular and impudent Parisian police. But, for greater security, I would recommend you to procure a passport for Henriette under an assumed name. Command me, if I can be of any assistance to you in obtaining one."

"I was about to say that I leave the execution of this also to your faithful friendship," replied Mirabeau. "It would be useful to us, if I could procure an English passport for .Henriette in Paris, which would accredit her as an Englishwoman by birth. It would be an easy thing for you, who have so many connections in the capital, and who frequent the society of distinguished and powerful persons, to obtain one for my dear friend. I think you have free access to the house of the British ambassador, the Marquis of Dorset. You are a man of great influence, my Chamfort, and we ought to congratulate ourselves in having found such a protector of our love."

"Chamfort has become a guardian of lovers!" he exclaimed, while a melancholy smile played around his lips. "But I think I can secure the passport. In the house of the Marquis de Vaudreuil are several English nurses, and it will not be extraordinary if I send the major-domo to demand a passport for one of them, who may desire to return to her own country. I will see to it that it be made out in any name you may select, and giving no difficulty at the government office. All you have to do is to decide under what name your beautiful Henriette is to travel."

"Let us ask her," replied Mirabeau, hastening to the cabinet, in which she had remained since the entrance of Chamfort. The count knocked and called so boisterously at the door, that Henriette stepped out of her concealment with an expression of undisguised fear. But Mirabeau quieted her apprehensions by the assurance that nothing unpleasant had happened. The question was to give a false name to her who otherwise was so ingenuous and true, in order to save her from future persecutions.

Henriette looked at him with an anxious and doubting smile; then her countenance assumed a sad gravity, and she slowly shook her head.

"I understand you," exclaimed Mirabeau,

"you neither will nor can deceive; you are too honest and noble! But you must not be too serious on this point. What is the name of a person but a domino, in which he has been admitted to the masquerade? Sometimes, as a jest, we turn the disguise, and wear it the wrong side outward. Our old friends, however, who always recognize us, only derive greater pleasure from our temporary concealment."

"Well, if you so turn and transpose the letters of my name, it is Nehra!" said Henriette, her natural cheerfulness returning, and her eyes again sparkling with happiness. "When we children in play turned our names, I often called myself 'Henriette de Nehra.'"

"Bravo!" cried Mirabeau, kissing her hands. "From to-day your name is Madame de Nehra.* Henriette van Haren has disappeared, and this anagram of your childish sportiveness shall become the happy sign of our union and of our future! Friend Chamfort will procure an English passport for that name."

"I beg to present my best congratulations to Madame de Nehra, on this occasion of a new christening," said Chamfort, approaching her, and offering her his hand with fervent zeal, which she received in her usually friendly manner. "Indeed," he added with his smiling thoughtfulness, "I anticipate the happiest results from your union with Mirabeau. Since you have gained your new name by transposing the old one, you obey the natural law of our era. Merely by rearranging affairs, a new and more beautiful life may be the result. Take the old letters and make new combinations, reverse them, resolve the old words into new, and we discover the names which embrace a joyous future. Just as the persecuted Henriette van Haren becomes the free and victorious Henriette de Nehra!"

She was obliged to laugh at Chamfort's comic manner while thus pleasantly bantering her, and frankly accepting his hand said: "Whatever my name may be, my nature remains the same; I

---

* Montigny, "Mémoires de Mirabeau," vol. iv., p. 146.

am nothing but a plain, silly girl, who is controlled, and ever will be, by her heart's emotions."

"So far we have very well settled with our friend Chamfort," Mirabeau recommenced. "But now we require his assistance in another very delicate affair. He knows what I mean. He is looking at me with that malicious smile of his, always lurking about his lips, when he has surprised a poor mortal in his weakness."

"Yes, I know what you want, or rather what you have not," replied Chamfort, laughing. "I have often been your father-confessor, in your affairs of the heart, and always succeeded better in extricating you from such difficulties than those of the purse. The latter must be the weakness you are at present bewailing."

"You are right," said Mirabeau, "you have hit the bird in the breast. I am again at that crisis when a man compresses a whole existence into the confession—'I have no mone !'" Henriette began to betray visible uneasiness during this conversation. Her cheeks flushed, and, in the deepest confusion, she cast her eyes downward. "She cannot bear to hear me speak of financial difficulties, the dear child," said Mirabeau, charmed at her aspect. "She blushes as if it were a shame for us all, for the whole world, that I have no money."

"On the contrary, it is a great honor for him to be out of pocket, Madame de Nehra !" said Chamfort, approaching her. "Count Mirabeau is, as usual, the representative man of his age, in having his finances in a continual state of disorder. He is passing through the same crisis, in regard to his treasury, as France, distressed in all her resources. When you are without money, thoughts of salvation occur to you; for you get an insight into your condition, the disease of your organization, and thus it is easier to make resolutions leading to improvement. That is one reason of the hope we entertain that Mirabeau will one day be the savior of his country, because like France he has constantly an empty pocket, and, under such circumstances, is better able to study about the prosperous and generous future."

"It makes me suspicious, Chamfort, that to-day you have so much to say about the philosophy of my empty purse," said Mirabeau, while his high brow became clouded. "If you can give me neither counsel nor assistance, say so without circumlocution. We only want money to travel as far as Brussels. There we are to get possession of a legacy, which will carry us farther. What do you say now, Chamfort? But a small amount will not take me even there. You know I cannot manage without a servant and a secretary, and I must have these people follow me immediately. Are you in funds ?"

"Our good mother Helvetius provided me with plenty of money when I took leave of her," replied Chamfort. "She said that, as I was reëntering the great world, I would have many new expenses, and ought to have sufficient pocket-money. In my desk, I think, are about eight hundred francs, and I would be glad if you take them, Mirabeau. Money disturbs me in my pleasant dreams, and in waking moments I am constantly thinking of what frippery I can purchase with it. I want no money in the house of M. de Vaudreuil. I live at the expense of the marquis, and, as for the few trifles I may need, I have the pension for which I am indebted to the beautiful Queen Marie Antoinette. I also intend to make a collection of my dramatic writings, and hope to obtain an academic premium. And now, farewell for to-day, children ! To-morrow early I will bring you the passport and the money. All the rest of your arrangements shall be certainly executed."

Mirabeau embraced his friend with an expression of the liveliest gratitude. Chamfort went to the door, then returned, and, drawing some folded papers from his pocket, said : "I had almost forgotten to deliver these to you. They are the promised contributions for your pamphlet against the order of Cincinnatus, partly written by me, and partly by Dr. Franklin, who, at the same time, sends you his greetings. You may make use of all or none, just as it may suit you. Condorcet and Cabanis send their excuses. They are both working at mathematics and natural philosophy, because they have no chance in politics.

Cabanis is killing himself in endeavoring to discover the connection between the physical and moral laws of the world."

After Chamfort's departure, Mirabeau said to Henriette, who was standing near him: "Well, my love, we have a great deal of work before us in making preparations for our voyage. Hasten, therefore, for we must carry with us our movable possessions. Above all, we must not forget to pack up our little Coco, from whom we cannot be parted. The little fellow is to make his first attempt at crossing the channel, and the question is, whether he is properly equipped. As you have undertaken the part of his protecting genius, you will attend, of course, to all that concerns his welfare."

Henriette nodded joyfully, and was about to attend to his requests, when something seemed to occur to her. She stood a moment thoughtfully in the middle of the room, and then returned hastily to Mirabeau. Clinging to him, she said, in a low, coaxing tone: "You could much better live without me than without little Lucas. Is it not true that he is nearer to your heart than every thing else? I shall always guard him as the apple of my eye; and yet I am often tormented about the mystery of his birth. You promised to solve the enigma, but you have not kept your word, Mirabeau."

"I will tell you now," replied the count, with a shade of solemnity: "The Princess de Lamballe is the mother of little Coco. She placed the child she had secretly borne under my care and guardianship, and I swore never to be separated from him. As I took this oath, I will keep it, because I am greatly indebted to the princess, and am glad of having an opportunity to do her service who was my friend in the saddest moments of my life."

"And is that the only reason why you have adopted Coco?" asked Henriette, slowly gazing doubtingly at him. "The child himself has really no relationship to you?"

"Silence!" exclaimed Mirabeau, laying his hand on her lips. "I shall never name to you the father of the child; but at some future time perhaps I will relate to you a long history about him."

Henriette did not seem quite satisfied with this explanation, but she dared not renew the question troubling her heart. Musingly and hesitatingly she left the room. Mirabeau's eyes followed her; smilingly and rapturously he contemplated the delicate, youthful figure moving before him, who seemed disquieted by ideas that proved to him how greatly she desired to believe herself in possession of an exclusive right to his heart.

CHAPTER VII.

THE TWO INTRIGUES.

FROM all parts of Paris the most brilliant equipages came to the representation of the "Wedding of Figaro," by Beaumarchais, to be given in the theatre-hall of the Hotel Vaudreuil. The quiet, aristocratic Rue de Bourbon shook with the rattling of the numerous carriages that rapidly passed along, conveying the company impatient to witness the comedy at the palace. The invited were assembled in the small drawing-rooms, which had a peculiar arrangement in the magnificent residence of the marquis. One was especially devoted to music, containing many different instruments. In another, all was arranged for the amateurs in painting; and, if any one wished to display his talent, even in society, he found paints, brushes, and pencils, ready to his hand, and could yield at pleasure to any improvisation. In a third, the tables were covered with all kinds of costly copperplates and other pictures. A fourth was in the richest and most comfortable manner supplied with books for those who desired to read. The marquis, a friend of the arts, who was proud of being called the protector of the muses, instituted receptions, at which, during the most lively conversation, diligent work was proceeding in these saloons. Many a great production was here canvassed and planned, which afterward carried off the prize of the day.

The marquis himself, one of the most brilliant members of society in those days, had been obliged to confine himself, as to any talent for the fine arts, to the cultivation of an excellent voice; it was extraordinary, and admired by all who heard it. It had been the means of introducing him to the highest court circles. He added so much grace of manner to this vocal endowment, that, although scarcely belonging to the more considerable minds of the age, he gained an influential position, assisted by his outward social superiority. His consequence among the literary men and artists of Paris was as great as the favor he had obtained at court. In that circle which had been encouraged in the immediate society of the queen, he was in fact the actual ruler. Its members were all present among those who were to witness the representation of the much-talked-of comedy at the Hotel Vaudreuil.

The beautiful and amiable Countess Julie de Polignac, and her sister-in-law, the haughty Countess Diana, who sometimes condescended to a little coquetry, were at the head of this court set. These ladies had a peculiar interest in the effort of M. de Beaumarchais, and it was owing to their influence that the queen and, through the latter, the king agreed to allow the piece to be played before an invited audience, after it had been pretended that the author had entirely rewritten it. Diana de Polignac, who had recently become lady of honor to the Countess d'Artois, also gained friends for the "Wedding of Figaro" from that portion of the court. She found those who aided her in overcoming the profound dislike of the king for this comedy, considering it as inimical to his government. It became suddenly a party affair for the friends of the Count d'Artois to oppose the king; and in this instance, in which he appeared narrow-minded and blind, they wished to show themselves great, and make a sort of concession to public opinion. The daring and arrogant Countess Diana, who had acted so remarkably in expressing her sympathy for Franklin and American liberty, stepped into the lists for the "Wedding of Figaro," and no one could easily resist her charming intrigues.

Before the commencement of the representation the two Countesses de Polignac, surrounded by a choice company of their friends and admirers, stood in the music-hall, engaged in earnest conversation. Their confidential words were spoken in a low voice, for they concerned the question of the day—the fitness for public exhibition of the comedy of Beaumarchais, in its less obvious and dangerous features.

"I answer for all the evil consequences that may arise from this evening's proceedings, dear marquis," said the beautiful Countess Julie de Polignac, in the proud security of the new and important position she had obtained near Queen Marie Antoinette during the preceding winter

"I am not uneasy about the consequences," said the Marquis de Vaudreuil, with one of his most elegant and respectful bows. "But my conscience is beginning to trouble me, and I think the poet might at least have erased some of the objectionable passages, which the king noticed with such decided displeasure."

"M. de Beaumarchais is obstinate; he would not do it," replied the Countess Julie, smiling so that all her white and beautiful teeth were visible. "But when the piece has once been played here, and such skilled and estimable courtiers as you, M. de Vaudreuil, and our charming colonel of the Swiss Guards, M. de Besenval, give evidence of its present freedom from dangerous sentiments, the king will be pleased to take back his former harsh verdict. He will certainly permit it to be performed, and then the general dissatisfaction among the public will be removed. We shall all have aided in recognizing genius, and you, marquis, will again have the triumph that at your mansion one of the masterpieces of the nation received its life." M. de Vaudreuil kissed her hand with all the exquisite politeness of French court society.

"Under the leadership of the Countess Julie, we may cheerfully enter the combat," said the Baron de Besenval, with formal gallantry. The colonel of the Swiss Guards was a man with snow-white hair. This venerable claim of respect and confidence, as well as the peculiar loyalty and simplicity shown in all his actions, gained him the high privilege of being intrusted with the secrets of the ladies. The rôle of confidant, however, did not prevent him from engaging in gallant adventures ; for, notwithstanding the snow upon his locks, he was still capable of attachments ; and his ardent inclinations toward the Countess Julie demonstrated his susceptible character.

" It is true we are assembled as conspirators," said Julie de Polignac, with that charmingly natural cheerfulness that added something so irresistible to her other attractions. " But having the brave and excellent colonel of the Swiss Guards under our banners, we may easily reconcile ourselves with the morality of our undertaking. Did he not lately sing for us the 'Ranz des Vaches' of his native country, while the tears actually stood in his eyes ? And when he tells us of the mountains of his native land, does not his noble heart reveal itself, and appear to us like an Alpine farm, where butter, cheese, honor, and gallantry, present themselves to the mind in an extraordinary and charming *mélange ?* When such a man conspires with us for the 'Wedding of Figaro,' we may certainly consider ourselves safe."

Those present burst into loud laughter on hearing these words, in which the Baron de Besenval, as usual, perceived no humor or irony, considering them rather as an expression of sentiment, indicating a favorable reception of his homage. He stood opposite the lady with delighted countenance, looking at her and sighing, thus heightening the merriment.

The Countess Julie de Polignac was not a beauty of the first rank, but she made that impression by the charm of her natural gracefulness, and an appearance that was brilliant in its remarkable simplicity. By such attraction she had gained entire possession of the queen's heart, when during the winter she first arrived at Versailles, drawn there by the splendor of the balls and other court entertainments. When Marie Antoinette asked her in surprise why she had not sooner come to Versailles, she answered smilingly and ingenuously, that she was poor, and feared the expenses of such festivals. The queen felt real friendship for the countess, and was so much attached to her that she became indispensable to her majesty, who chose Julie de Polignac as her daily companion. But this did not change the countess in any way ; she was as natural as formerly, wearing no jewelry, and only appearing with the sweetness of her fresh and cheerful manners.

At this moment Mirabeau and Chamfort entered the saloon. They remained at the entrance, to criticise the general outline of the company assembled.

" We have come very early," observed Mirabeau, sending his restless glances in all directions. " Only the court puppets, who have a special design to execute, are here. I am in such a fever of impatience, that all my limbs tremble. I wish this wretched comedy would begin, that we may proceed with our intrigue, and that I may be sure of Henriette's escape."

" We shall first have to witness a few acts of Beaumarchais's ' Figaro,' " replied Chamfort, in his sarcastic ease of manner. " But I pray you to look around a little, or, pardon my metaphor, turn over with your sharp eyes the leaves of the book of faces here opened before you. The people there are very happy, and laugh as if the world belonged to them forever. Ha! what a swarm of bees those courtiers are! They hum for nothing but honey. It is really a pleasure to see the assembly enjoying themselves, though all things are tending to their ruin. As to this comedy, of which they are speaking, it may be good or bad, but it expresses the very wickedness of those persons as in a mirror. Notice the Countess Julie de Polignac, and admire the deceitful show of innocence and naturalness she assumes in her new style of artful coquetry ! "

" The lady is not so much to be despised," said Mirabeau, slightly glancing at her. " A more sentimental heart speaks out of her beautiful brown eyes than her husband, the chief equerry of his majesty, is able fully to understand, harmonize with, or indeed appreciate. Yet her whole manner expresses the shallowness characterizing the queen's intimate circle, to whom this dear Countess Julie has given tone. Mind is banished entirely from that society, and they occupy themselves daily with the latest bon-mots—the little slanderous anecdotes of the court and city —the newest songs, whose refrains they use in a wanton and equivocal manner. Such is the favorite company of Marie Antoinette, from whom, as I hear, the intellectual Princess de Lamballe strives to keep aloof, to the great chagrin of the queen, who would gladly see her on a friendly footing with the countess."

"What have you to do with the minds of women?" exclaimed Chamfort, bantering him. "How often have we disputed this point, and you never would acknowledge that in them intellect could be a charm at all! And now, very suddenly, all the physical beauty in royal society does not satisfy you, and you ask for mental attractions in those surrounding the naïve Austrian, sharing the throne of France. Is there any thing more beautiful than that Countess Julie de Polignac in her super-refined simplicity, which is, by the way, the indwelling demon of coquetry."

"You approach the very reason why I require intellect of her," said Mirabeau, laughing. "Can a man with an imagination endure to see a woman before him in such a dress as suits this countess? Behold her, in contrast with the ladies around in the costliest and most artistic toilets. Hers is nothing but a *négligée*—tasteful and airy, it is true, but thrown over her fair form as if accidentally, and not even apparently fastened with any care. Can you wonder that that loose toilet should attract attention? A woman who has courage to appear in such a costume presumes much and hazards much. She does not even wear diamonds to divert attention from her physical perfections. If she were at least as learned and intellectual as the French Academy, of which you have the honor to be a member, my good Chamfort, a man like myself, while conversing with her, might think of other affairs than her dress."

Chamfort laughed, and Mirabeau accompanied him. They were in a better humor as they passed from one room to another, contemplating and criticising the company assembled in them.

"Why, there is Diderot!" cried Chamfort, pointing to a group of persons, in the midst of whom stood a tall man, with attractive features. "I did not believe the marquis when he told me that Diderot would be here this evening, for we are aware how he suffers; but M. de Vaudreuil knew how to rouse our dear encyclopædist. What a talent he has to bring people together in his drawing-rooms! And there is the charming old Baron d'Holbach, on whose friendly arm Diderot is leaning." As they approached, Diderot, as soon as he noticed the presence of his two friends, turned quickly to greet them, pushing his way through the people surrounding him. He gave his hand with especial predilection to Chamfort.

"You see me again risen from the dead, but only to make the acquaintance of the 'Wedding of Figaro,'" he said, in that clear and full voice that had lost little by age or sickness. Diderot was in his seventy-first year. He would still have been considered handsome, but for the many bodily sufferings he had lately undergone, and that left little hope of his remaining much longer among his earthly friends. His powerful frame was bowed, and gave signs of infirmity. But in his fine large eyes the fire of intellect burned undimmed. His lips were still eloquent, even in ordinary conversation, and few could equal him in the fluency and force of his words.

"I see a vacant corner which we can occupy for a short time," said Diderot, walking with Holbach to a sofa in a remote part of the saloon. Mirabeau and Chamfort followed, on receiving an invitation from him in a glance of his kindly eyes.

"It is sad," said Mirabeau, in a low voice to Chamfort, "to observe the bodily decay of this hero, whom all the strength of his intellect cannot protect from this mournful tribute to Nature! See how slowly and tremblingly he moves! And this is Diderot! he whose extraordinary mind has taught the French that all in existence is nothing but matter, and that the idea of a Supreme Intelligence is only a priestly invention. At his side is the no less renowned Baron d'Holbach, who is still bearing himself erect; he has been all his life a gourmand, and received the well-deserved nickname of 'steward of the philosophic skeptics.' Those two old men, who together wrote the 'Système de la Nature,' were once strong and ambitious, but they now walk unsteadily, and their own systems are well-nigh worn out. But, by the by, what have we younger men done, Chamfort, to demonstrate that we are worthy of succeeding them, at least in their opposition to despotism?"

"We shall, no doubt, gradually follow those Titans," said Chamfort, merrily. "The time of our friend Diderot has passed, but he has probably enjoyed his life. If he had not been guilty of the folly of treating the Empress Catharine of Russia as a woman whose cheeks you may pinch while talking to her, or to whom you may whisper an equivocal couplet,* he would have had a most brilliant position in St. Petersburg. That folly of his delighted me exceedingly. Although he had to leave the czarina in disgrace, it was a most effective jest which the philosopher indulged in with the empress. It would make a sort of title-page to the era of liberty and equality for which we are all longing."

Diderot and Holbach seated themselves on the sofa, while Mirabeau and Chamfort occupied two easy-chairs standing near it.

"Oh, you are Count Mirabeau that I see here, and only this moment recognize; like myself, you were imprisoned in the castle of Vincennes, and there meditated on the future of France!" said Diderot, in his pathetic and patronizing manner. Mirabeau bowed, and pressed the hand offered him with respectful fervor. "It was a momentous event for me," continued Diderot, "when I was suddenly dragged to Vincennes. The cause of this was the search made for my latest writings, that I had only partly finished.

I was seized, together with several proof-sheets of our encyclopædia that happened to be lying on my table. The police wished particularly to possess themselves of a little tale written by me, entitled 'The White Dove,' and which I had often read to my friends. It is true, this poetic trifle contained some irony that could easily be explained as having reference to King Louis XV., Madame de Pompadour, and the state ministers. However, the manuscript could not be found at my house, and I declared that I had no recollection of this improvisation. Notwithstanding this, I remained four months in Vincennes, and there I wrote some meditations with a pen made of an old toothpick, and ink manufactured of a piece of slate dissolved in wine. For paper I used the margin of a copy of Milton's 'Paradise Lost,' that I happened to have in my pocket. I united my criticisms on this great work with reflections on myself, liberty, and my native land. But what are those literary arabesques to the great works that my congenial successor wrote in that same dungeon! The book you composed there, Count Mirabeau, concerning *lettres de cachet* and state-prisons, is a masterpiece of its kind, and which I have studied with the utmost interest. It pleased me especially that you treated this whole affair not only from a political but a social point of view. Believe me—an old sorcerer, who will soon have uttered his last word—politics will soon be an indifferent, or, at most, a secondary thing in the new ideas forcing themselves upon the minds of men. The principal question will concern our social relations; that highest good which nations dream of and strive to obtain will always remain doubtful, and, in a mere political realization, delusive. The right, in any sense, of royalty will be severely tested, but perhaps will not be decided until the more important one of the community of property, is settled.* Think, hereafter, of Diderot, who, at the sunset of his life, saw far and clear into futurity. The words of Jean Jacques Rousseau: 'The fruits of the earth belong to all, but the earth to none,'

---

* "Mémoires de l'Abbé Georgel," vol. ii., p. 240.

* "Mémoires de Condorcet," vol. ii., p. 12.

will decide the national battles of the times. On that account I am interested in all I have heard of this new work of M. de Beaumarchais. In order to show the rottenness of the state, he begins in his comedy to attack society, showing its universal falsehood and corruption. I am curious to see how the former harp-and-guitar teacher of the royal daughters of his majesty Louis XV. executes this sublimely moral task. I will listen with the ears of both the past and the future. Such men as Beaumarchais remind me of the foretelling members of a rheumatic or wounded body, always aching when the weather changes, or the sky is laden with storms. It is a peculiarity of my nature that I have ever felt in better health and spirits when, during the night, I hear the wind howling and the rain beating against my windows—when the tempest sweeps by, overturning the trees in my garden, and shaking the foundations of my abode. I lie on my couch at such times with the greatest satisfaction, thinking: 'Only wait! storms will soon come such as no generation has ever witnessed; but Diderot will not rejoice in them, he will repose in death—in that sleep which will outlast the world's existence—which will still be unbroken when the firmament is no more!'"

A man of medium height appeared. There was a remarkable restlessness with much uneasiness in his aspect. He approached the group hastily, interrupting the strain of Diderot by presenting himself and pronouncing a few complimentary words. He was the author of the comedy, Baron de Beaumarchais, a man of about fifty years. In his sparkling eyes was an expression of great prudence and penetrating judgment, while his whole physiognomy was characterized by such shrewdness as at first sight is not apt to inspire a profound confidence. He was just entering the drawing-room, and seemed to have been behind the scenes, to oversee the necessary preparations for the performance, the commencement of which he came to announce.

"It is really fortunate that Beaumarchais has arrived," said Chamfort to Mirabeau, "for without his interruption Diderot would not have ceased to talk. I have never succeeded, even by the most adroit remark, in interrupting the fluency of Diderot's 'golden tongue,' as it has been called. I remember how this faculty of his caused the despair of the Abbé Raynal at a gathering at Madame Geoffrin's house. The abbé had a desire to talk incessantly, and, when his patience was overborne by the unending stream of Diderot's eloquence, he drew me aside, saying, with artful melancholy: ' If he would only take a pinch of snuff, cough, or use his pocket-handkerchief, he is lost; for then I can at once seize the opportunity to speak.'"

"Beaumarchais then provides just such an opportunity by which Diderot has been compelled to stop," said Mirabeau, regarding the author of the " Wedding of Figaro" with evident displeasure. " His impression upon me is always that of an insignificant person."

All were repairing to the magnificent theatre-saloon of M. de Vaudreuil. The numerous spectators were soon seated, impatient for the raising of the curtain. The representation was undertaken by the actors of the Théâtre Français, the same who had been engaged when the king previously interdicted the play.

The comedy began with the half-comic, half-uneasy conversation between Figaro and Susanna, who, in view of their approaching marriage, were disquieted by the thought that Count Almaviva intended to assert certain well-understood claims in the case of Susanna's wedding—an old feudal right possessed by the lord of the soil over his vassals. Hardly is it seen, in the comedy, on what hollow ground all the characters are standing, and that Count Almaviva's castle is nothing but a symbol of the degeneracy of society, when the page Cherubin appears to complain to Susanna of his misfortunes; for the count resolves to drive him from the castle, being jealous of a boy who seems to be a favorite of the countess. M. Cherubin visits the women of the count's household, and is surprised in the company of the gardener's daughter. The page is about to make love to Susanna, when Count Almaviva is heard at the door. Cherubin is hastily concealed be-bind the easy-chair, and the count begins a tender conversation with Susanna respecting the feudal right, when Bazile's voice is heard outside of the house. The count seeks the same hiding-place in which his page is concealed, who creeps into the easy-chair itself without being seen, where he is covered with some of Susanna's dresses. In the following scene the count hears of the audacities Cherubin has been guilty of in his household, and suddenly jumps up, unable to restrain his anger; he soon discovers the page, and drags him out in no very gentle manner.

The audience burst into loud applause at the situation of Cherubin, interpreting as it did so many facts, introducing the conduct of well-known parties. Much amusement was caused by the procession of festively-attired servants, peasants and their wives, at whose head appears Figaro, to request the count, in a petition signed by all, generously to renounce his inherited ancient right. The countess herself joins in this entreaty, and thus adds interest to the scene. The curtain fell before a half-astonished, half-excited audience, who were left in a frame of mind never before experienced at any theatrical representation.

"Is not that quite an execrable family whose acquaintance we have made through the poet?" said Chamfort to Mirabeau, in a low voice, between the acts. "In their crimes they cling together like burrs. Each desires to profit by and abuse the other, and the end of all is only to find out who is the most guilty and deserves the greatest punishment. This is the moral of the present state of society. In fact, all are to blame that social affairs have come to such a pass. Yes, Mirabeau, this comedy raises the questions: Who will be condemned? Who will be absolved? Who will escape?"

"Well, I think that Figaro, the man of the people, is not only the wisest, but also the purest of them all!" replied Mirabeau, thoughtfully. "I wager a thousand to one that, if he remains as courageous and enterprising, he will bring his bride home as a well-earned and innocent possession—an exception to the demands of an oppres-

sive and hateful feudalism. Figaro is an honest fellow, and it is generally the position of the people to be for evermore in antagonism to those in power, who use as their property what has never been adjudged to them by any law of nature or morality."

In other parts of the hall various remarks were made. "The author has represented the countess in the play very judiciously," said Diana de Polignac (who made pretensions to be a judge of the beautiful), to her neighbor, Colonel de Besenval. "She has a truly aristocratic appearance in this dark groundwork of society, and is evidently the only pure character of the company. Although she is hurt and deceived by her husband, who is faithless and dissipated as all cavaliers, she remains reticent and noble, only endeavoring to renew their union of love. Surely, her innocent amusement with the boy Cherubin cannot be considered wicked. Oh, when the heart is heavy and sad, you sometimes rejoice in the sudden apparition of a frolicsome creature near you, and you hastily stretch out your hand after him. But, after all, nothing is purer than the movements of an unhappy woman's heart!"

"I do not see how any one can be interested in this countess," said Julie de Polignac. "She is of noble descent, but you can easily perceive that she was the ward of Dr. Bartholo of Seville, and received her education in his house. It was a great honor for her that Count Almaviva carried her off from such plebeian surroundings, and it has always given me the greatest satisfaction to see the 'Barber of Seville' of M. de Beaumarchais acted at the Théâtre Français. But this dear countess ought to appear more grateful. If a real nobleman like Count Almaviva has a few weaknesses she ought not to play the simpleton, uniting with common people against her husband." The Marquis de Vaudreuil, to whom these frank remarks were made, kissed her hand delightedly, and pointed with an impatient gesture to the rising curtain, announcing the second part of the performance.

This act begins with the confidential conversation of the countess with her chief maid Susanna, from which her friends in the parterre discovered with some perplexity that her dallying with the handsome page had much to do with her heart, taking as her excuse the many infidelities of her husband, and at which she eagerly caught. Figaro and Susanna, from mere love of intrigue against the count, assist their mistress, and during the absence of her husband, bring to her the page, who was still concealed in the castle. The young and pretty actress, who played the role of Cherubin, sang the couplets of the romance with such seductive coquetry that the heart of the countess is finally captured. Then begins the scene where the countess and her maid, in playful pastime, attire the youth in a maid's dress. Susanna compares his white arms with her own; and her mistress, with a tincture of jealousy, reproves her for it. In this doubtful occupation they are disturbed by the unexpected return of the count. The page is hustled, just as he is, into the cabinet of the countess, and, after knocking a long time, her husband, suspecting what has been going on, is admitted. The turn things now take has a most curious and uncomfortable effect. The countess, in her confusion, begins to make confessions. She then pretends that Susanna is in the cabinet, and, when the count threatens to break open the door, she acknowledges and tries to excuse the presence of the page in the most natural manner she can think of. When the door at length is opened, Susanna is discovered. Her mistress comprehends at once the artful work in which the maid has been engaged. She had taken an opportunity to glide into the cabinet, while Cherubin descended by the window. The count fancies that his wife has been amusing herself at his expense, thinking that she merely told him the story about the page to rouse his jealousy. The countess soon reconciles herself to the role her husband tenders her. She begins to love intrigue for its own sake, and at the end of the act she is engaged in making preparations to disguise herself as Susanna and meet her husband at a rendezvous he had arranged with the maid in the garden.

"I think your beautiful Countess Rosina de-

generates considerably," said the Baron de Besenval, when the act was over, turning to his neighbor, Diana de Polignac. "She places her white hands into the midst of this dark intrigue, and soon will be the most defiled of all. If this continues longer, I shall have to throw the first stone at her; I cannot help myself."

"Then you would be doing her a great wrong, both as an honest Swiss and as a French cavalier," replied Diana, warmly. "You must own that the Countess Rosina only agrees to this intrigue to win back her beloved husband. She is certainly using questionable means, but has a good purpose in view; and I think, in a case of this kind, every woman should be a Jesuit, for the question is the possession of what is most important to her—her heart."

"I must compliment your penetration," remarked the Marquis de Vaudreuil to Julie de Polignac, who sat beside him.. "You foresaw that the education the Countess Rosina had received in the house of a doctor of Seville would declare itself."

"Do you see," replied Julie, coquettishly, tapping her hand with her fan, "this person does not shudder to dress herself in the clothes of her maid, in order to confound her husband, a Spanish grandee, a man who has just been appointed ambassador to London? How can one of honorable birth endure to wear the dress of a domestic? I have my doubts as to the noble descent of this Rosina, although the author has labored to make us believe it in the 'Barber of Seville.'"

"Well, how do you fare, friend Mirabeau?" said Chamfort to his neighbor, who was dreamily looking about him. "Is there not something in this comedy that is very attractive and curious, influencing the audience to thoughtfulness? I shall soon make up my mind as to who is the cause of all our present social infirmity. In my estimation, all the sinners in the comedy are involved in the sin of their master. If Count Almaviva were a better man, not given up to his passionate will, and wholly egotistic, heartless, and dishonorable, those surrounding him would be decent, well-meaning people, free from intrigue and sin. I think, Mirabeau, we must make the master answerable for the wickedness and misfortunes of his servants, and that is a very practical lesson, evidently taught by the play."

"You are a poet," replied Mirabeau, "and naturally more apt than I am to interpret the meaning of this shallow piece. I am really only thinking of Henriette: the dear girl must be very anxious at home, and my heart beats violently in anticipation of the unravelling of the plot. Do not forget to leave in season. Our arrangements are, that, immediately after the third act, you are to depart. As soon as you reappear in the hall, I take it for granted that all is right, and that the carriage with Henriette and the child is safely concealed in the court-yard of the palace. Then I take leave of you for some time, Chamfort!"

Chamfort replied with a nod and a glance, showing that he remembered and would be faithful to his agreement with Mirabeau.

The curtain rose for the third act, which called forth repeated applause. Especially those humorous passages directed against the aristocracy, were enthusiastically commended by spectators who were of the highest rank. Either they supported the author as patronizing a certain tone recently pervading French court society, or they thought it better only to see the witty side of weighty truths, and to be greatly amused. Thus the diplomatists and statesmen present extolled particularly the ideas of Figaro, in which he declares, with his natural good sense, what his opinion of social and state policy is, denouncing the times as characterized not only by levity, but positive vileness; and where Count Almaviva interrupts him by the weak criticism, "That is not policy but intrigue!" this ingenuous expression of a partisan and a defender of all that is pernicious, occasioned great merriment. The company were thrown into a frame of mind of which perhaps they had thought themselves incapable. The swift action of the comedy, hardly giving them time to breathe, led them to take sides, especially when they witnessed the scene in which Count Almaviva holds a court of justice in the midst of

his vassals, to decide the cause of Marcellina, who makes pretensions to the hand of Figaro. The boundless folly and wickedness of the old system of administering justice are here derided in the severest style. Then suddenly the situation takes the very frivolous turn that Figaro is recognized, by a mark on his arm, as the illegitimate son of this Marcellina, who desires to espouse him. She then asserts herself as the advocate of the social oppression of women, and undertakes the chorus. On the wings of wit the comedy rises to the heights of philosophy.

As the curtain fell, Chamfort left the saloon. Mirabeau became very restless; the impatience with which he looked forward to the return of his friend increased every moment, and he was agitated by the most painful thoughts. The Marquis de Vaudreuil and the Countesses de Polignac endeavored to draw him into conversation, but their efforts failed from the unyielding manner in which he bore himself toward them, answering only in monosyllables, and hazarding his reputation as a talented and brilliant speaker, beginning to be known at court.

The fourth act commenced. Mirabeau was scarcely in a condition to follow attentively the progress of events. His head involuntarily turned again and again to the door by which he expected to see Chamfort enter at every moment. But his return was retarded, and Mirabeau gave himself up to tormenting fancies, supposing that, notwithstanding all their arrangements, Henriette had been recognized and seized by the police. While anger and sorrow occupied his heart, he felt how dear his new love already was, and his yearning for her presence became irresistible. He was not in a state of mind to be interested in what was performing on the stage.

The marriage ceremony of Figaro and Susanna takes place. The countess is dragged further into difficulties by the fault of others as well as by accident and passion, and is on the way to become herself one of the guilty. Among the maidens forming the procession she discovers a young shepherdess, who pleases her particularly, and she cannot refrain from kissing her. It is hardly possible not to believe that the countess knew that it was Cherubin thus disguised, and whom the count discovers and very roughly drags out from under his mask. In the midst of the wedding festival the count makes his final arrangements for his meeting with Susanna at night, for whom his wife intends to substitute herself, in the most cunning manner. The conspiracy against Almaviva becomes more complicated. The tyrannical lord of all is in danger of being the deceived of all.

During this time Chamfort did not make his appearance, and Mirabeau's anxiety reached its highest degree at the end of the fourth act. His impatience was so great that he could not remain in his seat; he rose and went to the antechamber, through which his friend would have to come.

The fifth act began, and Mirabeau stood at the door of the saloon, undecided whether to remain or return to his dwelling to gain information of what had happened. On the stage they were just acting the scene of the nightly rendezvous, in which all his misfortunes visit the count; and the universal judgment begins, punishing the guilty through their own acts, permitting each to receive nothing but what belongs to him according to the order of justice. Figaro is gliding around in the dark, closely enveloped in his cloak, as if in philosophic melancholy, beginning that remarkable monologue in which he meditates on destiny, life, and society, applying his thought to the rank and exclusive position of the count, with a very solemn voice, but with very clear reasoning. With satanic art he delivers the passage: "Nobility, fortune, rank, honorable distinctions, all these make a man proud. And what have you done to possess them? You have only taken the trouble to be born—nothing more; otherwise you are precisely like other people." *

Some one touched Mirabeau gently from behind; turning, he perceived Chamfort, who nodded to him as if in confirmation, giving him to understand that all had been executed according

to their wishes. While the rest of the audience were perseveringly applauding Figaro's monologue, Mirabeau seized the opportunity to depart. He followed his friend through the anteroom; and, not until they reached the staircase, did they dare to exchange a word.

"We had a narrow escape from discovery," said Chamfort. "The police, guarding your house with the watchfulness of a Cerberus, had some suspicion of the pretty Provençal country-girl with whom I was going to slip into the carriage. They demanded information respecting her and our destination. I pointed, as you told me, to the equipage, bearing the name and crest of the Marquis de Vaudreuil, told them a long and circumstantial history why your child and its nurse were to be brought to the marchioness; then I lifted your Henriette quickly into the carriage, begging them to make further inquiries at the Hotel Vaudreuil. The police - officers nearly frightened me; you know I almost cease to breathe when I come near them. Now, however, we are safe here, and Henriette longs ardently to see you."

Chamfort led his friend to the coach, concealed in the carriage-house, and Mirabeau entered quickly, laying his hand on Henriette's lips, as she was about to utter an exclamation of joy. Little Coco was fast asleep on her lap. Chamfort stood a few moments longer at the door, heartily wishing them a happy voyage. Then he carefully drew their attention to the English passport, which he handed to Mirabeau. He recommended Henriette to change her costume as soon as possible; every thing necessary would be found in the carriage, and she would now have to pass for an English nurse. She pressed his hand affectionately in her hearty and frank manner.

"And now farewell, my friend Chamfort," said Mirabeau, embracing him. "Give my compliments to all those Almavivas in the theatre, whom I am compelled to leave for a while. I fear a frivolous comedy will scarcely amend them; we will soon have a graver play in France. I will write to you how affairs are going on in England.

---

* "Le Mariage de Figaro," Acte v., Sc. iii. "Vous vous êtes donné la peine de naître, et rien de plus : du reste homme assez ordinaire."

I shall naturally study English liberty. Farewell!
I love and honor you, Chamfort! Love me also!"

The carriage rolled away, in a short time reaching its destination. At the foot of the Montmartre, at the appointed place, was the travelling-
coach, for which they exchanged the equipage of
the marquis. The secretary, Hardy, and the valet
de chambre, were waiting to receive them. Miss
Sarah, who of course could not be dispensed
with, was among the *compagnons de voyage* awaiting Mirabeau. She showed her delight at seeing
her master by capering about and barking. The
party immediately put themselves in order of
motion. Mirabeau lifted Henriette into the carriage. She had much trouble in quieting little
Coco, who had been awakened by the dog. The
secretary took his seat by the coachman, and the
valet behind. Thus the well-laden vehicle rattled
merrily along the moonlit road to Brussels.

CHAPTER VIII.

A WALK THROUGH LONDON.

MIRABEAU and Henriette had been in London
for several days, dwelling, as was his custom, in a
large and expensive house, in one of the most
fashionable streets in the West End. The funds
obtained through the legacy left to Henriette
were already considerably reduced. It was a
beautiful summer's day, when Mirabeau, who had
been attending to some out-door business, returned early to persuade his charming friend to
accompany him in a walk, for since her arrival in
London she had not left the room. He hoped
that the sunny day and the inspiring air would
be the best remedy for the reëstablishment of her
health, which the voyage had greatly weakened.
Henriette gladly assented. Her pale cheeks,
bearing traces of real illness, were for a moment
faintly tinted with something like that color
formerly glowing on them. She arose quickly,
laying aside her work, to hasten in making her
toilet for the promenade; but, with a melancholy

smile, she felt that she could not move with so
much alacrity as formerly. Her feebleness was
the result of the hardships of the voyage, for
twice they were seriously endangered while making the transit from France to England: once a
violent storm overtook the vessel on the open
sea, so that it was nearly lost; and again, it was
almost wrecked in sight of the harbor. Added
to these perils, she was attacked by continual
sea-sickness, and on her arrival in London was in
such bad health that Mirabeau was obliged to
send immediately for a physician.

"Poor child," said Mirabeau, contemplating
her weakness, "it is evident that you have been
travelling with me; for I have never yet been
abroad but some misfortune threatened me. If I
travel on land, the wheels of my vehicle break;
on the sea, it only requires my presence, like
another Jonah, to marshal all the storms of
heaven against the craft that carries me. Every
trifle is a matter of life and death with me; and
I have associated you in the destiny of such a
man, my lovely, innocent Henriette! I am afraid
that the terrors of this voyage have seriously in-
jured you."

"But I have determined to be perfectly well,"
said Henriette, "for my present condition really
irritates me, and has become quite unbearable to
us all. Besides, the physicians in London make
too extravagant charges for me to indulge in the
luxury of illness. A guinea for each visit is altogether too much, and would soon ruin us."

"Ah, I recognize now my charming miser," exclaimed Mirabeau, laughing.

"I do not care for the miserable money itself,"
replied Henriette, gravely looking at him with
her frank, confiding eyes. "But it grieves me
when you are uneasy about money; and I wish
our stock would last forever. But it has not
that appearance, and I have a terrible fear that
some day you will sadly say to me, 'Henriette,
what has become of the money?'"

"You may be perfectly indifferent on that
point, for I am about to gain considerable funds,
my dear Countess 'Yet-Lee!'" said Mirabeau
(calling her by her pet-name—thus pronouncing

the final syllables of Henriette Amélie, and prefixing the title of countess, by which she was known to the servants). "I must live respectably," added Mirabeau, after a pause, during which Madame de Nehra endeavored to hasten her toilet. "It is true, our money is gradually disappearing—but how it is I cannot explain; the ebbing of the ocean is not so difficult to understand as the law that governs our purse. But never mind, Yet-Lee, I have taken some precaution. I have great literary enterprises in my mind, that cannot be unsuccessful. This whole morning I have been running about in London, summoning the army of publishers to my standard. Our affairs will mend, Countess Yet-Lee, rely on it. My manuscript against the order of Cincinnatus I have already disposed of; it will appear in a few months; it will be the first work in which I shall come before the public in open visor, and with my full name. The time is near when it will be necessary to take an unquestioned stand—man against man, tooth against tooth! The publisher gives me only ten guineas for my book, but, with the sale of every hundred copies, I am to receive additional compensation. The production must find a ready market; it cannot fail. Then, I have promised another bookseller to write something about the free navigation of the Scheldt, about which the Dutch are disputing with the Austrian Emperor Joseph, and which may easily be the occasion of a European war. I must, of course, write in favor of the Hollanders, who levy an impost at the mouth of that river according to a treaty a century old; and thus cut off the possessions of Austria from free communication with the ocean. But what do I care for Austria, the native country of Queen Marie Antoinette, to whom we patriots and agitators of France dare not make the least concession? I shall only receive a few louis d'ors in return, but I shall gain many friends both in London and Paris. And, besides, Yet-Lee, my mind is full of literary projects that must bear golden fruit. It is all the same to me with what I may be engaged; but I mean to work, though employed on a geography or a Chinese grammar. My secretary Hardy sits in his cabinet all day, making extracts from books and newspapers, which I intend to use for a particular purpose. You see we cannot be in want, and the publishers will soon come to me instead of my running after them."

Henriette in the mean time finished her toilet, and was standing before her sanguine friend, assenting gladly to his last words. He looked critically at her dress, and passed judgment on her general appearance. "Come," said he, kissing her hands. Beneath his kindly eye her beauty grew fresher, and the roses of her innocent youth seemed to be blooming again on her cheeks. She now took his arm, and soon regained her strength. Their walk led them first through several of the principal promenades of London. Mirabeau expressed his astonishment in a most lively manner at the peculiarities of the different streets, while Henriette endeavored to compare London with Paris and Amsterdam.

"I feel in an extraordinarily good humor," said Mirabeau, "for wherever I turn my eye, I see purity and independence, worthy of man. Even in the street, I have the elevating consciousness that I am in a country in which the people are considered something, and that every one enjoys the free development and exercise of his talents. Look even at the pavement, on which we are walking thus leisurely and unimpeded; its fine structure and cleanliness convince us that here even pedestrians are held in some estimation. Let your eyes roam over this vast area, larger than that of any other city of the Old World. It is true, London is like every other place where men herd together for business or pleasure—it has its broad and narrow streets, and is neither more nor less like Paris or Pekin than human circumstances make it. People huddle together in vast masses for numerous reasons, though they shorten their life by the impurity of the air they breathe and rebreathe, and where the unending combat goes on of the poor against the rich, the select mob against the common mob, the neglected and dishonored against those by whom they are neglected and dishonored. But then this remarkable cleanliness of London has almost equal attractions for the eye and the mind. It is a certain sign that the people are in a healthy political as well as physical condition; that they are free, having the desire and the time to take care of themselves as communities, and accurately to avail themselves of the privileges of their existence as social beings. This is truly a sovereign city, in which even the tiles on the houses seem to know that the dwellers rule by their own will. Most of the edifices are of brick, and very few built in noble style; but that is the glory of this city; every thing has the appearance of nationality, comfort, domesticity, safety, and independence. The river seems to ask: 'With what can you compare me, to which the ocean from all quarters of the globe daily brings tribute?'" *

"I shall soon be jealous of this London," said Henriette, pressing her friend's arm. "I cannot bear to hear you extol any thing, though it is but a mass of brick and mortar."

"Why, you were taken for an Englishwoman while in Paris," replied Mirabeau, laughing; "and when we strolled along the Boulevards, I often heard voices whispering behind us, 'Ah, look at that fair Englishwoman!' And you will soon see a change in me, if I continue to feel as well as I have hitherto done. Instead of Honoré Gabriel Riquetti Count de Mirabeau, I shall become a most portly 'Jacques Rosblf!' Then I shall be lost to France, and the question arises whether I can be of any use in this country, where all are so devoted to royalty."

"You cannot show me any thing to equal the Parisian Boulevards in this city," said Henriette, as they turned into the colonnade in Regent Street, and found themselves suddenly in the midst of the bustle of this thoroughfare. The crowds of pedestrians, and the numerous vehicles passing in different directions, never for a moment became confused, but a remarkable order and propriety controlled all their movements.

"Here you find more than Parisian Boulevards," replied Mirabeau, as he directed her attention to the life around them. His countenance

was cheerful, such as his companion had not seen for a long time. "Here you find a people—a nation—safely and industriously earning their livelihood, and moving onward like a stream that obeys only its own laws of motion. In Paris, my dear Countess Yet-Lee, there is no nation; and it is doubtful whether we can make one of the dull masses huddled together at the foot of an absolute throne—a people knowing their rights, and maintaining them by means of knowledge. Those you see on the Boulevards display only the variegated skin of some mighty serpent, lying in ambush, and whose victim is Paris. It is true all kinds of creatures roam about on the Parisian Boulevards; but they are not the nation; they are mercenary intriguers. We appear among them, discontented idlers of rank, speculating on the time when France will be a nation, and to whom my friend Chamfort has given the appellation of 'philosophic noblemen of the epoch.'"

"The people are looking at me jeeringly and maliciously," observed Madame de Nehra, after a pause, clinging to Mirabeau's arm with some fear. Several persons, among them a few intoxicated sailors, were just passing, and Henriette insisted that she noticed in their gestures that she was the object of their amusement, having taken offence in some way at her appearance. "In London, it seems, I am not considered so good an Englishwoman as in Paris," said Henriette, directing the attention of her friend to what was occurring. "I fancy it is my foreign toilet that gives umbrage to the people; for I am attired quite in Parisian style. I suppose it is especially my plumed hat that astonishes them."

"Do not let us be concerned about them, and quietly pass on," said Mirabeau. "We can soon change your costume in the most becoming manner. In this respect, the inhabitants show a want of understanding. They laugh at every thing that may appear odd only to themselves, and think they have a right to do so, from the fact that they are isolated, and have not the largest ideas of the rest of mankind, and their predilections and habits. Parisians show more cultivation in never permitting their own weakness to

---

* Mirabeau, "Letters à Chamfort," p. 52.

become apparent, for they do not presume to set themselves up as the supreme authority in any matter, or deride every one who does not bow to their standard."

So they continued their walk, and the count did not observe that several rude persons left the group that had amused themselves at Henriette's appearance, and, following, made all manner of ludicrous motions and exclamations, directing the attention of the passers-by to the foreigners. Henriette was becoming more and more frightened, and begged earnestly to enter a coach. Mirabeau now could not help remarking the crowd behind them; but considered it cowardice if he suddenly essayed to escape. At this moment they met a lady and gentleman, whom they recognized as travelling-companions, having made the passage from France in the same ship. They were an Irishman, and a Parisienne who had apparently eloped with him. She had manifested so much kindliness and intellect during the voyage, that Mirabeau had pleasure in her conversation, and quite a friendship was the result. Greetings were exchanged, and while they stood in the street to make inquiries after each other's wellbeing, the curious mob at the heels of Mirabeau and Henriette seemed to find additional food for ridicule. The Parisian lady wore also an immense plumed hat, that being the most recent fashion in France, and the rest of her toilet was even more remarkable than Henriette's, at least to an English street public.

The people assembled about the strangers began to indicate their more offensive humor by loud laughter. A man of wild and ungovernable appearance, carrying a large trumpet in his hand, suddenly stepped out, placing himself close to the ladies, who regarded him with real terror. He made them a ridiculous bow, thus gaining the applause of his accomplices. He was apparently a well-known buffoon from one of the public-houses, of which there were many in the narrow streets, and was greeted as the "Honorable Lord Trumpeter," which seemed to be his nickname among his comrades. His reputation as a jester appeared to be quite considerable, for his companions became still and attentive to see what he would do. He began to play the part he had devised by making the most frightful grimaces, displaying his characteristic and skilful ability. He intended to reproduce by his gestures the grotesque effect made on the spectators by the toilet of the ladies, and particularly by their head-dresses, and executed his pantomime very well, distorting the muscles of his face sometimes to a funny, and again to a repulsive expression—in in this manner so accurately describing their costume that they could not help recognizing the public opinion of them in the caricature.

After having finished his polite performance, Lord Trumpeter suddenly blew a blast on the instrument he held in his hand, as if to advertise his profession. He repeated this several times, and the applause of the multitude rose to the most frightful demonstrations of delight. Henriette acted wisely, at first laughing at the impudent capers of Lord Trumpeter, which reminded her of the days of her childhood, passed in Amsterdam, where street-scenes of this kind are not unusual. The Parisienne, on the contrary, became angry from the beginning of the affair, and now could no longer restrain her indignation. Like a true Frenchwoman, she began to abuse Lord Trumpeter, though her English was somewhat imperfect, and would scarcely have been understood by herself in her cooler moments. Caring little for the danger to which she was exposed, she did not hesitate, her large black eyes sparkling with resentment, to make use of the most violent and insulting expressions in reference to British nationality. She nearly succeeded in involving her Irish friend in the same outbreak, for, obeying her signals, he placed himself in position to fight the whole party of street blackguards.

Count Mirabeau stood quietly looking around with his arms crossed, maintaining his intrepid indifference, and meditating an escape from this absurd predicament. The national humor of the Honorable Lord Trumpeter had not yet reached its climax. After blowing a satiric melody, he turned again to the ladies and began to sing a popular song for their especial benefit. The lines were by no means poetic, but exceedingly vulgar, and, uttered with apparent simplicity, called forth increased applause from the mob, especially as the song was accompanied with fanciful gesticulations.*

This scene, however, was beginning to be noticed by others than those immediately engaged in it. Equipages and equestrians stopped to see what was occurring. Several gentlemen, apparently of rank, dismounted and entered the crowd, dealing out blows with their whips on the most tumultuous, who were evidently intoxicated. Mirabeau received advice as to the best manner of escape, but unfortunately he did not understand the counsel given him, and was on the point of losing his patience, as he could no longer be a witness of the insolence the chief actor permitted himself toward Madame de Nehra. Mirabeau seized the man by the throat, shaking him with his powerful arms, so that the rascal uttered a loud cry and fell on his knees, as if unconscious. This would doubtless have been succeeded by a dangerous complication of affairs, if at the moment a tall, slender man had not managed to make a way for himself through the crowd, just breaking out into violent tumult. The stranger wore a civilian's dress of dark color, and Mirabeau, who had a keen eye for the discovery of character at first sight, took him to be one of the reformed preachers from Geneva, many of whom, together with other political fugitives, were then in London. The new-comer, a rather young man of vigorous and determined appearance, succeeded in engaging the angry mob by an adroit address. He spoke a fluent English, and was master of many popular expressions. Among other flattering things, he called on them, as noble and magnanimous Britons, to go home, and allow honorable foreigners, visiting hospitable Albion, to remain unmolested. His accent betrayed his Swiss origin, but he made himself fully and impressively understood, aided by his powerful voice, reminding one of the style of a preacher, which his im-

posing demeanor corroborated. When he saw that his high-toned and slightly-religious speech was having some influence, he confirmed its success by flinging money among the rioters, thus turning their thoughts to a scramble among themselves. Lord Trumpeter himself, having escaped from the lion-like grasp of Mirabeau, was not a little surprised to find several sixpences in his hand, where he had not seen so many for a long time. The Swiss then gave him a thump on his back, ordering him in a commanding voice to go immediately to the nearest cab-stand and bring two carriages for the strangers of rank, against whom he had so grievously sinned. After the ringleader had disappeared, it was easier to disperse the rest by supplying them with money. The preacher then turned to Count Mirabeau, and, in the most obliging terms, requested him and his friends to enter a neighboring coffee-house to await the arrival of the vehicles, and generously offered to be their guide. Mirabeau accepted his friendly services with the most lively expressions of gratitude.

They had to wait a long while in the coffee-house, but the stranger would not leave until he saw them safe in the cabs; and, in the mean time, indicated his great conversational talents. He spoke frankly and freely about his own personal concerns, saying that his name was Duval, that he had filled a pulpit in Geneva until within eighteen months, and had been exiled from his home and position after the revolution of 1782, during which he had sided with the defeated popular party. Mirabeau seemed to take an interest in Duval, but hesitated to make himself known, considering neither the time nor the place suitable for such a disclosure. The keen-sighted Duval divined this scruple, and said, anticipating it: "I know that it is Count Mirabeau with whom I have the honor of becoming acquainted on this occasion. I have heard much of you, and my political friends and companions, who are here eating the bitter bread of exile, heartily welcome Count Mirabeau to London. We, the men of the Geneva democracy, have the greatest desire to obtain your friendship and sympathy. A few

* Mirabeau describes this scene in his "Lettres à Chamfort," p. 54.

days ago, as we were sitting in the Café de Paris in Haymarket, you entered, and your name was mentioned by some one present. We spoke of your great work on despotism, which is read in all our Swiss valleys, and we agreed that it would be of vast advantage to us and our cause if we could hold a secret council with you. The condition of our native land, and the hopes of European democracy, we would like to make a subject of consideration with Mirabeau. To-day I may perhaps consider this wish as favorably received, as accident has caused this meeting, and the humorous ignorance and narrow-minded inhospitality of this English mob have given me an opportunity of being noticed by you."

Mirabeau pressed his hand gratefully, and gave him a card with his address, requesting him to call at an appointed hour, and claim in any manner pleasing to him the thanks he merited.

At this moment Lord Trumpeter seemed to have returned, as the renewed cries of the crowd were heard, most of whom had not yet dispersed. Duval went out first to see whether the cabs were ready, returning with the intelligence that the buffoon he had sent had brought only one, capable of holding but two persons, saying that no other was at the stand.

Mirabeau, turning to the Parisian lady, who, in consequence of the fright, and excitement she had undergone, seemed to be suffering severely, remarked that there could be no doubt as to who should have the preference in attempting an escape. "I shall remain here with the Countess de Nehra," he remarked, "until another conveyance arrive. This cannot be long delayed, as we are under the protection of our friend Duval."

The condition of the Parisienne grew worse, so that there could be no thought of refusing the offer. She was almost fainting, and the count and the Irishman were obliged to carry her. While Mirabeau was thus making himself useful, he did not observe that a fashionable equipage was standing in the middle of the street. The owner was greeted with great respect by those around, while he sent his powdered footman, dressed in a rich livery, to make inquiries as to all that had occurred. Soon after the servant approached Mirabeau, requesting him and his lady to take seats in the carriage of his master, the first lord of the treasury, Minister William Pitt. Mirabeau glanced in astonishment at this gentleman, who kindly saluted and beckoned to him. His acquaintance with William Pitt dated only from the preceding day, when he paid the minister his first visit, to deliver the letter of introduction from Count d'Entraigues. Mirabeau did not hesitate to accept the invitation, hastening into the coffee-house to bring Madame de Nehra, and both entered the carriage of the generous Englishman, who insisted, with the amiability peculiar to him in private life, that his guests take the seats of honor opposite him.

William Pitt was at the head of the English cabinet, although only in his twenty-fifth year. In affairs of state he was much older than his contemporaries, while his grave and piercing intellect, ever calm and confident, often conquered his opponents before they began the conflict. In familiar intercourse the freshness and liveliness of youth became predominant, and an attractive smile returned to those classic lips that both betrayed his eloquence, and softened the austere wrinkles which thought had furrowed on his brow. Mirabeau was charmed in making this discovery of the minister's genial nature, for at the visit he paid on the preceding day, and on which he placed many hopes, he beheld only the wary and cold statesman, weighing every word, and treating him with inflexible precision. Pitt, with good-natured solicitude, occupied himself particularly with Madame de Nehra, thinking that he must console and tranquillize her on account of the ridiculous scene through which she had passed, although in reality she had not for an instant lost her good-humor.

The carriage went in the direction of Mirabeau's dwelling, for the minister insisted on taking home his protégés.

"It was only our rudest and most ignorant people," repeatedly remarked Pitt, "that committed such improprieties against honorable strangers. You must not judge us all from what you have seen to-day, count. Our people as a nation are good, honest, and respectful, and bear with equal dignity and obedience the laws of the strong government under which they live and are happy. There are, you know, uncultivated and insolent persons in Paris as in London, or in any other large city, where bad men find refuge, and the commotion that has dishonored our streets might as easily have happened anywhere else."

"Mobs are certainly by nature everywhere the same, nor do the aristocracy differ from them," replied the count. "From this fact, the deduction of course is that these two exclusive spheres of society are similar in Great Britain as in France, and are, in essentials, one and the same class."

Pitt violently bit his underlip at these words, but, immediately recovering himself, regained his expression of kindliness and even modesty. "In our country the aristocracy widely differ from the mob," he replied, with an apparently gentle smile, but at the same time casting on the French count a piercing side-glance. "In neighboring countries, it is possible that the nobility may be aiming at a tumultuous dissolution of the state government; fortunately, we know nothing of the kind here. We are old-fashioned; we have laws that reach every one, and an aristocracy similar to that worthily and rightfully becoming a civilized kingdom."

"France is not so fortunate," said Mirabeau, his countenance touched by sadness. "There, all are fast constituting a mob, if we do not succeed in creating a new and sound national body from the universal corruption. The people in their virtue and power will then be discovered, like the precious statue of some divinity, long lost beneath the ruins of an ancient city. But I will maintain, even at the risk of contradicting your lordship, that the Paris mob never could have been guilty of such behavior toward respectable strangers. Our lower classes are too cheerful and childlike, and at the same time too polite, to give offence through any notion of national hatred. To-day, in our own persons, we have experienced the

mere spite—the old prejudice—of the British against the French. I would not have believed it, lord chancellor, that the legacy of your noble father, the Earl of Chatham, who was a lusty hater of France, would be executed in the streets of London."

"This hatred was no legacy, but a state principle," replied Pitt, with dignified calmness. It was part of the political system of my father, and this was founded on the idea that France is the natural enemy of England; and that the latter, to become great and powerful, must be isolated, and collect within herself all her resources. Even if it had been necessary to subdue France, in order to raise England to her true position, Lord Chatham would not have hesitated a moment to go relentlessly forward with his system; but he was not a barbarian—he did not refuse to recognize in individuals those qualities that are to be expected in such a highly-cultivated and honorable nation as the French. And I esteem myself happy in being their friend, although I know how to prevent my country from making an imprudent treaty, and thus ruining her. However, we are not so segregated from France and the rest of the world as not to learn, and, adopting what is good, promote our own greatness."

Mirabeau bowed respectfully, at the same time permitting it to be seen that he ascribed such liberal sentiments to the accustomed diplomatic tone of the British minister. "I am not," he said, significantly, "such a friend of France, as to be blind to her faults and her degeneracy. But, again, I love her so much and so seriously, that I would gladly see her whipped with scorpions, if such chastisement would reëstablish her social as well as political morality, and make her strong and healthy again. If a humiliation of France by England could lead to such a result, I would gladly offer my head and hands for such a purpose. I know that your great father entertained an unbounded hatred of France; he shuddered in all his limbs at the mere utterance of the word Frenchman, and grounded his ideas on the absolute supremacy of either France or England. He seemed to regard it as a law of Nature, that, if

5

the latter is to be great and powerful, the former must be annihilated. We are, however, approaching a new era, in which all states that are free, honest, and vital, can occupy the same rank and stand together in closer relationship. We shall have to force France to become independent and happy, and whoever thus coerces her, in whatever manner, is her benefactor. Yes, your lordship, England has a nobler mission to execute than to hate her neighbor. Let us attack and conquer France; free England offers the best position from which the onset can be made. But it must have, for its principal object, the restoration of the French kingdom to its senses, and the gift of independence to the people. These thoughts, as I intimated to your lordship yesterday, brought me to London, and I would be happy if the ministry of Pitt should find it reconcilable with its policy to make use of the services of Mirabeau."

Pitt politely smiled, and looking down he seemed to indulge in an ironical silence, at the same time assuming a certain complimentary friendliness. His sharply-defined countenance, easily asserting a hard and repulsive character, had a certain charm of intellect, which gave to his cold superiority that mildness and consideration with which he listened to Mirabeau's remarks.

The carriage was passing St. James's Palace, and Pitt glanced searchingly at the windows of the royal residence, as if he desired to make some discovery. Then turning to Mirabeau, who was waiting for a reply in the greatest suspense, he said, quickly: "The policy of Pitt's ministry, my dear count, will gladly make use of all prominent minds, but its aim must always be conservative. In England we must defend the cause of royalty, whatever may happen. The people constitute, after all, only a doubtful idea—a phantom—about whose existence the most heterogeneous conceptions are evermore debating. It is always sought where it is not found, and found where it is not sought. How unreasonable and dangerous it would be to build the policy of a state on such a changeable notion, that never can stand any practical test! Although England

protects and represents national liberty at our hearth-stone, she is interested in preventing the success in France of any such popular policy, for that would occasion a universal national mania, plunging Europe into an abyss! We desire to live here in quiet and comfort; we are no idealists, count; we are Englishmen, and liberty must fill our pockets as well as our heads. We must become rich—that is our destiny—all else depends on the wealth of a state. We must firmly hold to this true and only foundation of our policy, if we are ever to become powerful. Mind alone is the mere efflorescence of a nation, and a beautiful ornament; but opulence is solid and resistless strength. Pitt's idea is to raise altars to wealth in our green fields and along our streams, in our factories, and commercial ports. Our conflict with other nations must be that of peaceful emulation."

Mirabeau felt himself nonsuited. He was silent for a moment, considering whether he should give free utterance to his indignation or not. "Your lordship must forgive me," he said, "that, in having an enthusiastic admiration for your form of government, I would gladly see its beneficial influence applied to France! I envy every Englishman as possessing more individual freedom than any other man on the globe. And this constitution, a masterpiece among all known systems of human liberty, must have wonderful inherent life. A nation, originally by no means the noblest and most gifted, has attained the highest rank by this charter of liberty.

"The British in themselves, by the way, are mere animals, incapable of the higher aspirations —they are stupid, superstitious, prejudiced, unreliable in business, and governed by mercenary lust. And such a nation is protected against its own ignorance and immorality, because it has recognized the right of civil freedom! What would not this country become, if the pure principles of its public law could be extended to its administration—if the evils yet remaining in the one could be pervaded by the spirit of the other.*

---

* "Lettres à Chamfort," p. 69; also "Lettres de Cachet," and "Considérations sur l'Ordre de Cincinnatus."

The present situation of England proves to me more than ever what a bulwark against all accidents and weaknesses of the reigning power is its form of government. It is the fountain of health, even when the ruler is physically and mentally diseased. It is said of your King George III., that the light of his mind is setting, and a night of insanity is likely to envelop the British throne. But that cannot injure the country or the wellbeing of the people. Your charter does not decay, and by its own strength accomplishes that which is best; it is lucid and rational, even if the intellect of royalty be obscured and impaired, because it is the power that distributes blessings, and therefore it is of little consequence what ability is associated with the head of the state. George III., as report has it, falls asleep while reading important and urgent papers—a representative indeed of a happy people—of your political paradise! Happy the nation whose king sinks into slumber in the midst of business, and to whom it is indifferent whether their monarch be awake or asleep while the great affairs of the world are discussed!"

The countenance of the British statesman was losing its amiable expression while Mirabeau spoke. A certain angry hint, often prominent in Pitt's demeanor, was a slight quivering, which, however, on this occasion almost immediately disappeared, for by a skilful turn he controlled his displeasure at some of the rude and false words of the impulsive count. "His majesty King George III. is perfectly well," said the minister, gravely and impressively. "For a long time the health of his majesty has indeed not been very good; but, God be praised! we may consider the kindest and most glorious of monarchs forever freed from the infirmity to which you allude. The contrary would be a great misfortune for England. Without the vital and personal cooperation of the king for the good of our country —without his strength and skill in governing, the real basis of our happiness would be wanting. The English constitution is not a self-acting machine, spreading opulence and liberty by the mere movement of its mechanism. Your Montes-

quieu has, however, made you Frenchmen believe this. He saw in our government a universal remedy—a sort of catholicon, that need only be applied to any nation to create or renew all the blessings of political happiness. No, Count Mirabeau, it is no such instrument—it could not be; and if a wise king is not felt in its administration, it is of no use. Guard yourself against that folly of seeking identical state institutions for all mankind. Your Montesquieu has drawn after him a swarm of philosophic saviors of the human race, who are all brooding over the possibility of attaining and confirming in one scheme political freedom and social happiness. I should be sorry if you also waste your talents in attempting to fill this leaky vessel of the Danaïdes. In state affairs you deal with individuals, not with systems. How could I manage with the parties surrounding me, if I considered them other than persons who feel and act as human beings, and therefore can be influenced by their fellows? I do not myself despair of uniting with me, for the benefit of the whole, even my most dangerous opponents, such as Fox, Burke, and others. The question of the day is to build the edifice, and it matters little whence the materials come."

"Fox, for example, who introduced the India Bill, and the great democratic Burke, who, during the American War, dared vindicate the principle of popular government?" asked Mirabeau, shaking his head.

Pitt seemed not to care about entering into details of this kind. Not noticing Mirabeau's question, he turned to Madame de Nehra, asking her pardon for the strictly political turn the conversation had unexpectedly and unduly taken. He drew her attention to a large millinery store they were passing, displaying ladies' hats in its showwindows. "Would you allow me to choose an English hat for you?" he asked, smiling, and making a motion as if to stop the carriage. "It would be nothing but justice that the prime minister of England should atone for the offence that frightened and insulted one of the most charming ladies in London. Your permission would give me the greatest satisfaction; for I desire your favorable opinion of me, not as a tiresome politician, but a man of taste in the fine arts. The large French hat of the countess was certainly that which excited our 'stupid, ignorant, superstitious, and corrupt people,' as Count Mirabeau has done me the honor to designate all my countrymen; let William Pitt therefore present you with an English hat, such as adorns the prettiest heads in this country. We cannot change the fashions of those among whom we temporarily reside. Every land has its own peculiar ideas of taste, in dress especially, and as strangers we owe them consideration."

Henriette cast down her eyes in perplexity, while at the same time she sent a questioning glance to Mirabeau, who seemed still occupied with the last expressions of Pitt. After receiving a sign of approval, she bowed to the minister with graceful frankness, declaring she would accept his present. The carriage stopped, and Pitt, with all the grace of an accomplished cavalier, offered his arm to Madame de Nehra, to accompany her into the store. Pitt showed considerable tact in this gallantry, and Henriette was delighted with her fashionable acquisition, with which she immediately replaced her enormous Paris hat. Mirabeau, whom the statesman seemed rather to avoid, had gone, unperceived, to the counter, and paid for the purchase. After Madame de Nehra had expressed her satisfaction, it was requested that the bill be sent to the minister's house, who was sadly mortified on being informed that payment had already been made. Looking rather out of humor, he invited them to reënter his carriage. Mirabeau, however, asked permission to take one of the cabs standing near, as his dwelling was not very distant, and lay in a contrary direction, and he did not wish to abuse the kindness shown him. Pitt cast a cold, scrutinizing glance at him, and consented, slightly bowing. They separated, with an evident mutual misunderstanding.

On his return home, Mirabeau threw himself in great displeasure on the sofa, exclaiming violently against the disappointments and vexations that he experienced everywhere.

Henriette approached him, laying her hand soothingly on his burning brow. "Why are you so dissatisfied, my friend?" she asked, gently and lovingly.

"I am at war with myself," he replied, sighing. "Accident placed me in a most favorable situation, in which I could converse familiarly with the first statesman of England. And, instead of taking advantage of it, I lost all prudence, and blundered in the most absurd manner. I was always passionate and rash, but I can never forgive myself for being such a blockhead as to utter uncalled-for truth, when I ought to have been reserved and calculating. I conversed with the British prime minister much as I would have chatted at a dinner with Chamfort or Condorcet. My dignity may have been perhaps gratified, but I was very foolish, especially for one who imagined that he would find in London diplomatic employment, or serve Pitt's ministry by secret missions. I could not have thought it possible that my natural frankness would play me such a trick. Instead of revealing my ideas and intentions, I ought to have enacted a kind of comedy, and, with a mingling of ingenuousness and perfidy, accredited myself with ability to read his most secret thoughts, and thus use all my skill in executing, as it were, variations to his tune. Instead of that, I play my own notes on my own instrument, and when I find he does not like my music, I almost knock him down! Well, if I cannot do better than that, I may as well commence at once my Chinese grammar, to save us from starvation!"

"Do not feel so provoked with yourself, Mirabeau," replied Henriette, caressing him with her hand. "You are as good as this English minister, and I like to see men boldly defend their views. If he will not employ you, we can dispense with him. We are not without brains, and a great future is before you! Let us be merry to-day; I feel as well and cheerful as I ever did. The walk with you has almost had the effect of a miracle, and I seem to myself like another being. And have I not gained a new hat by our adventure?—a hat so light and pretty that Titan‮‬, the fairy queen, might wear it—and chosen for me by his lordship, Minister William Pitt, but honestly paid for by my lover. Shall I make you laugh as I formerly used to do?" She hastened away, calling loudly for Miss Sarah, who rather unwillingly left her comfortable place on the sofa, at her master's feet. Henriette took the old Paris hat she had brought home with her, putting it on the dog's head, and tying the ribbons around her neck and paws, although she did not appear to appreciate the head-dress, moving about in it very uneasily, and finally retiring to a corner of the room. Henriette stood before the pet, making ridiculous grimaces and gestures, evidently endeavoring to imitate Lord Trumpeter in his assault upon the Parisian fashion. Mirabeau could not withstand this comic scene, and rewarded her with hearty laughter, that interrupted his melancholy humor. Delighted at her success in so readily dissipating his gloomy thoughts, she ran to him, and expressed her thanks with a kiss.

CHAPTER IX.

THE GENEVA FUGITIVES IN LONDON.

MIRABEAU was in his study, apparently occupied in writing; but, on observing him more closely, it was evident that his eyes wandered from the paper, first to the window, and out into the foggy London sky, and then sadly to Henriette, who was sitting opposite, engaged in some domestic employment.

"It is impossible for me to collect my thoughts to-day," he said, impulsively rising and approaching Henriette, who also discontinued her work, looking at him scrutinizingly.

"This fog is really detestable," she said, seizing his hand, and leaning her head against it, as if wearied. "I cannot comprehend how people can live in a country where the day is turned into night. I really shudder, and all the ghost-stories of my childhood seem realized. How those heavy mists heave as a sea over the roofs of the houses! See that grotesque form dancing past our window; does it not seem to fold its hands above its head? Mirabeau, that is on our account; the phantom laughs at us because we are still in London, uselessly wasting time and money."

"The phantom is right," replied Mirabeau, sadly and dejectedly. "We have passed many months in London, simpletons as we are! If I were a manufacturer of boot-blacking, I have no doubt I would soon make a fortune, but my literary works I offer in vain to all those publishers. I make new projects every day, extend my preparations to all quarters of the globe, and as a reward I am received with a shrug and a heartless glance. During these fruitless efforts, our money has again disappeared like the smoke in a chimney. For several weeks we have been making all manner of retrenchments, and have been scarcely able to procure necessaries; if manna does not drop down on us to-day, we can neither breakfast nor dine to-morrow. To cap the climax of my derisive destiny, I am writing a sermon on the immortality of the soul."

"A sermon?" asked Henriette, surprised. "Are you becoming a preacher, Mirabeau? and can you take that role so easily without preparation?" She sprang from her seat, and, approaching the desk at which he had been writing, seized the sheets, and glanced quickly and eagerly at their contents. "Why, sure enough, it is a sermon on the immortality of the soul!" she exclaimed. Her countenance became grave and thoughtful, and she regarded him half shyly, half reverentially. Her attitude was so ludicrous, that Mirabeau regained his good-humor.

"It is simply a kindness for a friend that has made me a preacher, but only for one discourse," he replied, taking up the sheets and contemplating them with a certain self-sufficiency. "You remember Duval, the man who rendered us such an important service on the day of our Regent-Street adventure, delivering us from the mob. He has asked me to do him a service, which I cannot refuse. You are aware that he is one of the Geneva fugitives, exiled in consequence of the revolution of 1782, and whom the English received and protected. He has been seized by that anti-cosmopolitan disease, home-sickness, and is making arrangements to return to his country. The gracious aristocracy now governing the Republic of Geneva, are promising that his wishes may be gratified; that he may even be permitted again to resume his position, making, however, the humiliating condition (as I consider it) that he must send them some evidences of his doctrines. Among these is a demand for a sermon on the immortality of the soul. They consider it possible that a revolutionist, who fought for popular government, may also have entered into some conflict with the faith of his church. In this difficulty he has addressed himself to me for a sermon, written in the purest and most forcible French. He has long been an admirer of my style, having heard it favorably spoken of, and I fancy that he saved us so energetically from the hands of Lord Trumpeter, in order to have a claim on my rhetorical favors. I hope that by my aid he will pass a good examination. It amuses me to fancy myself a clergyman, maintaining with a sort of pompous liberality a doctrine so sublime. I will read my sermon to you this evening at tea." *

"Do you not believe in the immortality of the soul, Mirabeau?" asked Henriette, softly, looking tenderly and searchingly into his eyes.

"Wait until tea-time, my child," replied Mirabeau, smiling, "and you will learn from my sermon how generously I promise an immortal paradise to every man. I will furnish any one, wishing to make use of proof and desiring a future life, a complete arsenal of arguments. Eternal life is an inheritance every one may claim who is satisfied of the existence of his own soul. But all claims are not paid, and some inheritances fail to reach their heirs. How do we know what

may be lost in the suit that death institutes against us? I cannot draw even the revenue my father, the Marquis de Mirabeau, not only promised me, but which was conceded as a right. He takes into account the debts he formerly paid for me, and I am at law with him about them. Suppose immortality should thus be withheld from us. Suppose it be taken into account how much of the original dowry of the soul we have wasted in the pitiful things of this earth, and that nothing remains to be paid. Alas! it is not unreasonable to think that annihilation awaits many a reckless child of Adam. Against my father, I can at least employ an advocate. I have engaged the renowned lawyer Target in my affairs in Paris. There then is a hope for me, though a slight one; but what advocate can I employ when the Father of the Universe closes the book of reckoning—when my wretched soul appears before him, and receives the judgment that there is no balance due me?"

Henriette anxiously clung to him, entreating and pacifying him with her loving eyes, as she always did when his wild and derisive temper was mastering him. She smilingly asked whether he would not again be a good and brave man.

"You are right in scolding me to-day," he said, with a melancholy mildness. "The fog without, and this sermon within, at which I have worked like a poor scrivener all the morning, have made me ill-humored. It is becoming a mental disease with me that all I think of leads me back to the miserable difficulties I have with my father. They poison all my purest contemplations, and demoralize my whole being in every nerve and fibre. I must make an end of this business, whatever may be the consequence. Target wrote to me yesterday that there was little prospect of his gaining my suit against the marquis. I would immediately return to Paris, and venture, as a last resource, to have a personal interview with him, and see what final impression I can make; but I am not sure whether our despotic laws do not still give him power over my person. I am ignorant as to the continuance of that parental tyranny, by which he incarcerated me, and ap-

* Vide Montigny, "Mémoires de Mirabeau," vol. iv., p. 174.

pointed my residence wherever it pleased him. If he can still do so, in consequence of the former orders of the king, I must be very careful how I meet my loving parent. In any other case, I would personally undertake the conflict with him. I should also like to know what my bosom friends—my creditors—think of me, so that I could decide as to the judiciousness of my return."

Henriette arose in great animation, and seemed to be meditating on some plan. She stood before him with downcast eyes and heaving bosom, but, presently lifting up her bright and resolute face, she said: "Send me to Paris, Mirabeau! I will reconnoitre and arrange every thing for you; and you will discover that your Yet-Lee is the most adroit and reliable agent you can find. You must remain in London awaiting my letters and return. You have no conception yet of my activity and enterprise when the question is to accomplish something for you, or even to encounter extreme danger. Oh, I will go to the ministers at Versailles, and endeavor to convince them that those abominable regal judgments which bound you so helplessly to your father's despotic will, ought not to be in force any longer. Then I will visit the merchants to whom you owe money, and, if possible, make an accommodation with them, asking to leave you unmolested until your financial affairs are in better condition. After that I will call on the booksellers in Paris, speak to them of your literary plans, and gain the favor of some rich publisher for the journal you intend to edit, entitled *Le Conservateur*.[*] My friend, I shall not slumber in Paris until I have succeeded in accomplishing something for you. You may rely on me."

Mirabeau contemplated her with joyful surprise, and pressed her passionately in his arms. "That is a capital idea!" he exclaimed; "and I really believe that by making such a raid on Paris you will assist me materially. Henriette, by the intervention of your beauty, you could adjust my difficulties, and smooth the way for a return, much

better than I could do with my impulsiveness, which ruins every thing almost before I have attempted my purposes. There is something of magic in your appearance, so that no one you address can very well resist. What more effectual agency can I employ than your charming appearance, your sweetness and grace? Your pure and smiling lips, pleading for me, cannot possibly be disregarded, even by a barbarian!"

Henriette, with an exclamation of delight, put her arms around his neck; but presently left him, walking up and down the room in evident excitement, apparently occupied with her preparations for the voyage.

"But it will not do," added Mirabeau, after a pause, his expression changing to sadness. "No, you might be exposed to dangers—to complications—which I would not care for you to hazard. You are not safe in Paris; you will be recognized as the former fugitive from the convent, and be returned to the dominion of your prioress, who will reclaim you by order of the police. I shall be indeed undone if you are snatched away from me."

"Why have you so little faith? why are you so timid, Mirabeau?" she replied, all her characteristic determination visible in her features, giving a still nobler bearing to her whole appearance. "Trust me, they neither shall nor can recognize me. Am I not an Englishwoman, having a passport in regular form? Besides this document, do I not possess a much more genuine English hat, so that on my arrival I shall be considered as an *Anglaise* of undoubted origin? I shall boldly dispute my identity with the former Henriette van Haren. And, in fact, am I the same person? Has not your love changed me, so that I bear little resemblance to what I formerly was? In those days I was startled if I met a cat in the silence of the cloister garden; now I feel courage enough to accept the gauntlet from the whole world, to fight in your favor, and travel not only to Paris, but to the Feejee Islands, as your messenger and agent."

Mirabeau was still undecided, but Henriette continued her urgent entreaties, uniting them

* Peuchet, "Mémoires sur Mirabeau et son Époque," vol. ii., p. 805.

with vehement and obvious reasons. He began at length to consider the execution of the plan, and unfold to her his wishes and views. At the same time he was glad to think that Chamfort was still in Paris, from whom she could expect protection and assistance. The departure was fixed for the following day. Mirabeau intended to write a concise memorial on the condition of his circumstances, which Henriette was to hand to the minister, Baron de Breteuil. He wrote with such uncommon rapidity that one night was sufficient to accomplish this; and he began to occupy himself with matters preparatory to their separation. Suddenly he remembered a fact of great importance. This was in reference to travelling expenses. When Henriette gently touched this point, after making prudent arrangements for every thing else, Mirabeau started, striking his forehead with an agonizing movement.

"Money! Money!" he exclaimed, walking up and down the apartment. "Where shall we find it for your voyage? We have not a single penny in the house; I know of no helping hand, which would replenish my pocket. Really, dear Countess Yet-Lee, you cannot travel without funds, and what are we to do?"

"No money for travelling expenses!" repeated Henriette, casting down her eyes in confusion. "And, I suppose, we have no credit to raise any?"

"A thought occurs to me," replied Mirabeau; after some musing. "What do you think of addressing ourselves to Elliot? You know—I am on intimate terms with him; for we were fellow-students and sufferers in the school of the Abbé Chocquart. During my stay in London he has often proved his fraternal affection for me. Go to him immediately, and say that I find myself in a painful difficulty, and that he would greatly oblige by lending me one hundred guineas. The case is urgent, and Sir Gilbert Elliot the only refuge of my wrecked treasury. Will you?"

A slight blush tinted Henriette's cheeks. She hesitated to reply, appearing to be in some embarrassment.

"You can go boldly to his dwelling, continued

Mirabeau, for he lives with his amiable family, ranking with the most esteemed and distinguished in London. I should like you to execute this commission for me, for I have no other reliable person whom I could send on such an errand. Our servants are ill-humored, because for some time I have not been able to pay them their wages, and, besides, they do not live as well as formerly in our house. Therefore, my love, do you go yourself. Sir Gilbert Elliot is a noble cavalier, who thinks a great deal of you; he is of that class of Englishmen who, in money matters, manifest a truly royal soul. He will consider it an honor, as it really is, to serve a friend with such a trifle as a few hundred guineas."

"If you think I ought to go, I will," said Henriette, after a pause. "You must always point out to me the path of my duty." She hastened to dress herself for her visit, as usual offering him her farewell kiss.

"You will take a coach," he said. "The mists outside are so dense, that I fear you may not be able to find your way to Belgrave Square, where our friend resides. Besides, it is too far for you to go on foot."

"And, for all that, Countess Yet-Lee would confront greater inconveniences than a London fog," said Henriette, laughing merrily. "The purse of Count Mirabeau just now does not belong to those that can afford even moderate expenses. In its bottomless depth not even a few shillings, to pay a vehicle, could be found." Courtesying, she quickly left the room, which Mirabeau paced restlessly and thoughtfully. Seating himself again at his desk, he began to sketch the memorial on his relations with his father, which Henriette was to deliver to Baron de Breteuil in Paris. The sermon on the immortality of the soul was temporarily laid away in a drawer. Just as he was in full flow of composition, and his pen could hardly express his thoughts fast enough, some one knocked loudly at the door, and entered on hearing his rather reluctant "Come in."

The visitor was of middle age, his physiognomy characterized by insolence and daring. He was small in stature, but indicated great energy, and his whole bearing was that of an adventurous man. His dress had a dash of the whimsical; and his gray hat, which he did not remove until he had already reached the centre of the room, was remarkable not only for its round, broad-brimmed shape, but for the flaming red ribbon with which it was bound.

"Ah, welcome, Etienne Clavière!" exclaimed Mirabeau, rising from his seat and warmly welcoming the intruder. "I hope you have not come to say farewell. It is said that you Genevans, although reposing here on beds of roses, are not quite satisfied with the hospitality of England, and are thinking of changing your asylum to some other country."

"Several of us intend to depart," replied the stranger, discontentedly. "Siordet, Janot, and others, are going to Neufchatel, to try their fortune there under that magistracy which, according to my idea, will scarcely protect revolutionary fugitives. Grenus, Ringler, and many more, are to retire to Constance, under the dominion of the dear, absolute Emperor of Germany, and a large number depart for Brussels. You see, count, the Geneva democratic refugees cannot live peaceably on British ground.—But I remain in London."

"You are right," said Mirabeau, "your compatriots are committing a political blunder, in separating and fleeing to all points of the compass. They ought to have remained together in this city, forming a steady and strong revolutionary community. Even if but a small club in the beginning, it would gradually have attracted all the elements of liberty in Europe, and have been a centre whence could have originated insurrections against tyranny, especially that of France."

"I have not given up that hope," replied Clavière, solemnly, and with a flash from his brilliant eyes. "Duroveray, D'Yvernois, and I, continue here, composing a revolutionary committee, that will soon be strengthened by the arrival of other Genevans entertaining similar doctrines. Among those who will join us, are Dumont, Chauvet, Marat, and Melly. We shall complete the organization aiming to subvert the govern-

ment of your country, and I have come to announce this to you, and take counsel with the strongest intellect of France, whose vocation it is to liberate her." He seated himself on the sofa, awaiting Mirabeau's reply, and playing with the ribbon on his hat.

"I shall not fail you when there is something to be done," said Mirabeau, standing before Clavière, "but, first, tell me why so many of your countrymen leave London, where they have found such a hospitable and excellent reception, not only privately, but by the government? The Geneva democrats who were exiled in the struggle of 1782, are the real favorites of the British people, and all the world knows that the government secretly abetted the attempted revolution, and promised assistance of every description. You let me perceive as much, or rather acknowledged it, Clavière, when I appeared in your counting-room in Geneva the same year, and when you so promptly extended your confidence to me. You were at that time the rich banker, and I the poor author, who presented at your desk a check with which a Swiss publisher had blessed me in exchange for one of my manuscripts. You immediately cashed the draft, although it was not quite in order, and we entered into a familiar political conversation, sympathizing in the same sentiments. On another occasion, you informed me that an outbreak was expected, in order to throw off the yoke of the aristocracy that was ruining your republic, and, in its place, to found the only true government—by representatives of the people. You introduced me among the patriots of Geneva, who afterward managed the revolution, yourself, Duroveray, and D'Yvernois, being the leaders. I then made the acquaintance of many whom I have since recognized as exiles, and with whom we consulted on the future of France, that country being important in reference to the stability of your free government, as well as for the liberty of all Europe. And why do these men withdraw from you and your cause? Have they become disloyal to their principles, and will they not betray and endanger our plans?"

"No," replied Clavière, "they are not recreant,

but their discontent with the English government drives them away. It is, however, short-sightedness to give up a position because you cannot immediately gain personal advantage from it. It is true, we refugees have been here a long time, and cannot exactly catch the roast pigeons with which the ministry and cabinet of George III. allured us. It was promised to us, and to the whole democratic party of our country, that we should found a new Geneva in Ireland, and settle there with all our manufactures, home-traffic, and industry, enjoying a safe refuge for our political and religious principles. The building of this new city, however, which we were led to expect would be a Zion of popular freedom, is still delayed. We would gladly work in laying the foundation if only a tract of land were allotted us for our colony. But this new Geneva as yet floats in the air—it is one of the phantoms of an English fog; thus we are discontented, doubting the sincerity of Great Britain."

"That is wrong," exclaimed Mirabeau, "for when England allots money for a purpose, she is in earnest; and have you not already a fund for your support, amounting to fifty thousand pounds sterling, intended expressly for the benefit of the first thousand immigrants from Geneva? You yourself, Clavière, in conjunction with Lord Grenville, are at the head of the distribution of this money; and, I may say, your financial talent and your political character are honored by your position. I should think that nothing could give you more confidence as to the intentions of this government." *

"This fund is certainly in existence," replied Clavière, "and I am still one of the committee of management; but it will be used only for its original purpose when something more definite has been decided for the erection of our new home in Ireland. In the mean time, the money is used for different objects, mostly through the influence of the British minister of state, William Pitt. The English members of our management, who are in the majority, immediately executed the proposals of the prime minister, and we Genevans voted with them with the greatest pleasure. The first lord of the treasury desires the interest of this fund to be used, for the present, in settling premiums on distinguished men who would work, write, or fight, to propagate the idea that England is the true protector of political freedom, and also to deepen the hatred against France, as a state where despotism is generated and nursed. He sent a list of names to the committee through Lord Grenville, commencing with that of Count Mirabeau, who was mentioned with especial marks of esteem."

"Is it possible?" exclaimed Mirabeau, in joyful surprise. "In this I recognize the wily William Pitt. I have met him accidentally, and in a most adventurous manner, and had a conversation with him, during which he rather scornfully repulsed me in my suggestions that from this country great influence could be exerted on the events of the times. In the face of all I said, he did not change his opinion, and while apparently checking me in order not to compromise himself, he excites the Geneva fund society, and absolutely accepts my proposals, and disposes of my talents. But what have you decided to do?"

"I have been sent by my colleagues," replied Clavière, emphatically, "and the real object of my visit to-day is to deliver to you in this pocketbook a bank-note of one hundred pounds sterling, with the respectful request to receive it as an acknowledgment of gratitude from the Geneva committee for your writings in favor of political liberty, and a petition that you would continue to exert your influence not only for our cause, but for that of all Europe."

"I take all you say and offer in the sense in which you tender it," said the count, receiving the pocket-book with visible satisfaction, but throwing it on the table as if with supreme indifference.

"You were always the defender of our republic," continued Clavière, "and as formerly you

---

* Vide Soulavie, "Mémoires historiques et politiques," vol. v., p. 264, where the "Acte du Gouvernement d'Angleterre, qui accorde cinquante mille livres sterling de secours aux six commissaires des bannis de Genève et au parti revolutionnaire de cette république" (of April 4th, 1783), is completely detailed.

wielded your pen for us—when our aristocracy escaped destruction only by the assistance of French bayonets, and when you addressed a memorial to the French minister Vergennes, showing in your impressive manner that the recall of these troops was an affair of honor for France [*] —so now labor for our Geneva—that is, kindle the indignation of the rest of Europe against your country."

"Yes, I love your Geneva!" exclaimed Mirabeau, enthusiastically, "and I shall be proud to serve your cause, which is also mine, and that of all patriots! I love your countrymen, so brave and enlightened, and who, by an unequalled assiduity, have ennobled the little republic. Your watches, for example, ticking in men's pockets over the civilized world, tell of the conquests of your skill and industry—they not only announce the right hour of the day, but it is natural to fancy that they mark the right year of liberty for our age. The energy of your people will make the first practical assertion in Europe that the true government for man is one of freedom! Our great Voltaire, by the way, had an enthusiastic admiration for your watch manufacture, pronouncing upon it, in his Ferney, the blessing of a free spirit. Are you not one of the first states of comparatively modern date that, even in the eleventh century, set the example of driving from your midst the aristocracy, with its princes and oppressors, and aimed at the establishment of the rights of man by a popular government? Since that time you have passed your lives in political commotion—one revolution after another you have attempted, brave men that you are. This whole century has been one continued struggle between the nobility and the people—between democracy and feudalism. The example on the shores of your beautiful lake has not been in vain —it has awakened other nations. The political books and pamphlets that sprang from your conflicts vied with the works of our Montesquieu, Mably, and Voltaire, to educate the national spirit, both in France and the rest of Europe; to give a new impetus to the people; to undermine the old monarchical institutions, and place democracy in the front of all governments. It was from Geneva that the first note of popular liberty was sounded, and it will not be long before all that can move in France will answer it—nay, the whole world will arouse itself to the great duty of deliverance from despotic rulers. Believe me, your country will assist mine in the coming contest. The same country that in your last effort forged your chains, defeating the people's party with bayonets, and driving its chiefs into exile, will ascribe her elevation to you. Let that be your revenge against the French monarchy!"

"France is the principal adversary of European liberty!" said Clavière, a sharp irony distorting his features. "With her we must make a beginning, if our principles are to succeed. France, as she is, must be overthrown, and upon the ruins of her *ancien régime* must arise a nobler system than that of the aristocrats. This great resolution, for it affects the future of Europe, the popular party in Geneva took in 1782, when your Louis XVI. sent his troops against our republic (engaged as it was in civil war), to free the aristocracy we had imprisoned, and reward them for their secret attachment to him. Then the scales dropped from our eyes; we were convinced that the French court had given orders to the government to suppress our democracy. The two parties in our country disagreed about the remodelling of our laws, and we soon saw that the influence inimical to the people, forcing itself into our constitution, originated with the King of France and his minister M. de Vergennes. When we left the gates of Geneva behind us, on that first dark night of our exile, we took a terrible oath that we would carry the revolution into the heart of your country. By this oath we have become your fellow-citizens, Count Mirabeau, for we share the same patriotic labor." [*]

"We are fellow-citizens and brothers in the empire of freedom, Etienne Clavière!" exclaimed Mirabeau, with flashing eyes, embracing the Ge-

---

* Montigny, "Mémoires de Mirabeau," vol. iv., pp. 114–139.

* Soulavie, "Mémoires historiques et politiques," vol. v., p. 251.

nevan. "As to M. de Vergennes, he was the only French statesman that had a clear conception of the whole situation, and expressed even at that time the fear that the struggles in Geneva would be but the beginning of a subversion of existing governments in Europe! He therefore insisted on suppressing the liberal party in your country by armed force, and to him I consequently addressed my memorial in your cause. I explained to him that the task of France ought to be that of succoring you, and of reconciling the parties in the republic; for France, who had just shown herself the liberator of America, could not at the same time appear as the oppressor of Geneva! Such inconsistency would lower my country in the eyes of Europe. I was the first to point out of what importance the reception of the exiled patriots in a colony in Ireland might become. I painted in gorgeous colors the future of such a settlement, that would give still greater power to the commerce of England by certain manufactures, so easily fostered in a land almost free from taxation. I showed that several German monarchs, among them the King of Prussia, Frederick II., had made efforts to direct to their countries the migration of the Geneva democrats, on account of their genius for the arts. I also pointed out that such settlements in any land would be refuges for all the discontented from the different countries of Europe. But M. de Vergennes remained firm in his opinions, which, I must own, were correct from his point of view, as ours were from our own. When I personally communicated with him, he merely said that the Geneva revolution was an epidemic disease which might invade France, and that was the idea on which he based his advice to the king." *

"It will always remain a grievance that France could not see of what consequence Geneva was to her interests," replied Clavière, "if only as a mart for the commerce of the south with Switzerland, Italy, and a large and important part of Germany. France has drawn profits of all kinds from us—from our industry, as well as from our

pecuniary resources. Did she not borrow one hundred millions from our republic during the administration of Necker, by means of which she was able to repair a considerable hole in her treasury? I will not mention that Geneva is the only military point by which France can be covered from the Rhone to the Mediterranean, preventing an invader from crossing the river. Would one not suppose that common-sense would lead your country to desire Geneva to be powerful, populous, and flourishing? But the policy of the government had no such sense; it cannot comprehend now that my native land, becoming powerful, not only by agriculture, but by manufactures, requires for its development free institutions. And what folly to turn us over to her natural rival, that she may enrich herself by our industry! Whether the intentions of Great Britain are selfish or not, we owe her thanks, and more especially are we indebted to William Pitt, who, since his association with the ministry, has redoubled the hospitality bestowed on us. It will be the duty of Geneva, whatever may happen, to keep on good terms with England."

"Be friendly with Albion, but do not trust her!" exclaimed Mirabeau, violently. "She receives fugitives only because at some future time she means to use them for her interests. You are now the whip with which she intends to punish France—well, that is all right! You must settle your own accounts when the latter country is free and in union with you. Then, as a return to Geneva for having given birth to our Jean Jacques Rousseau, we can secure such freedom to you that your republic will be the fairest star in European democracy. You are men of thought, and, if we wish to save ourselves from the actual degradation of the epoch, we must not despise new conceptions of what ought to be. Jean Jacques Rousseau, in his 'Contrat Social,' first opened to us the golden gate which leads to political happiness. This is also the merit of Necker: the second genius from the same republic, who came to France to inoculate the dying monarchy with salutary ideas. However he may have failed in his financial administration (I am not, remem-

---

* Soulavie, "Mémoires," vol. v., p. 250.

ber, one of his personal admirers), he has never-theless labored for a reformed France. He indi-cated his birthplace in the fact that he displayed his inventive powers, and believed that he ought to do so, as secretary of the treasury, and there-fore coined new money. Yes, Clavière, I also will belong to Geneva. Did not the words 'sover-eignty of the people,' and 'the rights of man,' originate there ? *—Here is a tribute, by the way, I bring to my adopted country. I have com-menced, you see, to write a history of Geneva." Mirabeau took a manuscript from his desk, and handed it to his friend, who glanced at it in sur-prise.

Just then an extraordinary noise was heard on the stairs, and the count, whose sense of hearing was very acute, thought he recognized Henriette's voice, as if uttering groans and painful ejacula-tions. He rushed to the door, which was opened as he approached by Hardy, the secretary, upon whom Henriette was leaning. Mirabeau caught her in his arms, carrying her to the sofa, with expressions of sorrow. She was half unconscious, but, on noticing his presence, she opened her eyes, and a slight color suffused her countenance, which before was pale as death. She smiled, and told him that he must not be uneasy on her account. She was, however, still too weak to relate what had happened to her.

All Mirabeau could learn from Hardy was, that having business to attend to in another part of the city, and passing through the street in which Christ's Hospital is situated, he saw a crowd gathered before it, and among them Madame de Nehra, who was just fainting and falling on the pavement. Assisted by some persons near he took her to a carriage, fortunately standing in the neighborhood. On the way home she became unconscious, and recovered as he was taking her up the staircase, complaining of headache.

Mirabeau immediately made an examination to see whether in falling she had hurt herself. Cla-

vière, proposing to go for a physician, departed. But Henriette declared that she had received no injury, and had entirely recruited her strength.

"And what happened to you, my only love ? " asked Mirabeau, kneeling before the sofa, and kissing Henriette's hands with passionate anxiety.

"I had executed my commission at Sir Gilbert Elliot's successfully," Henriette related. "He gave me the hundred guineas without hesitation, sending them to you with his compliments. It is true, he again permitted himself to express over-whelming words of friendship, which almost caused me to return the money to him, if I had not remembered the purpose for which it was destined. I put the purse he gave me into my bosom. The same good fortune that had guided my steps to Sir Gilbert's accompanied me on my return, until I arrived in the vicinity of Christ's Hospital, where I found myself in the centre of a crowd before I was aware of it, on account of the dense fog. The countenances of those I noticed were any thing but agreeable, and their exclama-tions revealed fearful news. They spoke of a woman who had fallen in the street with symp-toms of the plague. She was carried into the hospital, and the peopled assembled, loudly and violently demanding that measures should be taken for the safety of the community. Some said that the building ought to be surrounded by troops; others that the hall into which the pa-tient had been carried should be walled up. Quite unexpectedly the report became current that three similar cases had occurred in another district of London, and that it was an incontro-vertible fact that the plague was again in the city.* A universal lamentation arose from the people, who shouted and swore terribly. I have never witnessed any thing so shocking. Over-come by an indescribable emotion of fear, the crowd seemed to me like spectres in the thick mist. I lost my self-possession and fell. As Hardy raised me, I heard the exclamation : 'Another victim! She has the plague!' Seated

---

* Soulavie, "Mémoires historiques et politiques," vol. v., pp. 249-282. In the letters of the Geneva dem-ocrats, Duroveray and D'Yvernois (about 1783), is first cited the expression "les droits des hommes."

* From the unpublished correspondence of Mirabeau with Madame de Nehra.—Vide Montigny, "Mémoires de Mirabeau," vol. iv., p. 151.

in the carriage, I had sufficient presence of mind to hand the purse to the secretary; but I still fancied I heard the cry resounding after me: 'Do not let her escape, she has the plague!'"

Henriette was so exhausted by the recital of the dangers she had undergone, that her head fell back on the sofa. Mirabeau requested Hardy to bring restoratives, and at the same time deliver the purse which Madame de Nehra had intrusted to him. The secretary executed his commission, but, in reference to the money, he declared laconically that he knew nothing about it, as Madame de Nehra had given him none. Mirabeau was startled, not knowing exactly what to think of the whole affair. But Henriette sprang up hastily, anger restoring her strength, and exclaimed: "What! You deny that I confided a purse to your care? Mirabeau, I often defended that gentleman when you entertained suspicions of his honesty. Now I must accuse him, if he continues to deny having received a hundred guineas from me."

Hardy burst into scornful laughter, turning from Mirabeau to Madame de Nehra with provoking insolence expressed in every feature of his defiant face.

"Wretch!" cried Mirabeau, with his temper aroused, and seizing him by the throat, "you dare, in the presence of such testimony, to continue in your denial even for one instant, and behave so insolently? Kneel in the dust, you scoundrel, and make your wailing confession, just as a condemned spirit would make his in presence of an angel. Acknowledge what you have done with the money, if you are unable to return it! Such a sum is no trifle with us at present, and we cannot afford to play hide-and-seek with it."

"I reiterate," replied M. Hardy, in the most offensive manner, and without losing his self-control, "that the countess did not even give me one hundred sous, much less the sum you name. Besides, I do not see how so much money could belong to any of the family of Count Mirabeau. You demand a hundred guineas from me, and yet you owe me my salary for the current year.

Why, sir, even the coat you wear is mine. I lent it you from my wardrobe, because yours was torn and faded, and you had no means to have new clothes made. Have you ever paid me for it? You are my debtor, count, and you accuse me of theft!—you who do not really possess a decent coat to your back!"

Mirabeau was for a moment perplexed. His cheeks burned red with shame, and his lips quivered. He convulsively seized the coat, of which Hardy had so inconsiderately spoken, and seemed very much disposed to tear it to pieces. "I will deliver you over to the courts of justice," he said, in a loud voice. "Here in England they have no great consideration for rogues of your description, and you deserve the rope. If I find the money upon your person, I will content myself in dismissing you ignominiously from my service. If you have disposed of it, I will deliver you to the constable, for whom I will immediately send."

As Hardy still denied any knowledge of the stolen property, voluntarily turning his pockets inside out, Mirabeau rang the bell, and ordered the servant to bring a policeman. He soon arranged matters, as it was sufficient for Count Mirabeau simply to charge a person in his service with theft, to have the accused at once arrested.

After the secretary was led away, Mirabeau turned to Madame de Nehra with renewed and tender anxiety. The excitement which the last occurrence had caused did not improve her condition, and she appeared to be suffering. The physician whom Clavière had sent now entered. He soon announced that there was no danger, and that rest and a little nursing would soon restore her. Henriette was, however, obliged to retire. Her only grief was, that the means obtained for her voyage to Paris were lost almost as soon as obtained. But Mirabeau went to his desk with a triumphant air and brought her the pocket-book containing the bank-note he had received from Clavière. He handed it to her, and with surprise she listened to the story of its possession.

"Now I am content, Mirabeau," she said, looking joyfully at him. "Believe me, I am already quite well, and I shall be able to depart to-morrow, to prepare a home for you in Paris, and free you from your fetters!"

"To-day you must rest and sleep," said Mirabeau, kissing her. "You are, my dear child, as charming as courageous. Your beauty would raise you to the highest rank in society, if you did not prefer to remain at my side, blessing me with your love, and aiding me in the struggles of my life! There must necessarily be a Supreme Intelligence and a Supreme Good, say what we may, and that will reward you, and all like you, for benevolence and self-denial. In the depth of your soul's secrecy, do you not think so, Henriette? And now, good-night!"

CHAPTER X.

THE ARCADES OF THE PALAIS-ROYAL.

ON her arrival in Paris, Henriette scarcely gave herself time to have her trunks taken to an *hôtel garni* and hire a small room. Thinking only of Mirabeau and his affairs, she changed her travelling-dress in great haste, and, not permitting herself to take either rest or refreshment, she was again in the street on her way to the residence of Chamfort, to demand the assistance of this tried friend, according to Mirabeau's arrangement. With swift feet she reached the Hôtel Vaudreuil, in the Rue de Bourbon. , Feeling herself sustained by her resolution and courage, she needed no protection, beyond her own probity, to attempt any thing in the performance of what she considered her duty.

At the palace of the Marquis de Vaudreuil, Henriette experienced the first disappointment since the commencement of her mission, in which every thing hitherto had succeeded to her wishes. The porter standing at the door rudely repulsed her inquiry, telling her that the house now belonged to another family, to whom the marquis had sold it, and that M. Chamfort occupied a

small dwelling in the Arcades of the Palais-Royal. She repressed the momentary sigh forced from her by fatigue, and, making a cheerful effort, continued her walk, soon reaching the quarter where she had been told she would find the domicile of Chamfort. These galleries had lately been built by the Duke de Chartres, around the gardens of his palace. They arose from his avarice, and were rented not only for dwellings, stores, and literary cabinets, but for halls of questionable amusement, such as gambling-rooms, drinking-shops, and dens of all iniquity.

The houses opposite to the Palais-Royal formerly possessed greater value on account of the unobstructed view of the gardens, and the ready entrance by those living in the adjacent dwellings. The property had therefore considerably depreciated, and the proprietors questioned by law the right of the duke to build the Arcades. All France was interested in a process which so deepened the well-founded indignation against the prince, that public utterance was given to it; but the decisions of the courts were in his favor. And yet in these new buildings all the vice of Paris was nurtured and developed without fear of interference, that being the principal object in their construction—an idea suggested by the mercenary disposition of the prince.

Madame de Nehra walked up and down these crowded arcades, making numberless inquiries before she found him whom she sought. At last she received the desired information in a reading-room in which Chamfort was known. Her heart beat violently as she ascended the staircase leading to the entresol looking upon the Rue Richelieu, in which she was told he lived. Her anxiety arose from a certain reluctance she always felt on meeting one of Mirabeau's friends, and which time had not been able to remove. Free and unembarrassed as she generally felt herself in the innocence of her heart, at such moments she was deeply conscious of the only false step of her life; afterward, finding herself treated with sincere esteem, she regained her sense of security and ease. Then could she speak of her relation with Mirabeau in burning words, and give expression to her enthusiasm for the object of her love.

Timidly she knocked. Chamfort himself opened the door, and her eye fell on his mild, quiet countenance. His melancholy features brightened, and he expressed the most undoubted friendliness. He conducted her to an easy-chair opposite him, and seemed so surprised and uncertain that he looked at her silently for some time, although in such a manner as to awaken her confidence.

Henriette immediately perceived, with feminine penetration, that Chamfort seemed to be doubtful as to the continuation of her union with Mirabeau, and therefore questioned her in a very reserved manner. This almost inclined her to burst into laughter, but she was restrained by the thought of the grave purpose for which she was in Paris. Hastening to inform him of the real object of her mission, and explaining what was necessary in order to procure an honorable and safe return of Mirabeau to his native country, she fluently described her plan, the first step being the delivery of the memorial Mirabeau had written in reference to his life and situation; this she must give personally into the hands of the minister of the royal house, Baron de Breteuil. She then added, that she was commissioned to demand the assistance of Chamfort's tried friendship in obtaining an audience of the minister, in which the close connection existing between the former and the Marquis de Vaudreuil would be of material importance.

Chamfort, after a moment's silence, replied: "Of course I shall procure an interview for you with the baron, and, if it suits you, we shall go to-morrow morning to Versailles for that purpose. But my good De Vaudreuil will be of little service to us on account of many considerations. My noble friend is himself in disgrace. The representation at his palace of the 'Wedding of Figaro' made him enemies at court, and he has been blamed as being the cause of the public performance of this wretched comedy, having declared it purified from the poison which it still retained. He did not obtain the position as governor of the

Dauphin, which he eagerly sought, and he is almost in despair, although there is no necessity for him to trouble himself about such trifles. He sold his mansion in the Rue de Bourbon, because his magnificent halls daily reminded him of that fatal evening, and this also was the cause of the change of my residence. The marquis had purchased a more splendid dwelling, offering me, in the most obliging manner, a home in it; but I seized the opportunity to become independent again, explaining to him that this separation was necessary for the better prolongation of our friendship. Thus we parted, but are still the best of friends.* That is why you find me in the Arcades of the Palais-Royal, where I have located my philosophic hermitage, for I hope good purposes."

At these words Henriette, for the first time, glanced around the room, observing that Chamfort had accurately described it. The arrangements in this apartment and an adjoining cabinet were very simple; nothing was contained in them but what was absolutely necessary. Before a small decayed lounge stood a diminutive table, serving both as desk and bookcase. Notwithstanding the twilight in the room, occasioned by the curtains being drawn over the low windows, Henriette thought she perceived a completely exhausted inkstand, causing her to smile, as she thought of Mirabeau's frequent lamentations at the fewness of Chamfort's letters, and that one of the most distinguished minds found so little pleasure in work. On the other hand, small scattered leaves lay about on the table, covered with writing in lead-pencil, on which Chamfort wrote his celebrated ideas and reflections, often expressing great truths with wonderful brevity and poignancy. While this dwelling was quite retired, and really appeared like a hermitage, the peace of its studious inhabitant must have been disturbed by the tumult of the world about him, the hum of voices, the rattling of dominoes and billiard-balls, the ringing of the money in the gambling-houses, and the cries of those who pro-

* "Notice sur la Vie de Chamfort" (Œuvres de Chamfort, vol. i., ch. xliii.).

6

claimed the curiosities and amusements to be found in the neighboring halls.

"Yes," said Chamfort, "is it not strange, that accident has led me into the very dragon's den of Paris? Yet I feel comfortable here, and the louder this clamor is, the better can I indulge my thoughts as to the future of France. Often, as I stand at my window, I hear many a word that affects me, proving how strong the public political feeling is in this city. I overhear long and excited conversations in the café underneath my apartments, and I fancy that many people come here regularly at an appointed time to exchange opinions about the court and ministers. I hear many a true word from my philosophic watchtower, and I know that the time is not far distant when my friends and I, who are almost suffocating from the weight of our reflections, may descend into the streets as practical men, and preach liberty from every lamp-post! And all this we should credit to this blessed Duke de Chartres, who by his speculation has concentrated all the fermenting iniquity of this city, and thereby given us an insight of our real condition. It is said to be the chief object of the prince to make these buildings notorious as the focus of all that is infamous in the capital, and to open an extensive market for it.* There is a secret and almost fabulous reign of orgies in his palace, in which he is both lord and servant; and, in addition, he desires to found a public rendezvous of vice of every description. Another report about this prince, who regards money as the highest good, is, that he levies a certain amount of special taxes on all occupying his buildings."

Chamfort was continuing to explain the character of the neighborhood, and to indulge in his accustomed satire, when he observed Madame de Nehra leaning her head back with every sign of complete exhaustion, her brow and cheeks so pale as to suggest a fainting-fit. He quickly approached to assist her, but she reopened her eyes, smiling languidly. After drawing back the curtains and opening the windows, he returned, regarding her long in order to discover the cause and remedy of her indisposition. "Poor child," he then said, in a voice of great sympathy, "I comprehend why you are so weak. You may consider what I am about to say ridiculous, but it is necessary—I fancy you have eaten little or nothing during the past twenty-four hours. Am I right in my conjecture?"

Henriette nodded, and a blush colored for a moment her pale cheeks.

"Yes, that is what ails you," continued Chamfort. "I know you are one of those noble characters who could starve while occupied for the benefit of others, and take no rest until their loving efforts succeed. But the physical organization does not always support this heroism. Food and drink are necessary. Wherefore do I live in the Arcades of the Palais-Royal but to offer my services to you? Let me arrange matters for your benefit. I have a machinery here such as can scarcely be imagined in a fairy-tale. Two pulls at this bell-wire, which reaches to the kitchen attached to the café below, and the story of Roland's table-cloth is satisfactorily fulfilled. An active waiter hurries up, prepares the table, and my little dinner is eaten quickly and contentedly. On this day the graces will be present, if Madame de Nehra accepts my invitation, and for such a festival more worthy preparations must be made. Allow me, therefore, to absent myself for a few minutes."

Henriette urgently entreated him not to take any trouble on her account, adding that she felt much better, and would return to her hotel to take dinner. But Chamfort would not listen to her objections, leaving the room and soon returning, accompanied by a waiter, who began his preparations in the middle of the apartment, while Chamfort took a rosebush blooming at his window, and placed it in the centre of the table, that it might not be entirely wanting in ornament. He cut off one of the freshest of the flowers, placing it near the cover intended for Madame de Nehra, and leading her to a chair with his usual politeness.

"You ought to have a branch of laurel placed

* Soulavie, "Mémoires historiques et politiques," vol. ii., p. 108.

there for you," he said, when seated opposite her. "You deserve it, for magnanimity is of greater value than genius. You have crossed the ocean alone, in your youth and beauty, to work for your friend in this vile and selfish city; and does not a brave love merit the crown of honor? But laurels never would flourish in my household, and I have not a single leaf to offer you. Those I gained as a poet are withered; they could not thrive together with political wormwood."

The dinner was served, and the philosopher played the host very creditably, encouraging his guest and waiting on her so gracefully that Madame de Nehra felt perfectly secure and comfortable. Her natural cheerfulness soon returned, and the true friendly feeling existing from the moment Mirabeau introduced them to each other, found expression in hearty and confiding words. The kindliness of Chamfort's manner, notwithstanding his satirical expressions, enchanted those who associated with him. In the present instance it was the more remarkable, as he felt it a duty to treat one in her lonely situation with more respect than he was in the habit of paying to most ladies. He was especially pleased to notice his success in encouraging Madame de Nehra to recruit her strength. A glass of wine was drunk in honor of the absent friend who was sad and solitary in London—a toast Chamfort proposed with great enthusiasm, and to which Henriette could not refuse to respond.

"But we must not forget what we owe to Mirabeau," said Henriette, looking gravely at Chamfort. "The affairs concerning which he has sent me here, of course permit of no delay; but as it would be of no use to go to Versailles to-day, I am satisfied to leave it until to-morrow. What means are we to employ? What success can we expect? You see I am urgent."

"I have not ceased for a moment reflecting about it," replied Chamfort. "But I think it is of more importance for Madame de Nehra to occupy herself quietly with these *côtelettes aux fines herbes*, and await the results of my mental review of all my friends and patrons at court. One of them will undoubtedly do us the favor of speaking a good word to the Minister Breteuil, and procure us an audience; but I confess that precisely the right person has not yet occurred to me. Although, by a curious concatenation of events, I have had relationship with these people, and a real friendship with some of them, it was my mishap somehow to have disagreements, and a subsequent estrangement. It is true, I have often enjoyed the charm of their society, yet I could never forget that they are the people who have caused all the political and social trouble in France, and will finally effect their own ruin. It is well, for by their unspeakable follies and extravagance despotism will be overthrown. I carried my frankness so far as to give them advice, which, of course, they did not follow; but since I lately prophesied their approaching destruction, which I was ingenuous enough to do, their confidence has ceased, and the utmost I could obtain from them was, that they would not hate me. This is also the history of my otherwise pleasant residence in the Hôtel Vaudreuil."

"Alas," exclaimed Henriette, sighing, "where then are the hopes we placed in you? Mirabeau reckoned on your influence at court, who, as he always said, were so blinded as never to observe that you only considered them as a study of all that is corrupt."

"Those aristocrats are too well educated to betray any feeling," replied Chamfort, laughing. "They are capable of dancing a minuet with their enemy, and without once missing a step. They play and trifle with their opponent as long as possible, to persuade him and themselves that he really does belong to their party, and may be worthy of bearing their train. In this way the fashionable world amused itself a long time with that dangerous book of Helvetius 'On the Mind;' it lay on the toilet-table of the high-born ladies, and no one wished to see the serpent lying beneath the flowers. Who, besides, were the colporteurs of Voltaire's blasphemous and at the same time democratic witticisms? Were not the great men of Europe—even kings and princes— the first to glorify him? The death of Diderot, last year, was bewailed most in the fashionable society of Paris, and his funeral celebrated with sincere mourning.* The last time I saw him was at the Hôtel Vaudreuil as a spectator of the 'Wedding of Figaro,' on that memorable evening when Madame de Nehra was carried off by Count Mirabeau, during the representation of the comedy. Oh, the mansion of a marquis is useful in many respects in these days! By means of the aristocrats we are fast drifting into the epoch of liberty. Without them it would be but a popular dream. The nobility aided in destroying the people to set up a throne, and now, as the real *advocati diaboli* of society, they urge the people to overturn that throne."

The dinner was over, and Chamfort lost himself in his own thoughts, as he often did. Suddenly he sprang up, exclaiming with a laugh: "Am I not a fool? I quite forgot that two days ago I was nominated as a kind of reader or secretary to the Princess Elizabeth! This interesting young lady has taken a great fancy to my attempts at poetry, and has promoted me to this honorable position in her household, although I hope I shall seldom be called on to do much. She has ordered me, however, to write a commentary on La Fontaine's fables, and I have commenced this work.† I will go and read my introduction to her, which I have attempted to write very carefully. She is in the city to-day, at the house which the king, her brother, lately bought for her in the Avenue de Paris, and in which she is to reside until her twenty-fifth year, that is, for five years: but who knows whether any house in Paris will then occupy the spot it does now? However, I will beg of her a favorable word for Mirabeau. The king is very fond of her, and she may perhaps have the proscription withdrawn that hangs over the head of our friend. The first chamberlain of the princess is also brother-in-law to the minister, Baron de Breteuil,

and I will ask him for a few lines, by means of which you will gain an immediate interview at Versailles to-morrow. That will do, and I hope for the best."

Henriette pressed his hand in the most earnest manner, and her eyes beamed with gratitude. They made arrangements for the next day, when Chamfort was to accompany her to Versailles. She left for her hotel, while he hastened to be announced at Madame Elizabeth's palace.

CHAPTER XI.

THE QUEEN'S DIAMONDS.

CHAMFORT came for Madame de Nehra at the appointed time on the following morning, entering with her the post-chaise running from Paris to Versailles. He was in good-humor, and expected that they would be successful, in consequence of the promise he had received from the Princess Elizabeth, as well as the recommendatory note for Madame de Nehra addressed to the minister of the royal house, M. de Breteuil. The four leagues were soon passed over, and the travellers, after leaving the carriage, stood together on the Place d'Armes, that extended before the castle of the kings of France. Henriette was seized with trembling fear, and begged Chamfort, whose arm she had taken, to delay a few moments, before they approached the principal gate.

"A person is apt to lose his breath, when he beholds before him this enormous structure!" said Chamfort. "It is the eighth wonder of the world; it is said to be the admiration of all who see it, and is considered the largest and most imposing palace in existence. Even the Asiatic despots could never boast of such magnificence, and our Louis XIV., who made this edifice what it is, has here, as in every thing else, shown himself the master-architect of a despotic era. His successors have in these apartments done honor as well as they could to his principles. The present proprietor is somewhat better than his race, and

---

* Diderot died on the 31st of July, 1784.

† Chamfort's commentary on La Fontaine, one of his most brilliant and delicate works, was in the library of the Princess Elizabeth, bound in manuscript, but was lost in the revolutionary storms that overtook her. It can hardly be doubted that it is still somewhere in existence.—Vide "Biographie universelle," by Chamfort.

history teaches that the
:ally visited upon the com-
ooking at Versailles from
:es the impression of an
e manner in which the
grandeur of the buildings
give just such a perspec-
' thing dear to nations has
y in this place. Now, my
:eed boldly, entering into
with a sense of our own
:rmit mere outward splen-
ity and tranquillity of our

:d his arm to his compan-
ide the gilt railing that
of the castle, entered the
:urt-yard, rising like a gla-
Here they beheld the
: which the ministers and
:sided. The Swiss senti-
:ted out to Chamfort the
f the royal house; but the
not at home, having been
of the king. They were
gallery of the castle, and
:ster, as was often done, on
al presence. Passing into
ed that some remarkable
:ed to explain the commo-
ng. The servants and offi-
n the corridors and ante-
'hispering, and from time
:aculations.
nto the large court-yard,
mpanion had noticed an
'ort at once recognized as
nence Prince-Cardinal de
:er and poet had a peculiar
: meaning of affairs about
able to inform his friend
:rrived half an hour ago in
ving been sent for by his

is occurring in the royal
said, comically looking up

as if he expected to make some discovery. "Any
one accustomed to the air of Versailles, must be
competent to ascertain in the courts of the palace
whether there is any thing unusual in the temperature—whether any strange ingredient has entered among the elements of the atmosphere. I
fancy, at least, that it is possible for me to attain
this faculty, although the honor of my acquaintance with the court has always been through
others, and therefore my olfactory organs are by
no means sufficiently cultivated to make such
nice discriminations. But to-day I am certain
that something is wrong—some failure, may be,
of royal favor; or perhaps some financial embarrassment preceding the bankruptcy of the state.
The Baron de Breteuil and the Prince-Cardinal de
Rohan, as all Paris knows, are sworn enemies,
and if these two have an audience together in the
cabinet of the king, the question must be about
an extremely involved business, and I expect
something amusing."

"May not this be unfavorable to us?" asked
Henriette, anxiously, as they proceeded through
the gorgeous range of anterooms, unobstructed
by the lackeys, whose attention was engaged. At
last they reached the Hall of War, on the walls
of which France and Bellona were painted, and
where hung trophies and military decorations of
all kinds, as well as representations of some of
the heroic actions during the reign of Louis XIV.;
through this they gained the large gallery, opening before them in its surprising beauty.

"It will depend on the state of affairs in the
palace of Versailles," replied Chamfort, standing
at the entrance of the gallery, and glancing along
it with his criticising eye. "From all I can hear,
the minister, M. de Breteuil, is more intent than
ever in ruining Cardinal de Rohan, or at least
preparing for him a discomfiture endangering his
life. Since yesterday Paris has been full of the
strangest reports, that I had forgotten, until I saw
the equipage of Prince de Rohan. If the latter
cannot prove his innocence in this bad business
ascribed to him, Breteuil will be beside himself
with joy, and while in that humor he will grant
all we ask. At court, to gain your object, you

must always regard the lucky color that happens to be fashionable for the day."

Henriette and her friend continued their walk through the gallery, containing seventeen enormous windows, and as many arcades with their stupendous mirrors. Their position was so ingeniously contrived that they had a magical effect in reflecting the park behind the palace, which could be seen in its whole extent from this apartment, thus affording a charming *coup-d'œil*.

"We shall have to wait here for some time," said Chamfort. "Let us rest by the two antique statues standing in this niche, one of which is a Germanicus, the other a Venus. We have a complete view of all that may occur in the gallery; for on that side are the state-rooms and cabinet of the king, and on this the apartments of the queen. We can miss nothing, and in the mean time we can admire the paintings of Le Brun, in which he has represented a part of the history of the great Louis XIV. But are we in a condition of mind to enjoy all this magnificence? As far as the eye reaches you see nothing but trophies and goddesses of war, among them a few satyrs, and every possible interstice crowded with crowns, suns, lilies, and insignias of various kinds. Even in the velvet tapestry the triumphs of the earlier campaigns of the great king are inwoven. It was wise to write history in this way, but the display is greater than the facts—a pompous egotism has obscured the simple truth. The '*l'état c'est moi*' was only a boast after all. And how do you feel affected at all this, my musing Madame de Nehra?"

"Nothing here inspires me with confidence, especially in reference to our cause," replied Henriette, glancing sadly at the splendor around her. I do not comprehend how we can arouse sympathy for such a man as Mirabeau in such a place."

"Sympathy?" replied Chamfort, laughing almost too loud. "Really, Henriette, you are the first noble mind that ever sighed for such a sentiment in the gallery of Versailles. In the region where we are now, all calculate on accident, and must know how to turn it to account. If that

were not the case, I would not have ventured to come here in the interest of our friend. He has again given umbrage of a very hateful kind, as the Princess Elizabeth gave me plainly to understand, when I saw her yesterday at her palace. The ministry suspect him of trying to operate in England against France, and accuse him of being in the secret pay of Great Britain, as well as in collusion with the revolutionary Geneva refugees now in London. Our diplomatic spies have ferreted out all this and sent in their reports. Yet he has friends at this court, and Madame Elizabeth is one of them. She expressed to me the very judicious thought that talents like those of Count Mirabeau ought to be gained over to the interest of France. That is the reason we came here, although we must acknowledge that we are at present merely waiting for an uncertain opportunity. If we fail in an interview with the minister, we return without accomplishing our purpose, notwithstanding the favor and wise suggestions of Madame Elizabeth. It is quite a revolutionary idea of this little princess to attach any man of genius to the interests of this country. France, as it is at present, requires no talents and never will, until completely overturned. A man of genius can now do no other service to his native land than to aid her in occupying a new position, and I consider it one of the most wonderful signs of the times that such a thought should occur to a princess of France."

Madame de Nehra looked at him uneasily, for the sound of his imprudent words was passing along the polished marble walls to the doors of the king's apartments. He also became aware that Henriette's gestures for him to cease talking were timely, for several officers of the bodyguard stood at the extreme end of the gallery, apparently for a certain purpose, among whom he recognized the captain of the guard, Duke de Villeroi, whom Chamfort had often met at the house of the Marquis de Vaudreuil, and who always seemed to take special pleasure in conversing with the poet.

The duke scarcely saw Chamfort when he hastened toward him with all his accustomed politeness, greeting him and asking if he could be of service to him. "In truth," added the young duke, smiling, and gallantly bowing to Madame de Nehra, "you owe it to the enviable circumstance of being in the company of so beautiful a lady, that I did not immediately command you to leave this gallery. I have been sent here by the Baron de Breteuil with strict orders to clear this part of the palace of visitors. You arrive at Versailles when very strange things are happening, M. de Chamfort."

"I am not curious," replied Chamfort, quietly. "It is dangerous for us of the lower classes to know the secrets of the great. We only desire to have an audience with M. de Breteuil, in an affair concerning this lady, Madame de Nehra; and if the Duke de Villeroi, with his usual amiability, will assist us in our object, he would render us greatly obliged to him."

"When you can see the minister it is impossible to say at this moment," answered the young captain of the guard, mysteriously. "But I beg you and Madame de Nehra to step into this hall, parallel with the king's large apartments. As soon as practicable, I will inform M. de Breteuil of your presence. You cannot remain in the gallery, for my comrades have received the same orders as myself, and we must obey. It is only owing to the consternation of the attendants of the palace that you were permitted to enter the place, which is to-day forbidden to the public."

Chamfort gave his arm to Madame de Nehra, to conduct her to the apartment pointed out to them. He remained standing at the door to converse with the Duke de Villeroi.

"Tell me, duke," said Chamfort, "in what quality is the cardinal at present in the cabinet of the king?"

"Without doubt as grand-almoner of his majesty," observed the duke, evasively. "He arrived about an hour ago, to attend to his official functions—at least that is the general opinion. A half hour after, M. de Breteuil sent a special order to my comrade Count d'Agout, several other officers, and myself, to repair to this gallery and await further commands. The cardinal seems

to have been arrested in the king's cabinet, and the queen has left her apartments also for those of his majesty."

"Ah," replied Chamfort, "the queen's presence is doubtless very necessary in the affair, for the question is certainly about diamonds. Marie Antoinette is very fond of them, but latterly has had much trouble on their account."

"What, you know something about the matter?" exclaimed the captain of the guard, in the greatest astonishment; and added, in an undertone: "All sorts of reports are whispered about in Versailles, in reference to some diamond ornaments with which the queen is associated, and about which the Cardinal de Rohan is said to have acted very equivocally. The king was never known to be so excited and angry before as he is to-day."

"This secret, then, only now comes to light at Versailles," said Chamfort, with a gloomy smile. "I have no doubt that you know all the rumors in Paris. They do not spare the queen, and therefore I refrain from remarking about them in this place."

"It seems you Parisians are better informed than we who dwell at the fountain-head of events," said the captain of the guard, fixing his eyes keenly on Chamfort.

"You are precisely in the condition of many persons in the immediate vicinity of a waterfall. They really hear little of it, and it is only on removing some distance that they perceive any noise at all. At Paris we have the sharpest and surest ear for all that occurs at Versailles. It is well known that the queen has been in great alarm for some time about a diamond necklace, which the crown-jeweller Böhmer made, valued at one million six hundred thousand francs. The diamond-loving queen, however, is said to have refused this expensive jewelry several years ago, conjuring the king not to urge him to accept it at a time when there was so much suffering in the country. Notwithstanding, it is said (understand me, I am speaking only of the corrupt and profligate Parisians) that the diamond necklace by some means did come into the possession of

Marie Antoinette—that an unknown friend of the queen, having in view her favor, became surety for the purchase-money, and even paid some of the instalments. But this mysterious friend had more imagination than funds, or he did not trust in the curious bargain he had made. He did not pay regularly, and Böhmer began to make trouble, complaining of various persons of the court. So much they know at Paris, and it is natural that malicious additions should be made, especially sullying the reputation of the lovely queen. The real intrigante in this fraud is said to be an adventurous Countess Lamotte, and Marie Antoinette is accused of secret collusion with this woman, by whose means the Cardinal de Rohan—for is the generous admirer of the queen—was enticed into this dangerous adventure."

"Let us speak of these things another time," said the Duke de Villeroi, looking anxiously toward the door leading into the king's cabinet. "You are aware of my sentiments," he added, with a stealthy glance, shaking Chamfort's hand, and then returning to his post.

"These young nobles fancy themselves in opposition to the government," said Chamfort to his companion. "But in reality they are seized with fear and trembling as soon as they hear a downright word touching their courtly relations. It amused me to embarrass the duke on that point."

An extraordinary noise was heard in the gallery. The door leading to the king's apartments was violently thrown open, and the voices of those emerging from them became audible. Chamfort, with Madame de Nehra, retiring near the door of the side-hall, could see what was to take place. He recognized the Baron de Breteuil, who appeared first and in great excitement, beckoning to the two captains of the guard, the Duke de Villeroi, and the Count d'Agout. Behind the minister came the Cardinal de Rohan, dressed in the robes of his ecclesiastical and princely dignities; but in his countenance could be noticed traces of intense anxiety.

"Follow me, as his majesty has decided!" said Breteuil, in a harsh voice, to the cardinal, who, at sight of the guard, stood perplexed and helpless, glancing at the minister in an uncertain and questioning manner. The tall, elegant figure of the cardinal swayed and trembled. The unaccustomed position in which he found himself, seemed to have so affected him, that he was not capable of reflecting or resolving, but resigned himself to whatever disposition might be made of him.

M. de Breteuil delivered the cardinal into the hands of the Duke de Villeroi, to whom the former whispered a few words. The duke offered his arm respectfully to M. de Rohan, leading him away a few steps, and giving him in charge of the Count d'Agout and a sub-lieutenant of dragoons, who received him in military style.

"To the Bastille!" cried the minister, in a shrill, exulting voice, looking after them with an indescribable expression of triumph.

"To the Bastille!" repeated the Duke de Villeroi, and the walls of the gallery echoed the dreadful words. When the cardinal heard them, he raised both arms to heaven with a beseeching and terrified gesture, and nearly fell in weakness and agony; but the guard supported him, and he quickly disappeared.

"In fact, the princely churchman is borne away by a military escort!" said Chamfort, in his astonishment. "The handsome Prince Louis is dragged to the Bastille! What! Dare the police of despotism stretch its arm toward the scarlet mantle and red hat of the cardinal? Signs and wonders seem to take place in broad daylight. His eminence, Prince de Rohan-Guemené, is also an illustrious scion of the former sovereign lords of Bretagne; if such men are sent to that fearful prison, an altar will be erected there for other victims, and the lesson taught of the abolishment of differences of rank. The king will have the honor of having founded the worship of equality in France."

Chamfort and Madame de Nehra again entered the gallery, for all was silent and empty. Not long after, however, the young Duke de Villeroi reappeared, who, in the mean time, had followed Baron de Breteuil into one of the antechambers of the royal apartments. "Hasten," he said to Madame de Nehra, "the minister has consented to receive you in yonder room; he is waiting to hear your story, as I have announced you to him. You have arrived at a most favorable moment. He is in the happiest humor, and I am convinced that he will grant every petition addressed him." The young duke conducted Henriette to the door of the baron's apartment. Chamfort did not accompany her, remaining in the gallery to await her return. The captain of the guards stood opposite, nodding gravely and significantly.

"Did the cardinal make any confession?" asked Chamfort, in a lively manner. "Is he the deceived or the deceiver in this curious affair?"

"No light will probably ever be thrown on it," replied the Duke de Villeroi. "According to what I have heard, the cardinal's confusion was remarkable. Both the king and queen questioned him closely and angrily. The cardinal acknowledged frankly that he bought a diamond necklace from Böhmer, being induced to do so by a letter from the queen, addressed to the Countess Lamotte. He produced it, but their majesties pronounced the handwriting a forgery; the cardinal's attention was particularly directed to the signature, as a most bungling fraud. The king reproached him violently that a prince of the house of Rohan, and a great almoner of France, could have taken the words 'Marie Antoinette of France' to be authentic, since it is so well known that the queens of this country always sign their maiden name, and that 'Marie Antoinette de Lorraine' is the queen's proper signature. The cardinal repeated, tremblingly, that the wish to please the queen, and the idea that, by undertaking this commission, he would pay homage to her, blinded his eyes. This declaration increased the queen's indignation, whose personal dislike to him is well known. At this point the scene became very painful; as his eminence could scarcely stand, much less make any further defence, he was allowed to enter an adjoining room, to justify himself in writing. Fifteen minutes after he reappeared before their majesties with his written declaration; but this did not in the least solve the difficulty, and the king quietly commanded him to leave. It seems that the result of this examination was foreseen, as M. de Rohan on his exit was received by Baron de Breteuil."

Chamfort listened attentively to this account, and, shaking his head, said: "It will always be considered incomprehensible that this affair is made so public. If there is a case that requires concealment, this appears to me to be one. The court are generally well versed in this art; but now, what occurs behind the scenes is brought to the light. The good cardinal, notwithstanding his fifty years, and the ravages they have made with his former reputation of beauty, intended to play the lover to the fair queen. Whether his error was that of the greater part of the people, who consider Marie Antoinette as a woman of light character, or whether he was a victim of deception, trifled with by dishonest agents, with or without the queen's consent, will never be known. But forward, mischief! If this transaction receives notoriety from the courts of justice, then harm will come of it, do what you will. It would not be wise to call upon a tribunal to pass judgment in a case reaching to the recesses of a queen's heart—it would be a curious trial, where justice would have to do with a lady's passion for jewelry, and the silly gallantry of an enamoured dignitary of the Church! How imprudent of their majesties to open such a budget, probably sent to them by the Evil One himself! Nothing but discreditable stories can be contained in it, and the monarchy only increases its disfavor with the people. But I see Madame de Nehra approach, with a countenance announcing good tidings."

Henriette entered, her features beaming with joy. She hastened to Chamfort, and informed him that her interview with the minister had been successful beyond expectation. M. de Breteuil had received her with the utmost urbanity, accepting the memorial of Mirabeau, which she delivered to him, with the promise to read it at once, and consider it in its most favorable construction. He expressed himself in the most friendly manner in reference to Count Mirabeau, adding, with special kindness, that, according to the minister's view of the case, the former cabinet order of the king, placing the count in unconditional subjection to his father, could no longer be valid. Henriette was dismissed with the assurance that, on the following day, he would lay her case before his majesty, and immediately forward the decision to Madame de Nehra's address.

"We came to Versailles at a very opportune moment," said Chamfort. "Strange events have occurred in these court regions to-day—a cardinal to the Bastile, and a Mirabeau back to France! That Breteuil will now have unbounded influence with the king cannot be doubted; he will have control of every thing. My blessing on the affair of the necklace, and our best thanks to you, duke!" The captain of the guard kindly accompanied them on their return to the great gate of the palace.

CHAPTER XII.

COUNT CAGLIOSTRO AND HIS WIFE.

In the Rue St. Claude, in the Quartier des Marais, was a small house, that for some time had a peculiar attraction for the fashionable society in Paris. All day long splendid equipages stood before it, in which the neighbors recognized with astonishment the most famous ladies and gentlemen of the court, the most renowned dignitaries of the aristocracy, and even ecclesiastics of the highest rank. These visitors, whose stay became every day longer, came to see a stranger who had rented this house several months before, and inhabited it with other persons as mysterious as himself. Crowds of poor people also appeared at certain times, receiving presents at the hands of richly-liveried servants, and pronouncing blessings and prayers for their unknown benefactor, who had first arrived in the neighborhood in a carriage with post-horses, accompanied by his wife, a young and very beautiful lady, and fol-

lowed by a suite of servants, consisting of couriers, valets de chambre, and lackeys. He took up his abode in this quarter, after ostentatious and costly preparations had been made.

Count Cagliostro, a name to which he soon added all kinds of titles and dignities, was a man apparently not over forty; although at times he could assume in a wonderful manner an expression of countenance and demeanor reminding a spectator of the fabulous personages of a primeval age. His personal appearance was not advantageous, this disagreeable impression being produced as much by his bowed and heavy movement, as by his odd costume, composed of a blue coat of taffeta trimmed with braid, stockings interwoven with gold, and velvet shoes with buckles set with precious stones. His head was always covered with a hat adorned with white plumes, in whimsical harmony with the powdered and twisted plaits falling upon his neck and shoulders. Costly diamonds sparkled on all his fingers, as well as on his shirt-frill and gold watch-chain. When the air was cool, he threw over his person a bluish fox-fur, with a hood of curious form. The arrangements in his house were no less unusual and mysterious. The apartments in which he received his company were garnished with fabulous extravagance, and there were also small private cabinets, filled with strange figures, instruments, and apparatus of all descriptions.

Cagliostro was alone in his studio, attentively reading a ponderous folio, and casting occasional glances at the crucibles standing on fire-pans, and which broke the silence with their crackle and bubbling. He did not observe that a lady stood behind him, who smilingly looked over his shoulder, and at last ventured gently to touch him. He turned quickly with a cold, transient smile, greeting the Countess Cagliostro, who begged him to listen to her a moment.

"What do you wish, Lorenza?" he asked, manifesting his displeasure at the appearance of his wife, whose substantial and beautiful figure was revealed by her light negligee.

"I must really recall you to the present, though

at the risk of troubling your presence in Egypt, or among the guests of the marriage-feast at Cana," replied the countess, with mock gravity. "But something has happened. It is reported in the city that the Cardinal de Rohan was yesterday afternoon taken to the Bastile, and therefore will hardly appear as guest at our dinner-party in spite of his promise. Must we postpone the affair, and send messages to the rest of those invited?"

Cagliostro sprang from his seat, impulsively raising his plumed hat, but, as was his custom, replacing it immediately. "Do you think I was not aware of that?" he exclaimed, looking at her with his bright eyes, in which lay his great power of attraction. "Returning at midnight from Fontainebleau, and entering the streets of Paris, I had a vision showing me the cardinal in a dungeon in the Bastile, and I knew then that what I had long foreseen had happened. Had I desired to postpone our dinner, I would have informed you of that fact this morning, countess. But I see that you sometimes still doubt me."

"Certainly not," replied Lorenza, with pretended gravity, inclining herself apparently with great solemnity. "Since you have become Grand-Kophta, and your mighty mind has introduced us into the secrets of Egyptian free-masonry, I am more than ever amazed at your influence, and bow beneath it as a flower to the breath of heaven. But your mysteries do not seem to involve the concerns of the kitchen and cellar, Count Alessandro Cagliostro. Your spirits appear punctually, whencesoever you may call them, but roasts, pastries, fricassees, and all the trappings of a dinner, require considerable skill and labor, and hence my anxiety that, if our company are to assemble at seven o'clock this evening, nothing may be neglected, or in disorder."

"I see the Countess Cagliostro is still the same merry soul she was when Lorenza Feliciani," exclaimed Cagliostro, embracing her. His regular features expressed but for one moment a happy humor, for, suddenly reassuming his solemnity, he said: "I promised M. de Rohan that he should sit at my table in company with Richelieu. I

have in the mean time used all the energy at my command to put myself in communication with the spirit of the great cardinal, and I am certain that, when I summon him to-day, he will not only immediately appear, but, as I shall demand, unfold to us the future of France. It is immaterial to the spirit of Richelieu of what persons the company, may be composed. As the Cardinal de Rohan will lose the interview by his folly, I invited M. Chamfort this morning to take his place —he is one of the wittiest and selectest men in France, who has several times asked me to permit him to be present at a revelation of the modern Egyptian mysteries. This man is of importance to me. He is a member of the Academy, and I should like a report of my new science to be made to the renowned forty. I hope to be able to compel them to a recognition of the fact that, on this earth, there exists a mental faculty reaching beyond and spurning the laws of time and what we call Nature—a faculty which, to those who understand its secret action, may be exercised in a sublime and holy service for all mankind. I do not need any formal assent of the French Academy, but it might aid the truth in its reception by the mass of mankind. M. Chamfort promised to come, asking permission to introduce a lady from England, and, in the name of the Countess Cagliostro, I gladly consented to his wishes. Besides these we shall receive to-day a German baron, M. de Hohenfeld, lately minister of the Elector of Treves. He is a man of the world, paying court to all the ladies in Paris, very rich and extravagant—I recommend him to you, for once before you showed considerable tact in managing a German mind. He will be introduced by my friend the Marchioness de Barbeyrac, at whose last soirée a violent dispute arose concerning the spirit empire. The marchioness, as usual, wittily declared her unbelief, and the ex-minister, in his politeness, did his utmost to coincide with her opinions, and heroically attacked me. I have invited them both, that they may to-day, by their conversion, become illustrious examples."

"You are the master, Alessandro, and I obey you, as always," said Lorenza, roguishly glancing at him, and pressing his hand. "The dinner shall be ready at the appointed time. But I am beginning to feel that I cannot understand your lofty mind; nor can I comprehend your indifference at the arrest of the Cardinal de Rohan. In your place I would have ordered post-horses instead of giving a party; but, I suppose, as you recently reproached me, I am viewing things in the same commonplace and vulgar way as when in the house of my father, the coppersmith Feliciani."

"You are sometimes foolishly sensitive," said Cagliostro, as if repulsing her. "What in the world have I to do with the cardinal? I could not save him from the Bastile. He allowed himself to be driven by his passions, as a deer by the hunters, and finally fell into the snare. I am a man of ideas, and through men's passions I can direct their destiny. If the cardinal really fancied that the beautiful Queen Marie Antoinette would listen to him, he has only affirmed to what a height his presumption could reach; but such follies are beneficial, for they often aid in the concocting of great events—in dissolving the existing relations of men and things, and producing new and interesting combinations. On this account I made use of his confidence in me to guide him in his own chosen path. But of what consequence is that to us?"

"Well," replied Lorenza, with a cunning smile, "he came to you for advice, as to his negotiation for that magnificent diamond necklace, and to know whether the queen would listen to his suit if he purchased it for her. You did assume a fearful importance on that occasion, my friend. You sent for a dove, as in your language young maidens are called. After laying your hands on her head in your quality of Grand-Kophta, thereby giving her a power of communication with the spirits of the middle regions, you placed her before a crystal vase, filled with pure water, that she might read the future. The child saw in the vessel nothing but prosperity and joy for his eminence, and thus you consecrated the solemn fraud with your high-sounding and mystic terms, great Cagliostro."

"It is true," said the alchemist, momentarily forgetting himself and breaking out into a coarse laugh; but, recovering his seriousness, he added, "people that discredit what is really reasonable and true, are the most superstitious—they believe in a girl prophesying from a vase of water what is absolutely unknown. The cardinal ran boldly into the trap; he arranged every thing with our excellent friend Countess Lamotte, who worked upon him by an autograph letter from the queen; he bought the necklace, and our countess received it from his hands to deliver it to Marie Antoinette. Does any thing of all this attach any blame to me? I only acted the part of benefactor in aiding the imagination of a prince of the Christian Church. As I permitted the noble Louis de Rohan to have interviews with Semiramis and Cleopatra, and to sup with Marcus Aurelius and Henry IV., I also allowed him the pleasure to dream of love with a Queen of France. I committed no crime against her more than against the Egyptian queen, whom I caused to appear floating in a cloud of perfumes, and who, at my command, led the cardinal to a bower of roses."

"But M. de Rohan will accuse us of having betrayed him into these deceptions," said Lorenza, on whose countenance anxiety showed itself more plainly. "I fear we shall be regarded as accomplices. The cardinal is a half-insane and babbling visionary, who will expose all the intercourse he has had with us. You have taught him to search for the philosopher's stone, and he has paid enormous sums for the secrets of the Rosicrucians. But, in spite of the knowledge he obtained in the art of transmuting gold, he has become poorer, so that he could not even pay his instalments for the necklace, and thus the whole affair became public. Nor did your philosophy cure him of his folly; he has become more fantastic than ever, never dreaming of your impositions. You have certainly carried your charlatanry very far, and, if nothing else causes our ruin, it will be that mad rendezvous that you originated in the grove of the park at Versailles. Mlle. Oliva, whom you hired from among the notorious women of the Palais-Royal and disguised as a queen, may have been a very superior Marie Antoinette, who completed the work of turning the poor cardinal's head; but now that the case has gone before the courts of justice, that woman will betray you. I beg you, Alessandro, be prudent—let us leave Paris at once!"

"I do not comprehend why you are so cowardly," replied Cagliostro, in an irritable tone. "Must I remind you of the fearless spirit that formerly animated you, and considered no adventure too dangerous? And now, by a sudden flight that must bring suspicion upon us, you would lose the advantages we have gained in Paris. I will not leave; and, if accused, I shall know how to defend myself with all the means at my command. My influence, felt even by the princes of the royal family, aims at universal dominion over the minds and pockets of men, and we ought not to abandon this purpose in an impulse of foolish fear!"

"I am not timid," exclaimed Lorenza, her eyes flashing darkly, "but you know I always had a correct presentiment of danger. You remember I saved you and myself twice from imprisonment, once in London and again in Madrid, by urging you to leave in time, while you were insisting that no harm could happen you because you lived before the flood, and accompanied Noah into the ark."

Cagliostro burst into laughter, and for a few moments permitted the entreating caresses of Lorenza. As if to pacify her, he said: "All suspicion will fall on our noble Countess Lamotte-Valois; and, therefore, I was very urgent in advising her to flee. This morning, before break of day, she left Paris for Bar-sur-Aube, where I have procured her a safe place of concealment at the house of a grave-digger with whom I have business relations."

"That is why I searched the whole house for her in vain," replied Lorenza, thoughtfully. "But her disappearance will be of no advantage to us, Giuseppe Balsamo," she added, with renewed importunity. "As this was her place of abode, our house will be considered the source of her intrigues, and investigations will be made. The necklace will be sought for here; as the queen has not received it, it must be somewhere else."

"Not a trace of it will be found," said Cagliostro—"not a gem of it now sparkles in this house. You know we separated the costly trinket into parts, and Lamotte's husband has reached London before this time, and is turning the diamonds into money."

"You ought never to have had dealings with that wretched woman," said Lorenza. "By her art she deceived the cardinal, but she will also be your destruction as well as mine. I tell you, I never believed in her noble ancestry—it is an impudent invention. A person of this description cannot possibly be a descendant of the old royal family of France."

"Why not?" laughed Cagliostro, with a mocking grimace. "You women are not capable of doing justice to one another. Can an intrigante not be a daughter of an ancient royal house? My child, genealogies plainly prove that the Countess Lamotte-Valois dates her descent from Charles de Valois, Baron de Saint-Remy, a natural son of King Charles IX. of France. Her destiny made a vagabond and a beggar of her, and when I formed her acquaintance, she was living miserably on the alms thrown to her by the courtiers revering the name of Valois. I whispered to her of enterprise, and she repaid me as a useful and skilful instrument in my plans. Was it not an interesting comedy to see how the last of the house of Valois forced herself upon the daughter of the Cæsars, who wears a crown to which the poor outcast intrigante had many claims? The diamond necklace becomes a means of vengeance on this proud queen!"

Lorenza shook her head, and without a word approached the door of the cabinet.

"Make every preparation for our dinner-party this evening," Cogliostro called after her, impressively. "All must be choice, punctual, and brilliant. I rely on you, as I always do." He reseated himself at his table, and was soon absorbed again in his studies.

CHAPTER XIII.

THE SPIRIT-DINNER.

THE appointed hour for Count Cagliostro's dinner came, and those invited did not delay to appear. The count received his guests in his usual costume, which he never seemed to remove, and to which the fashionable society of Paris were accustomed. His wife, however, had made an enchanting toilet, which, with her sufficiently polished and effective manner, she knew how to wear.

The first that arrived were the Marchioness de Barbeyrac and her escort, ex-minister Baron de Hohenfeld. She was a lady of uncommon beauty, who, although about forty years of age, retained almost full possession of her early charms, and, where there was any deficiency, it seemed to be replaced by a certain kindliness and matured intellect. She was celebrated in the polite society of the time, and was sought for not only by those attached to the court, but by all who were distinguished in Paris. At present she held in her chains the German Baron de Hohenfeld, a man of stately figure, somewhat over fifty, indicating in his cheerful manners the character of a man of the world, as well as of a German cavalier who had gradually received impressions from French life.

Chamfort and Madame de Nehra arrived almost at the same time. The latter consented to pay this visit with Chamfort, as she knew that it would satisfy a curiosity of her absent friend. The life and actions of the magician had attracted Mirabeau's attention, and in his later letters to Chamfort he reiterated his desire, for several reasons, to have a full account of the renowned performer of miracles. Chamfort therefore resolved to form Count Cagliostro's acquaintance, and Henriette accompanied him in the happiest frame of mind, for she desired to show herself much interested, as Mirabeau's agent, and, besides, felt that she had obtained favorable prospects for him.

Cagliostro awaited his guests at the foot of the inner staircase of his house, behind him a crowd of attendants, dressed on this occasion in a rich mourning livery. The countess was in the drawing-room above, where she gracefully received the company conducted to her by her husband. All the guests had not yet arrived. General de Lafayette was expected, for he had accepted the invitation to dinner, feeling himself more powerfully than ever attracted by magnetism and magic, which had become fashionable in Paris on his return from his second voyage to America. At length, he also made his appearance, and the folding-doors leading to the dining-room were opened by the steward.

The saloon chosen for this evening's entertainment was decorated in a very peculiar manner. It was entirely hung with black velvet tapestry, interwoven with golden stars, whose brilliancy was not dimmed by the dark background. Every thing in the large apartment seemed intended to make an impression of solemnity and mourning, with which the magnificent mirrors and chandeliers formed a remarkable contrast. In the profound silence an effect was produced withdrawing the mind from the outward present, and plunging it into unusual thought and expectation.

The table in the centre of this mystic room was laden with the rarest luxuries. There were nine covers on it, although the company consisted of only seven persons; but Cagliostro explained this by remarking that not all who had been invited had come, unforeseen circumstances preventing them. He requested his guests to take their seats, but did not have the superfluous covers removed.

The suspense with which the company entered this magnificent apartment gave place to astonishment at the manner in which the dinner was served. No attendants were visible, their places being supplied by automata made of ebony—and a machinery, novel at that time, conveyed from below what was necessary for the repast, returning with what was no longer required.

The Marchioness de Barbeyrac, who came with the boldest and haughtiest doubts, was at first somewhat surprised, and fell into a deep meditation. Her attention, however, was aroused by the interesting conversation of Chamfort and the Marquis de Lafayette. She joined in it with her accustomed vivacity.

"I suppose people in America are so busy with material things, that they have no time to look for spirits?" asked Chamfort, in his usual sarcastic manner, turning to Lafayette. "The journals relate your triumphs everywhere during your second visit to the American republic. You helped to complete the temple of transatlantic liberty, general, and such a labor is really godlike. Having returned to France with the title and rights of a United States citizen, you must find time passing heavily here in Paris, where as yet there is nothing for us to do. And this *ennui*, by the way, originates spectres, miracles, and such things. Thus I explain your continued attachment to mesmerism; for, I hear, you are still an admirer of the German doctor, and ere wpresent at his magnetic cures, performed in the Place Vendôme." Chamfort, in his careless way, had spoken the decisive word in reference to the situation in which they found themselves. Lafayette, whose youthful countenance suddenly became very grave, hesitated to answer, while Cagliostro was sending his glances to each guest, endeavoring to discover, by the searching power of his eyes, the probable character and temper of those about him.

The Marchioness de Barbeyrac was the first to resume the conversation, her charming features expressing her ironical doubt. "If M. de Chamfort is right in his witty remark, I fear—what I hoped from the beginning—that we shall see no spirits at the table of Count Cagliostro; for I think we are amusing ourselves admirably, and if idle tedium evokes spectres we are safe from their intrusion to-day. What do you say, count?"

The magician smiled, disclosing his white teeth, which gave his mouth a peculiar charm. He replied in broken French, artfully magnifying his foreign accent: "The spirits care little for our amusements. Does the evening zephyr care for them? It kisses our temples, and passes by. Do even great natural principles, often unappreci-ated for centuries, care whether we comprehend them or not? That is our business—not theirs. Air, spirits, truth, are all one and the same thing, and it is our fault if we do not know how to employ them. They exist, in the fulness of their purpose and their adaptation, only when we comprehend them; and to him who is so silly as to suppose that there are no present problems in Nature, affecting his well-being, and which are capable of solution—to him all is conceit, doubt, and infidel superstition—an impenetrable wall separates such a mind not only from the invisible and eternal, but positively from the knowledge of material facts belonging to the sensible system of things of which for a time he constitutes a part."

"And I beg you most earnestly, count, not to penetrate that wall!" said the marchioness, forcing herself to a gracious smile. "I have certainly come here as a thorough unbeliever, and with ideas of conversion; but the nearer the moment approaches the more I feel a nervous discomfort. Perhaps the Marquis de Lafayette will first tell us something of America."

"For example, it is said that there are no donkeys in America," interrupted Chamfort, merrily. "I have long desired information on that subject. Is it true, general, that formerly such animals were not known in that country? It is owing to the wisdom of the great Washington, who is now as successful a planter as he was a hero, that donkeys have been introduced into his native land, and I should think that Europe, being overstocked, would gladly accommodate him."

"That matter was not quite so promptly accomplished," replied Lafayette, smiling. "It is true, my friend Washington felt the want of such animals at Mount Vernon, and I informed him what a superabundance there is in Europe.—But he would not be satisfied with a specimen of the common species, wishing to possess such as are found in Spain only. We endeavored to obtain some, by making application to his Catholic majesty, through Mr. Harrison, and the king gave orders for the purchase of two of the finest in all his kingdom, sending them as memorials of his esteem. The great American was pleased at the flattering attention of a crowned head, and he personally remarked to me that he felt under great obligations to the donor." *

"Heaven grant that this dangerous gift may not make him recreant to his republican principles!" exclaimed Chamfort, with a droll gesture; "for, by these Spanish donkeys, monarchical ideas might be introduced into America. I suppose, that the example of the great Washington is very influential in the United States, and if the defender of liberty is touched by such regal presents all the transatlantic democracy may feel as he does toward royalty. There seems to be some sequence then in the belief that the reëstablishment of a monarchy in the republic of the New World is not improbable, but yet my confidence in the principles entertained by the people has been confirmed by the accounts of your last triumphal procession there, General Lafayette. We have drawn the happy conclusion that the Americans paid you so much honor only on account of the independence you assisted them to achieve, and that the friendship of the transatlantic States for you signifies that liberty must at last dawn for all oppressed nations."

"The eyes of America are especially directed toward our country!" replied Lafayette. "The Congress confided to me a letter to King Louis XVI., whom the American Indians call the great Ononthio. In this epistle the thanks of the United States to France for her aid is expressed very seriously. Liberty has become, as it were, the breath of that continent. Repress it, and the nation dies. While smoking the last pipe with my friends there, wishing them, at parting, good health, fortunate hunts, inviolable unity, and the realization of all their hopes, the thought of the future of my native land overwhelmed me. The farewell tears filling my eyes were full of meaning; they were such as are shed at the parting from a friend to whom are confided our ideas, plans, and hopes. We must envy the Americans their good fortune. They will not only receive European donkeys, but open an asylum for the

oppressed among men. General Washington wrote to me lately to induce every one, who desired peace and happiness, to migrate to his country, and establish a new home, by mechanical or agricultural labor, in a rich and bountiful land."

"Long live Lafayette!" cried Chamfort, raising his glass to touch it with that of his neighbor. Count Cagliostro, however, made a gesture with his hand stretched into the air, at the same time inviting his guests to pause an instant in drinking the toast. Suddenly two of the automata rose through the floor, bearing a stand of decanters filled with precious wines. Cagliostro himself filled some of the glasses with the costly beverage.

"This is Syracusan," said Chamfort, tasting his wine with the air of a connoisseur. "We hope the count has received it in the usual way; for, although he doubtless possesses spiritual resources even for his wine-cellar, the timid ladies of the party would rather taste a growth that they are sure was pressed by the brown hands of an Italian peasant."

Count Cagliostro pointed to the wine-glasses, his manner having something good-natured and cheerful.

Chamfort raised his glass: "And now I drink, in this pearly Syracusan, the health of General de Lafayette! May his arm, dedicated to the liberation of nations, and his heart, beating for the emancipation of the negroes, continue strong and hopeful! He has devoted his services to all who are deprived of the happiness and dignity of man —to the unfortunate negroes beyond the ocean, as well as to the oppressed Protestants in France! Long live Lafayette! and with him all the disciples of national freedom and the rights of man, of whatever race or creed!"

The glasses were emptied. Even Cagliostro transcended his usual abstinence—for he seldom indulged in wine, and shared sparingly in the enjoyments of his table, scarcely touching any thing except a little Italian pastry. Lafayette contented himself with a grateful smile in acknowledging the toast with which he was honored. The marchioness, however, remarked to

* "Mémoires du Général Lafayette," vol. ii., p. 127.

Count Cagliostro: "It is with pleasure we join in drinking a toast which remembers even the American slave. General Lafayette has become, so to speak, one of the proficients of the black art by his interest in the negroes, in whose cause he has established an agency in Paris. You see, count, that sorcery is regarded here as one of the loftiest sciences, for a magician like M. de Lafayette wishes to summon before us the spirit of a fairer future. And now, count, tell us, what pretensions you yourself will verify—what decisive proofs of your mastery will you give us to-day? Is it all imagination, magic, illusion, or truth, that we are to expect from you?"

Cagliostro, at this question, looked quietly down, and seemed to lose himself in his reflections. Then the long plaits on his neck trembled as in magnetic motion, and the marchioness could scarcely disown that she saw bright sparks fly from his head. Presently he raised his countenance, looking at her with that extraordinary attraction which the most unbelieving acknowledged did characterize his glances. Madame de Barbeyrac felt herself singularly influenced, drops of perspiration fell from her brow, and, nearly fainting, she was obliged to sustain herself by seizing the hand of her neighbor, Baron de Hohenfeld.

"Gracious Heaven, you are pale, marchioness!" exclaimed the German baron, who had been an attentive observer of what was passing. He endeavored to wait upon the lady to whom his gallant services were devoted; but, quickly recovering, she refused assistance, declaring that she was quite well. "I feel already that I might possibly become a pupil of Count Cagliostro," said M. de Hohenfeld, with one of those polite bows so natural to the genuine cavalier. "And I think we are in a favorable state of mind to approach our real object. Were we not invited to enter the spheres of an invisible kingdom, under the guidance of our great master, on whose brow we may plainly see the signs of consecration and rank? I think I hear the opening of the golden gates, revealing to us the glories of the spirit-world!"

The marchioness looked in astonishment at her companion, who, after remaining silent so long, was thus suddenly moved to enthusiasm. She was on the point of indulging in some merriment, when she again felt the eyes of Cagliostro, and voluntarily turned to him, rising from her seat and following him. The sorcerer pointed to the chair, in which she again seated herself, sighing. He then said gravely, and with much dignity: "I beg every one to remain where he now is. I remember well what I promised you, Madame de Barbeyrac. This art, however, cannot be designated by any earthly color—the knowledge that avails here is neither black, white, blue, nor red. Pure science, illuminating the mind, must bear us on its strong wings far beyond the reach of the vulgar vision! I ask nothing of you but to name the persons you desire to see."

The marchioness started, but was silent. She appeared to have no courage to answer, and the company felt anxious and solemn.

"I will try to read your mind, marchioness," said Cagliostro, looking at her with a triumphant smile. "I think I can see fluttering there one of the names of such persons you wish to appear—that of the Cardinal de Richelieu."

"Yes," replied Madame de Barbeyrac, breathing freely, "let us see the eminent cardinal. And then I should like to see my well-beloved maternal grandmother."

Scarcely had the marchioness uttered these words, when Cagliostro approached a magnificent looking-glass on the wall opposite Madame de Barbeyrac, which, until that moment, had reflected the image only of this charming woman. The count bowed profoundly toward the mirror, and soon something on its surface seemed to move. At first, shadows gathered around it, as of the coming on of night, and solemnly affecting the mind; these were transformed into mists, and again into cloudy folds, like a rich drapery swaying to some evening air that whispers of youthful hope and love. The expectation of the company became a terror, and almost a breath could be heard, when an actual form of life resolved itself to the eyes of all.

A figure in the full canonicals of a cardinal, as if summoned by a kindred spirit, stepped forth from the mirror. It resembled exactly, in all its features and dress, that portrait of the great statesman and ecclesiastic still shown in the Hôtel de Richelieu. With increasing astonishment those present regarded the tall and dignified form approaching the table, and greeting the company with a gesture expressive of the repose of the happy dead.

The marchioness did not seem afraid of the apparition, but, on the contrary, resumed her self-possession and cheerfulness. She returned the salutation of the shadow with her accustomed grace and amiability; but the baron was seized with a feeling of the most distressing fear. He scarcely dared turn his countenance to the spectre as it passed, touching him with its garments. Chamfort and Madame de Nehra looked at each other in perplexity. The former essayed to laugh, but the grave look of Henriette reproved him for his levity, entreating him at the same time to observe the scene quietly and thoughtfully.

The marchioness regained complete control over her mind, and ventured to address the apparition in the usual conversational tone, excusing herself in the courteous language of a well-educated lady, who unhappily, and by some accident, had dared to disturb him. The phantom smiled, and appeared to listen to her with some interest. The marchioness, however, became almost talkative in her excitement. "The policy of the Duke de Richelieu I always greatly admired," she exclaimed, in all her drawing-room confidence. "It is a pity that the present ministers of France have entirely ceased from following the traditions of the great master of state policy."

The spectre prepared to reply by raising his arms solemnly, and said in a deep voice, having something mournful in its sound: "I cannot but bewail the incompetency of the present ministers of France; for heavily will this poor country pay for the sins of my successors. A sea of trouble will inundate altar and throne. Pharamond's dream will be realized; but a second and more fearful flood will come, whose bloody waves will deluge the land. And my happiness is troubled, in the place assigned me, only by the consciousness that the real result of my earthly activity is victory to the enemies of the Church. There is no salvation either for thrones or peoples but in the bosom of the Church of Christ. I first made France great, by bringing to her support the pillars of religion, and I considered it as an act of consummate policy to succor the Protestants of Germany, and thus humble the house of Austria. Woe is me! In this way I sowed the wind by which France will reap the whirlwind. But if you embrace the true faith you will be saved, body and soul, and outlive the most fearful trials."[*] At these words a brightness passed over the spectre's countenance, but suddenly it changed to an expression of dark irony. Stepping forward, the figure stood in the immediate neighborhood of the Marchioness de Barbeyrac, and, in a hollow voice, prophesied: "You yourself will die the death of a criminal. I tell you this as a punishment for disturbing my rest!"

The phantom disappeared. It seemed to have suddenly mingled with the surrounding air. No one noticed the manner of its withdrawal. Breathless silence reigned in the apartment. The marchioness again became pale, and trembled, while the baron immediately occupied himself in endeavoring to explain that the very ungallant expressions with which the great cardinal took leave of her, were the result of the hurry of his departure—that he had probably but a few moments longer to tarry with mortals, and, becoming confused, lost his correct judgment of the usual relations of persons and things.

---

[*] From a report made by Baron de Hohenfeld, and found among other family papers. It gives an account of this dinner at Cagliostro's house, and the summoning of the spirits. "I know not what became of the figure," says Hohenfeld in this paper, "so greatly was I moved by its speech. I have retained an indelible impression of the appearance of the phantom, and witnessed a similar majestic bearing during the reign of terror, especially among the ecclesiastics of the French Church."—Vide "Rhenish Antiquary," vol. ii., div. ii., ch. ii., p. 776.

"The words of the shadow remind me of our friend Mirabeau," whispered Chamfort to Madame de Nehra. "He fancies that this Cagliostro is employed by the Jesuits, and practises his deception for the purposes of that order. The speech of his spectral eminence, that we have just heard, seems to confirm this idea. We must not forget to report it to our friend in London." *

Henriette nodded approvingly, but remarked at the same time, in a lively manner, that he must redouble his attention in observing the development of the next scene.

The second apparition, like the first, became visible by its formation in the interior of the mirror. The solemn shadows were soon succeeded by a definite outline, and another figure began to move. It was an aged lady, in an old-fashioned night-dress of brown stuff, covered with lace, who approached the table with grace and dignity, turning in a kindly manner to her grand-daughter.

The marchioness approached with the greatest vivacity, stretching out her arms to embrace her grandmother, whose loved image she saw before her.

"Touch me not, my daughter," whispered the phantom, receding a few steps.

After the marchioness was seated, her grandmother took a chair near, and they began an interesting conversation, touching family affairs, but continued by Madame de Barbeyrac with joyful emotions. The lively marchioness seemed soon to forget by what extraordinary means she was permitted to speak to her aged relative; she lived again in the past, feeling herself at the hearth of her paternal castle, confidentially discussing the woe and weal of the whole family. The old lady was about to recur to the early days of her grand-daughter, showing a most surprising memory for all the little occurrences that characterized her at that period. She seemed to remember more than was pleasant to the marchioness, for, carried away by her volubility, she touched on certain youthful reminiscences, and, not quite with the delicacy of a spirit, brought into grotesque light the levity, wildness, and obstinacy of Madame de Barbeyrac, her disobedience to salutary precepts, and the consequences resulting. The marchioness could only save herself by laughing rather louder than was precisely proper when in company with a phantom. The loquacious old lady spoke of a page, named Pery, whom she called a dear little rogue, and who, at the time of which they were speaking, completely turned the head of her grand-daughter. Other and probably not very desirable revelations would have followed, when the marchioness, in her fright, and to put a stop to these disclosures, hastily moved her hand to seize her grandmother's arm, when the apparition exhaled like a vapor.*

The Countess Cagliostro prepared to leave the dining-room, rising from her seat, and inviting her guests to follow her to the drawing-room and take coffee. The company acceded to this request, and for a moment silently regarded one another with various sentiments. The reaction and depression that followed the unusual excitement, caused them almost immediately to take leave of their hosts.

At this moment heavy steps were heard in the antechamber, and several loud voices asked imperiously for Count Cagliostro. The folding-doors were thrown back, and two police-officers entered rather noisily, approaching the master of the house, and showing him a warrant of arrest for himself and wife. Their orders were to carry him and the countess immediately to the Bastile.

The magician received this news with unshaken tranquillity. "Do you know any thing of the cause of this arrest?" he asked, indifferently, returning the warrant to the officer after slightly glancing at it.

The officer shrugged his shoulders, replying, with an expression of contempt, that the Countess Lamotte-Valois had also been seized at Bar-sur-Aube and taken to the Bastile. "And I presume," he added, "that this lady has made confessions that lead to the incarceration of Count Cagliostro and his consort."

---

* The paper of Mirabeau, "Lettre sur Cagliostro et Lavater," gives this view.

* "Rhenish Antiquary," vol. ii., div. ii., ch. ii., p. 777.

The countess screamed aloud, and ran toward her husband, clinging to him and imploring his protection.

"Be of good courage, Lorenza; clouds come and go—all things aggregate and disperse by their own laws!" said Cagliostro, solemnly. Then approaching his guests he excused himself for thus involuntarily being obliged to abridge his duties as host. He hoped to grow in knowledge by means of this trial, and therefore he received joyfully all that happened to him. His countenance had an almost triumphant air, and with dignity he delivered himself into the hands of the officers, who were becoming impatient. They did not even give the countess time to change her gorgeous toilet, and she was forced to accompany them just as she was. A close carriage, standing at the door below, received the two prisoners and their escort, and they were quickly borne to their destination.

The company remained for a short time in the drawing-room, sadly conscious of their strange position, and involuntarily looking at each other with a peculiarly comic smile.

"It is well that the police did not disturb us in the midst of our spirit-company, but waited politely until we were at our coffee!" Chamfort remarked, interrupting the silence that followed the departure of their hosts. "And yet they troubled us at a very important moment, for to digest Cagliostro's phantoms is no trifle. What would have been the consequences if the avenging messengers from the Bastile had found among us his eminence, or the grandmother of the marchioness! It would have disconcerted the cardinal to come immediately in contact with the police on his revisiting France; and the dear old lady might not have talked so much and of so many family affairs, had she known herself to be under the surveillance of those officers; I fancy she would at least have been silent in reference to that charming Pery."

"I am convinced that we have been sadly deceived in this house," said the Marchioness de Barbeyrac, beginning to recover from her terror.

"I assure you, on my word of honor, that I never even heard the name of Pery, much less in connection with a page. And a man who allows his spirits to relate such untruths, is unworthy of confidence, either personal or scientific."

"I wish I had asked him to summon my father," exclaimed Chamfort, laughing. "I only knew my mother; and, although I must have had a progenitor, I never saw him. I wonder if Count Cagliostro did not also find my *ci-devant* father among the mystics in the Egyptian temples? If his manner or appearance had not suited me, I could have acted in the same way as others do in the case of the pretty page: I would have denied his existence."

The marchioness hastily took the arm of her companion, the continuance of this conversation not being very palatable to her, but on her departure expressed herself as courteously as if nothing annoyed her. General Lafayette, who seemed to have retained his favorable opinion of Cagliostro, followed, whispering to Chamfort, that the interference of the police proved nothing against a man of such extraordinary gifts; for was not the Bastile the home of the best and noblest in France?

"But the police are very eager in collecting proofs against our host," replied Chamfort, as they descended to the hall below, which was still guarded by policemen and soldiers. It could also be observed that a strict search was proceeding in the house. "Hunt everywhere," added Chamfort, "something must be found in the workshop of the sorcerer. A few spirits may perhaps be in some dressing-room, changing their costume; try to catch them. It is possible that in the cellar you may discover the great Althotas, the universal old man, from whom Cagliostro has learned the Oriental sciences, and who accompanies him everywhere to complete his education."

In the street the poor and the sick surrounded the house. They generally received gifts and remedies from Count Cagliostro about that time, and loud were their wailings and blessings when they beheld him carried away.

THE SWINDLERS.

CHAPTER XIV.

A MORNING AT SAINT-CLOUD.

QUEEN MARIE ANTOINETTE was at the castle of Saint-Cloud, which had been transferred from the hands of the Duke d'Orleans into the possession of the queen, having been expressly declared to be her personal property. All the officials and servants of the palace, as well as the Swiss guards on duty, wore her livery, and all the printed regulations, affixed to the gates and placarded in the environs, bore the simple signature: "By the Queen." This was something so unprecedented in the usages of the French, that it began to excite great attention, not only among the people, but among the higher grades of society. Complaints against Marie Antoinette increased, especially among the latter. They accused her of endeavoring to undermine the customs of the old monarchy, going so far as to say that it was impolitic as well as immoral that castles and lands should be in the exclusive ownership of a Queen of France.* The lower classes also drew from this fact new reason for complaint and hatred against her, and there were not wanting discreditable constructions of her conduct in various respects.

This prevalent excitement aided very decisively in strengthening the inimical feeling against the

* Campan, vol. i., p. 274.

court, while carrying on a process against Cardinal de Rohan. Since the latter was taken prisoner, together with such persons as were declared his accomplices, this suit was taking its regular course, and was about to be decided by the Parliament at Paris. The king and queen anticipated this moment with anxiety, nor were they ignorant of the danger that threatened the authority of the throne in this matter, for Louis XVI. soon saw what a mistake he had made, in committing, not only to courts of justice, but even to the Parliament in full session, the dark and inextricable affair of the diamond necklace. This idea of the king originated in a bold and magnanimous feeling, but one that, for his own interest, could not well have been worse, or more unhappy in its results. The Parliaments had been so long the customary enemies and rivals of the royal power, that they had no sympathy even with their restorer, for as such Louis XVI. might be considered. It was rather to be expected that the passions always animating this political body, would influence them, as usual, to sacrifice the authority of the king. As, on the one hand, it was well known that the queen desired the punishment of the cardinal, so, on the other, all were convinced that she could only gain her purpose by expressing the wish that the Parliament should find him innocent. All at court understood this thoroughly, and the uneasiness daily increased.

The king had never been known to act with such decision as in this disagreeable business.

He thought that he owed it to his love for and confidence in his consort, that this affair should be investigated, regardless of every thing; and, to a certain extent, be transacted before the eyes of the public. The foul suspicion, whispered everywhere in reference to the queen, had gone so far that she was accused of a secret agreement with the adventurous and criminal Lamotte, and of being the real author of the whole intrigue, by means of which the necklace came into Marie Antoinette's possession, at the cost of the unhappy cardinal, using for this purpose his foolish love. Many unprejudiced people entertained this opinion, and could not be induced to alter it. So much the more the queen thought it her duty to enter into this public contest for her personal honor and dignity, as well as for the moral purity and power of the throne. She was threatened on all sides. The clergy and nobility united in the most violent expressions of indignation at the imprisonment of an ecclesiastic prince, and many persons of elevated rank, as the Prince de Condé, who had married a daughter of the Rohan family, manifested their disapproval, becoming daily more violent and resentful in their complaints.

During this painful uncertainty, the queen found the quiet and solitude of Saint-Cloud more congenial, while the king often remained at Versailles, together with the ministers and their secretaries. The palace happened to need repair and remodelling, on account of new court arrangements, and the preservation of the beauty and security of this royal residence. Louis was busily engaged with the architect Micque concerning these improvements on the very day that the decision was to be made in reference to the queen. The greatest difficulty was found in arranging the expenses of the palace restoration, in view of the condition of the royal treasury; on that account the king's opinion was, to protract the work during ten years, completing it at the end of the century.

On the same day, the queen, according to her custom, was taking an early walk in the park of Saint-Cloud, endeavoring in its beautiful shade to forget her uneasiness, which had driven

sleep from her eyes. She sought a respite from her unhappiness in her gardens, and the society of her favorite friend, the Duchess Julie de Polignac and the latter's sister-in-law, Countess Diana. Marie Antoinette attached herself to these ladies of her court from a sincere feeling of friendship; and, next to the Princess de Lamballe, they enjoyed her confidence and love. Julie de Polignac had lately received the title of duchess, which the queen's friendship obtained for her, and also the position of governess to the royal children of France, so that she was permanently attached to the court. Thus Marie Antoinette was associated with her in a double interest: she had opportunities for a more confidential and less ceremonious intercourse with her chosen friend, and at the same time could exert a personal influence in the education of her children. And it was the amiable character of the duchess, so like that of the queen, that induced the latter to make her a confidante and companion for life. In the midst of court intrigues, the queen earnestly desired a true bond of friendship, and it declared in favor of her own heart, that she chose a woman of such simple and unassuming manners as the Duchess de Polignac.

A most happy familiarity existed between the queen and her favorite, who was a source of consolation to her patroness in the days of care and anxiety during the process against the Cardinal de Rohan. She could not bear to be separated from the duchess, to whom she could tell all her sorrows and the most secret emotions of her heart. Her friend united to a sympathizing tenderness a cheerful temper, and a talent to withdraw the queen from her sadness and tormenting fears. This was especially Julie de Polignac's task now, as they walked in the gardens of Saint-Cloud, when the Parliament of Paris, in full session, were preparing to pass sentence on the accused.

Marie Antoinette had arisen before day, and, after making her morning toilet in great haste and without assistance, she passed quickly into the park, to meet the duchess at the appointed rendezvous. Julie and her sister-in-law Countess

Diana, who was on a visit, were on the terrace ready to receive their unhappy sovereign.

"Is it not very cruel on my part," said the queen, heartily embracing her friends, "that I have deprived such lovely eyes of their right to finish their morning slumber? But they are looking at me as cheerfully and consolingly as ever, and that is what I desire; for your friend Marie Antoinette is overwhelmed with grief!"

"The morning is fair, your majesty," replied the duchess, in her melodious voice, "and there are no sorrows in these peaceful groves. Why should you not be happy in this fragrant air? If your majesty will do us a favor, and read in our eyes the petition we dare not express, it is that you would once more be yourself; despise the blind judgment of the people, and be thoroughly convinced that the sacredness of your person will at last affect the whole nation, and be joyfully recognized."

"No," replied the queen, bowing her usually haughty head in sadness upon her bosom, "this confidence I have long lost. I came to France with this expectation, and intended to win the love and gratitude of the people; but I begin to feel that the secret discord existing between myself and my subjects is assuming a power grieving and alarming me. This day I am appalled when I think of what is taking place in Paris. All the night long I was troubled with tears as I lay upon my sleepless couch. I am lost, if the Parliament absolves the cardinal." She took an arm of each of the ladies between whom she was walking, and went toward the pavilion, upon which the first rays of the sun were shining. As she sat down to enjoy the prospect revealed by the early morning, she seldom appeared more lovely, notwithstanding the sorrow with which her heart was overflowing. The manners of the court were forgotten by herself and her companions, who accompanied her with a natural and heart-felt sympathy.

"On looking at your majesty," said the lively and intellectual Countess Diana, "the happiness and power of beauty may be almost worshipped; and those who can associate evil thoughts with you must be criminal. I pray you to be as cheerful as you owe it to yourself."

"You are as amiable as usual, good countess," replied the queen, kissing the lady's brow. "But you have a stronger mind than I have; you are engaged in pursuits of literature and science, and have to do with studies of which I have never even dreamed. I am really obliged to my sister-in-law, the Countess d'Artois, for giving you a few days' leave of absence, to stay here in Saint-Cloud with us. She is to be envied in having such society about her at all times."

"If your majesty strengthens our Diana in her learned caprices, we are undone!" exclaimed the duchess, in a bantering banner. "Notwithstanding her youth and beauty, she is already a walking library; I have no doubt that soon we shall see her appear in a head-dress composed of books fragrant of past centuries. See, there is a volume actually visible from behind her fan, with which she is trying to conceal it!"

"We have caught her, and if it be a questionable book, we must ridicule her," exclaimed the queen, who seemed to have regained her cheerfulness. The volume which Diana had brought, and until now had concealed, was seized by Marie Antoinette to ascertain the title. After reading the name, she replaced it carefully on the table, covering it again with the countess's fan, indicating an uncomfortable dislike for it.

"It is a French translation of Homer's Iliad," said Diana, blushing, and lowering her eyes. "Can Father Homer, the greatest and best of poets, not find favor in the mind of an enlightened queen?"

Marie Antoinette laughed, but made a motion to reject the book with her beautiful hand: "No, no, for the sake of all the saints, spare me your Homer! From all I have heard of him it is my opinion that his Trojan heroes do not concern us in this country. They cannot pay court to us; we cannot expect them to join even in a tolerable contra-dance for our amusement, and we must say *fi donc!* when they roast a whole ox and consider it their greatest enjoyment. Do you give me credit for having made some acquaintance with your ancient friend, countess?"

"And I will sing you a song to show Diana how well I also have studied her poet," exclaimed the duchess, gayety and raillery laughing in her brown eyes. She arose, and, standing in the centre of the pavilion in a ludicrous position, sang in the manner of an itinerant begger: "Homer was blind and played the hautboy." * Then she began a burlesque dance, executing it with such success, that Marie Antoinette was forced to laugh.

"Yes, you are right, let us be merry," cried Marie Antoinette, accompanying the duchess in her dance. "Let us think of nothing but amusement and nonsense," continued the queen, with a sort of wild levity beaming in her eyes. "Sadness, reflection, literature, and all that, must be banished from the court of France! Shall it not be so, my dear friends?"

The young Countess Diana was in such confusion, that the duchess, who could not bear to see any one's feelings hurt, approached her and kindly took her hand, repeatedly kissing her while making the most tender protestations. Then, turning to the queen, she said: "Your majesty must not quite despise my Diana and her learning! She is a dear, good child, and, what is more, can invent and practise as many foolish pranks as either you or I. She intended to read to you something from her dear old Homer, at sunrise, to cause your majesty to forget the silly process against the cardinal. Was not that a freak suitable to your programme of nonsense? She has interviews with other old people, as I will betray to your majesty. She is most tenderly attached to a certain Virgil, who has written eclogues, and even a poem on agriculture, in which every thing is, no doubt, very pastoral and proper. She read to me from that old master, and I exhausted two vials of my finest perfumes when she transported me among his lowing cattle."

The queen laughed, and, kissing the countess, said: "You shall read that to us when we are all assembled at my farm at Trianon. Then I will compare your poetical descriptions with the reality. I am sure I shall like your Virgil, and I am glad when I think that ancient poets extolled the country. In fact, how happy might we be in this sad world, for every thing from the hands of Nature is good and beautiful! I consider it a favorable sign of the times that my subjects are trying to return to primitive modes of life, throwing off more and more the follies of mere conventionality, and again becoming an agricultural people. I can almost regain my faith and confidence, and think that all will end well, however dark and threatening these transient days may be!" The queen again became grave, and her sweet countenance grew thoughtful and melancholy. She seated herself on the green bank, resting her head on her arms, and fell into deep meditation. "If I only knew why I am so little loved in France!" she exclaimed, clasping her hands, and her eyes filled with tears. "What have I done, that I see none but persecutors in my path—that I experience estrangement and hatred where I hoped for gratitude and attachment? The nation despises me—I feel it more and more every day; and yet I gave to it my whole heart. I thought Frenchmen were men of honor—cavaliers—who would at least do justice to the woman, if not to the queen. But their slanders reach me in my most sacred relations as a woman, and thus embitter the joyful practice of my duties as a queen. Oh, I am often sorrowful when I think that I stand in such an unhappy position in reference to my people!"

"No!" exclaimed the duchess, with enthusiasm, "you are loved, queen! I am bold enough to remind you of that speech of Marshal de Brissac, whose sentiments reëchoed in the heart of every Frenchman. It was at your public entry into the capital, after your marriage with the dauphin was concluded. Pointing to the people that were crowding at the feet of your majesty, the governor of Paris said to you, in chivalrous devotion: 'Madame, you behold on yonder square two hundred thousand lovers, in rapture with your beauty.' And I could cite many such scenes, where the people met your majesty with an unquestioned

---

* Composed by the Duchess de Polignac, in imitation of a song of the times: "Ton père était aveugle et jouait du hautbois."—Campan, vol. i., p. 147.

regard, and were glad to receive a smile from your charming lips."

"So much the worse for me, that I have lost this favor, and without knowing how, or by what error!" sighed the queen. "You have not reminded me of that day in my life in a very happy manner; for was it not followed by that terrible disaster, when at the fireworks the crowd became so fearfully uncontrolled that there were more than four hundred dead and wounded? I am beginning to understand many of the omens of my royal entry into France, and which have been so maliciously explained by the satirical songs of my enemies."

"But there are also poems written in praise of your majesty," said the countess, kneeling at the feet of the highly-excited queen. Who knows not by heart that of Voltaire on the beauty, amiability, and generosity of the best of queens?* And he was one to whom little was sacred on the altar or the throne, but whose proud spirit was obliged to confess itself conquered by your charms."

"You are endeavoring to console me with those precious reminiscences, and I thank you!" exclaimed Marie Antoinette, rising hastily and leading the countess with her. "Memory is often a very useful endowment, helping us to pass lightly away from the disagreeable present; but the danger of to-day is too great for my poor beating heart. A few faded flowers from the past can give me no balm for these fresh wounds. Advise me, how can we pass the intervening time until we receive news from Paris, and learn how the suit has ended?"

"An idea occurs to me, your majesty: let us anticipate all, and drive immediately to Paris!" said the duchess, thoughtfully. "There we must see whether we can do any thing to turn the scale in our favor. We shall certainly reach the city long before the commencement of the Parliamentary session, and will have time to enter into confidential conversation with some of the members, among whom I have at least three good

friends. As soon as we arrive at the Tuileries we can send for these gentlemen, and give them a hint of the just wishes of your majesty. What do you say to my proposal?"

"I think it is excellent!" exclaimed the queen, in a lively manner. "Ah, I am so helpless and undecided, that it seems like a light shining in the darkness and uncertainty of my mind. The king will be engaged all day at Versailles; and, although I would not take a single important step in this business, he would not be angry with me, if, to allay the torture of my heart, I attempt to discover beforehand the inclination of the Parliament. Opinions may be influenced, and as my honor and reputation depend on this high judgment, no one can blame me for anxious curiosity. We ought to have moved in this affair before; and yet the king, who thinks too nobly, hopes to obtain a favorable decision on account of the justice of our cause and the conscientiousness of the judges."

"Then I will hasten into the palace, and order all preparations for your majesty's departure," said Countess Diana.

"Yes, hasten, I entreat you!" replied the queen. "The fleetest horses must immediately be harnessed, for I intend to pass the distance from Saint-Cloud to Paris in a shorter time than has ever been known before. Both of you must accompany me, my friends; I feel well only in your society, and at your side I shall have some courage to act in the presence of my enemies."

Countess Diana's slender figure almost flew with the orders of the queen to the castle, while Marie Antoinette, leaning on the arm of the Duchess Julie, walked slowly along the park avenue.

CHAPTER XV.

THE PARLIAMENT AND THE QUEEN.

THE greatest excitement prevailed the whole day among all classes of Paris. They awaited the decision of the Parliament in the cause of the

----

* "Mémoires de Weber," vol. i., p. 46.

accused cardinal with feverish suspense, manifesting itself in every street and square of the capital. Since early morning, more than ten thousand persons, composed of every rank, stood before the palace where the sessions were held, and besieged all the entrances. Some of the people penetrated into the halls and antechambers, in order to be the first to learn the sentence.

The prisoners in the Bastile had been taken to the Conciergerie during the night by the officers of the Parliament; and the public heard with special satisfaction that Cardinal de Rohan was treated with the consideration due to his high birth and position, being confined in the cabinet of the principal recorder of the prison, under the guard of the royal lieutenant of the Bastile. The examination began at eight in the morning, and was not ended when the evening approached, so that the people became impatient. Sometimes a rumor from the interior of the hall of justice would reach the anxious crowd, when it could be observed how every thing relating to the person of the cardinal was received with the greatest sympathy. The senior president permitted M. de Rohan to be seated during his examination, because he seemed to be very uncomfortably affected at the beginning of the trial, his countenance turning pale and his knees trembling. Afterward, however, he spoke almost half an hour with great eloquence and force, answering the questions addressed him by the president with a dignity and clearness undeniably proving his innocence. When he concluded, he bowed to the judges and counsellors, who arose at his salutation, returning it respectfully—a proceeding without precedent in the case of one accused before that tribunal. The preliminary affairs and incidents of the court were received and rumored among the masses in the street with shouts of joy. Many ardent exclamations of regard for the cardinal were heard, showing without doubt, and remarkably, which side the people had chosen, and on what grounds they desired to have the accused declared innocent and formally released.

A travelling-carriage, laboriously continuing its route through one of the streets near the palace, was finally forced to desist from the struggle with the crowds pressing against it on all sides. It was driven into a gateway standing conveniently open, while the passengers descended to attempt a way through the surrounding multitude. One of these was Mirabeau, who was on this day returning to the French capital, recalled by the encouragements he received from Madame de Nehra, as to the results of her mission. Henriette, with the faithful Chamfort, had gone even as far as the barrière, to receive and accompany him to Paris, as in a sort of triumph; for they rejoiced not only that they had regained their friend, but had the satisfaction of knowing that by their successful efforts he was released from his old bonds—from all that had oppressed his life, and could return to Paris as a free man. Mirabeau gave Henriette his arm to conduct her through the restless crowd engaged in shouting and gesticulating against both the court and the queen. Chamfort followed near, to aid in protecting Henriette. Little Coco, the inseparable travelling companion of Mirabeau, whom he had brought back from London, remained with his nurse in the carriage, until the streets became passable.

"My return to Paris could not have been celebrated with more congenial music than these noisy voices of the people!" said Mirabeau, allowing himself to be pressed forward by the crowd, taking good care of Henriette, whom he pressed close to himself. He was endeavoring to gain the route leading immediately to the Parliament-house, to be near the events transpiring, in which he was deeply interested, after Chamfort had related to him what was going on. "I love to see the people," said Mirabeau, looking eagerly about him, and breathing deeply. "Nothing to me is so grand as an excited crowd. They remind one of the future—they are like a vast field preparing for the hand of the sower, and the deeper the soil is ploughed and enriched the greater the harvest to be expected."

"This sounds rather aristocratic-revolutionary!" cried Chamfort. "A count with such noble ancestors must be a somewhat different friend of the people than myself, born in a hut. Your Countess Yet-Lee, however, has freed you from the arrogance of your father the marquis. With her beautiful eyes, which even a minister could not withstand, she obtained a new order from the king, that gives you the freedom of your person, and protects you from the power of the head of your family. Inhale then the breath of the people, and (if I also may speak figuratively) exhale it as a flame to set France on fire!"

Mirabeau and Henriette laughed heartily at these remarks, made in a very serious manner.

"Henriette has conferred many favors on me," said Mirabeau, glancing tenderly at her, "but now she has surpassed herself. On account of her personal appearance, which has an indescribable *je ne sais quoi*, even the severe mind of the Baron de Breteuil was turned in my favor, and I am really grateful to this minister. Nevertheless, I cannot appear as his partisan in this place to-day. Whatever right there may be in the intrigue he has contrived to bring against the cardinal, I do not desire to see M. de Rohan condemned. Although I entertain not the slightest sympathy for this enamoured prince of the Church, I have a great desire to see him honorably acquitted!"

"Bravo!" cried a man dressed in a blue blouse, who had been pressing behind them for some time, and, observing them attentively, tapped Mirabeau's shoulder approvingly. "You look like a man of rank, yet your intentions are good. We desire the cardinal's innocence, because that will declare the queen's guilt."

"And what interest have you in finding the queen guilty?" asked Mirabeau, returning the greeting of the man in a polite manner.

"She is proud and haughty toward the people —she despises us as of no account and contemptible, while she herself is mean and hypocritical!" exclaimed the man, an angry and resentful expression deforming his face. "My wife washes for the park gardener at Versailles, and, happening to be there on the day in question, she gossiped too long, and found herself belated in the garden. She says she is certain that it was the queen who granted the cardinal an interview in the grove. My wife never tells falsehoods, and is ready to take an oath as to the truth of her assertion."

"If your wife is handsome, we must receive her declaration without an oath," said Chamfort. "But I can tell you, my friend, that one of my fair neighbors in the Palais-Royal, where I live, is said to have represented the queen in a most whimsical disguise, at that rendezvous. This woman's name is Mdlle. Oliva, who resembles the queen from head to foot. From my window I have often listened to confidential conversations among the companions of Mdlle. Oliva, who rove through the Arcades of the Palais-Royal. Thus I know that it was an understood thing among them; that she had been hired to play the role of queen, to unsettle completely the poor cardinal's brain. For this the artful lady will have to pay at the high Parliament."

"You appear to side with the court," replied the husband of the laundress, scanning Chamfort contemptuously and threateningly. "I suppose you are one of those who riot in idleness, while the people suffer want, and sometimes starve in the midst of their hard work."

"No, good man," said Chamfort, laughing; "I work also, and if I am not starving it is because my appetite is not so good as yours. I envy you your health and strength, and hope you may always have a sufficiency to satisfy your hunger, and, believe me, you will soon find more than enough."

The friends were driven further on, and found great difficulty in remaining together in the multitude pushing and swaying continually. They met Count d'Entraigues, who, to his great surprise, was pressed almost into Mirabeau's arms, whom he immediately recognized, having been forced in that direction by a movement in another part of the crowd.

"I take this embrace as a punctual reply to the last letter I sent you to London a few days ago, Count Mirabeau," said the new-comer, warmly shaking hands with Mirabeau and Chamfort.

"I did not receive it; my departure was quite sudden, owing to favorable news," replied Mirabeau. "I have just arrived, and we meet already, running against each other, as we are borne along on the tide of this popular commotion. What has become of your work on 'Privileges,' Count d'Entraigues?" *

"I was writing to you about it: it is again in suspense," replied the other, an elegant and slender man, with a very aristocratic bearing. "I will resume it at some future time, when I have gathered more materials."

"On such an occasion as this you can gather plenty," remarked Chamfort. "Is it not so to-day that the French people desire nothing more ardently than a guilty queen? This expresses an abolishment of privileges by a more decided fact than any other that you could find. Formerly it was a prerogative of the king that he could do no wrong; now, as soon as guilt is discovered at the fountain of authority—on the throne itself—others must suffer; their assumed claims must cease to exist, for the same law must be applied to all who enjoy special favors. None will henceforth dare to be rich at the expense of his fellow-man."

"That remark is unusually striking and subtle," said Count d'Entraigues, politely. "Much is now at stake for the kingdom and the so-called privileged classes. The court, however, have this time set a rather cynical example concerning those recognized prerogatives; for they have seized a cardinal, a consecrated dignitary, who formerly had only to give an account to his spiritual judges; and, like a common criminal, they have brought him before a secular tribunal; and its judges, obeying their inherent opposition to royalty, will avenge the cardinal, by exonerating him, thus pronouncing suspicion as to the queen —in fact, her actual guilt."

"Then it is supposed in court circles that the verdict will be in favor of the cardinal?" asked Mirabeau.

"The queen herself must be intensely anxious,"

replied Count d'Entraigues, "for very early this morning she drove into the city from Saint-Cloud, requesting the presence of several of the members of the Parliament to attend her at the Tuileries. There a long conference took place, in which the Duchess de Polignac and her learned sister-in-law engaged with great interest. These gentlemen were doubtlessly influenced by the irresistible beauty and address of the queen, but whether they in their turn can influence others remains to be proved. The probability is, that the cardinal's acquittal will be pronounced by a smaller majority than was expected."

At this moment a noisy exultation was heard from the direction of the Parliament-house, and reëchoed by ten thousand voices.

"The sentence must have been pronounced," said Mirabeau, as he and his friends at last found themselves in the immediate vicinity of the palace of justice.

The decision had been rendered, and the people near the palace, who received the first news, related to each other the particulars of the trial, accompanying them with renewed cheers, and many severe and ungallant remarks, as well as moral applications. The cries, "Long live Cardinal de Rohan!" "Justice declares his innocence!" prevailed, although exclamations against the queen were mingled with them, and the ill-will and execrations of the public became every moment bolder and more undisguised. The statements rumored everywhere among the people, and confirmed by well-known persons present during the trial, were, that Prince Louis de Rohan was declared innocent by a majority of three; that the real deceiver, however, the Countess Lamotte-Valois was sentenced to be publicly whipped, branded on both shoulders, and imprisoned for life; that Count Cagliostro was fully exonerated from all blame, and that the other persons involved should receive greater or less punishment, according to their supposed deserts. "Long live the Parliament!" resounded through the streets of the capital.

"The guilt of the queen appears to satisfy the crowd—they cry long life to the Parliament of

---

* "Essai sur les Privilèges," by Count d'Entraigues.

Paris!" whispered Chamfort to Count d'Entraigues. "If only those old institutions were better, we would gladly permit them to live. Will not the dear people, now crying themselves hoarse, require a very different body to represent their rights and pretensions? This old Parliament seems to have an aversion to its own existence, and to avenge itself on its own restorer, Louis XVI., who ought to have left it among the relics of the feudal age. The members of this present court of justice avenge themselves in insulting the crown and dishonoring the queen. The good king ought to have let those institutions belonging to a dead past go with it! He ought long ago to have called the General Estates of the nation; and his honest heart, beating for the welfare of France, would have been appreciated."

"It is true, the throne of France trembles to-day!" said Mirabeau, raising his head, and glancing over the crowded square. "Why should we despise this ancient ministration of parliamentary law? Has it not gained new honors in fighting against royalty? And the members of the court to-day have really behaved well, for, in sentencing Lamotte-Valois to the most degrading punishment, they intend to reflect upon the king's house. To whip and brand a descendant of the royal family of Valois is a considerable satire upon the worshippers of those in whose veins flows the blood of the ancient monarchs of France!"

The crowd separated at the entrance of the palace, for a close carriage passed through slowly, and then took the road toward the Bastile. It bore away the Cardinal-Prince de Rohan and Count Cagliostro. A report spread among the astonished people, that it was the special request of the queen that both the accused, although acquitted, should be sent back to the prison, and be released only on the next day. Count d'Entraigues confirmed the report by repeating what he had heard in court society—that the queen, incited by her hatred of the cardinal, had indeed permitted herself to issue an order to that effect, preparing an insulting removal for the man to

whom she owed the most humiliating and afflicting event of her life. Marie Antoinette knew how to effect this beforehand, in case of the cardinal being discharged, and was well assisted by those members openly and secretly devoted to her, as the sequel proved. But the revengeful queen did not consider that she increased only the public triumph of M. de Rohan. This was shown upon the first movement of the horses, for the prisoners were loudly applauded, and the crowd so arranged themselves as to form a kind of triumphal procession, escorting the carriage to the Bastile.

Prince Louis de Rohan appeared at one of the side-windows, occasionally leaning out, thanking with smiles and bows the unceasing and enthusiastic exclamations in his favor. He was in the full costume of ecclesiastic honor, but his robe was of violet, the mourning color of cardinals; his breast was decorated with many orders, but his pale face, brightening at the voice of popularity, still bore the traces of painful excitement.

"The affair might have turned out badly for the handsome Prince Louis," remarked Chamfort, as the carriage passed them. "It can easily be seen that the queen almost gained her object with the gentlemen of the Parliament, for an acquittal by a majority of three votes is rather a narrow escape. And then they have put him into the same vehicle with Count Cagliostro, sending the proud priest back to the Bastile in the society of a notorious charlatan, instead of liberating him immediately as a recognition of his innocence.— See how the sorcerer makes good use of his opportunity! He endeavors, if possible, to surpass his colleague the cardinal in pathos and dignity, greeting the people, from the other side of the carriage, with the gravity of a prophet, pretending to believe that part at least of the public applause is for him. He smiles continually in his ecstatic manner, and now he graciously lifts his plumed hat, as if called upon to express special thanks. He actually had the hardihood to appear before the high court of the Parliament in his magician's costume."

"So that is the world-renowned miracle-per-

former Cagliostro!" said Mirabeau, observing the
necromancer with particular attention as he
passed opposite the party. "I perceive, Henriette, that in the description you gave me, in your
charming letter, of your spirit-dinner, you pictured this person so accurately, that I would have
immediately recognized him. The appearance of
the man confirms me in my opinion of him.
Every feature and every motion shows the instrument of the Jesuits, and now I have done with
him. His eyes do not please me—he is a trap-
per, and all he catches he delivers for a consideration to the Church."

"He might have done something more for his
pupil Louis de Rohan," remarked Chamfort,
when the carriage had slowly passed, accompanied by its cheering escort. "By means of his
magic arts he introduced to the cardinal the
queens of ancient times, but he could not exorcise
the hatred of Marie Antoinette. What did it
profit M. de Rohan that Cleopatra and Semiramis
often visited him in secret? The Queen of France
rejected the lover of fifty, and—that is all! If I
had been in Cagliostro's place, I would have infused a little of the elixir of youth into the poor
prelate—perhaps that might have assisted him in
winning the favor of the modern queen."

In the distance could now be heard the voice
of the multitude who had accompanied the carriage as far as the gates of the Bastile; but the
people would not leave until the cardinal, after
extending his hands over them and blessing them,
disappeared within the gates.

Mirabeau and Henriette hastened to find their
carriage, after separating from Chamfort and
D'Entraigues, the latter inviting them to dine at
his house the following day, and taking no refusal. Henriette was very impatient to see Coco,
and as soon as she observed her favorite she hurried forward to embrace him. They soon passed
through the now empty streets to their dwelling
in the Rue de Vaugirard, which Madame de Nebra
had taken, and arranged with all her usual care
and taste.

CHAPTER XVI.

THE WIFE OF THE MINISTER OF FINANCE.

MIRABEAU had been in Paris several weeks.
His object in returning to the city was to finish
an historical and political work, and thus attract
the attention of the ministry, in order to obtain a
place suitable to his rank and talents. In his
restlessness and indecision he at first intended to
return to his native Provence, and take possession
of Castle Mirabeau, which was at present unin-
habited, and devote himself wholly to literary
labor in a retirement he so much needed. He
hoped, at such a distance from the capital, to be
able to live on the small annuity allowed him by
his father, who had finally consented, through the
mediation of mutual friends, to pay it regularly.
He was prevented from adopting this plan by the
illness of Coco, and remained in Paris, where he
made acquaintances that seemed to him of importance to his labors and prospects.

Henriette sat at the bedside of the sick child
tenderly and anxiously nursing him. For several
days she had constantly attended him. Mirabeau
at this time appeared absent-minded and busy,
spending most of the day abroad, sometimes returning only at daybreak. After a short but
kind conversation he was about to depart again,
hardly seeming to have time to kiss the fevered
brow of little Coco, when Henriette said, with
some sensitiveness: "You scarcely remember us
now, Mirabeau. All day you leave us alone; I
seldom hear your voice, and without it every day
appears to me void and melancholy; if I must be
deprived of you much longer in this way, I shall
certainly become very miserable."

"My dear child, you must have patience and
indulge me," replied Mirabeau, drawing her hand
to his lips. "I have entered into a new current
of business, driving me hither and thither, but
you know there is but one thing that constitutes
my happiness: to be in your presence, and hold
your head in my arms.

"I am not vexed with you," said Henriette,
playfully pouting. "Every thing would be well

enough if that Clavière had not come to Paris, and taken complete possession of you. I do not know, but even in London a certain fear troubled me whenever he entered our dwelling, and I really trembled. Now I can explain this feeling; for since he is here you seem to associate with him only! He will draw you away from me altogether, Mirabeau."

"No, my good child!" exclaimed Mirabeau, quickly, but, with visible signs of haste, seizing his hat. "No Clavière, no angel, no demon, will ever alienate me from my Countess Yet-Lee. We are united for ever, heart and soul. But, believe me, my friend Clavière deserves your confidence. He has a strong, active nature, and, since his arrival in Paris, my ideas have been enlarged. I owe him much; in company with him I have entered a new course, in which I hope to attain my great aims."

"Clavière has not a very attractive countenance," replied Henriette, in a low voice and with downcast eyes. "His features quiver, and his eyes have a glassy, spectral look—in his presence my old habits of the cloister recur to me, and I secretly make the sign of the cross. We have not become happier on his account, and "—she added, blushing, and scarcely audible—"no richer!"

"What, not richer!" answered Mirabeau, warmly, replacing his hat on the table, and taking a small box filled with gold-pieces from his desk. "Look at this! Do you know how much was here? but, by the good counsels of our Geneva friend, the original sum has increased tenfold during a few weeks!"

Henriette shook her head, after casting a slight and distrustful glance upon the gold.

"Do you remember the hundred guineas in London that caused us such trouble?" continued Mirabeau. "You went for them to my friend Elliot; on your return a very singular accident happened to you, and the knave Hardy stole the money out of your pocket. The English courts, however, discharged him on account of insufficient proof. But, on the day I left London, I found the whole amount among some old rubbish

in a hole in the wall. Luckily I had no immediate use for the money, and since my arrival here I have other resources; thus I saved a little—an accident that never happened to me before—and began to speculate, according to Clavière's advice. I bought stock of a newly-organized commercial company with part of my money, and with the rest I make time-bargains, as they are called —that is, I deal in stock without really delivering any, agreeing to win or lose at a certain time the difference of the market-price." [*]

"I do not understand one word of this business," said Henriette. "But I must say that I have no confidence in riches thus acquired. I do not believe that money so handled is apt to remain. It is like the gold in the fairy-tale—some day when you come to lay your hand on it, you will find nothing but ashes."

"Your criticism of my new financial adventures is not so bad, my child," replied the count, laughing. "But we cannot well avoid the follies of the day. Our luck may favor us, and thus we may aid others in gaining wisdom. And that is the idea of Clavière and myself — to that we devote all our strength and mind. France is plunged head and ears into this rage for speculation. Gambling in various public funds, government loans, commercial stocks, and jobbing of every kind, seem to constitute the only life of our present society. It is a disease, but I hope the country will pass through it. In the mean time, the men of progress will fill their pockets—that is their duty. Speculation is an epidemic that easily seizes every one. We were infected with it by the Dutch and English; it has become domesticated in France, and will run its course. The race for money will finally become a race for liberty. When all the property of a nation has been driven into such channels and evaporated, new resources must be opened, and that can be done only by social and political freedom. This wild speculation is always the forerunner of dangerous storms."

"And what says our friend Chamfort to all

---

[*] Peuchet, "Mémoires sur Mirabeau," vol. ii., p. 341.

this ? " asked Henriette, thoughtfully playing with the locks of little Coco.

"Chamfort has gone for several weeks to Auteuil, to visit Madame Helvetius," replied Mirabeau. "His ill-health prevented him, as he intended, to pay you a farewell visit, and I had almost forgotten to mention his regrets. He does not believe in business — he is too idle and dreamy an epicure—he is afraid of taking cold at the Exchange. On his departure he said to Clavière and myself: 'You must provide well for the financial disease of the French. For myself, I will remain the poor Cinderella of the revolution, and stay at home guarding the flame of liberty. After you have made bankrupts of your fellow-citizens, and swindled them out of their money, send them to my hearth.'"

Some one rapped at the door, and Etienne Clavière entered. Mirabeau greeted him with much heartiness, while Henriette hardly raised her eyes, finding it difficult to conceal her ill-will toward the new-comer, and negligently returning his salutation.

Clavière's appearance had remarkably improved since his residence in the capital. His manners were more courteous, or, at least, betrayed an intention and effort to produce a more polite effect, and his burly figure had gained almost as much grace in its movements as it was capable of. The barbarian energy expressed in his face seemed, however, only to conceal itself behind a shrewd diplomatic patience. The democratic costume he wore in London, as a political refugee, was replaced by a fashionable toilet, and the gray, broad-brimmed hat with the red ribbon, was succeeded by one of Paris fashion. On entering, Clavière approached Madame de Nehra, to play the graceful gentleman, although she obviously sought to escape his notice. He asked her pardon for again depriving her of the society of the count, whom he came to conduct to an assembly of admirers awaiting him.

Henriette replied, with a sad inclination of her head, that she was accustomed to the object of his visits, and that all she felt was a little curiosity to ask whither they were going—to a socie-

ty for the amelioration of the condition of the negroes ? the American Club ? a dinner at the house of the banker, M. Panchaud ? or a rendezvous of black, white, and gray speculators from every quarter of the globe ? She uttered these questions with such sensitiveness that Clavière smiled; and Mirabeau, to appease her, caressingly took her hand.

"It is quite probable that the count will return very late to-night," said the Genevan, with lurking ridicule. "Almost all those you enumerate with such charming indignation unite to-day at a feast, and Count Mirabeau is indispensable. The beneficent society for the blacks, and the American Club, give a dinner in one of our most magnificent halls. Many and important speeches will be made, and every one anticipates some eloquent passages from the lips of our friend. It will be worth while to attend, for the philanthropists who desire the abolition of slavery are to be sustained by the new *Club des Américains*, and they intend to further such an object with all the means at their command. The members of both societies wish also to make a collection for the promotion of their common purposes. Money will not be wanting, for among the guests are the most brilliant and best names on the Bourse. You are again right—M. Panchaud, my prudent countryman, will be there; and among them will be several literary characters, and 'philosophic noblemen,' as Chamfort calls them. Is not this an assembly for which a man may, for an hour or two, leave his wife and child ? "

Henriette blushed and smiled, looking up at Mirabeau with her recovered good-humor.

"And do you know that Calonne will be there ? " added Clavière, turning with a significant glance to Mirabeau. "I have just left his cabinet, and he promised me faithfully to be present at the 'Club.'"

"Ah, that is what we all desire," exclaimed Mirabeau. "By this visit the minister of finance will not increase his friends at court or among the aristocracy. It is, however, time for him to raise his mask a little on that side. After throwing away the government money by handfuls, like a genial gambler, he must let the king know that it can only be regained permanently and with interest, by a radical reform of the whole state, and all belonging to it!"

"I am laboring for that daily and hourly," replied Clavière, with a vulgar grin. "And the movement is near—it cannot certainly be very distant, as I can satisfactorily prove."

"If it is near, it will be through the efforts of an irresistible spirit, named Etienne Clavière!" said Mirabeau, smiling. "Really, among all your satanic ideas—and you overflow with them—the happiest was, that you knew how to make yourself private secretary to the minister of finance. You have in this way become the secret master of the revolution of the state, for which we sigh, from day to day, as the farmer for rain on his withered field. But why have you not put on the uniform of the ministerial officials, since you are formally accepted as private secretary of M. de Calonne?" *

"It is not necessary for me to be so punctilious as to my official character," replied Clavière. "M. de Calonne has need of me, and therefore sought to attach me to his ministry in a suitable capacity. Calonne is a man of the world, and has perhaps too much wit to occupy himself with thorough financial labors; so for some time I have been making his mathematical calculations, when they require long and connected reasoning. He is well satisfied, and thus I urge him gradually to the very point where we desire to see him. Yesterday I finished the new financial scheme, and immediately delivered it to the minister. Many of your ideas, Mirabeau, are mingled in it, and I hope you will be satisfied. I have brewed a charming drink, that must by its own action have a powerful effect on the political and social mind of France. You will soon see of what use is a Geneva banker, like myself, who has thoroughly mastered financial science, and who, besides his practical skill and business preference, is driven by the very demon of state revolution!" Clavière burst into boisterous laughter, as was his

custom when he had expressed himself to his satisfaction. Then he urged Mirabeau to depart with him, adding that they must not let the company wait, especially as he, Clavière, had undertaken to make the opening speech. "I am so full of malice," he added, "that I can scarcely retain it. If I have to suppress my oration much longer, it will burst from my mouth in bright flames. Let us go quickly, and assist me in renewing my excuses to Madame de Nehra, that her gracious anger may not descend on my devoted head."

Quickly taking leave of Henriette, she returned their compliments in silence. Seating herself at the bedside of the sick Coco, she concealed her sorrow in pacifying the crying child.

Mirabeau and Clavière rapidly passed on through the thoroughfares until they reached the Boulevard Montmartre, thence to the faubourg, where, in a remote street, was the edifice, surrounded by a garden, which the recently-formed club had rented for the purpose of holding their meetings. On the way, Mirabeau intentionally turned the conversation to the financial minister, asking, in rather a decided manner, when M. de Calonne intended to arrive at the banquet, and whether he would remain.

"The minister promised to be present at my speech," replied Clavière, "in which I wish to criticise all the present tendencies to social reform. I shall try especially to explain that the efforts to restore to society liberty and human dignity are on a par with those to fill men's pockets with money, and make them all opulent. The curiosity of M. de Calonne was excited when I hinted at the points of my speech—he wished to know how I could bring this subject to an issue; and, although this morning he was suffering from the consequences of a night passed in dissipation, he promised to attend punctually at six o'clock. I made him give me his word that he would remain during the whole banquet, to have a fair view of the activity of the minds of the present day—a matter instructive and absolutely necessary to a financial minister. We shall have such men as Cabanis, Condorcet, Hol-

* Condorcet, "Mémoires," vol. i., p. 227.

bach, and Lafayette. What an exposition of new ideas we shall enjoy! And M. de Calonne has at least one strong faculty—inquisitiveness. He wishes to know what is passing in the sphere of thought, and I have made him in some measure see it as a duty, telling him that a man in his position must make money out of ideas. I have therefore excited that prominent and by no means uncommon faculty, which he has inherited from Mother Eve, and I hope it may give him knowledge."

Mirabeau looked at his watch, standing at the corner of a street, and begged permission to take leave of Clavière for a short time, remarking that they would probably not meet again until toward the close of the banquet.

"Then you will not hear my address?" asked Clavière, irritated. "And why do you so suddenly become indifferent concerning subjects of which you seemed but just now to express your entire approbation?"

"I will certainly appear toward the end of the feast," replied Mirabeau, smiling, "and will then have sufficient opportunity to notice the effect of your speech. It is not indifference to your great eloquence, which no one admires more than I, nor insensibility for the great thoughts you intend to illustrate, and about which we may speak another time; but I must go, for I have a rendezvous elsewhere—I must profit by the opportunity, cost what it will."

"Now I understand your inquiries in reference to Calonne's visit to the club," exclaimed Clavière, fixing his searching eyes on the count. "You intend to pay a visit to Madame de Calonne. But I pray you, commit no folly—attempt no intrigue, into which you may be led simply for its own sake. The minister, although the most capricious and unprincipled man in Paris, is of jealous temperament, and watches his wife with the suspicion of a Herod. If he has any distrust, you assuredly will lose your game with him, and I can never revive his interest in you, which may be of great advantage!"

"It is my way," replied Mirabeau, again looking at his watch, and holding it toward his friend that he might see how near six o'clock it was.

"Go, Clavière, and deliver your address on liberty, human dignity, full pockets, and all that, or on the art of turning the bankruptcy of society into resources of wealth. In the mean time, because it suits me, I shall pay my visit. Not long ago I met Madame de Calonne at a dinner given by the Countess de Riancourt; her equipage failed to arrive, so I induced her to enter my carriage and had her driven to her residence. You know that it is dangerous for any woman thus to accompany me.* When we parted, Madame de Calonne gave me permission to visit her. You know, as well as I, that she and her husband are on very bad terms, although it is scarcely two months since they celebrated their marriage, and I may have much to suggest in view of happier connubial relations."

"Their wedding-day was very unfortunate!" replied Clavière, taking Mirabeau's arm, and preparing to accompany the latter a short distance; probably hoping to succeed in inducing the count to return, and appear with him in the banquet-hall of the club. "The lady was dreadfully insulted on that day by her husband," Clavière recommenced. "It must have made a strange impression, when a bridegroom sat deliberately down to a game of ombre, at the moment the carriage came to carry him and his bride home. He played on with his usual perseverance whenever he handles a card. The parents of the lady were confounded, and she herself was ready to sink into the earth in her indignation and shame; his friends twitched him anxiously by the sleeve, but nothing could divert him from the game. At last his mother-in-law plainly asked him to return home; but he begged to have a few moments more, and requested her to descend and enter the carriage with her daughter, as he would follow immediately. When they had gone he forgot them, until the relatives united to drag him forcibly from the room. They even had to carry him down and push him into the coach, where he met his bride in tears." †

"Yes, that is the incident which has prompted

---

* Peuchet, vol. ii., p. 320.
† Condorcet, "Mémoires," vol i., p. 230.

my favor with Madame de Calonne!" said the count, smiling. "Good-evening, Clavière; I hope to return in time to assist in the advocacy of your schemes of philanthropy."

"I will not let you off," replied the Genevan, holding Mirabeau's arm. "You must not play the tempter, for it may be detrimental to you in important matters at present under consideration. If Calonne ill-treated his wife on their wedding-day, that gives you no right to speculate on her fidelity."

"Clavière as a preacher of morality is really quite a comedy!" exclaimed the count, again making efforts to free himself from his anxious friend. "You, the teacher of the French in all arts of speculation—the greatest gambler on the Exchange, and who have done more to demoralize the people in money matters than any other man—you are suddenly playing the defender of morality!—To please you, and because I hoped to obtain a position from the minister, I wrote against this singular passion for sudden fortunes by stock operations, but you well know I only did so according to your orders, to give a check to the business of certain companies, and transfer the movements of the Bourse to your hands, by depreciating as much as possible all paper but your state-bills."

"We know, friend, what you have accomplished, and what your genial pen may yet accomplish, if you enter into our plans," said Clavière, gravely. "Your two pamphlets against the bank of discount and the Spanish bank, have caused quite an excitement, and greatly aided our financial operations.* To the minister it was as convenient as agreeable, to have brought to the notice of the public certain ideas that he considered it right to impress on them, and you have executed his wishes in a truly masterly style. You may rest assured that he will show his gratitude in a decided manner, provided no folly 'à la Mirabeau' destroy the existing good understand-

ing. Your attacks are masterpieces of financial logic, and in a tone of sublime social morality. The bank of discount, founded by Turgot, was formerly highly meritorious in reference to the commerce and money-market of France. Its business involved large and small amounts from all corners of the land, and the dividends increased enormously; but at length its favor with the public so fluctuated that the institution was endangered. The mania for stock-gambling ruined small capitalists in particular, and Calonne, who had been endeavoring to sustain the credit of the bank by government laws in its favor, now thought best to destroy it. Then you wrote your pamphlets, my friend, by which you sought to depreciate the stock, both financially and morally. You were even stronger in your second pamphlet against the Saint-Charles Bank, which the famous Cabarrus established in Madrid three years ago. This concern pretended to be supported by commercial enterprises in Caracas and the Philippine Islands, just as the banker Law turned into money the Mississippi gold-land fever, when the anticipated commerce of Louisiana inundated us with a flood of bank-bills, threatening to carry away all our solid resources. A country like Spain, to which flow abundantly the precious metals of the New World, sends us paper of no value, but which is nevertheless more sought for in Paris than in Madrid. The strength of Mirabeau dealt mighty blows on the Spanish bank. In fact, you revealed the unsoundness of the whole financial policy universally adopted, and accompanied your argument with a most eloquent description of the manners of the present age. That is a sad picture indeed of those who exchange real property for paper of whose worth and origin they are ignorant, and which serves, so to speak, as admission tickets to debtors' prisons or insane asylums. The government has been obliged to interfere, for if all capital is to be transmuted into these bank-bills, whence is to be derived the necessary court revenues? The Spanish bonds this day still sell for double their nominal value at the Paris Bourse."

"My dear Clavière," said Mirabeau, laughing,

* "De la Caisse d'Escompte" (1785); "De la Banque d'Espagne, dite de Saint-Charles" (1785); "Lettre du Comte de Mirabeau à M. le Couteulx de la Noraye" (1785).

"I see through your noble intentions. You begin a .broker's conversation with me to change the current of my thoughts. But I cannot help you; I only care at present for my contemplated visit to the wife of the minister of finance, and I do not in the least trouble myself about stocks. I have worked enough for them—let me have a holiday. I am afraid you employ me and my pamphlets in raking out the chestnuts from the hot ashes, for your special benefit; and, say what you will, you draw considerable profits in negotiating paper for whose depreciation I have been employed. Yes—you and Panchaud, and the rest of the Geneva financiers, who are' ploughing the revolutionary field of Paris, are feeding your friends with the proceeds of a system which I have been called upon to expose and denounce. I am certain that M. de Calonne does so, although he surpasses me in his manœuvres to sink the paper of the bank of discount. I have lately heard, in fact, from some ladies in the Palais-Royal, that he makes them presents of candies wrapped in the bills of that establishment." *

An equipage passed at this moment, in which sat a gentleman whom Clavière greeted politely, and Mirabeau also lifted his hat. "M. de Calonne!" said Clavière, laughing. "He has a very keen ear, and it is possible he may have overheard the words 'candies' and 'bills!'"

"I will relate this story to his wife," replied Mirabeau. "And, now, my friend, hasten to the banquet; for you see your minister is punctual, and you must not let him wait for your speech, intended to make all mankind happy. I shall arrive soon enough to say a few words myself." Mirabeau and Clavière separated, going in different directions.

CHAPTER XVII.

THE BANQUET OF THE AMERICAN CLUB.

THE philanthropic assembly in the large and brilliant hall was numerous, and graced by the presence of many distinguished guests, even from the higher classes. The entrance of the minister of finance made quite a sensation. Many surrounded him, with congratulations, pretending to pay him homage in flattering allusions to the success attending his recent financial operations. Others remained at a distance with visible reserve, avoiding any probability of introduction. Calonne, however, with the tact he possessed in perfection, endeavored to approach those who, not without design, seemed to shun him. In this group were Cabanis and Condorcet, toward whom the minister advanced with great cordiality.

The Marquis de Condorcet received M. de Calonne rather coolly, holding himself erect, and scarcely touching the hand extended to him; but this did not in the least disturb the minister, who was determined to have some friendly discourse with these men. On the contrary, he began to converse with his usual versatility, all he said sparkling with wit; even Condorcet, who was this evening more than ever taciturn, found his icy reserve melting away before he was aware of it.

"My object in coming here was to meet such friends as the Marquis de Condorcet!" said the minister, in his courtier manner, and with great geniality. "Tell me, marquis, may a poor financial operator, who becomes poorer as he makes more money, reckon on the approval of such superior minds? You are happy in your intellectual empire, where you have no currency but thought, and all requirements are satisfied by an exchange of ideas—there you have no deficit! You philosophers take good care that in your system all is well balanced, and that reason shall not accumulate debt upon debt, and loan upon loan, upon mere supposition, as a financial minister of France is forced to do.

It was difficult, even to the measured and straightforward Condorcet, to withstand altogether such charming urgency. His broad, thoughtful brow began to show a little more friendliness, and the face of the marquis expressed a shade less of contempt. "We mathematicians and philosophers," he replied, smiling slightly and even rather good-naturedly, "do not trouble

------

* "M. de Calonne tout entier," par M. C . . . . (Carra), Bruxelles, 1788.

ourselves so much about errors in our calculations, because the people do not suffer starvation as the immediate consequence. Financial ministers have in this respect a much harder task to perform. There is, however, a very good proverb: 'The pitcher is carried to the well until it is broken!' We shall soon discover whether the pitcher we mean is made of indestructible gold, as it is said to be, and in which are treasures for every court official, if he will only receive them. Perhaps, when we see the fragments, we may remark better on the material out of which your money is manufactured. The present scheme of finance, encouraging, as it does, all sorts of gambling, and disturbing an honest and reasonable desire for profit, introduces a vast amount of mischief into our society."

"Bravo!" cried Calonne, clasping his hands. "Can we desire any thing better, my dear friend?" His refined and pleasant countenance beamed with an expression of humor, generally containing a slight sting of satire, and used with such art that it was not quite clear for whom it was intended. There was, however, considerable attraction in his manner and appearance. He was at this time in his fifty-first year; but his tall, slender figure and highly-polished manners made the impression of a much younger age. His conversation often suggested that he was a pleasant-tempered roué—one, moreover, who conceded every thing, from mere indifference and indisposition to disagree.

The minister passed quickly to another group, after having spoken a few courteous words to Cabanis, inquiring in a flattering manner about the success the latter had obtained in his medical practice since his removal from Auteuil to the French capital.

It began to be more lively in the brilliantly lighted and decorated hall. Cabanis looked with thoughtful and melancholy eyes at the symbols and standards ornamenting the ceiling and walls, among which were insignia belonging to the two associations united for this evening. In the centre was a large portrait of Washington, a present from Lafayette. Over it waved the American flag, with its thirteen stars. On both sides of this fine likeness were pictures, exhibiting negroes undergoing punishment, in positions of entreaty, or prostrated beneath the lash. Each embellishment was surrounded by an American and a French flag, having an important meaning of union and friendship.

"The walls tell terrible tales!" said Cabanis to Condorcet, as arm in arm they promenaded through the hall. "Those slaves impress me with a painful feeling, and challenge every man to do his best, that such dark accusations against humanity may cease! But if we wish to make fair and happy all that is black in our present society, we must go beyond these 'puristes libéraux,' as the gentlemen of the American club call themselves.* Purification in their sense is washing the negro white, and that is known to be rather an unsuccessful business in this world. It is nothing more than a philanthropic delusion, which in my opinion is of a piece with the financial administration of the charming M. de Calonne, who has just honored us with his gracious notice. Such whitewashers are worse than the slaveholders. And we, my friend Condorcet, what color are we striving to obtain?"

"Oh," replied the marquis, with gravity, "we must strive to be tyrannized by no particular shade; for there is illusion in every color, and, so long as we are controlled by it, we endure untruth and injustice. Let us return to Nature, as our Jean Jacques Rousseau advised us—all healthful development is the result. In her society we rest free from all deception. Whatever she represents herself to be, she really is, and whatever is offered we may take and enjoy without question. Those ideas of social happiness with which the priesthood and the monarchy have so long amused us have very little practical existence. One fact remains—the world progresses, but only in and through Nature. That is why I was so glad, Cabanis, when you began to translate Homer. You will make the French acquainted with an old poet, who sang about the only true

* Challamel, "Histoire-Musée de la République française" (Paris, 1842), v. i., p. 28.

system of human life, showing that king and people, religion and state, liberty and custom, have their origin in the same beneficent source. We have need of that ancient author. The greatest satisfaction I have ever had is, that we have commenced to write on the same subject: the indissoluble union of the physical and moral nature of man!"

Cabanis pressed his friend's hand, saying, in a low voice: "All we can do now is to record this new gospel. It is not exactly the right way to begin, for it should be preached to men from the housetops, that they must renounce what is artificial, if they intend to attain and enjoy the object of their existence. If we once liberate man from the unnatural in politics and religion, we put him in possession of all liberty. Of course, it is a humiliation that such men as we can only use our corrosive ink to unloose the chains of our fellow-men. I often become irritated in the midst of my labors at the superstitions of society, and prefer to visit my indigent patients, believing that there is something more real and noble in curing some poor cobbler's wife of a fever."

"Excellent, doctor!" cried a jovial voice behind them, and Cabanis felt a friendly tap on his shoulder. He turned and saw Baron d'Holbach, who welcomed his friends and colleagues with hearty greeting.

"Ah," said Cabanis, smiling, "even Baron d'Holbach does not disdain to appear here! It must mean something that we thus assemble; the lieutenant of police will certainly discover a dangerous tendency somewhere."

"My good friends, I have only come to give my mite for the emancipation of the slaves, and incidentally to hear any new idea that may find utterance," replied Baron d'Holbach, in his usual happy mood. "You know I am always suffering from lack of news. The world is becoming more tedious. What are the latest rumors?" The eyes of the old philosopher beamed with a curious expression, that might have been somewhat gloomy if so much real kindness had not mingled with it. His appearance was plain and simple, almost approaching the patriarchal style; yet,

without apparent contradiction, the cheerful man of the world might be seen in all his deportment—a fact of which his well-nourished person gave good evidence. The celebrated thinker, so much feared in his day, could be discovered in his high brow, on which appeared inexorable decision and audacity.

"If you desire any thing new you must discover it yourself," replied the Marquis de Condorcet. "For all that we hear is old. A large assembly, however, seldom think, and the longer they remain the more thoughtless they become."

"But you will find something new at the table," said Holbach. "And I really feel consoled in noticing the preparations. To eat and to think are one and the same operation—the only difference being that the organs are dissimilar. He that eats continually reproduces himself, and the better you dine the more profoundly you think. All spiritual ideas are gradually absorbed with good food into the physical organism, and my own well-conditioned body is the real pantheon of ideas."

"This application which you make of your celebrated system always pleased me, on account of your personal amiability," replied Cabanis. "Your book has had influence—it is indeed a fountain whence we draw most of our ideas, and I hope our greatest deeds also will be accredited to it. Really, Baron d'Holbach, if the gay Abbé Galiani called you 'steward of philosophers,' it is not because of your Sunday dinners, with which for years you have regularly entertained your thinking and eating friends, but on account of your 'Système de la Nature' as well as your other writings. They are to the world as a hospitable and pleasant inn, so to speak, in which mind (and mind is matter) feeds itself from already provided resources, and just as it is convenient. At best, mind is a result of matter manifesting itself in ideas."

"We shall not be surfeited with good things to-night," remarked Cabanis, dryly, calling attention to the dishes. "I see nothing but very ordinary fare, and to a higher mind, accustomed to the dainties at Holbach's table, they give little promise of ideas. Who can originate great thoughts from sour-krout? Banquets by subscription are, however, in Paris, not always the choicest, and I see many men of Holbach's school present, who will suffer terribly in the process of thinking. It would be some consolation if this feast were quickly begun and ended."

"I hear that the hosts are waiting for Etienne Clavière," replied Condorcet. "He is also a philosopher, and is to make the opening address. No doubt he has been belated at the Bourse, for he is the secret agent of Calonne, and attends to all the financial and other swindles his master undertakes. This whimsical man has no doubt many good traits, but his rough manner has something so bloodthirsty about it that it always makes a mysterious impression on me. It is said that he is also paid by the English ministry for the part he acts here. He is the principal spring in the stock-gambling machinery at work in Paris, and, uniting deeper plans with it, he aims to produce anarchy in our whole social fabric; but I do not trust him; he is no Frenchman, and I do not like to see foreign hands tampering in our affairs."

"If he desires anarchy, he is as welcome as one of ourselves!" said Holbach, smiling complaisantly. "You will remember that anarchy, as the real principle of life, I have preached in my work on Nature. Repulsion and attraction constitute anarchy in all its phases, more or less active. That is the only condition by which both the physical and the moral worlds live and maintain their equilibrium; for all laws originate and are valid by force of some sort—their elements must fight and be fought against, before what we call law rests on any sure foundation. Perhaps this Clavière may be a pupil of your old Holbach. I have often asked you, Cabanis, to bring him to my house some Sunday to dinner."

"He belongs to that class of people whom you can seldom secure," replied Cabanis. "Otherwise, your hospitable dinners, that for thirty years have made Sunday in Paris a feast of mind, would have attracted him. He is a dismal fellow, but he knows every movement in the market as well as the value of every bank-bill, for he trades in

them with the activity of a demon. Such men are seldom docile—they are bad pupils, and they rush into experiment, sometimes deceiving, and sometimes being deceived."

"I do not see Count de Mirabeau," remarked Holbach, holding up his eye-glass and glancing around on those present. "He positively promised to meet me here. I know he is your hero, Cabanis; you not only love but study him, and in your new philosophic researches, which I expect to be more progressive than mine, you look to such a hero of human nature as we see represented physically and mentally in Mirabeau. He is the man of nerve; and I hear you advocate the principle, that every thing is only nerve—that all ideas are the production of the senses, and that thoughts are formed in the brain because it is the centre of the nervous system.* I comprehend how Mirabeau has been your model for this explanation of human nature. I have never seen a man so highly organized and gifted; and if France, in her present effeminacy, is destined to witness great deeds, he will be the one by whom they are to be accomplished."

"You do not appreciate him too extravagantly, but you do more than justice to my own modest efforts," replied Cabanis, a slight blush suffusing his usually pale countenance. "You cannot help thinking of such a nature as Mirabeau's when you essay to explain the human organization. Truly, in him is nerve: and I have observed that it has a reciprocal action with his ideas, and controls his objects and purposes. I must confess, that while engaged in my labors on the physical and moral peculiarities of man's structure, I often think of him, although I have lately seen him but seldom."

"Well, my dear friends, it all depends on what we understand by our terms," said Baron d'Holbach. "In my system I consider the stomach as the real source and centre of man's being. If your stomach is disordered, your nerves and brain receive no nourishment, nor do you produce ideas. It will therefore always remain the seat of the

* Cabanis's "Rapports du Physique et du Moral de l'Homme."

human mind; and your philosophy, Cabanis, is only a polite style of making all ideas originate in the nerves instead of the stomach, which is by many considered too grossly material. But materialism is the science of the day—the science of matter and force—a secret which we have won from Nature, because we ventured to confide in and made her our divinity. What says the meditating Marquis de Condorcet?"

"You know I sympathize with you in your more important doctrines," replied Condorcet, awaking from his dreamy silence. "Stomach, nerves, and brain, are the immediate agents of life, and what is called mind exists in them only —no rational man can dispute that. But you forget one important fact, of which I beg to remind you—that is, development, without which humanity, or any thing else, has of course no progression."

"Ah," laughed Holbach, his whole body shaking, "you will not supplant us in that way! what you call development I call digestion. Can any thing under the sun be clearer? He that has nothing to digest has no development. You would elevate the human nature, no doubt, but by your law you provide for it Icarian wings that will not bear it to the clouds."

"No," replied Condorcet, in rather an animated tone, "the law to which I refer has greater power. It reminds man of what has been in his history, while you lead him to material Nature. He can only become perfect by that growth which lies in his will, and without which your machine of skin, bone, stomach, and nerves, remains but a puppet that has no yes or no. Give man a will, and power of progression, and he has at once lofty purposes—he mounts the horses of the sun, and reaches the limits of his hopes. The law of progress is so strong, that after its power has been fully recognized, he can perform miracles, and transport himself beyond the sea, with no such wings as you allude to. Materialism is a just idea if rightly understood—I admit that. Indeed, it involves wonderful facts—it will teach men to journey in the air, and, when thousands of miles from each other, they will correspond

swifter than an eagle's flight. Every one, as soon as he thoroughly comprehends the development of which he is capable, will lengthen his life by centuries." * The tall form of Condorcet swayed as he spoke, and a deep color suffused his face.

"M. Etienne Clavière has made his appearance," remarked Cabanis, drawing the attention of his friends to the short, corpulent, but active man entering at the principal door, and quickly working his way through the crowd. "The spirit of speculation seems to be in a great hurry," continued Cabanis. "You have a good opportunity to notice his importance; he advances with the assurance of a harlequin, who knows that with his entrance the comedy begins. There is your man of strength and matter! Materialism is not only the parent of atheism, but also of stock-gambling. What do you say to that, Baron d'Holbach?"

"You know I am always glad to see any thing new," replied Holbach, looking piercingly at Clavière's physiognomy. "Do I not go from one coffee-house in Paris to another to obtain knowledge? Priests and royalists call us heretics and children, because we consider certain human functions paramount; and now suddenly appear men who see mind in money only, and who worship at the stock-board. It is possible that they are a worthless rabble, who dissipate all cultivation, and who will finally turn society into a horde of swindling idlers. We must, however, cautiously discover what perchance is concealed behind those men of physical strength — whether they have any thing besides their impudence and the beggar's pride.—But Clavière is really making a figure. If I were not too old to prophesy, I would say: 'That man will one day become minister of finance after France has been revolutionized.' † However, let us take our places, and sit together, gentlemen, that we may exchange our opinions on passing events."

The whole assembly, consisting of several hun-

---

* Condorcet's "Esquisse d'un Tableau Historique des Progrès de l'Esprit Humain," a posthumous work.
† Etienne Clavière really became financial minister in March, 1792, through the influence of Brissot's party.

dred persons, took their seats around the table, and in considerable excitement, which was greatly heightened by the address that Clavière soon delivered, as to the meaning and objects of the night's festivity.

Clavière was a brilliant speaker, distinguished for bold and new thoughts, striking images, and a certain art by which he conquered the heart of his audience. He commenced by assuming the appearance of a very honest man, speaking of the necessitous circumstances of France, and which threatened the peace of society. Then, with a peculiar smile, he made prominent the utility of money in the state and among the people, because a just and satisfactory division of it was an expression of true harmony. Skilfully introducing American liberty, he explained how it had already begun to produce prosperity in that country of immense mineral and agricultural resources, while in France provisions were becoming scarcer and of worse quality, in the midst of a deluge of paper-money, in which all would long ago have perished, if a man of noble and creative mind had not used his judgment and influence in directing anew the financial affairs of the country.

This flattery, administered with great discretion, in reference to Calonne, who was sitting opposite the speaker, was received with applause, causing the minister's cheeks to glow, and eliciting congratulatory gestures from the courtiers near him. Even General Lafayette, who was well acquainted with M. de Calonne, and sat at his side, whispered agreeable words.

Clavière now passed on to a compliment on Lafayette and other officers present, known to have fought in the American war of independence, asserting that after France had taken such a conspicuous part in aiding the United States, by sending her best and bravest sons to her battle-fields, she ought to finish her work now in the name of all that suffer and are oppressed. The speaker went on to say that the society for the deliverance and civil equality of the poor slaves was formed in France through the activity of the Marquis de Lafayette; but that, unfortunately,

in this as in other cases, nothing decisive could be done without money—that large sums were necessary to lay a foundation at all adequate to the object in contemplation, which was to promote the abolition of slavery, and to continue the agitation of the subject, by pamphlets, associations, and a liberal outlay.

M. Clavière averred that a great deal of money must therefore be contributed to make even a small beginning; and that nothing is more characteristic of a man than the way in which he applies his gold; for if it is for a good purpose, he is good himself, and he who gives for the cause of freedom, must feel free himself.

"Money," said the Genevan, with considerable profundity, "is the sinew of life, and in your sinews live mind, ideas, and all that is divine, as one of the most distinguished and intellectual men of France, now honoring us with his presence, has well and truly said in a recently-published work."

"How very subtle this man is!" said Holbach to his neighbors. "He approaches us all in turn, and makes us a present of a paper of candy; but I have no confidence in him; he has not quite art enough to conceal his real purpose—for he brings us back too often and too zealously to pecuniary matters, about which, no doubt, he intends to sound a trumpet in honor of his minister and companion, M. de Calonne."

Clavière continued to remind the assembly that a good condition of society is characterized by the amount of money spent—the more the better. "The expenditure itself," he said, reproduces funds, as well as ideas, useful to society—economy is the worst financial system. That is the rock on which my great Geneva compatriot was wrecked while administering the finances of France. Necker's mind was the greatest of his time, and as such he must be recognized. He united financial and state reform, and at least endeavored to give the people political rights for the taxes imposed on them; but unhappily he misconceived in reference to economy as an effective remedy for the condition of the country, and thus he lost credit. No one could believe in a frugal minister of finance. Under a good administration the currency must be as abundant as if it descended in showers from the clouds—new paper must therefore often be issued.

"The beneficent genius of the French finances has the seat of honor at this table. When M. de Calonne entered on his duties, he found in the state treasury two bags containing twelve hundred livres opposite a six-hundred-and-four-million debt, and a yearly deficit of eighty millions. He immediately began by urging a loan of one hundred millions—a productive and wise idea. It is true loans have multiplied, but there has been no stringency in the supply of currency, and all the capital of the nation has been put in motion. In the present year (1785) one hundred and thirty-six millions have been issued in treasury notes.* Gentlemen, gold glitters in all corners of France; she has more to spend, and consequently will receive more. France will become rich, and her people free and happy!"

As Clavière uttered these words, immense applause resounded in the hall. Some of the guests cried, "Long live Calonne!" others, in stern voices, commanded silence. Clavière paused a moment, contemplating the excitement in the assembly with flashing eyes.

"He has actually brought out a cheer for Calonne already," remarked Cabanis in a low voice. "And the minister does not appear in the least abashed that his merits are trumpeted by one of his own agents. A man, such as he, has not much choice or modesty in his gratifications. There is some ambiguity, I think, in the flattery that money almost grows in the streets during Calonne's administration. It is true, such management, or rather mismanagement, of the public funds is designed to soothe our real misery for a short time —it is an attempt to blind the nation, under pretence that the treasury is overflowing. Calonne buys every thing merely to show that he is able to do so. Estates, castles, islands, forests, dukedoms, and I know not what, he has purchased for the state, and all without any reason for making these acquisitions. Any one desiring a state en-

dowment had only to say so, and he is sure to be received with open arms — all pensions are bestowed in perpetuity, and he that already has a life revenue may have it extended to all eternity. Even the most greedy and importunate courtiers are astonished at the blessings provided for them." *

Clavière saw that this was the proper moment to resume his speech, which had only been interrupted by its effect. "Economy is not wisdom!" he began again. "In financial matters it is an exception. In a good monetary system, I repeat, the currency must flow abundantly, as a river from its source in the impenetrable mountains. Gentlemen, our country, great and beautiful as she is, may congratulate herself on her return to a natural order of things. This idea the present era seems to recognize everywhere. Behold the mothers of France, who are generously beginning to nourish their own children, instead of intrusting them to the care of hirelings! A good government, if it wishes to be great and strong, must also exercise such devoted and beneficent maternal love on all its citizens!" He was again interrupted by boisterous applause.

"Now he drags Jean Jacques Rousseau's ideas of a return to Nature and maternal affection, into Calonne's financial swindle," said Baron d'Holbach. "What is to become of us in the hands of this rollicking fellow, who makes use of our convictions only to delude us? I suppose the next thing he will demonstrate is, that the real prosperity of France consists in the deficit of her finances."

"He that understands how to spend well and richly, has no consciousness of deficits!" said Clavière, just at that moment. "A non-defaulting administration would be a picture without shading. But painting, gentlemen, is the art of shading; and so financiering, to be perfect, must be mellowed by occasional losses."

"He is transforming his friend Calonne into a Raphael!" exclaimed Cabanis, rubbing his hands. The last flight of the orator, however, seemed

---

* Louis Blanc, "Histoire de la Révolution française," vol. i., ch. v.

* Louis Blanc, "Histoire de la Révolution française," vol. i., ch. v.

to cause some dissatisfaction, for many of the guests began to hiss; while others, with more politeness, complained that the public misery should be treated in so trifling a manner, and the well-known ruinous condition of France brought into ridicule by one who seemed to rejoice in his charlatanry.

Mirabeau entered the hall. Wherever he appeared he was sure to produce a sensation, but especially on this evening, and the eyes of all were turned toward him. He was very grave and pale, and could not repress a curiously sarcastic grimace, on hearing the last remark of the Genevan about deficits. He took the seat reserved for him at Clavière's side. The latter hastened to conclude his address, uttering a few brilliant thoughts, by which he successfully managed to unite his audience in full and favorable recognition of his opinions generally.

The banquet now really commenced. Several other orators, with shorter addresses, were heard. Mirabeau refused all invitation to speak, and seemed to have a little disagreement with his neighbor Clavière, who was endeavoring to urge him.

"When a man comes to dinner late," remarked Mirabeau, helping himself from the dishes before him, "he has to attend to other affairs than to display his eloquence. Besides, you have spoiled the business, Clavière, for the company do not seem to take kindly to your representation of deficits—many, in fact, seem to feel quite ill from the effect of your eloquent argument. I fear that I should only increase the excitement against us, for I see many opponents. I have already more enemies than I ever had in Paris, on account of my recent publications. Shall I tell you some news? The police are about to forbid the circulation of both my works, the one against the bank of discount and that against the Spanish bank—this is to be done at the request of my amiable patron himself, M. de Calonne."

"Who told you that?" asked Clavière, eagerly. "It was to remain a secret from you for a few days longer."

"The wife of M. the Minister just announced it

to me, in order to give me a proof of her friendship," replied Mirabeau, smiling.

"If she gave you no other token of regard, you are really to be pitied!" said the Genevan, looking at the other derisively. "Poor adventurer that you are! you must have had a dull interview with the fair lady, if you were occupied with state affairs."

"That is not my opinion," replied Mirabeau. "If you wish to obtain the good-will of any one, you must know how to treat him. Once I disputed about an Arabic grammar, with a person who had long lived in the East, and our very disagreement became a basis of true friendship. Madame de Calonne is one of the best ladies in existence, but I soon saw that she was prouder of being supposed conversant with state affairs, and competent to pass judgment on them, than of her beauty and her very pretty foot, which is one of her principal attractions. So I amused myself by conversing with her as I would with her husband. I asked her for news from the financial administration, and whether my two pamphlets on the question of stocks had received her approbation. At first she looked at me in apparent astonishment, and then burst into laughter. She said, looking charmingly important: 'I will show you, count, that I am in possession of a secret. Both your pamphlets will be dénounced, and confiscated by the police, and M. de Calonne himself has demanded this. I accidentally heard him speak about it, half an hour ago, with the lieutenant of the Parisian police.'"

"And did Madame de Calonne also tell you the reasons for this measure?" asked Clavière, in a very irritated tone.

"Of course, I pretended to be overwhelmed with sorrow, and I regret now that I did not ask for the reasons of this strange action of the minister."

The Genevan laughed aloud, but then said with some anxiety: "Speak in a lower voice, for Calonne (who is sitting opposite) has very keen ears, and I fear he may overhear our conversation."

"I am not concerned about that," replied Mirabeau, with comic naïvety. "He cannot possibly hear what we are saying. But why does he act so equivocally toward me? He first induces me to write those pamphlets, and then forbids their circulation."

"I am surprised at your not immediately understanding his intention," said Clavière, excitedly. "The minister has two objects in view, which I myself advised: first, he does not wish the Exchange to suspect that the opposition to stock-gambling—a movement you inaugurated so effectually—is permitted by him, much less that it owes its origin to his influence; secondly, he thinks that your works will be more effective when they have the charm of being obnoxious to the government."

A collection for the objects of the association had been proceeding for some time, and the plate approached Mirabeau; he took a well-filled purse from his pocket, and cast it in with some ostentation, so that the minister was attracted by the metallic sound. M. de Calonne nodded kindly to him, making inquiries about his health, and why he had kept away from the ministerial mansion.

The count replied, without the least embarrassment, that he would not have done so if he had known that his visits would be agreeable.

"I thought," said the minister, bending over toward Mirabeau, "I heard you speak with M. Clavière about your two pamphlets? Can you imagine such a thing, count, that the police intend issuing an interdict in reference to them?* It will probably be made public to-morrow, and unfortunately I could do nothing to prevent it!"

"I thank your excellency for your sympathy," replied Mirabeau. "The prohibition, however, will greatly increase the demand for the pamphlets, for we all find forbidden fruit the sweetest."

"Indeed?" asked M. de Calonne, slightly wrinkling his forehead. At this moment he remarked a ring, with a peculiar jewel, sparkling on Mirabeau's hand, and regarded it with increasing attention, apparently making great efforts to decipher the letters engraved on it. Involuntarily the count withdrew his hand from view, placing it under the table, and for a moment became visibly uneasy. The minister was disturbed in the curiosity which suddenly possessed him in so strange a manner, by a remark from his neighbor General Lafayette.

"I am afraid you have been very imprudent," said Clavière, from whose sharp eye nothing escaped, in a low voice to Mirabeau. "The ring you wear attracts Calonne's attention."

"He recognizes it," replied Mirabeau, smiling. "It belonged to his wife, who placed it on my finger at parting."

"That was to console you for the prohibition placed on your pamphlets, I suppose?" asked Clavière. "And, with your usual carelessness, you did not take it off on coming here! I beg of you, my friend, do so now, and conceal it for the present. Here, take mine, and put it on quickly under the table. If M. de Calonne approaches you afterward he will find that he was mistaken. I am anxious for a good understanding between you and him; he must raise you to the position due your talents."

The count shrugged his shoulders, but followed the advice of his more practical friend.

The banquet was over, and all rose to greet those they had not yet had an opportunity of accosting. Calonne had scarcely left his seat, when he hastily forced his way through the congratulating crowd and crossed to the other side of the room, where Mirabeau and Clavière met him. He received the compliments of these gentlemen very kindly, offering his hand to the count in an especially friendly manner. He held the latter's hand for some time, uttering the most flattering phrases, evidently examining the ring, and suddenly brought it nearer to his eyes, but looked surprised, as one disappointed in some sure expectation. He released Mirabeau's hand, and a few minutes after disappeared from the hall.

"I know him well, and doubt that he is altogether convinced," said Clavière, looking after the minister. "His suspicion is often assisted by

---

* Peuchet, vol. ii., p. 377.

a remarkable presentiment, leading him, even in business affairs, to the most concealed traces of what he desires to discover."

"I am surprised that a man of his character can be so unreasonably jealous," replied the count. "A general lover, such as he, is usually not inclined that way, and it is the more remarkable, as he does not pretend to have the slightest regard for Madame de Calonne. If his friends should happen to pay her compliments, he ought rather, as a man of the world, to be obliged to them. And if he does not appreciate his own gold, why should not others?"

"That reminds me, by the way, of the coinage of our louis d'ors!" laughed Clavière. "You are quite a financial genius, Mirabeau. I can tell you that the edict ordering the alteration of gold coin in France will shortly be made public. I have worked out the idea for the minister—the whole plan is mine. We shall remould the old louis d'ors according to a new scale, and hope to gain two, or one-fifteenth, on every thirty coins. Our dear public will easily submit to a small loss in the deterioration of the metal. But I think that any thing like deterioration in the case of Madame de Calonne would not exactly please the minister." *

"Let us resume our levity at some other time," said Mirabeau, taking leave, and turning to converse with other friends, among whom were Cabanis, Condorcet, and Holbach, who had been for some time awaiting his leisure.

CHAPTER XVIII.

THE MISSION TO BERLIN.

SEVERAL weeks later, Mirabeau sat in his room with Henriette, to whom he always returned with renewed affection. Contrary to his later habits, he had not left home during several days. He

* Louis Blanc, vol. II., ch. v.

seemed to be in bad humor, and his usually bright brow seemed to lower in vexation and despondency; he was seldom so much moved as at present, for his temper easily changed to any present impression.

Henriette was in her favorite position, on a tabouret at his feet, and engaged in some embroidery intended to adorn little Coco. From time to time she looked anxiously up at her friend, who was lost in thoughtful silence, hardly conscious of her presence.

"Mirabeau," she said at last, pausing in her work and touching his arm gently, "why are you so sad? I fear that some misfortune has happened to you. Why do you not give me a good scolding, and storm and rave around with your dear thundering voice? Or why not take a walk —go to a café—hunt up some friend and promenade the Boulevards, if you will not let me accompany you? How is it that you have not been to the financial bureau for several days? Rouse yourself! It is injurious to such a strong man to remain still."

"You are right," said Mirabeau, in a mellowed tone not usual to him, "I am wasting my time in idle melancholy—in I know not what thoughts, leading to no results. It is fortunate that you are by my side, Henriette; are you not at the same time my wife, my child, and my mother? You are careful for me, and your voice would encourage and rouse me. I thank you, for the breath of your ever-fresh lips reanimates me, and my soul already bestirs itself."

"Do you know, Mirabeau, that I would really be glad if you have no more business at the financial minister's?" said Henriette, beginning one of her cheerful conversations. "I do not think you gain any thing there in either temper or funds. At times, I confess, I have been really jealous of your visits at M. de Calonne's. I do not know why. You are accustomed to look so happy on departing; and when you say 'Henriette, I am going to the financial ministry,' I always console myself with the idea that you will soon be a rich man by means of your connections with the great monetary world; but nothing has yet come of it all, and you seem to be richer only in care and dejection."

"It is true," replied Mirabeau, springing up, irritably ; " I have now less money than ever, and I may thank this miserable financial business for it. The depreciated bills, of which Clavière gave me such quantities, and which were meant to pay me for my labor, have not again risen in value, but remain on my hands—mere packages of rubbish, with which the rats may build their nests. I sometimes fancy that I have been used only as a tool! They make me write against speculators and the Bourse, and promise me mountains of gold, but pay me in paper—the very trash that I myself aided in depreciating! Clavière tells me it is very deep strategy to become rich by what we do our best to render valueless in the market.

"These are Egyptian secrets, perhaps—but I have gone far enough in their solution. I, who detest speculation in my inmost soul—who see in it nothing but the degradation of society, and the moral and domestic ruin of the individual—must be used as an instrument for its defence!—must fight in the ranks and by the side of unproductive speculators, whom formerly I would scarcely have considered worthy of the honor of an insult. And why did I undertake such business? Because I was obliged to have something to do; I could no longer bear to remain idle, in shameful inefficiency, and dying from inaction. It serves me right that in my character of depreciator I have become intolerable to myself. And, to-day, my child, we may make a stew of our bank-bills for dinner, for I certainly do not know how we are to pay for it."

"You need not be alarmed on that point, my friend," replied Henriette, looking at him as if she felt pained, and secretly drying a tear. "You know I am a good housekeeper, and have saved a whole louis d'or of the money you lately gave me. I intended to buy a little present for you to surprise you, but now I am glad that my precious coin can come from its hiding-place to our rescue, Count Mirabeau. This is the last reserve." She hastened to her work-table, taking the gold-piece out of the drawer.

"That is a good friend, but unfortunately we must immediately dispose of it!" said Mirabeau, slipping the louis d'or quickly into his pocket with a very cheerful gesture. "Perhaps this may turn out a fortunate day for us, for when you find any thing unexpectedly, some other agreeable addition is generally made. You see misery has made me superstitious. Clavière promised to call on me to-day, to bring me the last intimation of M. de Calonne as to his intentions in reference to me. I am expecting him every moment with increasing impatience. I have sent word to the minister, that he must declare briefly and simply what he means to do for me, and if he does nothing, that I am weary of compromising myself any more for him and his financial intrigues. Not only do I gain no money, but by my writings I make a thousand enemies among the public, and not a single friend of any consequence in the *ministerium*. The opposition against me in Paris increases—my name and character are dragged in the most disgraceful manner into the journals ; and, what is most disagreeable to me, they refer to all the past sins of my life, and punish me in my private relations, going back so far as to reproach me with the abduction of Sophie de Monnier.

"I have just made a most cold-blooded opponent of Beaumarchais, the author of the 'Wedding of Figaro.' You know I published a small brochure last week against the new water company of Paris. I thought M. de Calonne desired to have arrested the excitement of the public for the shares of that company, because capital was withdrawn from the royal funds. The price of those shares had risen from twelve hundred francs to fifteen hundred and higher. I interfered, endeavoring to prove that the speculation, by which the Aqueduct Association were trying to accumulate their capital, belonged to the prohibited schemes of the Bourse, for it was involved in the late ministerial action forbidding any sales on time-purchase, and merely nominal values.* Now, this Beaumarchais, a speculator of the most reckless char-

* " Sur les Actions de la Compagnie des Eaux de Paris" (Londres, 1785).

acter, but belonging to the managing committee of this company, writes such a malicious reply, that I do not know whether I ought not to put my sword through his body. And M. de Calonne—since I broke this lance for him (if not for him, for whom else?)—does not admit me to his presence! I have not been able to see him for eight days; and now I have demanded a decisive answer through Clavière."

"What!" asked Henriette, in the greatest astonishment, approaching him, and anxiously looking into his eyes—"you have not spoken to the minister for eight days? Yet you went several times to his residence at the beginning of this week, and told me afterward that you had long interviews there. Did you speak to some one else? Are there any pretty ladies in the financial mansion? I have made inquiries on the subject, and was told that Madame de Calonne is very beautiful."

"You have broken your promise, my child," replied Mirabeau, threatening her playfully, putting his hand on her lips, and covering her cheeks with kisses. "You solemnly promised me, a short time since, not to be jealous, and now you have fallen into a relapse. If I told you that I was at the house of M. de Calonne, you may rely on it; I was really there, and if I held conversations, they were important, even if the person to whom I addressed myself was one next in authority to the minister himself."

Without replying, Henriette stood at the window, looking thoughtfully and doubtfully into the street. Then, on hearing a carriage approach, and seeing it stop before the house, she exclaimed: "M. Clavière is descending from the equipage—he is coming to pay you a visit. You must, however, permit me to absent myself, my friend; you know I do not deserve to see him, for I do not recognize his perfection. Besides, I have some necessary things to attend to, and will depart." She took her hat, and, after Mirabeau had kissed her repeatedly, she hastened away as fast as possible by one door, while Clavière entered as quickly by the other.

"At last!" exclaimed Mirabeau, impulsively.

"You have made me wait a long time, Clavière, and yet you know I am the most impatient man under the sun—my mind and body tremble to hear the decision!"

"That is why I hesitated to come!" replied the Genevan, clearly out of humor, throwing himself into a seat and remaining silent.

"You do not look like a messenger of good news," said Mirabeau, anger becoming visible on his countenance. "I suppose, the minister will do nothing for me. Well, then, let him fear my enmity!"

"He offers you a secret mission to Berlin," replied Clavière, "but he cannot give you a position in his bureau, and he will not use his influence for you here. In fact, he desires to have you removed from Paris."

Mirabeau stood a few moments with folded arms in the centre of the room, meditating. At length he said, vehemently: "Tell me something more about matters and things, Clavière!"

"Your affairs are in a very bad condition," the latter replied, "and all without doubt by your own fault!"

"The minister does not like my argument against the shares of the Aqueduct Company?" asked the count.

"It did not please him," said Clavière, "nor did I like it. We have paid the printing expenses for it, but M. de Calonne considers them as so much money thrown away. You were too violent, my friend, and have exposed many weak points to our opponents. The minister wished to have the public warned against this new speculation, but it does not suit him to have the originators of the enterprise, especially Messrs. Perrier, personally attacked as swindlers and cheating stock-jobbers. M. Constantin Perrier addressed himself to my chief, and succeeded, it seems, in changing his opinion, for the ministry intends to purchase one hundred shares of the company. M. de Calonne and his colleagues talk of nothing but the national and patriotic value of this scheme, and the minister himself is enthusiastic for the use of the steam-pump for the first time to come into practical use at this aqueduct, and for which the brothers Perrier have proposed many improvements." *

"You may go where you please with your financial ministry!" cried Mirabeau, passionately. "Does this Calonne think that the steam-pump will force all the gold of the Pactolus into the Seine? If he had told me so sooner, I would have been quite as charmed as he is with this new invention. But why does he wish to send me to Berlin? Is it possible that any man can have a secret mission to that city?"

"For some time past Prussia has attracted the attention of King Louis XVI.," replied Clavière, dryly. "A change of monarchs is soon expected there. The great King Frederick II., who has raised his obscure kingdom to a brilliant and powerful position, will soon have disappeared from among the living. It is desirable to know something of the intentions of his successor in reference to France; besides, it would be well to have a correct and more intimate knowledge of the circumstances of this suddenly exalted country. The French government wishes to estimate anew its position in Europe, and M. de Calonne proposed to send you, that you may give us authentic reports about the court of Prussia, as well as her resources and ideas. For the first month you are to receive two thousand francs, and the rest will be arranged afterward."

"To go to Berlin would not be so very disagreeable to me," said Mirabeau, after a pause. "I am disgusted with my residence in Paris, and I long to see other men. A fresh breeze, even from Brandenburg, would be grateful to my fevered brow. But, before I say any more, explain to me why Calonne desires my absence?"

"I never expected that Count Mirabeau, the hero of the future, would ever act in such an innocent manner," replied Clavière, rather petulantly. "But you carry your simplicity too far. I have warned you often enough, telling you that Calonne is jealous, and, besides, has the keenest faculty of discerning men's manners and motives."

* Peuchet, vol. II., p. 388.

"I have not visited Madame de Calonne for several days," said Mirabeau, evasively.

"Because she declined to receive you, my dear friend!" exclaimed the Genevan, with irony.

"Ah," replied the count, "M. Etienne Clavière appears to be well informed, not only of what occurs in the office of the financial minister, but in the boudoir of his wife."

"I never could understand your conduct in this whole affair," said Clavière. "At a public banquet you openly wear a ring, just received from a lady whose husband sits opposite you, and before whose eyes you expose it in such a manner that he is almost enabled to decipher the letters (to him well known) engraved on it. Calonne was not deceived by our manœuvre. His suspicion was aroused, although, according to his self-possession, he allowed no one to perceive it. I imagine, however, that some violent scenes have lately taken place between him and his wife, for she could not show him the ring he asked for, which was a present from him. Madame de Calonne feels that you have shockingly compromised her, and that is more dangerous for you than the minister's anger. He will avoid making any public demonstration from political motives, but he desires your absence from this city. We shall lose your pen, which would have been of great use to us; but, mark me! the lady will avenge herself—she is an Italian, and be careful how you cross her path again."

"Very well," replied Mirabeau, calmly. "I accept your proposal. Do you make all the arrangements, and I shall be grateful to you. I am off for Berlin. To-morrow, if you please, I shall be ready to start with my whole family."

"Yes, to-morrow," said Clavière, "for if you accept this position, the minister desires you to depart immediately. I will prepare all that is necessary to-day. Farewell, Mirabeau! I am sorry that we lose you in this manner; indeed, I am so greatly troubled that I almost feel disposed to call you to account for your folly."

"We shall meet in another way than with powder and lead," said the count, with a shade of melancholy. "We intended to accomplish a great deed; but it is not yet evening for either of us. My conduct separates us, but the tempest is coming that will bring us together again. Then we must support each other."

"It cannot be long before that period," said Clavière, with greater heartiness than usual, embracing Mirabeau. "In the mean time let us be busy with preparatory matters, and when you return, you will take your rightful place as master and leader of the movement! I hope the new financial plan I have worked out for Calonne will please you in your capacity of political sapper."

"What are your projects, at present?" asked Mirabeau, looking at his friend in a very significant manner.

"We mean first to deliver a memorial to the king, preparing him for Calonne's new system," replied Clavière, ardently. "This petition will demand nothing less than a complete remodelling of the French monarchy; and I can fancy the astonished countenance of good Louis XVI., when the spendthrift Calonne suddenly appears before him with the austere language of Turgot, Vauban, and Necker. France, hitherto divided by provincial and state privileges, is to be directed anew, so that she shall be a unit. She is to have a national representation. Taxes are to be decreased, and not paid, as formerly, by the citizens only, but by the nobles, the church, and

9

even the king. Justice and unity must reign in this country, and all privileges, differences, and distinctions, cease forever. Will that satisfy you?"

"I profoundly bow to you and Calonne!" cried Mirabeau, with solemnity. "It is true you still step very softly: you bind up the talons in cotton, for the national representation may be compared to cotton. But you will go farther, will you not, and give the talons their natural play? We must have pain ere we can have pleasure!"

"Mischief will come, but in good time," replied Clavière. "However, let us not stop to prophesy now; it is probable that I shall return to bring you more precise orders; for the present, adieu!" They shook hands, and Clavière quickly left.

"To-morrow we go to Berlin!" exclaimed Mirabeau, as Madame de Nehra entered. His voice had not sounded so cheerfully for a long time, and all the depression Henriette had essayed in vain to disperse had disappeared.

"To Berlin?" asked Henriette, standing in the doorway in surprise, and lookingly smilingly at the changed appearance of her friend.

"To Berlin!" repeated Mirabeau. "Prepare every thing. My whole tribe (as I always call you) accompany me—Countess Yet-Lee, little Coco, and Miss Sarah!"

CHAPTER XIX.

THE JOURNEY FROM PARIS TO BERLIN.

On the evening of one of the last days in December, 1785, a carriage, driven by a postilion, was passing slowly over the public road leading from Toul to Verdun. A heavy fall of snow obstructed the progress of the travellers. The route lay for some miles along the banks of the Meuse, and on its surface the moonbeams were trembling. It was midnight when the party entered a forest, whose stillness was broken occasionally by the sound of parting branches, or the hooting of an owl, in dismal keeping with the scene.

Those within the carriage were asleep; but the dog lying at its master's feet, uttered repeatedly a low howl, by which the young lady, dozing in one corner, was so often disturbed that she resolved to remain awake, and, after carefully and affectionately looking at her neighbor, wrapped in an enormous fur cloak, as well as at a little boy lying in the arms of his nurse on the opposite seat, she leaned her head out of the window. Her beautiful eye wandered over the forest, shimmering in the light, and her imagination transformed the trees into many curious forms.

"You are really unbearable," she whispered, bending over the dog, that again began to whine. "I believe you are afraid of this solemn forest. Do you see spectres, foolish Sarah?" But Henriette herself seemed to feel disquieted. With a hasty movement she put her head farther out of the window, but immediately withdrew it. Mirabeau's hand had accidentally fallen upon her lap, and she turned to him, as if waiting for a confirmation of some fear that possessed her, but seeing him so deeply buried in sleep, her anxiety was allayed. She looked out again on the landscape, and was so charmed with its beauty, that she felt disposed to blame herself for evil thoughts, and for being alarmed at her own fancies. At length, she could not help believing that dark figures were gliding around the carriage, and passing away into the darkness of the forest, again to appear with threatening glances at her and her companions.

"They must have been branches of trees, like this one," thought Henriette, breaking off a twig glittering with ice that had been forced into the window as the coach passed by. She seemed assured of her safety, as she glanced at her sleeping Mirabeau, with his vast strength and courage. "But I will remain awake, and watch," she said to herself, with regained confidence, looking out into the bright night. She almost fancied herself the guardian angel of her companions, now and then smiling at her friend and little Coco, who, by their regular breathing, showed how little they knew or cared about what was passing in her mind.

At this moment a pistol-shot was heard, entering the carriage from the bushes, and harmlessly passing through the opposite window.

"My friend! Some one is shooting at us!" cried Henriette, in a loud and terrified voice, clinging to Mirabeau, who was not quite roused until she shook him violently. Two additional shots were fired almost at the same time. One of the balls struck the interior of the coach, fracturing the door, and falling to the ground. Henriette's movement in awakeing Mirabeau was probably the cause of her escape. The dog howled fearfully, while Coco mingled his cries with the agonizing screams of Henriette and the nurse.

After Mirabeau recovered from his astonishment, he first examined the child to assure himself of its safety. Then he said to Henriette, with a slight shudder: "They were not highwaymen, for people of that description have more experience in their profession. If they had wished to rob us, they would not have fired three shots and then disappeared. They would have troubled us a little more, and at least defrayed the expense of powder and ball. They are mere amateurs, and have been hired to murder me; but they are very clumsy performers, and I wager a thousand to one that a woman is at the bottom of it."

"Is it possible?" exclaimed Henriette, with another shriek, clinging closer to Mirabeau. "You can protect us? You must, I know, have left bitter enemies in Paris, but I cannot comprehend why the ladies should desire your death. No, my friend, you merely imagine that. Why should they persecute you? Besides, I am sorry to say, you are not such a woman-hater, Mirabeau, that you could have slighted them. You know how often you have excited my jealousy!"

They now noticed that the carriage had turned round, leaving the public road and driving across a field-path, which probably led back to the village whence they had last started. The count called to his servant; but he was not at his post. The postilion said that he intended to return by the shortest route, as he knew the forest was unsafe. Mirabeau's servant seemed to have been driven by terror to take refuge in flight. No denunciation or entreaty could dissuade the postilion from his resolution; he only drove more rapidly, so that there was fear of being overturned every moment.

"And you really suspect that a lady hired some assassin to kill you?" asked Henriette again overcoming her alarm. She was meditating on the strange words the count had uttered. Her natural shrewdness betrayed itself; for when Mirabeau was a little disconcerted and hesitating to reply, she added, softly: "I have been told that Madame de Calonne is very beautiful, and she is said to be a native Italian."

"And what does that concern us, my child?" replied Mirabeau, laughing, but regretting that he had betrayed himself by his first imprudent exclamation.

"I have often read of the vindictiveness of Italians, and that they run to the dagger or poison, when they fancy themselves insulted," said Henriette, inclining anxiously toward Mirabeau. "Might not one of them make use also of pistols?"

"No, my love, I do not think so," replied the count, dryly, to this very ingenuous question, at the same time kissing her repeatedly, this being the easiest way to silence her.

They were driving so violently over the snow, and into the deep ruts, that the shaking and swinging of the coach made it difficult to converse, although Henriette was still deeply engaged with her subject, and seemed to have many questions on her mind.

"No, my child," said Mirabeau, after a pause, beginning to feel pity for her uneasiness, "there are no pretty ladies in Paris who could have cause for taking such revenge as to fire at me among the forest snows of Verdun. And it could not have been a homely lady, for I never give one of that class much reason to avenge herself. Besides, I assure you, Madame de Calonne is not handsome. Her nose is too long, her eyes are gray, and utterly hateful to me, as you know that color is, and on her thick lips a demon and not a Cupid might be supposed to dwell. I do not understand how your fantastic jealousy could select such a woman as that. I could hardly recognize her, having seen her but once at an evening party. Shall I tell you the name of the lady who hired those assassins? It is Accident, which I have ever considered of the feminine gender, coquetting with all and conspiring against them. Accident always persecutes me. When did I ever leave home without falling into danger on the road? Think of our voyage to London,—when, almost in the harbor, we came near being wrecked through the agency of this same lady, Accident."

Although Henriette was not quite satisfied with this explanation, she dismissed the matter from her thoughts, for the carriage was at the post-house, where every one was in great wonder at what had happened. Mirabeau's servant, pursued by fear, had reached the village before the coach, and thus the news had preceded the return of the travellers. He stood ready to open the door and assist the count to descend.

Mirabeau, in his powerful voice, immediately demanded the presence of the post-manager, and when this official appeared he was ordered to supply another postilion, or force the one present, who had returned against the wishes of his passengers, to continue the journey.

The postilion replied with oaths that he would not go by the same road, as the forest was filled with robbers and murderers, and he would not expose his horses and his own life. It was in vain to represent to him that no further attack need be feared, since the assassins must know that the authorities would be informed. But the driver persisted in his refusal, and, at length, the travellers were informed that they could not resume their journey for some hours, because the wheels of the carriage must be repaired, if they did not wish to break down on the road.

Mirabeau was obliged to yield, though not without many expressions of anger. The nurse and Coco were provided for in one of the small rooms, but the count and Henriette preferred to walk up and down before the post-house, awaiting the hour of their departure. The sky, in the clear, cold atmosphere, presented a most brilliant spectacle, and Henriette, sometimes looking up with a sigh into the infinite space above her,

pressed closer to her friend's side, who had partly thrown his fur robe around her delicate frame. She began to cough violently, for the fatigues of this journey plainly affected her health, which for some time had been very feeble.

"Tell me, Mirabeau," she said, after a short silence, "why you are in such a hurry? I do not complain on my own account, for I can bear a good deal; and in such an hour as this, when I walk beneath the starry heaven with you, my only beloved—separated from all, but united with you—my anxiety and suffering are compensated. But I fear little Coco's health will be endangered by this journey, if we travel by night."

"He is four years old," replied Mirabeau, lightly, "and I intend him to be a hardy, strong man, and he can only become that by early habit. He is not so badly off; he is well wrapped up, and his nurse, who continually carries him in her arms, is a stout Provençal peasant-woman, who shares with him her healthful warmth and vitality. However, I will tell you why I am in such a hurry," he continued, after a pause, his eyes glancing upward. "I travel fast, because the great men of the earth are like those stars. We behold, and, as it were, worship them; but they disappear, carrying all their glory with them."

Henriette, not quite understanding him, leaned her head on his breast, and looked at him with searching eyes.

"You regard me with astonishment," he continued, "and do not know that I am speaking of a great king in the North—to whose capital we are travelling—Frederick the Great. Before we started it was supposed in Paris that he was dying—his brilliant life is as that morning star, which will soon vanish. We are hastening to him, for I must see him before his departure. It is a blessing when the eyes of the great behold us in their last moments.

"The condition of Europe will change as soon as Frederick has ceased to live. That red aurora on the horizon yonder may remind us that the dawn of a bloody era is at hand. We must know the position France will occupy, and therefore we hasten to Berlin. Our government cannot trust the ambassador sent to the court of Prussia, because he is weak and a blunderer. It is necessary that the death of Frederick the Great should not only be immediately announced by a courier, but that just and decisive remarks on the condition of things in Prussia and Germany should accompany the news. That is the reason, my sweet friend, why we hasten to Berlin by forced marches, through night and storm, cold and danger!" Henriette was about to kiss his hand, but he pressed her ardently in his arms.

As the morning dawned the carriage was announced ready, and additional compensation being promised to the postilion, he had no further scruples in driving the count and his family to Verdun. They passed Nancy, Frankfort-on-the-Main, Leipsic, and finally reached Berlin in safety, on a bright January day in 1786.

CHAPTER XX.

THE MESSAGE TO SANS-SOUCI.

COUNT MIRABEAU temporarily took up his residence in the Ville de Paris, one of the best hotels in Berlin. It was situated in Brüder Street. It did not answer all his expectations, but he was told that he could find nothing better in the capital of the King of Prussia, which seemed to be behind other large cities in outward elegance. In fact, Berlin appeared to him and his companion at first like a desert; but as the count saw and heard more, his impressions were modified.

According to his custom, he passed the first day, even before attending to any business, in walking about the streets, to comprehend the city in its details, and make the acquaintance of its general every-day life. While Henriette remained at home, and endeavored with her usual skill to give a home look to the dark, many-cornered rooms assigned them, Mirabeau, in his activity, was running through the town, strolling into odd-looking places, loitering about the gates and the zoological garden. He went among the

people as much as he could; and, although he had difficulty to make himself understood in his imperfect knowledge of German, he managed to exercise his usual extraordinary art of questioning. He knew so well how to interest any one that came in his way by his interrogations, that there was no escape from his inquisitiveness. His manner was flattering, and the person addressed could not help feeling attracted by the burly catechiser.

He happened to meet an artisan on the Kurfürst Bridge, in front of the iron statue of the Great Elector. This man became the count's guide and companion through many a street and square, instructing him in the manner that just suited Mirabeau's character and present humor, and giving him much desired information. The stranger was a shoemaker, carrying on a stick a row of boots and shoes to his customers. The count, who had a peculiar talent in placing himself on a familiar footing with persons of this man's class, met the honorable disciple of St. Crispin resting himself, by placing his burden on the railing around the statue, and quite ready to enter into a political and patriotic conversation. The artisan, it is true, could not exactly tell who the Great Elector was, and Mirabeau could not help thinking of the lower classes in Paris, who generally have a thorough knowledge of every historical monument in their city. However, the shoemaker knew that the man on horseback had been a very brave and God-fearing man, who caused the French in his day considerable trouble; but all he had done was nothing in comparison with the great deeds of the "Alten Fritz," who gave them an awful whipping at Rossbach.

Delighted with this frankness, which added to the peculiarities of a man of the people of Berlin, was exceedingly amusing, Mirabeau asked him whether he was aware that he was talking to a Frenchman. This question did not in the least disconcert the shoemaker—he merely raised his cap with an ironic side-glance, smiling very good-naturedly, and said: "The foreigners here are almost all Frenchmen; one can easily recognize you by a certain genteel nonchalance, as you stroll through our thoroughfares; you always act as if nothing could come amiss to you. And then you mangle our dear German so miserably, at the same time putting on an air of such suffering, that you seem ill, and we feel like sending you immediately to the hospital to be cured."

"Your remarks are not flattering, my friend, but they are edifying," replied the count. "And if you have no objection, I should like to ramble in your society through this goodly city. Afterward you will return with me to my hotel, to take my measure for a pair of shoes, for I have arrived in a rather dilapidated condition as to my feet, and I think that the sharp Berlin pavement requires a strong sole."

The man was perfectly satisfied with this arrangement, making, however, the condition, that the way must go by the houses where his customers lived, and where Mirabeau would have to stay outside until the shoemaker returned.

The count was always in a cheerful and excitable humor when he first found himself in a new city. He accepted the bargain, and was especially delighted when his friend told him that their first walk would be to the residence of the minister of foreign affairs, because a pair of shoes were to be left there for M. de Hertzberg himself.

"Why, that is a very happy coincidence," said Mirabeau, laughing, and drawing out a pocket-book, to assure himself of a letter contained in it, which this name brought to his recollection. "I discover now where M. de Hertzberg lives; I have a letter of introduction to him from Paris, and will leave it with one of my cards at his house, so that he may appoint an audience. I should not be sorry if the minister would also give me something to do, for although, unfortunately, I am no shoemaker, but only Count Mirabeau, I know where the shoe pinches the governments of Europe, and I could give him some sound advice as to how Prussia, if she would only wear lighter boots, might become the first state on this continent. Do you not think so, M. Cordonnier?"

"My name is Sommerbrodt," replied the shoemaker, with perfect self-possession. "You are a count, and I a cobbler. Is it customary in your country for two persons of such different ranks to promenade the streets together without any ceremony?"

"People in France have not made so much progress yet," replied Mirabeau; "but the day will come when such associations will be made, first from policy and afterward from choice! Here in Germany, my friend, I believe you are much in advance of us, and if you would, you could soon surpass all other nations in fraternity and equality."

"I do not quite understand you, count," said M. Sommerbrodt, with a cunning smile. "You advise us to wear lighter boots, in order to advance more rapidly? Your French shoes are not so bad—I must even admit that they are vastly superior to our work in many respects. I remained in Paris for a time, during my travels as a journeyman, and I learned a great deal there; but I did not acquire the knowledge of manufacturing seven-league boots, for I do not think you could go much faster in them than in your light-leather pumps, however well you may understand the trade. I will, however, make something extra for you, count, if you give me your order—not with strong soles, they would not suit you; you have a well-shaped and small foot, and I will serve you so well that our bad pavement shall do it no injury."

"Excellent!" exclaimed Mirabeau, rubbing his hands with delight at the acquisition he had made in his new acquaintance. "In your company and with your shoes I should like to wander through all Germany; for I am desirous of knowing something of the whole of your country. I can tell you, M. Sommerbrodt, that I have always wished to gain that knowledge. Germany reminds me of the fairy-tale of the twelve sleeping virgins. How many states have you in your country? I believe more than twelve, if any one will take the trouble to count them."

"O yes," said the shoemaker, laconically, and he pointed proudly to the royal castle before which they were passing.

Count Mirabeau stood with folded arms to contemplate this splendid edifice, which especially attracted his attention. Master Sommerbrodt expressed his satisfaction at the interest the Frenchman took in it, and permitted himself to tap the count familiarly and approvingly on the shoulder.

"As to your twelve sleeping virgins," he continued, with a crafty smile, "you are wrong in likening the states of Germany to them. There are probably more than thirty, and their chamber is called the German empire."

"Your Prussian royal castle is large enough to unite them all, whatever their number, under its roof!" said Mirabeau, thoughtfully, still looking at the building. "And that is the Spree, over which we passed, is it not, my friend, on the other side of the palace? So if you could entice your maidens into the castle, you would not have far to go to baptize them. Your Spree is very patriotic, for it kisses the feet of the royal residence; and you dignify this little murky streamlet by calling it a river."

"Do not speak lightly of our Spree, count, for we regard it highly," exclaimed Master Sommerbrodt, with comic zeal. "The river reflects our national character: it flows as quietly and free from trouble as the thoughts of the natives of Berlin, and we rather like its muddy color. You cannot so easily measure its depth, while your Seine reveals many a sad story of your follies and sorrows."

"You are, I see, a judge of national peculiarities, M. Sommerbrodt," replied Mirabeau, laughing. "But your king, the great Frederick, on whose account I have come to this city, never dwells in this castle?"

The shoemaker shook his head, and replied: "You must go to Potsdam and Sans-Souci, if you wish to see Old Fritz. That is his home, for he never felt at ease here, much as we love him and desire his presence. The old gentleman will probably never feel well again in this world. He has conquered all his enemies but old age. Field-Marshal Gout is said to afflict him. His stick cannot ward off this foe; indeed, for several days we have heard very bad reports about the king's health."

"Then I suppose there is little prospect of seeing him, if I announce myself?" asked Mirabeau, continuing his walk.

"Latterly, he is said to have given audience to no foreigners," replied Sommerbrodt. "But since you are a Frenchman, it is very different. Those of your country are always men of rank, and it is an honor to be acquainted with you. Your countrymen are welcome wherever they may go. Old Fritz still likes to see them, and I wager that, even at the point of death, he would give audience to a Frenchman."

"And does the condition of his majesty really cause anxiety to the inhabitants of Berlin?" asked Mirabeau, earnestly.

"I can tell you," replied the shoemaker, somewhat mysteriously, "that things are going on badly at Sans-Souci. If you will wait for me outside the house of Minister von Hertzberg, I will bring you the most authentic news. His excellency is in Berlin to-day, and has always shown himself condescending toward me. We have had many a political conversation together, and he tells me all I desire to know. Others probably will not have such good opportunities of hearing the truth in this matter, because the ministers would rather keep it secret, and not let the public know what they are to expect."

"I will not trouble you to do so, Master Sommerbrodt," said Mirabeau. "It is high time for me to request an audience with your king, and I would rather return to my hotel, which is not very far from here. I will immediately write a letter to his majesty, and send it by express to Sans-Souci.—But you must not forget to call at the Ville de Paris and ask for me. I not only look forward with pleasure to the instruction I am to derive from your visit, but must beg you to take my measure for a pair of shoes, which must be something superior, as I intend to wear them at my interview with the king. And now, since I have asked you so many questions, permit one more. How is it that all the citizens we have met wear blue coats—I see that you wear one yourself?"

"That is not difficult to answer," replied Sommerbrodt, the smile disappearing from his countenance, and a solemn expression taking its place. "It is the color of the Prussian army, and we citizens and artisans prefer to wear it. We then believe ourselves dressed like our king, with whom we are always ready to enter the field, or perform any service he may require of us. Our blue coats show that we have our place in the king's army; besides, this is the color representing fidelity, and we feel ourselves every day more attached to our royal family."

"I respect such patriotism!" said Mirabeau, saluting the citizen in a friendly manner, and quickly returning to his hotel.

Henriette received him joyfully, showing him with a triumphant smile how far she had succeeded in unpacking and arranging, and rendering the rooms comfortable. The count, however, soon hastened to his desk, and, taking a sheet of paper, wrote:

"SIRE,—It is doubtless too presumptuous a hope to demand an audience of your majesty, especially when no affair of importance or interest is to be discussed. But if you will pardon a Frenchman, who, since his childhood, has been accustomed to hear of your fame, and who desires to see the greatest man of this or any other century, then condescend to permit me to come to Potsdam and do homage at your feet.

"I am, with the most profound respect, sire, your majesty's very humble, obedient, and submissive servant,

"COUNT DE MIRABEAU." *

After reading this note to Henriette, who had no fault to find with its flattering and careless tone, he placed it in an envelope, and rang for a waiter, whom he ordered to find a reliable man to send to Sans-Souci. Such a person was present in the hotel, who soon appeared before the count. The messenger's outward appearance betokened a pitiable and starving condition, as he stood with sad and downcast eyes to receive Mirabeau's orders.

"Who are you, and what is your name?" the count asked quickly, looking searchingly at the pale, drooping countenance, and the clean but

* Literally from the original.—"Œuvres de Frédéric le Grand," ch. xxv., p. 323.

threadbare dress of the man, who was considerably advanced in years.

"I am the ecclesiastic candidate Johann Ludwig Schmidt," he replied, in a timid voice. "I am also a poet and a critic," he added, with a slight tincture of self-appreciation.

"Ah," said Mirabeau, with an involuntary smile, "then this is a mistake, for which I must ask pardon. I cannot possibly commission a man belonging to the German Parnassus to carry a letter for me to Sans-Souci."

"I undertake all commissions and errands of the Hotel Ville de Paris, and the proprietor vouches for their execution," replied M. Schmidt, in a modest but decided tone.

"And why is a man of your talent not in a better situation?" asked Mirabeau, surprised. "Is it customary in Germany for intellectual men to act as servants?"

"Oh, I pray you," replied the candidate, a burning spot or two appearing on his hollow cheeks, "I am very well contented in this house, although perhaps there might be an improvement in some respects. I was tutor to the children for many years, and after completing their education I remained here as book-keeper; I also write the bills of fare, and go on errands. I still have leisure to write an occasional contribution to the *Berlin Monthly*, published by Messrs. Biester and Gedike."

"And are you really contented with such a lot?" asked Mirabeau. "If your poetry is creditable, and your criticisms advance good taste, why does not your great king do something for you—he is in a certain sense your colleague?"

"Pardon," replied Schmidt, "the German Muse is no pauper—she would not beg even of the king. But she will celebrate him as soon as the hero's eyes are closed in death, and with all the ardor and strength of which she is capable. I have already commenced an ode in Sapphic metre, and as soon as the sad news from Sans-Souci reaches us, my poem goes to the printer, and I hope it will be the first that appears in a German journal."

"What, are you in such a hurry?" exclaimed Mirabeau, in astonishment. "Well, then it is high time for you to be on your way with my letter, for it is my intention to see the king before his death. Hasten, take extra horses at my cost, and liberally pay the postilion to take you quickly to Potsdam. At Sans-Souci you will have yourself announced to one of the adjutants of his majesty; tell him that you are sent by Count Mirabeau, who requests to have this letter immediately placed into the hands of the king. You may also add that Count Mirabeau has brought a packet of books for the king from his friends in Paris. I require a reliable man, who knows all about Sans-Souci, for my servant does not speak a word of German, and is besides too awkward for such a commission—your countenance gives me the greatest confidence in you."

The messenger took the letter with many profound bows, promising to forward it immediately, and was about to leave, when the count called him back. "I wished to make a suggestion to you," said Mirabeau, "but it is in reference to your qualifications as a German poet and critic. You might daily read an hour in your language with me, and instruct me in its refinements. I feel the necessity of becoming master of the German; and you, Henriette, must join me. It is true, I studied this language with Cabanis, who commenced to translate into French a dramatic work of Goethe, I believe it is called 'Stella,' but I have found to my sorrow that, in the streets to-day, I could not converse even with a shoemaker—an educated man, by the way, for it seems artisans are such in Berlin."

"Then we shall read the 'Hamburg Dramaturgie,' by Gotthold Ephraim Lessing," exclaimed Schmidt, with sparkling eyes.

"I see you are the right man for me," replied Mirabeau. "You begin immediately with your Lessing, who, as I have heard, disputed so valiantly with our poets, and used, as it were, David's sling against our boastful court poetry. But, you must know, that I consider myself as working in the same direction—to combat old and existing things is my trade. Now go, my friend, and the better the news you bring the greater your compensation."

"I feel curiously here in Prussia," said Mirabeau, after a long pause, when alone with Henriette. "This country must be well studied to be understood—that must be now my task, and I shall devote all my time and strength to it. I will write a comprehensive work on the Prussian monarchy, There is a vast deal of intellect here—when I think of it, it almost makes me shudder. I made to-day the acquaintance of a shoemaker on the street, and he showed as much wit, understanding, and logic, as a member of the French Parliament. To-night we shall go to the theatre. Even if you do not understand the language, you may learn something, and you will see many sensible faces around you."

CHAPTER XXI.

MIRABEAU'S VISIT TO FREDERICK THE GREAT

THE letter Mirabeau sent to King Frederick was very favorably received, and answered on the following day. The king, in an autograph letter, appointed a very early audience at Sans-Souci, accompanied with most friendly and gracious expressions. *

Mirabeau felt more impatience than he ever remembered before, during the interval between the reception of the king's missive and the day for the interview. The count postponed all the visits he intended to pay, until after his return from Potsdam. He would be able to plan more decidedly his movements in Berlin, after his audience with Frederick the Great, as he would be guided by the impressions it would make on him and the hopes it would awaken. The only exception he made was in reference to Minister von Hertzberg, to whom he sent his letter of recommendation, and was received by that much-deserving and highly-cultivated gentleman on the same day, in the plain and simple manner that was so natural to him.

---

* "Œuvres de Frédéric le Grand," ch. xxv., p. 323.

The long-desired day at length arrived, on which Mirabeau was to approach Frederick the Great, behold his countenance, and hear his voice. Henriette, as usual, assisted the count in making his toilet, fancying that it ought to be very choice, but he insisted that he would only appear as he generally did in polite society in Paris. This was in a black coat in the English fashion, which required neither gold, silver, nor embroidery. As to his shoes, Master Sommerbrodt had honestly kept his word, and delivered the pair ordered of him early in the morning ; they were of the best workmanship, as he said that he did not wish Berlin to be behind Paris in the art of shoemaking.

At Henriette's entreaty, Mirabeau finally consented to wear a slightly-frizzled toupee, together with a cue. She sportively said that, in presence of so great a king, the count must not appear with his natural mane, but at least make a pretence to respectability and custom. Mirabeau gave way to her with a certain good-nature, although it was his intention to be as unrestrained as possible. After surveying him with pleasure, Henriette hung his eye-glass around his neck, which was indispensable to him, for, when not holding it to his eyes, he was in the habit of playing with it, so that he felt at a loss without it. *

The conveyance the count had hired to take him to Potsdam had arrived, and Henriette, quite proud of his appearance, accompanied him to the door. He travelled as fast as possible along the bad roads, arrived at the appointed hour at the palace, and entered without delay, passing but one sentinel at the gate. This impressed him so ludicrously that he could scarcely believe he was visiting a king, but some colonel or captain of the Prussian army.

Mirabeau inquired for Major-General Count von Görtz, as he had been requested to do in the king's letter ; and the sentinel pointing to a corridor, he passed through it hesitatingly, so solemn and silent did it seem. Then he reached a large hall, where sat a Prussian officer, warming himself at a large fire, who arose as Mirabeau entered, and, looking piercingly at him, approached a few steps, and returned the count's bow with a stiff military salute. To the inquiry for Count von Görtz, he made himself known as that gentleman ; and when Mirabeau introduced himself with some ceremony, M. von Görtz became very cordial. The count understood the formality of the general's military position, while he appreciated the honest and brave character indicated in his countenance.

Von Görtz remarked that he would have the honor of announcing Count Mirabeau to the king, and disappeared by a door at the other end of the hall. On his return, he said that his majesty would appear at the entrance of his cabinet in about a quarter of an hour. Mirabeau asked whether a packet of books which he had sent by mail the preceding day had arrived, and whether they were already in the hands of his majesty. Count von Görtz politely replied in the affirmative, adding that the king had ordered him to thank Count Mirabeau, and had expressed himself very curious to know what accident had brought a traveller like him to Berlin. *

Mirabeau's impatience prevented him from continuing a conversation with Count von Görtz, who was fortunately rather taciturn. When asked in a low voice whether the reports relative to the king's health had any foundation, the latter answered with a shrug of his shoulder. Then he added : " I think that the resolution his majesty took this morning is a bad sign ; he does not intend to be present at the military review to be held this year. This is the first time he has made any acknowledgment of his illness ; if it were not for that, there are moments, every day, when one would think that neither ill-health nor old age could bow his noble mind."

After the expiration of a quarter of an hour, the door of the adjoining cabinet opened, and the king appeared for a moment. Mirabeau scarcely saw the slight motion of the hand, but M. von Görtz told him, softly, that it was an expression

---

* Vide Rachel.—" A Commemorative Work," vol. ii., p. 65. Rachel describes Mirabeau's personal appearance as she herself saw him in Berlin.

* " Œuvres de Frédéric le Grand," ch. xxv., p. 394.

MIRABEAU AND FREDERICK THE GREAT.   p. 139.

of his majesty that he was ready for the audience. M. von Görtz then took Mirabeau's arm to introduce him to the king.

The self-possessed and confident ease of manner usual to the French count, almost forsook him when he found himself in the immediate presence of the great monarch, who received him with a quick, searching glance, replying with a nod to a really reverential obeisance.

The small bent figure of Frederick, who could scarcely support his trembling limbs by leaning on his stick, made at once a depressing and an elevating impression on Mirabeau. In a sort of dreamy embarrassment he looked at the king, on whose head, bowed by age and disease, he thought he saw all the glory the world can give, and he felt deeply moved. At first the count was surprised at the small stature of Frederick, and the necessity of looking down on him was by no means pleasant, but he soon felt like one much inferior to the monarch he came to admire; he recognized an imperial genius in the expression of Frederick's features, to which his weakness and suffering seemed rather to give additional interest.

The king, immediately on the entrance of Mirabeau and the general, made a sign to the latter to withdraw, which he obeyed, leaving the two alone in the royal cabinet. The count had been told in the anteroom that when Frederick wished to distinguish any one he granted him an interview without witnesses. The monarch sighed audibly as he sank into his arm-chair, near the hearth, pointing to a sofa, on which the count seated himself.

"Your visit, count, finds me a poor patient," the king began, in a full and strong voice, contrasting strangely with his decrepitude and illness, "But I could not withstand a greeting from France, although I am hardly in a condition to enjoy it. You have sent me some beautiful books from Paris, and I thank you; but I miss one which I sought eagerly among them. My friend, the Marquis de Condorcet, sends me pretty things, but not his 'Life of Voltaire,' which it is natural I should desire to see. Not long ago he wrote

me that it was completed; why does he keep it from me? Do you know—"

A violent cough interrupted the monarch, and when he began to speak again, his words were more indistinct and uncertain. Mirabeau, during these attacks, could not very well reply, and he improved the opportunity by noticing more particularly the sick king and his surroundings.

Every thing in the cabinet was arranged so unostentatiously that Mirabeau might have fancied himself in the study of one of his literary friends in Paris. The walls, instead of displaying extravagant pieces of art, were lined with shelves laden with various works. A small table was covered with books and papers, and the only ornament in the room was a gilt clock on the marble mantel-piece.

After surveying the simple furniture of the room, the count's eye returned with renewed interest to the wonderfully affecting aspect of the king. The coat Frederick wore was of the same color as Mirabeau had before noticed in the dress of the citizens, but it was exceedingly shabby and faded; his vest could not in any manner be considered clean, being literally covered with snuff. His top-boots, reaching above the knee, did not add much to his dignity, but partook rather of the grotesque. The count, however, acknowledged to himself that he was not altogether disappointed in his expectations, for the great intellect of the king was not obscured in a *physique* so oddly and meanly clad, and so anxiously endeavoring to husband its last vital resources.

Frederick, who had almost recovered from his painful fit of coughing, cast one of his piercing glances on Mirabeau, which seemed to fathom his character. There was a singular union of goodness and mischief, of mildness and irony, in Frederick's blue eye, and the count could not easily resist its power.

The king seemed now to expect an answer, and the count replied in a more reverential manner than he ever before assumed toward any one: "Sire, I feel myself happy in being graciously permitted to name myself among my great countrymen who sat at your feet, and heard your voice, although I do not merit so enviable a privilege. Condorcet has finished his 'Life of Voltaire;' it is now in press at Geneva, but seems to have been delayed. My friend wrote this book with continual reference to your majesty, for who could treat of Voltaire without endeavoring to gain the favor of the 'philosopher of Sans-Souci?'"

"Ah," replied the king, slightly smiling, "very soon nothing will be left of the so-called 'philosopher of Sans-Souci.' True philosophy seems to consist in coming to terms with physical disease, and retaining sufficient intellect to keep a cheerful countenance, notwithstanding one's sufferings. I hope, however, that our friend Condorcet has exhibited that scamp Voltaire in all his vagaries. I loved him, it is true; but I hated him also, and I could with pleasure have seen him hanged. He would make a bon-mot on any circumstance of his life, and mock at mankind wherever he found them. How often he made me laugh; and yet I am ungrateful enough to wish that he had brought up on the gallows, as I do on my crutch-cane!"

"Sire, Condorcet's book, I think, will not be a gallows on which to see Voltaire hang," replied Mirabeau, beginning to feel more at ease, and frankly smiling. "The object is to celebrate the ideas of liberty entertained by the great thinker, and this is adapted to the impartiality of Condorcet's mathematical brain. Prussia and France are not uninterested in the life of the 'philosopher of Ferney,' and thereby show that they are at the head of European nations, and commissioned by Providence to herald the new social era. In my country the people have accepted Voltaire's thoughts; in this advancing Prussia, it is the king himself who aids in disseminating them, thus manifesting his affinity with the French nation."

"That sounds well, spoken in your language, count," said Frederick, his head inclining on his breast, apparently meditating for a moment. He continued: "Abstract ideas do not warm us very well when we are old, and we seek vitality from other sources. An impracticable philosophy is tolerable so long as we have any thing to hope

for in its application; but when we have nothing left to look forward to, we become eminently practical. I am constructing turnpike roads through my country, draining marshes, making uncultivated tracts arable, and imitating the English in their artificial meadows. I am also gladdened with the success of my manufactures, having sold last year to foreigners linen amounting to six million dollars, and cloth to a million and a half. I have another favorite object which I will mention to you. I have ordered three hundred sheep from Spain, to improve the breed here. Can you imagine that I am anxious for the arrival of these animals, and cannot depart in peace before I see them? Yes, I am sometimes obliged to laugh at myself; for formerly I expected the visits of the philosophers and intellectual men of France with an impatience similar to that concerning my Spanish sheep."[*]

Mirabeau bit his lip at this remark of the king, fancying that it was intensified by an ironic twinkle in his majesty's eyes, but said quickly, and with all the courtier's deference: "This idea of your majesty is admirable. You are endeavoring to improve your sheep by this importation, but the intellectual men of France endeavor to ennoble the human race; and you, sire, have made use of them for that purpose. A wise king cannot be indifferent as to whom he governs, and Prussia has become a progressive country under your rule. Several years ago you abolished or ameliorated vassalage in some of your provinces, but we have not yet broken a single slave's chain."

"And what may be the object of your residence in my states, count?" asked the king, turning the conversation.

"Sire," replied Mirabeau, in a lively manner, "my object is gained in the admiration I feel for the prosperity of your majesty's states. I have appointed this place as a rendezvous for my brother, the Viscount de Mirabeau, who asks your permission to be present at the military reviews at Berlin. As to myself, I am completely ruined in

[*] Hertzberg, "Mémoire Historique sur la dernière Année de la Vie de Frédéric II.," Berlin, 1787.

my prospects in France, although I have performed important services in the financial department. Our minister of finance, M. de Calonne, hates and even threatens me, because I would not meddle with his last loan, nor defend his desperate economy of recoining our gold money; so I resolved to leave France until she should desire to recall me and appreciate my labors. This hope may be foolish, but it arises from my situation. I am forced to depend on my industry, and whatever talent I may have, so long as my father is alive, who will not share his fortune with me. These, sire, are also the reasons why I would accept with thanks a suitable position in a foreign country. I had an idea of going to Russia, and offering my services to that undeveloped country. I would not have thought of this, if your government were not perfect in its organization, so that I cannot hope to be useful to your majesty, which has been my favorite idea—my earliest ambition —but the troubles of my youth and the miseries of my native land always prevented the execution of my wishes." *

The king listened attentively, and remained silent for some time after Mirabeau ceased. He then replied: "It is possible, count, that you may do well in Russia, and I advise you to go there. I have no doubt that my fair and virtuous cousin, the Empress Catharine II., can appreciate your talents. I dare not deprive her of any more Frenchmen. She was irritated because Voltaire did not altogether belong to her, but still remembered his old friend the King of Prussia. If she should suspect that I had prevented Count Mirabeau from visiting St. Petersburg, I would have reason to fear her. You appear to me to be likely to gain the favor of the czarina; you are intellectual and muscular, and she has a special regard for such men—they soon rise at her court. I suppose, however, that you would have to conceal your opinions. Do you not think so ? "

Mirabeau began to tremble, as usual, when he

thought he could no longer control his passionate temper. He plainly struggled with himself, and, after overcoming his emotion, his countenance was comparatively calm, and indeed cheerful. With an appearance of ingenuousness, he asked: "What are opinions, sire ? So long as absolute states and tyrannic governments exist, opinions must be dressed in one uniform. I am, for example, a sincere friend of the Poles, and love that unfortunate nation with all my heart, but I am far from referring the dismemberment of Poland solely to Russia's barbarity and a tyrant's lust of power. There are historical events to be attributed more to surrounding influences than to the action of one individual; and during the excitement, the noblest are often hurried by outward pressure to the commission of unworthy deeds. Now, the division of Poland was not exactly the work of honest men, but it was done, and who is to be held responsible for it ? "

The king frowned, and looked down gravely and thoughtfully. His breathing was irregular and difficult, and he seemed distressed. Mirabeau was almost sorry for what he had said about Poland, but it was from a feeling of resentment at the manner in which Frederick had commended him. The king's appearance suddenly changed fearfully, for he seemed older and weaker than at the beginning of the interview. The count indeed wished to be dismissed from a presence that made such an impression on him. Frederick replying in a gasping manner, Mirabeau, for the first time, observed that age had deprived his majesty of all his teeth, if not of a desire to utter insolent words.

"It is a pity when a nation is ruined through its own fault," said the king, endeavoring to raise his voice. "For in no other way does a state cease to exist. If the Polish men had been like their women, their government would have been firm to-day, for the latter manifested an astonishing strength of character, and I consider the women the men of that country.* What future can a nation have that, boasting of freedom, is

<hr/>

* Mirabeau, in a letter to Frederick the Great, dated Berlin, January 26, 1786, explained more particularly the pretended purposes of his residence in Prussia.— Vide "Œuvres de Frédéric le Grand," ch. xxv., p. 325.

* The literal words of Frederick the Great.—Vide Ségur, "Mémoires," vol. ii., p. 136.

enslaved? A people broken up into parties—so intoxicated by a lawless freedom, that the veto of a single man in the Diet was sufficient to break down the popular will—such a national existence could only become food for other and more vigorous states, who naturally prey upon it for their own benefit. I am also an admirer of the Poles, count, but only of the women. I would never have given my consent to a suppression of the Polish ladies." The jesting tone which Frederick was endeavoring to give the conversation, appeared so ill-timed and sad, that the count could not immediately join in it. He was silent, and, after a pause, the king continued: "Tell me something of the Marquis de Lafayette, who paid me a visit last year, and left me the most agreeable recollections of his presence. Is it true that he has bought a plantation in Cayenne for the sole purpose of liberating the negroes on it?"

Mirabeau confirmed this, adding a few words of explanation.

"I am very glad of it; it pleases me!" cried the king, with an expression of liveliness. "Frenchmen are both intellectual and amiable, and we may be sure that you do that which is refined and benevolent. To buy an estate merely to free the slaves has something noble in it—it shows a great and wise heart. Yes, to have slaves is hardly right—and yet I have slaves over whom I am tired of reigning—who have grown under my feet, wherever I have turned, and when I neither sought nor desired them. The bondage of mind and character in a civilized country is worse than that of the body. Give Lafayette my greeting when you meet him in Paris. He was with me in Silesia to review my troops, and, with the Duke of York, we have often dined together. Tell him that I well remember those days."

Mirabeau bowed, and looked with renewed astonishment at the king, whose eyes now beamed mildly, giving to his whole physiognomy a kind and hearty expression.

"I shall rejoice the hearts of many in Paris by my letters, sire!" said Mirabeau. "Your majesty's admirers will learn from them that your health is much better than they were led to suppose, and your intellect is as fresh and vigorous as in former days."

"Oh, no," replied Frederick, shrugging his shoulders, "do not sketch me to my friends in the French capital different from what I really am. My strength becomes every day less—my gouty limbs have gone forward as an advance to the shores of the Cocytus, and my mind will very soon follow. In other days, I did sometimes manage to gain a victory with a ragged and exhausted army; but this poor body of mine cannot long maintain its position—I must soon submit to the most humiliating retreat I have ever made. All my members are in open mutiny; and when the foot will no longer execute what the head considers for the best, the whole organization must soon disappear. You may tell all my friends that I am about to retire from the battle of this world."

"But perhaps your majesty would not despise our physicians?" said Mirabeau. "Many men, distinguished in the healing art, might be of great service to you, sire. I venture to mention my friend Cabanis (whom Voltaire loved), as worthy of your honor and confidence. He is at the same time a thinker and a physician, uniting a childlike manner with an heroic mind, and as easily combating the diseases of the human frame as those of the nation and the age. The German medical men are not philosophic enough, and therefore cannot probably assist your majesty in the establishment of your health."

"I thank you, count," replied Frederick. "Do you not know that I consider pharmacy as mere quackery? My physicians have always had a difficult position with me, and I have often played them great pranks, for in the year 1785 I had such good health that I could do much without endangering it. I was accustomed to overcome any attack by the use of rhubarb, sulphate of soda, and emetic tartar, while the doctors bored me with their prescriptions about diet, and really made my illness worse. The physician who tried to prevent me from indulging in my favorite dishes, polenta and eel-pasty, I considered a charlatan. As to your medical philosophers I have had no lack of them. My poor Lamettrie once recommended a certain Nymphean syrup, and it really cured me. He wrote the natural history of the soul, and attempted to prove that man is nothing but a machine. At last, his syrup lost its effect, and Lamettrie died in consequence of an indigestion, having eaten too much of my eel-pasty, fancying that he could do all a king permitted himself. I will tell you something more, count. I have sent for the celebrated Knight Zimmermann, who is a philosophic physician, and I am curious to see how the author of ' On Solitude ' will treat the solitary king. I am the kind of patient he ought to have, for I am very ill and lonely." The voice of the king became inaudible, and in such a peculiar manner that Mirabeau approached the easy-chair of Frederick. He had fallen asleep. This was often the case, from the day his health began to fail. Bowing his head on his breast, his breathing was heavy and obstructed, and he seemed to be in pain.

The count left the cabinet softly. At the door, he turned to contemplate the powerless figure of the great monarch. It made him tremble to think that that small man, the picture of decrepitude and suffering, was Frederick the Great, and he hastily withdrew. Entering the anteroom, he mentioned to Count von Görtz what had happened in the cabinet. The latter remarked that it was of frequent occurrence, and considered one of the worst symptoms by all interested in the king's health.

Mirabeau did not feel much like himself until he gained his carriage, awaiting him at the foot of the palace, and felt the fresh air on his burning brow. He asked the postilion to be driven back to Berlin about as fast as he had been to Sans-Souci in the morning.

CHAPTER XXII.

THE CHINESE MAGIC LANTERN.

Count Mirabeau was domesticated in Berlin. He had left the hotel, and for several weeks dwelt in a private house, in the street under the Linden —a residence which he had arranged in quite a grand style. He also purchased a brilliant equipage and several horses, for it seemed necessary to maintain a proper position in the capital of Prussia. He had also increased the number of his servants, and in his cabinet two secretaries were continually at work. Even old Schmidt, who taught the count German, had found his way there, and was very useful, having become the literary errand-boy of his French patron, for whom he procured all the materials required from German works.

Madame de Nehra, as usual, when Mirabeau began to launch into extravagance, entreated him to restrain himself, but her petitions were less than ever regarded. He seemed to have a fixed plan as to his actions in Berlin, and this high manner of living was a part of it. Henriette, who had repeatedly witnessed the sad consequences of his lavish expenditure, wept many a secret tear.

But, on the other hand, the count led a more active and fatiguing life than Henriette had ever before known him to do; this was a new cause of anxiety to her. After moving about all day either in Potsdam or Berlin, making various acquaintances, paying visits of all kinds, and working a few hours with his secretaries, he seldom retired at night, but sat generally until early dawn, unceasingly writing. Daylight often surprised him with his pen or book.

One night Mirabeau was as usual at his studies, having given special orders that he was not to be disturbed. He had returned about midnight from a party at the residence of Councillor von Dohm, one of the most eminent officials in the ministry of foreign affairs. He slept one hour, and then found himself sufficiently refreshed to return to his desk. It was one of the coldest nights. The frost was upon the window-panes, and the fire, kindled an hour before, had burned low. The valet had been positively forbidden to attend it, because the count did not care to overburden those serving him. He himself was but scantily clothed, having on a quilted dressing-gown, but wearing neither vest nor stockings. He appeared, however, to feel so comfortable that he continued his work with a rapid pen.*

Suddenly, Mirabeau heard a slight noise at the fireplace, which, at first, he did not care to notice particularly, but, as it was regularly repeated, his attention was at last attracted. He looked up hastily, and beheld, to his great surprise, a snow-white figure bending over the dying embers. He was perplexed, but immediately rushed toward the object sitting on the floor, and with his powerful hand lifted up a trembling and sighing woman, whom he recognized, first angrily and then laughingly, as no other than his faithful friend Henriette.

"Is it you, Yet-Lee?" he exclaimed, reproachfully, while he carried her to the sofa and gently laid her down. "Against my express desires and entreaties you would rise, and almost frighten me by your spectral appearance!"

"And you almost choked me by your terrible grasp, my restless friend—you give quiet to no one about you!" said Henriette, still trembling with excitement. "I was only about to make a little fire for you. The servant would not brave your anger, because you had forbidden him to enter your cabinet. That is the reason I arose, thinking that I would rather be scolded by you than let you suffer cold. Besides, I hoped you would not notice me in your profound abstraction, and, I might as well confess it, I have been keeping your room warm in this way for five nights; but now you have caught me!"

He took her in his arms, covering her with kisses, and said: "You are cold yourself, in your light robe, and you wish to warm me, whose veins are burning with politics. In the sweat of my brow, I am writing down in cipher all I heard last evening at the house of M. von Dohm, and have to dispatch it early to-morrow morning to M. de Calonne at Paris. Such work makes me warm, and I rather desire cold. But now, child, you must return to your room without any contradiction, for I cannot permit you to remain here longer. A writer of secret dispatches, and

particularly in cipher, is a terrible creature, with whom a lady of heart and sentiment should not have any intercourse. Now, go; no fire shall be made here to-night."

"You will have your way in every thing, despot!" replied Henriette, pouting, and leaving the sofa. "But I declare that I will not go unless you allow me to kindle a fire. If I had known that Berlin is so frosty a city, I would have advised you not to come here. And the cold no doubt is increased by the faces of the inhabitants; if you only see one, he makes your arms, feet, and nose freeze. In such a city you propose to sit up all night and write in a room without heat! No, friend, a fire you shall have, and, if you had not interfered, it would have been burning brightly long ago."

"Well, let me tell you what we shall do," said the count, laughing. "I cannot remove you without physical force, and as I wish to finish my report as soon as possible, let us make the fire together—it will be done more quickly. Now, let us go to work, Yet-Lee." He went to the hearth, and Henriette followed; but laughed at him when he looked helplessly about for wood and coal.

"I concealed my wood here yesterday," she said, like a triumphant child. "There it is behind the closet, and because I could not bring it out softly enough, I made that foolish noise, otherwise you would have known nothing about it. I will hand you the billets, one after the other, but make as little noise as possible, for Coco sleeps in the adjoining room."

They knelt before the fireplace to begin their work, but Mirabeau was so awkward that instead of hastening he retarded it, and delayed the return to his desk. Henriette, however, was soon in a good humor, when she saw that the count could not place one stick of wood properly upon another.

"And now tell me on this occasion," she said, "what you can have to say about Berlin in your many dispatches to Paris. I could not find enough to fill two pages of note-paper. What in the world can it matter to France whether the

* From the unpublished memoirs of Madame de Nehra, and Montigny, vol. iv., p. 343.

old King of Prussia is still alive, whether the heir-presumptive has many debts, how many times Prince Henry sneezed, and whether M. von Hertzberg, that tedious gentlemen who paid you a visit not long ago, is a friend of France or not? All these affairs ought to be as indifferent to Louis XVI. as they are to me."

"If you were right, the world would be much better," replied Mirabeau, busily engaged with the fire. "But in the present state of politics, the most insignificant circumstances are the most decisive. I report to my government nothing but worthless stuff, that any valet de chambre could tell them just as well; but here is the difference —a servant judges from his point of view; I, from mine—and probably we both come to the same conclusion."

"But when you returned from your visit to the old king at Sans-Souci, you were greatly moved, and wrote your dispatch to Paris in a very grave and solemn frame of mind," remarked Henriette, casting one of those admiring and enthusiastic glances full upon him with which she generally regarded him when thinking herself unobserved.

"At that time I felt like one who had caught a view of what is usually invisible to the human eye in the process of creation and dissolution," replied Mirabeau, gravely. "I had seen human greatness in all the humiliation of decay. I thought I felt the presence of an irresistible destiny, whose progress we cannot mark but by final results. The letter, containing the details of my visit to Frederick the Great, and addressed to Messrs. de Vergennes and Calonne, is said to have made a deep impression on the King of France; so Clavière wrote me. Louis XVI. was especially struck with the passage where I mentioned that in Prussia all was ripe for a revolution. This idea I deduced from my conversation with the king." *

"And why must there be any commotion?" asked Henriette, pausing a moment in her work.

"It must be," replied the count, "because this state is called to play an important part in the future history of Europe. It must become a free state, or sink to ruin; in its fall it will bury the independence and well-being of Germany. This King Frederick was a great man; he has sowed among his people the seeds of a liberal national existence, and they must force their way up, although he may have cut off the first sprouts. Had Frederick governed with his intellect only, the standard of freedom would ere now be waving from every height in this country. But he was also controlled by his feelings—by a contempt for human beings in general, and for Germans in particular—and this led him, both from convenience and ill-humor, to bind upon his state the strait-jacket of his imperial will, and use his subjects as he pleased in a mere government mechanism. Nevertheless, he has in reality promulgated the law of liberty throughout Prussia, and he alone could prevent its practical development. After his death will arise a storm that cannot be calmed, and it is of the greatest importance to France to know what will become of this country. Austria can be bridled by Prussia only—that hated empire, which gave France a trifling and illiberal queen. If not counteracted, Austria will satisfy its desire for conquest first in Germany and then in other countries! You see how necessary it is to pay attention to even the smallest indication of progress. The condition of Europe requires a close union between Prussia and France, and to prepare the way for it is the task I have set myself, rather more than my government expects me to perform. Louis XVI. is said to have been pleased with my intimation as to a revolution in this state, but he has not fathomed its true meaning, for there can be little joy for him and his equals in such a change.* My idea is, that when liberty to the human race has been sounded in Prussia, the freedom of France must necessarily follow, if the two countries are united!" The count hastily sprang up and walked the apartment, leaving Henriette to finish making the fire.

"It will not burn to-night," she at last said, in an irritable tone. "Come, Mirabeau, and help me blow the flame, for you have lungs with more

---

* These words of Mirabeau are published in the work "De la Monarchie Prussienne," vol. v., p. 357.

* Vide Condorcet, "Mémoires," vol. ii., p. 72.

strength in them than all the bellows in Berlin."

He laughed, but bent down to aid his friend, for her breath was quite exhausted. Not long after, the fire was burning merrily, casting its red glow upon their countenances.

"And now, my love, I thank you for the trouble you have taken," said Mirabeau, intending to dismiss her with a slight pressure of his hand. "I have much to do to-night, for, after finishing my cipher dispatch, I have to add the last paragraph to my pamphlet on Cagliostro and Lavater, as I have to send it to the printer to-morrow. Then I wish to see whether I have sufficient materials for my work on the Prussian monarchy; and, if so, to arrange them—or, to explain in a few words, I intend to divide it into certain heads, and when I have decided on them, it will be easier for me to know what I still need, and on what particular points I desire to obtain information. But now retire, Yet-Lee, my midnight star! You are the confidante of all my plans and hopes, but there is no necessity for your companionship in these severe labors."

Henriette looked dissatisfied, but slowly departed into the adjoining room. Mirabeau seemed sorry at her departure without a more tender farewell. She returned when she heard her name breathed softly and entreatingly. "You must not think that I shall always be so busy," said the count, taking her head between his hands. "No, Yet-Lee, I shall shortly be, I hope, a very considerable man, and then we can have as much leisure as we please, and shall never be away from each other. I am already becoming rich. I am earning money from the French ministry, for the more they understand the services I alone can perform for them, the better they will pay me. On that point Vergennes and Calonne are trustworthy."

"My friend," replied Henriette, bowing her head, "you spend ten times more than you receive from Paris, for you do not appreciate economy, and soon you will have to borrow. I am afraid you are doing so already. Were not three Jews in your study yesterday, with whom you had a long and warm conversation? Without doubt you desired to borrow money from them, and, I suppose, you have discovered that the Jews in Berlin are as hard to deal with as those in Paris."

Mirabeau laughed aloud. "What a comic mistake on your part, my child, and what an insult to the gentlemen that called on me yesterday, and whom you mistook for usurers, ready to lend money on undoubted security! My good Countess Yet-Lee, they were the most distinguished of the Israelites in this city, asking me, as a deputation, to write in their favor, so that their condition as citizens may be ameliorated. Among them was the highly-respected Dr. Hertz; he may be a Jew, but he has a most polished presence. I have really taken a liking to him; he is a physician, and a man of high intellect, like our Cabanis, and his eyes and eloquent lips betray a brave heart. It would make me very happy if I could always associate with such persons. The Jewish community in Berlin have many such remarkable men. You meet among them bold and energetic intellects, ennobled and refined under the pressure of circumstances. The spirit of the venerable Moses Mendelssohn, whose writings I have begun to read, rests upon this community, and has given them a dignified and spiritual demeanor, and their conduct shows that they would do honor to any position, if the sovereign could only consent to treat them as human beings.[*] The capital of Prussia contains in them an important element, and I would almost prophesy that this race will one day become the ruling power. Not as a royal residence, but as the home of the Jews, will Berlin gain preëminence; and to have a good position in society here, it may perhaps be necessary to treat their religion with respect."

"And did you promise to write in their favor?" asked Henriette, looking at the count with a doubting smile.

---

[*] Mirabeau's words in reference to the Israelite community in Berlin.—Vide "Sur Moses Mendelssohn, sur la Réforme politique des Juifs," etc., and "Lettres sur Cagliostro et Lavater," in the "Œuvres de Mirabeau," vol. iv.

"Why not?" replied Mirabeau, amused at her curious expression. "These friends in Berlin fancy that whatever I write for them will be more favorably received because I am a Frenchman, for the Hebrews and the French generally have a sort of affinity, so that one may always reckon on the assistance of the other. I have no time to write any thing new or comprehensive, but I will compile a treatise in which I shall embody the pamphlet of M. von Dohm on the civil amelioration of the Jews."

The count took his seat with such a business air that Henriette knew he was really in earnest, and she dared no longer stay. After she left, he continued his work more rapidly than ever. His pen glided over the paper quickly, and nothing disturbed the silence save the crackling of the flames on the hearth. For several hours he did not even raise his eyes from the sheets he was filling with so much haste. When the dispatch was finished, and he had once more glanced over it, he folded and addressed it to Clavière, by whom it was sent to Vergennes and Calonne. He looked at his watch—the morning had come; but this did not cause him to cease his labors. Placing the dispatch on a table, ready for the courier, who was expected shortly, he passed on to other business, for which he seemed to have a greater liking.

A loud knocking was heard at the street-door, and urgently renewed, as no one was ready to attend at such an early hour. It immediately attracted Mirabeau's attention, and thinking that it might be an important message, he awakened his valet Boyer, in order to send him down and see what was wanted.

Boyer returned accompanied by a man whom the count recognized at once as one of his couriers, who appeared to have just returned from Paris. He handed a letter, saying that it was of importance, and that he had been ordered to deliver it as soon as possible on his arrival in Berlin. The address was in the handwriting of Clavière.

After making himself acquainted with the contents, the count found, to his no small astonishment, that his presence was suddenly required in the capital of France. The minister of foreign affairs, Count de Vergennes, was so anxious to see Mirabeau, that his departure was requested the same day on which he received the communication. Clavière intimated that the reason for this recall was, that the last accounts received about the court and the political condition of Prussia had made a profound impression on the French government, and that Louis XVI. and his ministers having exchanged opinions on the subject, it was desirable to have Mirabeau present, so as to be able to question him personally.

The count mused a moment, and an unusual cheerfulness took possession of him. He sent off the courier, intrusting him with the dispatch, and, as he would arrive in the cabinet of the minister of foreign affairs several hours earlier, he was ordered to announce the count's immediate arrival. He then called for his valet de chambre, to have his toilet attended to.

Madame de Nehra also appeared, having been awakened by the noise in the house, and suspecting a sudden departure of her friend. She rushed toward him, clung to his arm, and asked, almost breathlessly, whether she had heard correctly of his going to Paris, and when he would return, and whether it would not be better for her to accompany him.

Mirabeau tried to calm her in the most affectionate manner, but did not permit the valet to be interrupted in his duty of dressing him. He informed her that she and Coco would have to await his return quietly, as he was obliged to travel very fast, but hoped soon to have settled the important state affairs concerning which he was recalled, and would be back in four or at most six weeks.

Henriette was silent, but Mirabeau noticed the tears she was endeavoring to conceal. After he was fully and carefully dressed, he sent away Boyer on matters pertaining to the journey; then, approaching his friend, who was standing at the window, he embraced her and kissed away her tears, while she regarded him gravely and doubtingly. "Only be of good courage, Countess Yet Lee!" he said. "We soon meet again, and I shall be more cheerful than you ever saw me be-

fore This recall proves that the French ministry
is beginning to appreciate me. In Paris the authorities have finally discovered of what value to
them are my observations and knowledge of state
affairs as well as my insight into the real necessities
of the times. I will give my government all the
information it may desire, and show how in Prussia a‘party may be organized of great assistance
to us.   An alliance of France, England, and
Prussia, would give a new and successful turn to
European politics."

"And what thanks will you receive for all your
labors, Mirabeau?" asked Henriette, slowly raising her eyes.

"It will be seen," replied the count, stamping
on the floor, "that not to appoint me to a distinguished position in the service of the state, is
not consulting the interests of France! Is it not
a shame that a man like Count Esterno is ambassador from our government to the Prussian court?
That empty and unstable man, who knows and
hears nothing—who has no heart or head, eyes
or ears, for the advantage of his country—cannot
possibly remain here if my ideas as to a new
foreign policy receive any attention. I would
accept this place myself as soon as my views are
adopted.* I could make amends for the neglect
of my predecessor, and I am sure that is the intention of those who now send for me. I have
made myself necessary to them here, although I
would take any other position in Germany where
I could work for France according to my own
opinions."

Henriette cast down her eyes, shaking her
head at the exciting hopes of her friend.

"You may rely on it, this time, child," continued Mirabeau, "for has not the government
already shown itself liberal to me in money matters? I cost them much more now than as a
regular ambassador. The original sum for my
monthly expenditures was one thousand francs,
but this has been raised fivefold. I have, of
course, many extra expenses: our manner of
life, the expense of dress at northern courts,

the equipages and horses, without which no
cavalier can take a suitable rank in Berlin, cost
money; then, I have many private outlays, in
making journeys to different parts of Germany, to procure materials for my work. The
King of France, who undertakes to pay me from
his privy purse, will certainly soon have to increase my salary.* But in return I give him such
a thorough knowledge of the Prussian state, that
the future of the whole German empire can be
directed at Paris according to the pleasure of our
government."

Henriette asked, with a heavy heart, at what
hour Mirabeau intended to depart. He replied
that he would certainly leave in the evening—
perhaps sooner, if he could return in time from
some necessary visits he had to make. She left
the room to attend to her domestic affairs, and
make preparations for her friend's journey. Half
an hour afterwards she called him to breakfast.
Sitting opposite Henriette at the table, and endeavoring to amuse her by cheerful conversation,
he was asked why he was attired so early in his
choicest and most elegant suit, as about to attend
a court levee.

"Not exactly that," replied Mirabeau, lightly,
"but I intend to visit Prince Henry, the old king's
brother, for I do not think it advisable to return
to Paris without once more confidentially conversing with his royal highness. You know he
was a friend of mine, and guided my steps on
this new ground, giving me many hints how I
could further the interests of France in Prussia.
However, I do not know what his personal opinion of me may be at this moment. I must have
a definite word or two from him before I go, so
that I may have something important to announce
at the council to which I am called in Paris. I
am the more anxious to see the prince, because I
was told by a reliable person, at the party last
night which I attended at M. de Dohm's house,
that Prince Henry had intimate relations with the
French cabinet, especially with M. de Calonne,
and was in some sense the cause of my being

---

* Peuchet, vol. iii., p. 2.   * Montigny, vol. iv., p. 342.

sent to Berlin.* In becoming a diplomatist, one is in danger of also becoming a dupe."

"How is that, my friend—have you been deceived by any one?" asked Henriette, anxiously, clinging to him in her usual manner when uneasy about him.

"No, but I was influenced without being aware of it," replied Mirabeau, "for M. von Dohm, who is the best-instructed man in this city, and whom no state secret escapes, told me yesterday, in confidence, that Prince Henry had often advised the French government to remove the incapable Count Esterno from the position of ambassador to this court, and replace him by a man of more energy and character. In the political circles of this city it is taken for granted that I am to be the future envoy to Prussia, and that Prince Henry urged our ministers to send me here, so that I might become acquainted with the routine of business as well as the persons with whom I would have to associate. When I heard that, I remembered in an instant that Clavière told me before my departure that the prince desired the presence of an expert observer in Berlin, to act in concert with him, and to serve the French interest.

"By an especial recommendation from our cabinet I was told to pay my respects to the old gentleman, and he has always kindly received me. But as, in spite of much good advice, he has latterly treated me very cavalierly, I thought myself mistaken in considering him a useful patron. Now I will see if I cannot force from him, in the course of conversation, some expressions, showing how far he is inclined to assist the French policy, to which he is sincerely devoted. If I can take any thing so definite with me to Paris (and such intimations can be better communicated orally), I shall have an undeniable success in my mission here. Besides, I wish to ask him for a few lines addressed to M. de Calonne, telling him that Count Esterno must soon have a successor, who is in relation with the right men, and who has the confidence of their party. If I can see the old prince at once, I must depart before evening, for my presence is urgent in Paris."

"No," replied Henriette, "you cannot leave before to-night. Every thing does not depend on politics as far as you are concerned; you must also have a little consideration for Coco and Yet-Lee. This evening we are to have a Chinese magic lantern, as I mentioned to you yesterday, and you must be present at the performance, if you are a man of your word. We are about to enact a comedy in which all depends on politics, and where the paternally-minded Emperor Toutcequevousvoudrez makes his whole people jump over a bamboo-cane. Besides, a German song will be sung, which M. Coco, principal actor to Count Mirabeau, has been practising for several days, and who will doubtlessly acquit himself with great credit." *

"These are tricks of my valet de chambre Boyer, designed to retard my departure," said the count, smiling. "The good-for-nothing fellow has taught you these things, and they may be very amusing on a long winter's evening in Berlin. However, not to grieve you at parting, I will have a seat in the parterre of your theatre, and take my leave only after the conclusion." Mirabeau's carriage was announced, and he departed on his visits, the last one intended for the palace of Prince Henry.

Toward evening the count returned with some signs of ill-humor, telling Henriette, whom he found busy with preparations for the amusement, that all he had undertaken during the day had failed. "Even the miserable Count Esterno refused himself to me, and I was turned over to the secretary of legation, for the purpose of having my passport *viséd*. Minister von Hertzberg, to whom I wished to say a few farewell words, is in Sans-Souci with the king, who desires his constant presence, and cannot bear to have him out of his sight. He was, however, expected to-day in the bureau of foreign affairs; and I called four times, but in vain. I really am mortified to have so much trouble about a clerk, for what else is

---

* Thiébault, "Frédéric le Grand, ou mes Souvenirs," vol. ii., p. 194.

* Montigny, vol. iv., p. 343.

Hertzberg—what else are all Prussian ministers? I had about the same success at the palace of Prince Henry. Having been announced three times, I was told that his royal highness had not yet risen, and, on account of ill-health, would probably not receive visits all day. When I called the fourth time, I was told he had just left to take a drive. This was so contrary to my former receptions at the palace, where I was privileged to call when I pleased, that I could not help expressing my surprise to the prince's adjutant, M. von Knyphausen, and I did so in quite an irritated tone. However, I fancy the prince was only a little disturbed at my importunity, for I discovered by a smiling expression of the adjutant that his royal highness had not passed the day alone in his cabinet. His visitor was the young dancer Rollin, who at present has great influence with the hero of Hohenfriedberg and Prague."

Mirabeau's vexation was interrupted by little Coco, who, after great efforts, succeeded in gaining a seat on the count's knee, without being specially observed; but, at length, he could not refrain from kindly receiving the child's caresses, and regaining his good-humor. He was obliged to remain according to promise, and witness the magic-lantern performance, although he still had much to do preparatory to his departure. As soon as night set in, Mirabeau was led into the drawing-room, where the Chinese comedy was to be performed.

As he was generally on very good terms with his family, it was no great sacrifice to delay his departure for their pleasure, but his thoughts were already on the road to Paris, and he was mentally occupied with addresses to Messrs. Vergennes and Calonne. He even hoped to have an opportunity of personally communicating with King Louis XVI, and perhaps be permitted to pay his respects to the fair Queen Marie Antoinette.

While thus losing himself in his thoughts, the count scarcely perceived that he was already in the realm of the Emperor Toutcequevousvoudrez, and that the images on the wall were in conspiracy against the bamboo-cane, which was the only support of the kind monarch. The representation succeeded admirably; the figures moved like real actors (the invention of Boyer), Coco was delighted, and Henriette, who was always easily satisfied, almost forgot that she would so soon be separated from her friend.

"This is quite a terrible history," whispered the count, putting his arm around Madame de Nehra, who was seated near him. "It seems as if the subjects of this Chinese emperor do not understand him. He seems to have accepted his promising name as readily as our Louis XVI. that of 'Friend of the People,' and 'Long-desired.' This shadowy monarch bestows all that is wished for, but, like other sovereigns, he fancies the whip answers all purposes. The paternal bamboo is always striking the people in the same place, until they discover that some change is necessary. The mistress of the emperor is probably 'Public Opinion,' who, having also felt the cane of her lord, and, having a more delicate cuticle, cannot rest until she has organized a conspiracy among the populace. There is historical truth in this! The emperor, I see, holds his cane firmly, kisses it, and weeps (an act which subdues his subjects), and offers to resign it, when all voluntarily present him their patriotic bodies, upon which the cane is to be laid forever, and in a solemn ceremony jump over the bamboo."

Mirabeau arose; his time had elapsed, and he became impatient. The servant announced the arrival of the travelling-carriage. "I feel very sad at leaving you," he said, pressing Madame de Nehra to his heart. "Who knows whether I shall ever feel as happy as to-night, blessed in your pure love, and amid these innocent amusements? Your comedy is a good idea for me to reflect upon in my journey—you have reminded me forcibly of a despotic government. Your simple sports reflect wisdom, for you are right in your play of shadows, so long as the question in political systems is about any thing except the happiness of the people; then the cane will always represent the best and strongest government. If I were a sensible man (which I never pretend to be), I would remain with you in your cosy room, instead of rushing head-foremost in pursuit of some reality among unsubstantial expectations in Paris. Perhaps I am myself nothing but a shadowy actor."

The postilion blew his horn, which resounded merrily in the cold night air. Henriette accompanied her friend to the carriage, making him promise soon to send for her, should he not intend to make Berlin his future residence.

CHAPTER XXIII.

THE DEATH OF FREDERICK THE GREAT.

COUNT MIRABEAU returned to the Prussian capital after a short stay at Paris. With the exception of occasional visits to the courts of Brunswick and Dresden, he was more busily than ever engaged in his political observations, and awaited with profound interest an event which would affect the national relations of all Europe.

The midsummer of 1786 had come. The death-struggle of Frederick the Great had already lasted five months, and the long-expected catastrophe had not yet occurred. In the beginning of August favorable reports were circulated, for the king seemed to be deluded by an idea of recovery. The physician in ordinary, Dr. Frese, narrowly escaped disgrace for having dared to pronounce the word "dropsy," when asked his conscientious opinion of his patient's disease.

There were many, however, who believed that the hour of Frederick's dissolution was near; and Mirabeau, driven by his usually uncontrolled impulses, had one of his best horses brought on the night of the 16th of August, to ride to Potsdam for definite information. During several weeks he was ready at a moment's notice to be near the expiring monarch, for he was very anxious to send the news of his death as early, and with as full an account as possible, to the French ministry.*

* Mirabeau, "Histoire Secrète de la Cour de Berlin" (1789), vol. i., p. 56.

As Mirabeau was about to mount, he noticed a friend, with whom he had lately become intimate, hastening toward him. The count waited to salute the new-comer, thinking that he might have news to communicate. It was the Baron Noldé, a young nobleman from Courland, who had resided several months in Berlin, and attached himself to Mirabeau; they met every day in friendly intercourse, not only in society but in the domestic circle. Noldé was good-natured and childlike; having become a playfellow of Coco, and an attentive friend of Madame de Nehra, he considered himself as an indispensable member of what the count loved to call his "tribe," making himself useful in many ways. Mirabeau had further captivated the baron, by becoming the latter's adviser in some difficulties with his family, one of the first in Courland, who ardently desired Noldé's return to his native province, where an important position was offered him; but he preferred to withdraw himself, having a passionate hatred against Russia. He hoped to gain favor with the French government through Mirabeau's influence.

Noldé had shown himself indefatigable in bringing reliable information from Sans-Souci, having good opportunities, on account of his acquaintance with most of the diplomatists then in Prussia. It was now nearly midnight, when the young man hastened breathlessly toward Mirabeau, to inform him that the Saxon ambassador had just dispatched a messenger to Dresden, to announce to his court the probably immediate dissolution of King Frederick. The baron added that the Saxon envoy would not have done so if he had not received something reliable from Sans-Souci.

Placing his hand on the neck of his impatient charger, the count exclaimed: "We might do the same thing; for, if all we hear is true, the struggle cannot at most last longer than a few days. I also could have sent my courier to Paris. At the moment of his arrival in that capital, the death of the king would have occurred. If I were the regular representative of France I would certainly do so; but in my position I must be prudent, and I dare not waste money. But I cannot remain at home to-night. I must start for Potsdam, and it would give me pleasure if you accompany me, Baron Noldé." The young man gladly accepted this invitation, and they waited in the street until another horse was brought from Mirabeau's stable.

"The departure of the Saxon courier to Dresden annoys me," the count began, with evident restlessness. "How easily the news might reach Paris in that way, and when my messenger arrives at the French ministry—why, I have communicated no information that is not already known. I ran after our ambassador all day yesterday, to assure myself of his opinion as to the state of affairs, and discover what he himself may have heard; but, you know, when Esterno is wanted he is not to be found. First, I was told that he was dining at Charlottenburg; and, when I followed him, he had left long before to visit the queen at Schönhausen. I drove back to Berlin, donned my new court suit, almost killed my best carriage-horses, and hastened to the queen's residence. I entered about the same time as Esterno, and found a select company around her majesty, talking cheerfully of the most insignificant things. No one pretended to believe in the dangerous condition of the king, and the queen certainly had heard of nothing to make her uneasy. Every one chatted and laughed, and her majesty graciously took notice even of my breastpin, and conversed with me about it. She had been told that I had recently visited Castle Rheinsberg to see Prince Henry, and remarked how happy she was there when crown princess. You can imagine, however, how little I was blinded by all this, for I have had no rest since; and a conviction that the king's death is at hand drives me at midnight to Sans-Souci." *

The horse intended for Noldé was led up, when Mirabeau, with his friend, started at a gallop, permitting no servant to follow them. They took the shortest route to the Potsdam Gate, and then over the silent public road.

"The king must be in a critical condition," said

Mirabeau, "for I had intelligence by means of my doves this evening—they really serve me well. What a happy thought that was of yours, Noldé, to arrange a pigeon-post for me between Berlin and Potsdam! As soon as Frederick's death has occurred, it is to be expected that Potsdam will be closed, so that no messenger could depart. To-day my pigeons returned with a note containing these words, written by my correspondent: 'Violent fever and swelling.' I am afraid that we are too late to be admitted, for I was told that all the bridges around Potsdam would be raised as soon as the death of his majesty occurred."

They were passing through a village where a peculiar movement before the inn attracted their attention. At the gate lay a dying horse; and the rider, who had dismounted, was knocking vigorously at the doors and windows to arouse the landlord. When the latter finally appeared, the man demanded another horse in the name of the king, in order to be enabled to continue his journey to Berlin.

Mirabeau and Noldé alighted, to enter into conversation with this man, who appeared to be a royal messenger, hoping to gain information from him. They were told that from the preceding afternoon, King Frederick was unconscious, and all around him were in the utmost anxiety. The courier was on his way to Berlin for other physicians, when his horse failed him.

This recital so excited the sympathy of the inmates of the inn, that they hastened to arouse the inhabitants of the village, and everywhere could be heard exclamations of sorrow. A horse was soon provided for the messenger, and he resumed his journey with the utmost speed.

The count and his companion rode on in silence. The day was near dawning, and a cool breeze swept over the fields. "I fancy I see the dying king passing away with the morning mist," said Mirabeau, slightly shivering in his saddle. "Why does the hour of a monarch's dissolution appear of so much more importance than that of a poor laborer? The death of the great proves the insignificance of man. Every ruler while he lives might be a god, if he could only resolve to be a

---

* Mirabeau, "Histoire Secrète de la Cour de Berlin," lettre xiv.

man; but when he dies the delusion ends. People arc always ready to love their sovereign; and, when they do not, he himself has uprooted their affection. They honor in the monarch the possibility of the good, and accredit him with the power of its execution, for they are magnanimous and long-suffering. They feel, in their simplicity, as if there could be no greater calamity than the death of a king. Any one of the poor wretches in yonder village would sacrifice his best horse on a useless mission for the dying Frederick. And what has he ever done to ameliorate the condition of his subjects? They starved during his life—they will starve after his death."

The two riders, having rested themselves and their horses a short time in the forest, soon resumed their route to the gates of Potsdam, through which they passed at a gallop. The streets were silent, for the inhabitants of the city, for the most part, had not yet arisen; but here and there a light could be seen, and some citizen leaving his residence. When Mirabeau and Noldé reached the Brandenburg Gate, near the Egyptian obelisk, they noticed on the road many persons on a pilgrimage to the palace at Sans-Souci, to receive a confirmation of their worst fears.

The count and his companion did not halt until they came to the gate leading to the heights of the castle. The windows were in a blaze of light, and along the halls could be seen the hurrying up and down of the inmates. The crowd outside, having gained access to the highest terrace, added to the unusual and solemn spectacle. The silence was hardly interrupted by a whisper.

Marabeau and Noldé dismounted and mingled with the crowd, pushing their way to the principal porch, by which Mirabeau had entered so excitedly when he paid his visit to the king. The recollection of this remarkable interview never faded from his mind, although it had not fulfilled his wishes—that vision of royalty powerfully affected the count now when he thought of the last struggle of the great king.

Many equipages arrived with distinguished and noble persons, demanding admission into the palace. Mirabeau was too busy with his reflections to notice many of his more intimate acquaintances, who had come on the same mission. "These poor people move me," he whispered to his companion, referring to the sympathizing crowd; "they stand in their quiet grief as still as statues. They are nobler in their sorrow than their sovereign in his agony. When I think of him in his apartment, said to be shockingly offensive, and in clothes that he would not change for months, this picture is sad indeed, and I am compelled to look upon the populace as comparatively pure and spiritual. The monarch dies, but his glory lives in the people!"

Some one gently touched Mirabeau's hand, and, looking around, he thought he recognized in the dim light the figure of Prince Henry, who had just driven up, and leaving his carriage had found his way so far without attracting special attention. The aged prince seemed to find some difficulty in walking to the palace, and remained a moment near the entrance. He was accompanied by his adjutant, Marquis de Luchet. Mirabeau hastened to greet his royal highness with all the formality due him, but was restrained by an urgent gesture. The count noticed that his rather harsh countenance, which might easily lead a stranger to suppose him deficient in sentiment, bore an expression of pain, and traces of tears.

"How is the king?" asked the prince, familiarly taking the arm of Mirabeau, who replied that he had not been permitted to enter, and only appeared, as so many others did, to satisfy a sorrowful curiosity.

"This is the third time to-night that I have been here, to make personal inquiries," remarked Prince Henry, softly. "I am so overwhelmed with grief, that I have not ventured to enter the chamber of his majesty; but at the door I have heard his death-rattle—a fearful sound to me. I think I hear it now."

"It is the wailing cry of his last moments resounding through the halls," said the count, lowering his head to listen.

"Go with me into one of the side-chambers of the palace," replied the prince. "We shall there find Minister von Hertzberg or Count von Görtz, who can tell us all. I saw Councillor Selle when I was here at one o'clock. He told me a change had then taken place in the king's countenance. The good man wept, for his majesty was beyond the skill of physicians."

"It is just twelve minutes after two," said Mirabeau, looking at his watch. "The morning approaches. If your royal highness permit it, my companion and myself will follow you into the interior of the castle."

Prince Henry walked before them, deeply sighing. In the corridor he whispered to the count: "When the event has taken place, we must begin our political operations anew; but, whatever may happen, I remain the faithfully-devoted friend of France, and I beg you to assure M. de Calonne of this at the first opportunity. Under all circumstances I shall labor to make your policy the guiding-star of Prussia, for only as a member of that system can my country retain its position in Europe."

"But what are we to do with M. von Hertzberg?" asked Mirabeau, in a low voice. "His great influence seems to be exerted even on the successor to the throne of Prussia. I am more convinced than ever that it will be necessary to remove this minister. Great Britain has succeeded in forming an English party here, making every effort to gain influence. If Prussia become the ally of Great Britain, all our labor is lost. European politics will then take a different direction, and who knows what may happen?"

"As to Hertzberg, I have followed your advice, and will continue to do so!" replied the prince, in a lower voice. "You counselled me to disguise my hatred toward him, and pretend to a reconciliation, to lull my nephew and the minister into security. I have found this very salutary, count, within the last few days, and I thank you.* This, I see, is the only way in which we can make Frederick William accessible to my ideas, and perhaps we may succeed in saving our position, un-

consciously drawing Prussia's new monarch over to the interests of France."

During this hastily-whispered conversation they had passed through the corridor, and gained one of the anterooms, where the servants were in great excitement. On the entrance of the prince and his companions, a respectful silence ensued, and his royal highness was about to beckon to one of the attendants, when a side-door opened, and Minister von Hertzberg appeared in overwhelming grief. On seeing the prince he turned to him, as if to give some information, but the loud lamentations resounding through all the halls and chambers of Sans-Souci, told too plainly the sad tidings that the minister intended to communicate. Prince Henry could not restrain his tears. He leaned for a moment on the shoulder of M. von Hertzberg, whose honest face was full of deep and natural sorrow, while it was hardly possible to doubt the sincerity of the prince's friendship toward him.

"Frederick the Great is no more!" was heard on every side. The valet de chambre, Strützki, who had closed the monarch's eyes, came from the royal chamber and told those in the anteroom that, by the watch hanging above his master's head, it was twenty minutes past two when he ceased to breathe. The information passed to the people gathered near the palace, and was transmitted to the city, with every expression of heartfelt sorrow.

Prince Henry ordered his equipage, to return to the mansion in Potsdam, where he had taken up his residence for several days, his health not permitting him to stay longer at Sans-Souci. He took leave of M. von Hertzberg with a hearty shake of his hand, glancing at Mirabeau with an expression of as much secret understanding as intentional reserve, on account of the minister's presence.

Immediately afterward, M. von Hertzberg departed, and in great haste drove to Potsdam, to announce to Frederick William, now King of Prussia, the news so important to him.

Mirabeau asked his friend Baron Noldé to ride to Berlin as quickly as possible, and finish the

---

* Mirabeau, "Histoire Secrète de la Cour de Berlin," vol. i., p. 50.

dispatch, nearly ready on the count's table, by adding a few words communicated to him. The young man had shown himself so apt, that he could be intrusted with important commissions, and he left to expedite the courier to Paris, Mirabeau himself intending to remain a short time longer at the palace.

Scarcely fifteen minutes elapsed when Frederick William II. arrived, attended by M. von Hertzberg. The handsome figure of the young king expressed at this moment as much dignity as sorrow, and he was keenly criticised by the French count, who had withdrawn into a niche of the anteroom. The monarch and the minister entered the chamber where lay the remains of the great Frederick, but soon retired, as if in consultation. Not long after, M. von Hertzberg reappeared alone, his breast decorated with the order of the Black Eagle, which the heir of Prussia's throne presented to him as a token of gratitude as well as of unanimity of opinion and purpose.

Mirabeau departed in haste, and, as he proceeded to Berlin, he could not refrain from reining his horse in the middle of the road, as if to bow in worship to the beautiful autumn morning. Saluting the sun, he never felt more inclined than now to declare its eternal nature, for he sighed in remembrance of transient human fame. One of the most distinguished men in the world's history having just ceased to breathe, and his body fast passing to corruption, Mirabeau turned to the glory of the day as the best symbol of purity and unending life.

CHAPTER XXIV.

PRUSSIA AND MIRABEAU.

KING FREDERICK WILLIAM II., after assuming the affairs of state in Sans-Souci, rode to his capital, accompanied by his eldest son. The people everywhere received him with enthusiastic exclamations, following the royal cavalcade to the square before the armory and the Linden, where the troops were to take the oath of allegiance. Among the spectators were Mirabeau and his friend Noldé, who seemed to be greatly interested. At daybreak the soldiers had been mustered in all parts of the city and formed into close ranks, while the words of the oath passed from man to man.

"This ceremony has something grand in it," remarked the French count to his companion, and it would make a deeper impression if the formula were not quite so long. The whole meaning is: 'I am a king. I confide in my army because I am not sure of my realm!' * But these martial parades will probably have less prominence in future."

"The new sovereign is said to possess some military capacity," replied Baron Noldé, "and if certain intriguers, into whose hands he fell while crown prince, do not lead him further astray, he would be warrior enough to preserve the army of Frederick the Great, and become a renowned leader. I think, therefore, that it ought to be the object of the liberal party in Prussia to make a soldier of him, if possible, and keep him well posted in the traditions of his ancestors—to save him, in fact, from the Rosicrucian spiritualists, who will attempt to work upon his imagination."

"Ah," said Mirabeau, laughing, "these are the consequences of your introduction to the house of the fair Wilhelmina Rietz, and your invitations to the platonic banquets she gives to the learned. I know that this idea of yours is that of the Charlottenburg party, and gallantry induces you to subscribe to it."

"You are again bantering me, Mirabeau," replied Noldé, almost angrily. "Yet you know very well that it was only to please you that I asked the English ambassador to make me acquainted with this Circe of Frederick William. We often obtained important news from that source, and it would be a loss to us, if the Rosicrucian party, headed by General von Bischoffswerder, should influence the king so far as to remove Rietz. The new mistress, whom the cour-

* Mirabeau, "Histoire Secrète de la Cour de Berlin," vol. i., p. 60.

tiers wish to force upon the monarch, has already made the condition that her predecessor with her two children must be exiled to Lithuania."

"But the king will never consent to it," said the count. "I saw Mdlle. von Voss lately, and I will give you my opinion. Even if M. von Bischoffswerder should succeed in persuading Frederick William II. to accept this fair lady by threatening him with the displeasure of the spirits, a substantial beauty like Rietz need have no fear; after a few months her lover will return to her. Mdlle. von Voss is not pretty, and will not charm the king very long. She is too gentle and languid, and will probably fall into a decline, when Rietz will regain her ascendency; he will remember her beauty as one of the fairy tales of youth, that are seldom forgotten. I know women of her stamp—men who once come within their influence, always return, whatever may part them for a time. I believe that Wilhelmina Rietz possesses a certain honesty in her love, and the king may wander from but never remove her. Tell her so, baron, when you see her."

"I thank you for your commission," replied Noldé, laughing. "But I assure you, on my word of honor, that I have never attempted to be on particularly friendly terms with this lady. I think, however, that she unites amiability and frankness to very remarkable beauty, and that one may even talk sensibly with her. My interest is much heightened because the blockheads at court are beginning to slander her. They do not do so on account of any special interest in virtue, but they fear in this woman what is ingenuous and sincere in sentiment, because it might induce the king to act nobly, and then what will become of General von Bischoffswerder and his clique?"

The military ceremony at this time more particularly attracted Mirabeau and his friend. General Möllendorf stood near them, and seemed so deeply moved during the administration of the oath to him, that tears burst from his eyes. He beckoned the officers in his vicinity to approach, and, standing in their midst, exclaimed: "You have lost the greatest of kings, the first among

heroes. And I—what shall I say? I have lost my friend!" * The mournful manner of the old wounded warrior made a deep impression on all about him. Many wept, and even on the platform on which the diplomatic corps were, and near which this scene occurred, some emotion was visible.

"I have been astonished at the numerous indifferent countenances in the streets, especially to-day, and was inclined to make contemptuous reflections, but this sorrow for the deceased king changes my ideas," said Mirabeau to his companion. "These Prussian officers manifest much natural regret and honesty, such as I have seldom met with."

When the review ended, Mirabeau shook hands with Noldé, asking the latter to ride immediately to Charlottenburg, and pay a visit to the villa of the fair Rietz.

The baron was surprised, and seemed to ask an explanation, but the count said: "My diplomatic friend does not seem to comprehend why this visit is so urgent to-day. Nevertheless, go; for many reasons I should like to know how affairs are there. Mlle. Rietz is like a cipher-letter to me at present, from which I must discover what is to be expected in the future. The new turn in Prussian politics is closely allied with her charms. If Messrs. von Bischoffswerder and Wöllner succeed in displacing her by Mlle. von Voss, their party will have gained a victory over the inclinations of his majesty, and we may then report to Paris, that the mystic party, who had gained the ear of the crown prince, will have the decisive vote in his reign. For if he renounces a favorite who has been his from her fourteenth year, whom he educated, and with whom he read Rousseau and Shakespeare, this party must have obtained an extraordinary influence. The days would be indeed past when Frederick William and his mistress amused themselves with the story of Sir John Falstaff, and when the king predicted to her that he would resemble that brave knight, while Wilhelmina measured her

---

* Mirabeau, " Lettres à Mauvillon," p. 13.

lover to see how near was the resemblance already." *

Noldé was ready to execute Mirabeau's commission, promising to return as soon as possible, after having made his observations at the residence of Mlle. Rietz.

The count added: "On your report depends whether I pay a visit to-day to General von Bischoffswerder. If the Rosicrucians take possession of the field (and we shall know that from the fate of the lady you are going to see), it will be worth our while to attempt immediate terms with these people, and I must begin to-day with the general. I hear that he intends to remain in Berlin until evening, and then accompany the king to Sans-Souci. If Mlle. Rietz gain the victory, these gentlemen are mere bubbles on the surface."

"If Mlle. Rietz remain, she may thank you for it, count," replied Noldé, smiling, "for it would be owing to the memorial you sent the king yesterday, recommending to him a liberal reform in every department of his state. What a strange combination! The preservation of the king's old favorite, and the reception of the progressive ideas of the century, are in this instance one and the same thing."

"Whatever it may be," replied Mirabeau, thoughtfully, "the paper I sent Frederick William II. is good, reviewing many fruitful topics.† I worked at it in the last days of the former monarch, and finished it in a very solemn frame of mind on the morning of his death. Accompanied with a letter I sent it off yesterday, and am convinced that it has reached its destination. If Mlle. Rietz is still in a position to know any thing, ask her whether his majesty has received a manuscript from me, and whether he will honor me with a reply."

"From what you have told me," said the baron, "your ideas are beyond the weak intellect of the present king. His nerves can better endure some apparition evoked by the charlatans Bischoffswerder and Wöllner, than the ideas you conjure him to accept. And do you really believe, Mirabeau, that a young state, like Prussia, will accept them when they are too new even for France, and which your creative genius has conceived for the immediate well-being of your native country?"

"My friend," replied the count, "have you never heard of Archimedes? He required but a place for his lever beyond the earth, and then proposed to lift it from its orbit. Such a place I consider Prussia; my ideas are my lever in the coming revolution. And what was it I proposed to King Frederick William? First, I reminded him that he had succeeded to the throne at a most auspicious moment, living, as we do, in an age that every day becomes more enlightened, and in harmony with us. Then I begged him to give as much liberty to his subjects as they could bear and use, for by it his royal authority would only become strengthened and ennobled.

"He should accept the principle I have laid down in all my writings, that the world should not be governed too much. I recommended, as the first step to this reformation, the abolition of the military slavery in his states, for the barbarous law enforcing on every Prussian the duty of being in the service from his eighteenth to his sixtieth year, and even longer, is a dishonor to the nation, and ought to be replaced by a different system of recruiting, more suitable to the public and more in accordance with notions of freedom. I proposed, therefore, the organization of a national guard, the idea of liberty being best preserved and expressed in that way. Then I demanded, for all in the state, the right of voluntary and untaxed emigration; of the purchase of the estates of the nobles; the abrogation of the privileges of the aristocracy, and the limitation of the nobility, always a great curse to monarchies. I then combated the prejudice that had hitherto estranged the military and civil departments, by which the army may at last endanger the throne, threatening the government with anarchy. I demanded also that the judges should not be deposed, and that they be paid

---

* Related by Countess Lichtenau.

† Lettre remise à Frédéric Guillaume II., roi régnant de Prusse, le jour même de son avènement au trône, par le Comte Mirabeau. Berlin, 1787.

from the public treasury and not from the court-fees.

"Besides, I asked the King of Prussia to open public workshops, and be the first monarch in whose states all that desire may find employment —this is one of the first laws of Nature, and the true and only bond of society; for every man who is willing to use his skill or strength, and is idle, becomes a natural enemy of his race, and has indeed a right to carry on a war against society. Everywhere in the country—in the villages, in the cities—such facilities for labor should be given at the king's cost, and any man, no matter whence he comes, should have work, and enjoy its fair compensation, the whole nation thus learning the value of time, skill, and industry. I advocated also public instruction, the freedom of the press, and an unrestricted toleration in matters of religion. I denounced the whole system of political economy which Frederick the Great had adopted and left as a legacy, proposing to lessen the taxes, raise the imposts on landed property, and make exceptions in no man's favor; to open internal intercourse, and support honorable industry, promoting above all a free trade, which can flourish only where real liberty is known. Commerce requires nothing of kings, or any one else, but to be left alone." *

"I have been listening with great attention," said Noldé. "This is an array of good doctrine, Count Mirabeau. I shall have to think on what I have heard during my ride to Charlottenburg; but, as an obedient servant of the Emperor of Russia, I feel indisposed as to ideas of liberty that transcend my conception; like young Mai-kater, I cannot see the sun without sneezing."

"You know I like to hear you jest, while I lose myself in the enthusiasm of my convictions," replied the count. "And yet you natives of Courland have as much of the revolutionary fever in you as Frenchmen. Indeed, I am certain your family desire your return, because they think you are the best man to direct a public

movement.* But I must not let you go; you can do better service for France than in the land of czars and czarinas."

The friends separated in the heartiest manner. Noldé ordered his horse, while Mirabeau returned home, being anxious on Henriette's account, who had lately been by no means in the best health.

———

CHAPTER XXV.

THE remainder of the day Mirabeau remained at home, as he wished to undertake nothing until he had received Noldé's report from Charlottenburg. He was also very uneasy about Madame de Nehra, for whom he had engaged the services of his Jewish friend Dr. Hertz. Henriette was suffering from the same disease of the lungs that had afflicted her in London and for a short time in Paris—with her very delicate constitution, the physician feared for her life.

During the forenoon the count received an answer to the communication he had addressed to the king. A royal lackey delivered the following letter, dated August 20, 1786:

"COUNT MIRABEAU: I have received your memorial, with your note. I am much obliged to you for your attention, and thank you for the many compliments you pay me. Be assured that anything from you will give me pleasure; and I pray God to keep you under his gracious protection.   FREDERIC WILLIAM." †

"And that is all!" said Mirabeau, laughing, and throwing the paper on the table. "Any thing coming from me will give the king pleasure! That is very good, and proves to me how incorrigible are these princes 'by the grace of God,' on old as well as new thrones. They only think of what will please them, and thus they are irretrievably deaf to their own interests.

———

* Mirabeau, "Lettre à Frédéric Guillaume II."

* Baron Noldé in the "Histoire Secrète de la Cour de Berlin," lettre xvi., p. 52.
† Montigny, vol. iv., p. 345.

'*Tel est mon bon plaisir*' is the theatrical air of monarchs. The whole nation rushes into ruin with them. My ideas of reformation gave amusement to the King of Prussia! That would be desirable if it were not evil. I intended to give him, first pain and then conviction; but as my suggestions only amused him, all is lost!"

A cavalier approached in great haste, stopping before the door. It was Baron Noldé, who dismounted and entered the apartment with a gesture indicating that he had been unsuccessful in his mission.

"I bring strange news," he cried, as he met the inquiring glance of Mirabeau. "Every thing at the villa in Charlottenburg is in the wildest confusion, and I have just left Mlle. Rietz, weeping and wailing and gnashing her teeth. Her removal is decided upon. The new policy of the state is indicated by the fall of the king's mistress, who is not of noble blood; perhaps the Rosicrucians expect to exert a greater influence on his majesty by means of a woman of the aristocracy. Mlle. von Voss succeeds, and is raised to the rank of Countess von Iugenheim. She is religious, however, and demands some sort of marriage ceremony; the queen has been prevailed upon to favor this intrigue, and has actually given her consent. The consistory at Berlin has been applied to for an opinion as to this morganatic marriage which presents the fair-haired Voss to the left hand of the king. The queen has been promised that her debts shall be paid and her allowance for pin-money increased. The brother of the new mistress is to be intrusted with the portfolio of a minister of state."

"Well, then, we know what to do," replied the count, quietly. "I must immediately dress, for my visit to M. von Bischoffswerder cannot be postponed an instant." He rang for his valet de chambre, and gave him orders for the toilet.

"And how is that amiable creature, Mlle. Rietz?" asked Mirabeau, going to the mirror and inspecting himself. "Did you give her the consolation I confided to you? I still believe she is indispensable to the king, for she is the personification of all physical beauty—but only that.

Even at the courts of our French Sultans Louis XIV. and Louis XV., none equalled her in that respect; if they had ever seen her, they would have deserted their Maintenons and Pompadours."

"I am not sufficiently informed to pass judgment on that subject," said Baron Noldé, "but I must say that Mlle. Rietz in her grief really inspired me with pity, although sometimes she suddenly became very angry. I have no doubt she deserves better treatment. At first she was told that she must leave Berlin, and not approach within ten miles, when she began to wring her hands, and presently to pack her trunks; then came a counter-order from his majesty permitting her to remain at her villa. At this information she became so happy that I had to waltz around the apartment with her. She accuses Wöllner of being the cause of her misfortune, saying that the blow had not been given by Bischoffswerder."

"That is possible," replied Mirabeau, "for Wöllner was formerly a country parson, and is said still to be so much of a theologian that he actually preaches virtue to the king. Prince Henry (who first drew this man from obscurity by making him councillor of the board of revenue at Rheinsberg), at a confidential supper, related strange stories of the zeal of Wöllner. Such people endeavor to turn the state into a prison, where you have access to nothing but a hymn-book, and no one has access to you but some praying-machine man, under the supervision of the police. If he and his creatures succeed in remodelling the Prussian state, the alternative of its going to ruin or becoming an example of order and liberty, will soon be decided. Wöllner is, however, a good agriculturist, and is said to have made some propositions about the administration of the public revenue. Sound economy seems to have taught him that royal animalism ought not to remain uncultivated, but must be treated with prudence; so he considers a new, pious, and aristocratic mistress for the king a step in the right direction, and Bischoffswerder allowed himself to be persuaded into this measure by his colleague, who probably threatened the general with the avenging sword of the Rosicrucians."

Mirabeau went to the window to see if his carriage was ready; then he took a pamphlet from the table, putting it into his pocket with a peculiar smile. "It is my criticism on Cagliostro and Lavater, which I will offer to the general as a compliment," resumed the count, seeing that Noldé looked curiously at him. "I take it as a convenient matter with which to begin a conversation, and I hope to lead him to a favorite but difficult subject. Bischoffswerder is but another Cagliostro, with less style and geniality. My friend, the same causes produce the same sort of impostors everywhere. In the Italian adventurer I discerned an instrument of the Jesuits, and what else are these Prussian charlatans? Besides, I hear that the Rosicrucians, whose leaders doubtlessly in this state are Bischoffswerder and Wöllner, have gained ground to a great extent. In Berlin and Potsdam particularly they are said to have many disciples, and much has been said about their machinations among the people. Go around, Noldé, and see whether it is true that this deception has reached the lower classes. For, until the present time, the disciples of spirit-seeing, secret tinctures, and elixirs, are among the higher ranks. The essence of life which the general pretends to distribute is certainly only intended for the nobility, and that is probably the secret of his share in state affairs. The citizens do not need such aid, and I have always considered myself as belonging to them in that respect as in many others, but I will see whether I can gain any advantage from him." The friends descended the staircase, and Mirabeau took leave of Noldé at the carriage door.

General von Bischoffswerder was at the royal palace, where he occupied a suite of apartments during the presence of the king at Berlin. The count found his antechambers crowded with people, eagerly awaiting the moment when the man who was supposed to have the most powerful and influential position in the state, would condescend to admit them to a momentary audience. Mirabeau merely sent in his card by the valet de chambre in waiting, and quietly looked forward to the result. Not long after, the servant reappeared, politely inviting the count to enter the cabinet of the general, who was ready to receive him.

Mirabeau followed into the adjoining room and was in the presence of M. von Bischoffswerder, who stood with folded arms in an attitude expressing a certain degree of good-will. The count was surprised when beholding, for the first time, gentlemen whose appearance was different from what he expected, and he could scarcely repress an ejaculation at the corpulency of the general. However, the sagacity of the visitor suggested that it would be much easier to dispute with a man of that weight, as he was probably of a comfortable temper, as such persons are.

The general advanced a few steps with surprising ease and grace, considering all the circumstances, but Mirabeau remembered having heard that M. von Bischoffswerder was not only an associate of spirits—he was a huntsman and one of the boldest riders. In obedience to a gesture, the count seated himself on a sofa, while Bischoffswerder with dignity took a large easy-chair opposite. His small gray eyes twinkling for a moment on Mirabeau, he asked, in a gentle and musical voice, how he could serve him.

The general spoke in French, and the count was somewhat surprised, recollecting that the gentleman was a Saxon, who finds it more difficult than any other German to pronounce the French language in an intelligible manner.

"I wish to hand your excellency a pamphlet just issued," said Mirabeau, with an appearance of unconcern. "It is my criticism on Cagliostro and Lavater, and as it treats of certain movements in both France and Germany, I thought I could not better aid the people than by placing my observations in your hands. You are intimate with the most hopeful of kings, and will probably soon give to the politics of Prussia your own impression."

The general accepted the tract courteously, and after glancing at the title-page he laid it on the table. "I dare say I shall learn much from it," he said. "For I confess that both these men are strangers to me." He sank back into the armchair, showing signs of uneasiness. Mirabeau looked at him searchingly and saw that some drops of perspiration stood on M. von Bischoffswerder's brow.

"He recognizes the wolf prowling about the sheepfold," thought the count. "I wonder how he will resist my attacks?"

"I have no influence," said the general, piously raising his eyes. "I only desire to be the most faithful servant of his majesty." At these words he put his hand to his breast, covered with the insignia of his state uniform, which he had not taken off since the morning's ceremony.

"Indeed, in no country in the world do we find so much fidelity and devotion to the reigning royal family, as in Prussia," said Mirabeau, enthusiastically. "I must devote a separate chapter to this in my great work on the Prussian monarchy, at which I am now busy."

"I have heard much that is commendable about your preparatory studies," said Bischoffswerder, in an extremely friendly manner. "Is this little pamphlet an essay belonging to that work?"

The count endeavored to fathom the meaning of this question; but the general appeared perfectly tranquil and ingenuous. Mirabeau remembered having heard that questions of this description were usual with his excellency, who preferred to pretend ignorance, narrow-mindedness, and, to a certain extent, simplicity.

"Oh," replied the count, "the treatise on Cagliostro has no connection with Prussia. I do not know whether there are any Prussians like him, although it may be supposed that such impostors will occasionally appear in every part of the world. Wherever spirits are really revealed, necromancers are the order of the day. Cagliostro has certainly attained eminence in his art; he calls up for us spirits from all centuries; he has already made appear Semiramis, Marcus Aurelius, Henry IV., and many other potentates. The only spirits he has not succeeded in evoking are the German philosopher Leibnitz and the great Elector of Brandenburg." *

Bischoffswerder writhed for a moment, but soon looked as indifferent as ever, saying, while he clasped his hands more firmly: "All depends on this: whether we have the right faith. To him that believes, nothing is impossible; but he who desires miracles with a wicked heart, pronounces his own judgment. I am certain, count, that you do not speak about Cagliostro in any other sense; and what is your opinion of Deacon Lavater? Do you consider him a true Christian?"

"I consider him a rival of the Italian," replied Miribeau, quickly. "Lavater would gladly have been a Cagliostro, for whom in his writings he expresses great esteem, and whom he defends against all accusation. But the deacon, whatever powers he may possess, would have made a much greater figure, if he had determined to become a mountebank on a large scale. However, his German honesty interferes with such enterprises, and he is nothing but a puling religionist, where he could have been a knight and a magic hero. I believe that he deceives himself much more than he does others, when he essays to perform miracles. Lavater has often said what your excellency remarked just now, 'Nothing is impossible to a believer;' but as he had very poor success, I think my answer to your question must be, that he cannot be a good Christian." *

"Oh, I am delighted that we agree on that point, count," exclaimed the general, with almost a tender expression, as if he expected that this was only the beginning of a good understanding between him and his visitor. "Lavater is just as you say he is, chiefly because he is not a Prussian. It is necessary to belong to that nation, and especially as one of its soldiers, to be a Christian in the truest sense of the word, for only in the service of his majesty the king can the pure gospel be confessed and practised."

"I was under the impression that your excellency is a Saxon by birth," said Mirabeau, bowing deeply.

---

* At a spiritual meeting, which Bischoffswerder and Wöllner prepared for the crown-prince Frederick William, they introduced the pretended spirits of Leibnitz and the elector.

* Mirabeau, "Lettre sur Cagliostro et Lavater" (Œuvres, vol. iv., p. 498).

"A Saxon may become a Prussian, as a Saul became a Paul, and do you not think that Saul was a real Paul?" replied the general, enthusiastically. "If I am not an Old Prussian, I place my merit on the fact that Heaven has deigned to make a New Prussian of me."

"Lavater may fail in other things, but he is a good Jesuit, as all conjurers and spirit-callers are, in the present day, by whatever name they go," said the count. "Your excellency can, however, instruct me on one point. I have made the assertion in the treatise now lying on your table, that Lavater was a pupil of Schrepfer, and my visit to-day is partly for the purpose of receiving authentic confirmation about this from your own lips."

Bischoffswerder hesitated a moment before he replied; then he said, as innocently as possible: "Why do you suppose that I can give any information as to the relation existing between Lavater and Schrepfer?"

"Because the latter lived in Saxony, where he is said to have succeeded in forming a union between the Rosicrucians and freemasons," said Mirabeau, ingenuously. "It is possible that, during your youth, your excellency may have frequented the coffee-house which George Schrepfer kept in Leipsic. Every man sometimes takes coffee in a public saloon, and even converses with people with whom he elsewhere does not associate; although I never would believe that your excellency belonged to the pupils of Schrepfer, as several journals and magazines have affirmed."

"I saw him several times in Leipsic," replied Bischoffswerder, thoughtfully. "I was interested in him because he had been a Prussian hussar, and fought in the Seven Years' War—that is the only reason why I visited his café, for even as a young man I was enthusiastic in every thing having the slightest connection with Prussia."

"His coffee was rumored to have been weaker than his apparatus for the citation of spirits," said the count. "For he became bankrupt as a coffee-house keeper, while his credit in the spirit kingdom was unlimited, for the dead were ever ready to do his bidding. He is said, not only to have used concave mirrors, but to have invented frames covered with crape, in which all from the shadowy world were permitted to hide themselves. The nobleman, who inherited this apparatus, is doing a much better business, and will probably not commit suicide on account of his debts, as poor Schrepfer did, in the Rosenthal, near Leipsic."

Mirabeau was astonished to find that even his last intimation about the nobleman (Bischoffswerder), which he knew was quite impudent, had not the slightest effect on the general. The latter maintained his attitude in a masterly manner, not considering any thing the count chose to touch upon as being in any sense personal, but at times he looked with visible anxiety at a clock on the marble mantel-piece.

"And when will your work on the Prussian monarchy appear, count?" asked Bischoffswerder, turning the conversation in an indifferent voice.

"It requires still much labor," replied Mirabeau. "I have entered into communication with a Brunswick major, M. de Mauvillon, who will assist me in editing it. I made the acquaintance of this man (who is every way competent) at the court of Brunswick, where I have lately spent some time. But much is yet wanting for which I would wish to beg the favor of your excellency. Perhaps you may by your influence remove the difficulties which prevent me from using the royal state archives."

"Do you intend to write your book in a style similar to that in which you wrote the memorial you sent to his majesty several days ago?" asked the general, in a more austere tone.

"Ah, your excellency has read the latter?" replied the count, with flashing eyes.

"It was sent to me by the king with the gracious intimation to make a report of it," said the general. "But as I am now enjoying the privilege of personal intercourse with you, count, I may permit myself a few questions for my better information. What do you understand by the national guard that you recommend to Prussia, and by which you pretend to remove the faults in our present recruiting-system?"

"What do I understand by it?" repeated Mirabeau, surprised. "I mean by it to abolish the military slavery that depopulates and impoverishes your kingdom, and replace it by a national organization having some show of liberty. Is it necessary, that a people engaged in war must be driven like a herd of cattle to the slaughter? It is much easier to arrange the service in such a way that it may appear as an affair of honor and zeal, and thus you would gain strength for the safety of the state. Begin by encouraging your peasants to form companies in their parishes, and to practise the use of arms; let them nominate by vote who are to enlist, and let this be considered a distinction. Thus you will commence at the foundation of a system on which all else in the state may rely." *

"That would not be considered national in Prussia," replied Bischoffswerder, with quiet dignity. "Here we call measures by that name only when they come immediately from the king, and are executed by express command. Whoever is recruited by his majesty is considered a soldier. The idea of freely-chosen companies can never be permitted in this state; we do not manage our affairs in so experimental a manner."

"How!" exclaimed Mirabeau; "can any thing be conducted in a more dignified and safe manner than in an association where one acts for all, and all for one? On the contrary, sir, a decision by one person in the state, without the concurrence of all, is experimental. Allow me for a moment to call your attention to France. I do not know who he was that once said, 'The fairest kingdom, next to the heavenly, is France!' It is true, but, for some time, it has been visited with disorder and suffering. Financial embarrassments (and they express political neglect) become greater day by day; nothing can save us, but an assembly freely taking counsel and deciding on the state of affairs. This is my opinion and that of my friends; we have endeavored to promulgate

it in Paris. If the authorities still demur to call an assembly from the General Estates of the country, then a meeting of the notables will be necessary, consisting of privileged persons, but yet having a free national basis. I have lately addressed the most urgent representations to the French ministry on this point, and, as I was one of the principal originators of the idea, I have worked out the plan in detail, and sent it to M. de Calonne."

"I thank you, count, for your interesting information," said M. von Bischoffswerder, slightly bowing. "It is decisive as to our relations. We are Germans, and do not intend to concede any more to French customs. He who endeavors to effect a closer alliance between these two countries, is only thrashing straw. Prussia must become more German than it has ever been, and our present King Frederick William II. will be a German monarch. The affectation for France is at an end, and his majesty assumes an independent role. He would only become a very paltry imitator of the irreligious Frederick if, instead of being German and national, he were French and foreign. God forbid!"

"Is it possible," exclaimed the count, in astonishment, "that the memory of the great king, whose eyes have scarcely closed, already ceases to have influence for the state and its future? The works of a second-rate artist often outlive him; and shall Prussia show nothing of the mind of Frederick the Great? Really, that is sad! But many things have lately surprised me among the people. Much indifference and even dislike of the great monarch seem to be the order of the day, and, before his tomb is closed, the voice of his enemies is heard."

"Do not abuse those who would give honor to God," said Bischoffswerder, solemnly. "There is nothing higher than our revealed religion, and only in it can exist either king or servant. He that reigns without the pale of that faith does not really reign, and his subjects turn to him who will keep them in the faith, that they may not stumble, but stand firm under Christian officers. King Frederick is dead; but we shall destroy his

---

* "Lettre à Frédéric Guillaume II." (Berlin, 1787), p.24.

evil example, for we mean to live under a pious government."

"Then my memorial must have received your excellency's disapprobation in a religious point of view," said Mirabeau to the general, whose lips were moving as if in silent prayer.

"You are a friend of the Jews!" replied Bischoffswerder, with a pitying shrug of his shoulder. "I have unfortunately discovered that your religion consists in mere toleration ; you demand it to a greater extent than it existed even under the late king, and you wish us to publish an edict granting the Jews all civil rights. On what grounds can you justify an act that would open the gates of a Christian state to the arch-enemies of our faith ? "

"I have no other justification than what I have already expatiated upon in my memorial," said Mirabeau, with a very expressive smile. "The state would gain good and useful citizens ; its population and capital would increase. I conjure you, general, use all your influence with the king that universal toleration may exist in his realm, for only on such a foundation, liberty, opulence, and happiness, can be expected for the government and for society! May Frederick William II. disarm the prejudicial reports spread about him, that he has become a member of the sect of the Rosicrucians, and the agent of those merciless necromancers ! " *

"Count Mirabeau," replied the general, scarcely able to maintain his dignity, " his majesty has no doubt well weighed the principles by which he will govern, for he is a God-fearing man, anxious for the happiness of his subjects, but in his truly Christian mind no room can be found for what is called liberality ; it has the same signification as usury. He who desires religious liberty trades away his soul's eternal happiness for the miserable market-price of a present delusion. He who desires a blessed future life, must be intolerant, for to permit infidelity and wickedness, is in itself wrong. Truth in its essence and power is illiberal and exclusive. It would be like receiv-

ing earnest-money from the Jews for the purpose of buying our Christian state. I thought the Counts de Mirabeau were an old aristocratic family ? Can a nobleman of ancient descent defend Jews ? "

"Oh," replied the count, laughing aloud, " a man of ancient and noble descent can do much more than that—he can fight against himself. I have learned this in France and cannot forget it in Prussia. True aristocracy in these days, is to sacrifice all privileges and prejudices for the benefit of all, returning to the people what belongs to them. In my reforms, I ventured to suggest that the land-tax should be raised, but that not a single estate should be exempt."

"I noticed that," said Bischoffswerder. "But the Prussian nobility would not suffer the state to put its hand into their pockets. They honor the government by paying nothing. You wish to be tolerant in reference to God, and intolerant in reference to the aristocracy. Sir, the cause of the Gospel and that of freedom from taxation of the estates of the nobles, are the same thing. One must stand or fall with the other, for from the privileged classes a blessing flows through the whole land, improving all. I have observed this particularly as to my friend Wöllner, who is now privy councillor of finance and intendant of the royal buildings ; for what would he ever have become if he had not married the daughter of a nobleman possessing a free estate? Only through his union with the nobility, by means of such a family as the Itzenplitze of Gros-Behnitz, could he receive that consecration which made the poor country-preacher a companion of his majesty. This is an example, sir, of how a Prussian may elevate himself. Every thing else we refuse to accept."

"I must be satisfied with your decision," replied Mirabeau, impatiently springing from his seat, and preparing to take leave of the general. While the latter was slowly rising, the count continued : "A state may fail in its destiny as well as a human being. It happens sometimes that we fancy a country is becoming powerful, but when we take a nearer view, we perceive that its

---

* Mirabeau, "Lettre à Frédéric Guillaume II.," p. 52.

rottenness commences before maturity.* May the statesmen of Prussia remember that it is destined to become great!"

"It need not," replied M. von Bischoffswerder, raising his corpulent body with some exertion. "It shall be great before the Lord, that is true; but it requires no increase of power, and it will be happiest and mightiest if it possesses nothing but the sheepcotes of Brandenburg. Farewell, count!"

* "Pourriture avant maturité," the celebrated saying of Mirabeau in reference to Prussia.

With these words, Mirabeau was dismissed. In the greatest haste he passed through the ante-rooms and down the staircase, to reach his carriage awaiting him in the inner court-yard of the royal palace. He did not take breath until seated in it. Half laughing and half angry he threw himself back on the cushions, whispering: "The only fool in this business am I! Who else would have undertaken to dispute with a Bischoffswerder unless such an enthusiast as myself? I continually return to my labor of washing the negro white."

CHAPTER XXVI.

MIRABEAU'S CLOTH-STORE.

On a cold February day in 1789, Mirabeau emerged in great haste and excitement from a house on the market-square, in the old Provence town of Aix. He did not throw his cloak over his shoulders until he was in the street and felt the cold, reminding him that his health might suffer if not more careful, but his face was in a glow, and anger swelling the veins in his forehead.

"Why, my dear brother, is the session of the aristocracy over?" asked a lady, against whom the count almost stumbled in passing, and who now retained him by grasping his cloak. He recognized his sister, Madame de Saillant. She resided in Aix, and he had renewed the tender intimacy of their youth since his stay in the little town.

"The assembly has not adjourned, but I have finished forever with this fine aristocracy of Provence," Mirabeau replied, with a tragi-comic expression. "You must know, my dear sister, that the nobility and clergy have as good as turned me out; and you can now see how one looks who has been trying to maintain a proud appearance, (in which I hope I was successful). The reaction must be visible and awkward enough, so that I really must present a rather sheepish appearance."

"It could not be otherwise," said Madame de Saillant, in a cheerful tone; she was one who could not easily be saddened, and always had a consoling influence on her brother. "I admired the courage with which you came to this place, to enter an assembly who are your natural opponents, and against whom you have been acting your whole life. And now you have really succeeded in being turned out?—But it is cold, Gabriel. Accompany me home and tell me all the proceedings over a cup of chocolate."

"No, my dear Caroline, I thank you," replied Mirabeau. "A man expelled by the aristocracy and clergy has no time to drink chocolate—he must think of vengeance. I have a great deal on my hands to-day. But let me inform you of one fact: it was my former father-in-law, Marquis de Marignane, who demanded my expulsion. He arose and said that there was a rule which prohibited Count Mirabeau from a seat in the assembly, for they had lately declared that no one was entitled to participate in their proceedings who was not in possession of an estate in fee. This was a preconcerted affair; all they desired was to destroy my opposition by removing me, and, of course, the motion prevailed, so I had but one thing to do — take my hat and leave. I have arrived safe outside, and I despise and defy those gentlemen. They have anticipated a dangerous state of affairs for themselves, for as soon as I renounce the idea of being nominated a deputy from my own rank in the Assembly of Estates, I belong exclusively to the people and the Third Estate, and am certain of being elected by acclamation in Paris as their representative at the great session soon to be held!"

"And why did you not resolve to do so at first, Gabriel?" asked Madame de Saillant, glancing sympathizingly at the agitated countenance of her brother. "You would have spared yourself many disagreeable feelings in this paltry old place, full of prejudices against you. And I would have been saved much pain; for you know that from love to you as well as to Emilie de Marignane, I have been continually laboring for your reunion with her. She loves you still—her whole life is nothing but anxiety and sorrow for you; and since your arrival here in Aix, she sits at her castle, dreaming of you with pale cheeks and weeping eyes. When you came, my heart was filled with hopes for the realization of my plans, but now all is disarranged, and you are farther apart than before. You have again violently aroused the displeasure of her father in the session of the Provence aristocracy. He was the real cause of your divorce from Emilie, when you wished to be reunited with her; and now, when he might have been won to your interests, this new apple of discord—the election—has been thrown in, and I fear all my efforts for your happiness are in vain."

"You were always an amiable dreamer, Caroline," replied Mirabeau, caressing his sister's hand. "And yet you know that I can now make less use than ever of your kindness in this affair. The time has come for men to act, renounce, fight, and sacrifice themselves; who can now think of courtships and marriage, of old or new wives? I assure you, when I resolved to come to Aix, I never even remembered that Castle Marignane was within half a league's distance. I merely followed the invitation of the state recorders, calling on all property-holders to assemble, and I considered myself included on account of our family property in Provence. The question is about the elections of the Estates of the kingdom, with which Louis XVI. is endeavoring to sustain himself after he was forced to cast away that broken reed—the assembly of notables."

"If you had remained united with Emilie, you would have been a landed proprietor in Provence, and the unpleasant occurrence of to-day could not have happened," said Madame de Saillant, sighing. "I am certain that my dear friend Emilie will be in despair when she hears of it."

"Such proprietors have always intervened between her and me," replied Mirabeau. "And as to the session from which I have been expelled, I am glad that now I can shake the aristocracy from my shoulders. I acknowledge that, for a short time, I thought it best to become a deputy from the Estate of the Nobility, always thinking they ought to be the leaders of the people in a struggle for liberty; for, strongly as I love the Commons and their cause, I find much that is repulsive to me in them; I have often been vexed at their follies. They are altogether without plans, without enlightenment, sometimes irritated at small matters, where they are wrong; and yielding good-naturedly to great ones, where they are right. But the last quarter of an hour has completely changed my ideas."

While they were talking the snow began to fall. Mirabeau had ordered his carriage at the usual time—the close of the session—but as he had left earlier, could not expect it; he therefore proposed to his sister that they should enter a cloth-store, with the proprietor of which the count had lately become acquainted. Madame de Saillant hesitated at first, but finally consented to take shelter there until some conveyance could be procured.

"The noble Marchioness de Saillant is induced by her democratic brother to mix with low society, and accompanies him into a vulgar store to seek protection from the storm!" said Mirabeau, laughing, as he gave her his arm. "But you were always a friend of the people, Caroline. Even while we were together at our father's house, sympathy united me with your hopeful and great mind. I believe you always loved me, wherever I may have been, and however I may have been buffeted by fortune. I owe many a consolation in very dark hours to your letters and advice. May I not reckon on you in future, now that I am plunging into a doubtful conflict for the people?"

Caroline pressed her brother's hand tenderly, as they entered the store, near the door of which they could no longer remain, on account of the inclement weather. The owner, M. Le Tellier, was dining with his family in a small adjoining room, and had not yet noticed the strangers. The count did not wish to disturb him at his noonday repast, although they had often already conversed about the elections.

As they loitered in the store, Madame de Saillant again began to converse on the subject so near her heart. She related the profound mental sufferings of her friend Emilie, who, since her divorce from the count, enjoyed nothing in life but hearing of Mirabeau and his affairs, often driving from Castle Marignane to Caroline's house, to talk about the absent one and see his letters, kissing and weeping over them. Emilie would certainly come this evening between six and seven o'clock, and his sister gently hinted that a visit from him at the same time would be what she most desired.

"No, my dear Caroline," replied Mirabeau, gravely, "let us say no more on that matter. We have been separated, and can never be reunited. Six years ago I would have given every thing if Emilie de Marignane had inclined her heart toward me, pardoning and receiving me again, after my father's *lettres de cachet* tore us asunder. I desired to atone to her for many a wrong I had done her; but her father the marquis, and all her wealthy relatives, obtained influence over her and she declared herself my enemy. Since then my memory of her has faded away, and who can restore it? It is strange that, at this decisive moment of my life, she is again to be forced upon me. Does she wish to entice me from the glorious career before me by the bribe of her landed property? No, I pay homage to no such feudal love. Let her weep for me, for I am truly lost to her! The people have my affections, with whom I am about to be united in an enduring bond; for I will be a candidate for the representation of the Third Estate."

"Could such a connection as that with a certain Madame de Nehra really be strong enough to turn your heart from a woman like Emilie, who possesses beauty, amiability, intellect, rank, and wealth?" asked Madame de Saillant. "My dear brother, I do not know that lady—I have never seen her, and all the flattering things you have told me of her in your letters may be true; but persons in her position can always be set aside—she is neither more nor less than a sort of grisette, while a union with one of your own rank insures the happiness both of husband and wife."

"No, my learned sister," replied Mirabeau, quickly, "you are altogether mistaken. You have thought much at your life—you have been educated at your convent in philosophy, and can even understand Latin; [*] you may know something of sentiment, and have had an affection for your deceased husband, but you never understood so profound and honorable a love as mine for Madame de Nehra. She is an inseparable part of myself—nay, she is my better genius. She not only loves, but serves me—not only serves, but controls me. She is my dearest friend, if I may say so, for together we fight our way through the world—my agent, for she attends to all my business affairs—my messenger, to do my bidding with cheerfulness and fidelity. She crossed the sea from London to Paris alone, and in feeble health, to have the cabinet order repealed that placed me at the disposition of my father, and succeeded. Two years ago I returned from Berlin, and was forced to leave this faithful friend in the Prussian capital, because she was suffering from illness: but I knew that I would be unfortunate in all my undertakings without her protecting presence.

"I felt that my political position at Berlin was becoming unworthy of me, and fancied that I should receive, as a reward for past service, some situation under the French government. I thought I could make pretensions to the secretaryship of the convention of notables, soon to open its sessions, but I was repulsed, for the ministry never intended to do me justice. The assembly were not strong or courageous enough to arrest

---

[*] Montigny, "Mémoires," vol. 1., p. 270.

the ruin of the country, and Calonne lost his portfolio, having to run away from his creditors. The new financial minister was a prelate, the Archbishop of Toulouse, M. Loménie de Brienne, a man who had some predilection for the philosophic fancies of the age, but could make no money either out of them or his half-forgotten psalms. Then I published my pamphlet against stock-gambling—tearing the mask from hypocrisy.* I intended thereby to close all avenues to a reëntrance of M. Necker into the ministry by turning public opinion against him, but I expressed myself too strongly, and the government issued another *lettre de cachet*—the seventeenth in the course of my life.

"I was obliged to flee and hide at Tongres. And who became my savior? It was Henriette. On receiving the news, she immediately left her sick-bed, declaring herself perfectly well, and offered me her services. She hastened from Tongres to Paris; again implored M. de Breteuil for my liberty; went to every one whose friendship and influence she thought might be of avail, and did not desist until, by her entreaties and her charming address, she gained her object, and I was released from exile! At this moment she is unweariedly occupied with my affairs at the capital, while I, endeavoring to make the Provence aristocracy democratic, am expelled from their hall."

The proprietor of the cloth-store entered to greet Count Mirabeau, whose voice he had heard. He was a short, active man, with the dark, shrewd eyes of the Provençal, but his outward appearance gave signs of poverty.

"I am afraid that we have disturbed you at your dinner, Master Le Tellier," said the count, returning the man's respectful bow in a very friendly manner. "We are claiming the hospitality of your store until the snow-storm has passed."

"As to dinner, I cannot say much either of its quantity or quality in my house," replied Le Tellier, sadly. "With five children and no income, I might assume the name Monsieur Deficit,

* "Dénonciations de l'Agiotage, au Roi et aux Notables."

as they are at present calling Marie Antoinette Madame Deficit."

"The Parisians are witty in their misery," said Mirabeau, laughing, "but they are at least trying to bake new bread, and we shall soon have a new *boulangerie française*, with the sign of the Estates of the kingdom. You must be well represented there, you gentlemen of the Third Estate; for if we succeed in our present undertaking no one shall suffer hunger in France, even if he has twice the number of children you have, friend Deficit."

"Our hopes rest on you, count," replied the proprietor of the store. "And we were really sorry to see you associate with the nobility and clergy, as the intentions of those gentlemen are obvious. They wish during the elections to deprive us of our rights, by not permitting us to be fully represented. You belong to the aristocracy, it is true, but you have a reputation of being a friend of the people, and of having a heart not quite as tough as the parchment demonstrating your ancient descent."

"No, that you and your friends may be sure of," exclaimed the count, solemnly. "I was present at the meetings held in the hall yonder, just because I intended to combat for the rights of the Commons against a clique. For what is the object of those men? They wish to overthrow the decrees of the king, who has ordained that the Third Estate must be represented by a proportionate number of delegates, as the other Estates. I stepped into their midst to let them hear a free and true word from one of their own rank; but it is easier to preach to the deaf than to the obstinately wicked. When I found I could not reach them through considerations of justice and prudence, I endeavored to frighten them. But they care only for their own rank, and would absolutely protest against going to heaven if they thought that they could not carry their aristocratic privileges with them. They are taking measures for a solemn protestation against the king's popular order; and, that they might not be disturbed, they simply showed me the door—that explains my presence here, Master Le Tellier. Since I have been expelled from my own rank, I must look for something to do. I envy you your business; it must be agreeable—you know what you live for, and see the results before you. Will you take me as a partner in your store?"

"That would be an expensive movement, count," replied Le Tellier. "You must use capital, if you expect profit. You doubtless observe how meagre my trade must be; the stock is small, and I do not pretend to deal in the fine or more costly cloths. Alas! my sales are insignificant. Our country about here is impoverished; we have no means to make new purchases."

"I enter as partner from to-day," said Mirabeau, gravely offering his hand to Le Tellier. "As to the amount of money I am to bring in, we can settle that hereafter; I will pay one thousand francs down for improvements in the appearance of the store; it ought to look a little better. It will soon be a time of remodelling everywhere; all the old rubbish will be cleared out of the way, the signs newly painted, and every thing put in order. Let us have a new firm, my friend. But, first, take your money."

Mirabeau at once drew out his pocket-book, and looked for something, but, not finding it, he was embarrassed, and began to reflect. Madame de Saillant smilingly noticed this, and, without waiting to be asked, which she expected, as a matter of course handed her purse to her brother. He quietly took it, and counted out in gold-pieces the sum mentioned to Le Tellier, who was regarding him doubtingly: "Our new firm," he said, "shall be 'Count Mirabeau and Le Tellier.' While waiting for the new sign, we shall put up a temporary one, and it must be done promptly. Have you not a black board, or something of that kind, on which we can write the letters with chalk?"

Le Tellier seemed to comprehend what was required, and joyfully hastened to bring the necessary articles. The count, taking the chalk, wrote in large characters: "In this store Count Mirabeau sells cloth, for the purpose of newly apparelling all the Estates." Then he said: "We must fasten this on a post outside, so that all that pass by may see it."

Le Tellier was delighted at this idea, and moved about with more than his usual activity. In a few minutes the notice was conspicuously before the public.

"That is excellent, count," the cloth-merchant repeated. "When the noble lords and barons come from the hall, they can hardly pass without observing the new sign, and it will afford us some amusement to witness their surprise and fear. —They will understand the meaning of being newly clothed by Count Mirabeau. The jacket you will make for them will be a tight fit, and not unlike that for the people, count?"

"You are an intelligent partner," said Mirabeau, patting the man's shoulder. "Your comprehension is quick, and we shall no doubt do a good business. Certainly we must make a similar style of dress for all the Estates, and from the same cloth. At first, the material will be coarse, for we have nothing very superior. So much the better, for the higher classes should learn to wear jackets of coarse stuff. If we succeed, we shall have better goods after a while, so that the people may have what is fine and costly. What do you think of it, friend?"

The marchioness now remarked to her brother that it was time to depart, for she did not feel very comfortable during the conversation, and the snow-storm was over and the sky clear. The count, on leaving, said to Le Tellier: "Announce to your friends (and I know you have a great many in the coffee-houses and club-rooms of Aix), that I have entered into a partnership with you. If any one desires to trade with us he shall have a reduction of twenty per cent. on his purchases. The time is at hand when the most profitable business will be to belong to the people themselves. Tell your friends also that I shall attend at my store every morning from twelve to two o'clock, and that whoever appears at that time can ask me any question he pleases." On leading his sister into the street, Mirabeau saw that several persons had already noticed the sign, and were reading it with the greatest surprise."

"Let us amuse ourselves a little with these faces," said the count, in a low voice to Madame de Saillant, retiring again into the store. "They are my former colleagues from the session-house. The meeting has adjourned, and most of those standing there feel as if they had been poisoned by my business notice. They are endeavoring to laugh, but you can see that they feel badly. The noble gentlemen have doubtlessly passed a protest against the magnanimous order of the king in reference to the number of deputies, and walk proudly as they think of their ancient privileges. There is my worthy father-in-law, Marquis de Marignane! As he was entering his equipage he saw many persons around the cloth-store, and he is really condescending to mingle with them, followed by the Archbishop of Aix, M. de Boisgelin, who is putting on his spectacles."

Mirabeau's carriage now arrived, at the time the assembly usually adjourned. He beckoned to the coachman to drive up to the store. "It is time to go," said the count, escorting his sister out, and through the group at the door. Madame de Saillant blushed deeply, feeling greatly embarrassed at meeting so many of her intimate friends while in such a strange position.

M. de Marignane and the archbishop were still standing in animated conversation, and when they beheld Mirabeau and his sister their astonishment was so great as to embarrass them in saluting the marchioness. The count passed in his haughtiest manner, as if utterly unconscious of their presence.*

---

* The story of Mirabeau's store has been contested, but it has probably as much of historical truth as is accorded in this description. Chateaubriand's "Mémoires d'outre Tombe," vol. ii., p. 33; "Mémoires de Condorcet," vol. ii., p. 318; and the "Anecdotes du Règne de Louis XVI.," vol. vi., p. 267, give particulars of this cloth business, in which Mirabeau sold goods to the amount of three hundred louis d'ors daily, and on the first day to that of even fifteen thousand francs. Montigny and others have vainly endeavored to discredit this curious episode in Mirabeau's life.

CHAPTER XXVII.

BREAD AND MEAT.

Mirabeau was seated at the *table d'hôte* of the hotel in which he had taken up his residence at Aix. From the time of his arrival the number of visitors had so increased that the proprietor found it necessary to open several apartments adjoining the public dining-saloon, to make room for those attracted there by the presence of so celebrated a character. Outside, as usual about that hour of the day, a crowd had assembled, awaiting the appearance of the count, who never omitted to make some remark as he passed out, and even sometimes addressed them. He had become the popular favorite, not only in Aix, but in the neighboring towns of Provence, especially in Marseilles, where he often spent a day. He had risen in the love and esteem of the middle and lower classes, while becoming more and more openly the opponent of those of higher rank, and an object of hatred and persecution. The people came to him for advice and consolation in all their troubles, and he was present not only at the meetings of the citizens where debates about the elections were held, but he visited the poor, associating with them as both an equal and a benefactor.

Rumors were rife among the guests at the *table d'hôte* of a rising of the populace at Marseilles, caused by hunger, for the most necessary articles were sold at fabulous prices; also of commotions in one of the quarters of Aix, inhabited by the poorest and most oppressed of the people; and many supposed that these disturbances had some connection. Mirabeau went out, having observed a few acquaintances who dwelt in that part of the town. He was received with shouts of "Long live Count Mirabeau!" and was on the point of entering into conversation with several laborers who had long seemed suspicious to him, when an approaching travelling-carriage attracted his attention. It drove in great haste to the hotel, stopping in front of the principal door. The count heard his name called in a gentle and well-known voice, and was greatly surprised to meet Madame de Nehra stretching her arms toward him. He greeted her heartily, but with anxiety, knowing that her unexpected presence in Aix must be caused by something unfavorable to him, which she was trying to obviate. He conducted her to his rooms, while his friends and admirers in the street seemed somewhat surprised.

"That beautiful woman is his wife, I suppose, who is running after him from Paris," said a laborer, slyly winking. "Let us serenade them to-night, Master Le Tellier."

"If you do not wind your silk more to the purpose than you make this supposition, you will soon be turned out of your factory," replied Le Tellier, who had become of course a personage of some importance. "Count Mirabeau," he added, "has no wife, except the lady from whom he is divorced, and who dwells at Castle Marignane, and we and all our friends must pay her a visit of ceremony."

"What do you mean, Master Le Tellier?" asked several, surrounding him with expectant faces. "Yes, you are right; the time will soon come when we must assault the proud castles in this vicinity, for there we can obtain better wardrobes than we buy in your store, though many of us have been provided for in that respect by the generosity of Count Mirabeau."

"If I ask you to make a pilgrimage to the old castle, friends," exclaimed the cloth-merchant, smiling, "it will not be to storm it at present; we shall go to demand the appearance on the balcony of the fair Countess de Mirabeau. If she favor us in our request, as she will have to do, we will pronounce shame upon her for so shabbily treating a man like her former husband, who is the benefactor of the people and the savior of France. She must kneel before us, and swear that she will so kneel to him for pardon, and return all the property of which she deprived him. You shall have new clothing out of Mirabeau and Le Tellier's store for this festival procession." This proposal was received with shouts by the multitude, who disappeared in a side-street with their leader, the cloth-merchant.

The count was greatly concerned to ascertain the object of Madame de Nehra's journey, so suddenly undertaken, and she was no less eager to inform him. "New intrigues are forming against you in Paris," Henriette said. "They are afraid of your conduct in Provence; the court and ministry have received exaggerated accounts of you. I have heard from the best-informed persons that the government will do their utmost to prevent your election as one of the deputies from the Third Estate. Chamfort, who ferrets out every thing, has heard that your secret history of the court of Berlin is to be, or has already been used, as a criminal accusation against you; and then, as one condemned, you are ineligible in Provence. I thought it my duty to hasten to you, my friend, and inform you of this danger. If you do not care to have me stay, I will return to the capital, for I am quite strong again, and my lungs do not give me trouble. All you need is to tell me what I am to do, for something must be done; but I did not venture to act without your consent."

Mirabeau paced the room with an eye flaming in anger. "So these cowards intend to put me on trial," he exclaimed, in a violent manner, "and to answer for a book that in reality is not mine, but which the ministry had compiled by their agents without my knowledge or consent, partly out of the dispatches I sent to Vergennes and Calonne from Berlin. Besides, those intriguers falsified my reports, inserting passages against the present King of Prussia, which never originated with me, and are offensive to his majesty. I let these things pass at the time because they were indifferent to me, and I regarded the work as a worn-out coat that I never expected to see again. I ought to have known that it was intended to hurt me, and that they would use it against me whenever an occasion presented itself. But how did they begin this business? Tell me all you know."

"The state attorney formally denounced the book before the Parliament of Paris," said Henriette, her honest eyes sparkling with indignation. "The accusation says that the rights of nations have been violated, and the honor of the French nobility invaded, by one of their rank, inasmuch as the monarch of a friendly country has been insulted."

"This is pure invention," exclaimed Mirabeau, stamping; "and so it is fancied that I am to be caught in such a snare! I was sent to Berlin by order of Louis XVI., from whose purse I received my salary. Even if they said that King Frederick William II., or Prince Henry of Prussia, had entered complaints against me at the French court, I could prove to them the falsehood of such an assertion; for our old friend Noldé is still in Berlin, and has access to the highest circles. He wrote me lately, that at the Prussian court my revelations were received with the utmost indifference. It is therefore French intrigue, without doubt the work of the Provençal aristocracy."

"That may be," replied Henriette, " but I must also tell you, my dear friend, that Queen Marie Antoinette has especially shown her hostility to you. The Duke de Lauzun told me that she has made common cause with your enemies in Paris, to prevent your election. You are nicknamed the 'plebeian count' at Versailles, and that is really too bad! Something must be done, and your friends wish to know in what light you regard the affair, so that we may act accordingly."

"The gentlemen from Provence, it seems, knew how to obtain the queen's countenance," said Mirabeau. "For the honorable title of 'plebeian count' I have merited. It is a good name, indicating my career. The report of my intercourse with the populace of Aix and Marseilles has already reached the abode of royalty, and overwhelmed its inmates with fear. I do not see how my present associations are any the worse. The gentlemen of the mob are the gladiators of liberty, and if they are naked and dirty, freedom will clothe and wash them. And what harm have I done to Marie Antoinette? I have admired and pitied her in my heart—that is all I have ever had to do with that beautiful woman; and now she is attempting to prevent my election, while as member of the National Assembly I could be of great service to her!"

"The best thing you can do is to go immediately with me to Paris," resumed Henriette, placing his hand to her heart. "Believe me, your presence will solve all difficulties and turn them to good account; for no one can easily resist your persuading eyes."

"No, Yet-Lee, in politics nothing but evil eyes rule," replied Mirabeau, smiling. "I will return with you to the capital, but not to utter sweet words to my opponents; the time for that is past, but I will rend the web they spin. I will denounce the ministry to the whole of Europe as co-authors of the work concerning the Prussian court. They may do what they like with the book itself—that is a matter of indifference to me—but they must not associate my name and character with it."

"Then let us make arrangements for our departure, for no time is to be lost," said Henriette, quickly taking up her travelling-hat, which she had placed on the table at her entrance.

"We cannot go in such a hurry," he replied, looking at her, and pleased with her zeal. "The fair Countess Yet-Lee is no doubt very tired, and ought to rest. Besides, I must say farewell to my friends in this town, and promise them to return at an appointed time, that they may not lose heart at my sudden disappearance."

"I am truly much fatigued," replied Henriette, "but I wish you could make up your mind to come immediately with me. I confess that I am not too well pleased with your stay in Aix; in fact, I have felt sad about it. If you would do me a favor, you would never return; you can be elected deputy in Paris as well as in Aix, for, if you will have nothing more to do with the aristocracy, you may reckon on the people everywhere."

"And what displeases you about Aix, my Yet-Lee?" he asked, looking curiously at her.

"The town may be good enough, but the Countess de Mirabeau lives here!" replied the blushing Henriette, in a low voice. "During the night of your departure from Paris I dreamed that I lost you in the crowd, and when I saw you again, you were seated upon a golden throne, at the side of a beautiful woman, on whose bosom you leaned your head; and I, your poor wandering friend, could not approach you, for the proud glances of the lady drove me away." She ceased speaking, and tears streamed down her cheeks.

"Are you, too, concerned with a reunion of myself and Emilie?" exclaimed Mirabeau, somewhat indignantly. "I am almost led to believe in the existence of unseen intelligences peopling the space above and around us, and who come very near our thoughts, without our knowing how and wherefore! I came to Aix thinking of nothing but the elections, and since I have been here I have been annoyed in reference to a divorced wife. My sister harps on that string; some of my friends do the same; and now you come from Paris, chanting that ridiculous refrain. It is useless!—Let me explain your dream, Yet-Lee. That fair and proud lady on whom you saw me lean my head is Liberty, for she will soon ascend her throne, elevating me and all her oppressed sons to a sublime height. But I shall never forget my companion, my beloved friend. We are united forever, and the new era will only more firmly fasten our bonds. Do not cast me from your heart, for I shall need the blessing of your presence in the approaching day of anarchy and conflict."

Henriette kissed his hand with a grateful smile. Just then the valet de chambre entered, delivering a letter sent by express from Count de Caraman. Mirabeau hastily broke the seal, and presently went to the window where Madame de Nehra had withdrawn, and communicated the contents.

"I cannot go with you to Paris for several days, Henriette," he said. "This letter is from the commander of the province, now at Marseilles. The outbreak among the people there is of a serious character. They have armed themselves in large numbers to obtain a reduction in the price of bread and meat. So far no acts of violence have been committed, except against a few obnoxious baker and butcher stores; but the carriage of M. de Caraman has been pursued by the worst and most excited among the populace, annoying the worthy man with various threats. He attempted several times to tranquillize his assailants by addressing them with his usual firmness,

but did not succeed. The mayor of the city was obliged to take flight, and good men anticipated very violent deeds. The greatest danger is expected on account of promises made by certain of the magistrates, at the city hall, to ward off from themselves the furious mob. They pledged their word that bread should be sold at two cents a pound and meat at six. This pledge was required to be redeemed, and was immediately announced to the rioters with a trumpet—this was a present peace-offering, but a very dangerous one. Now, as bread is worth three and a half cents, and the meat seven, Marseilles will soon need these necessary articles, or the city must refund the loss of the tradesmen, which, as the sums required are enormous, it cannot do very long. Count de Caraman entreats me to go to Marseilles, and assist him by my advice, which he pretends highly to esteem, as well as to use my influence with the inhabitants. It is true, they confide in me, and have always shown their attachment, whenever I have visited their city. I must therefore restore peace to Marseilles before I can accompany you to Paris, and you must await me here, Henriette."

Madame de Nehra ventured to make a few objections, showing him the necessity of his presence in the capital, where so much that was personal was at stake. But Mirabeau replied that it was more urgent for him to go where human beings were suffering, and where, if their wants were not treated in the right way, greater distress would ensue. "When I have reëstablished order in Marseilles," he added, "I will stand before the ministry at Paris, demanding of them by what right and in whose interest they are endeavoring to arrest and denounce an influence like the one I wield. I will show them that I have become a tribune of the people, but that the state and society will be the better for it. But you, by dear Henriette, shall in the mean time make the acquaintance of my sister, the Marchioness de Saillant. I will leave a few lines for her. She has long desired to see you, and I am sure you will become great friends."

The count hastened to give orders to his servants, so that he could start as soon as possible. In half an hour all was ready, and he passed so rapidly from Aix to Marseilles, that he was on the shores of the Mediterranean long before night, and entered the streets of the city, which were by no means in a quiet condition. He ordered his coachman to drive slowly, so that he might make observations, which were far from satisfactory. Numerous patrols of citizens were moving, endeavoring to maintain order, in which object they were often prevented by gatherings of the populace, who passed with songs and cheers. It was plainly seen that violence threatened the city. The guards were unarmed, and used only weapons of persuasion with these turbulent men, who apparently yielded, but reunited in larger numbers.

Mirabeau, who had a keen eye for such movements, soon discovered that the rioters tended toward the same point, as if to execute some preconcerted plan. He heard that they were fearful lest the reduction in the price of bread and meat would be discontinued, as the more wealthy in-inhabitants refused to pay so much into the city treasury as to cover the difference between the present price and the actual value of the food. The excitement had reference to certain prominent persons, among whom were especially mentioned M. de la Tour, intendant of the province, and a person named Rebuffet, who had made himself unpopular by monopolizing the collection of the city tolls.

Mirabeau drove to an hotel, and without resting ordered a horse, intending, notwithstanding the lateness of the hour, to ride through Marseilles, and particularly some districts well known to him, inhabited by sailors and day-laborers. Before, however, entering these dangerous precincts, he had himself announced to the military commander, Count de Caraman, whose summons he had so promptly obeyed.

The old count, with whom Mirabeau had associated on intimate terms in Aix, was in a most depressed humor. He was glad that his friend had come so quickly, but he did not conceal his fear, that the outrages of the coming night would be fearful. He was in doubt how far he should make use of the troops, if at all. The regiments stationed at Marseilles were in their barracks, awaiting the signal for action. The commander desired to have Mirabeau's candid opinion, after having put him in possession of all the facts in the case, with clearness and gravity.

"Let the troops remain in their quarters, whatever may happen, I conjure you!" exclaimed Mirabeau, vehemently. "I will not rest to-night, but remain on horseback in the streets. I shall soon succeed in finding my old friends, and through them I shall get reliable information. By the interference of the soldiers, the affair would gain an importance which I wish to prevent at the very beginning. Military power is the most unfortunate that can be employed in a popular riot, particularly at the commencement. It can only be quelled when its causes are explained, and its difficulties treated with justice and frankness. I know the people of Marseilles —most of them are as brave and honorable as any in the world, and I have a true friendship for them—some of them have often rowed me about in the harbor. On the public market square I will argue with them the question of the value of food and its reasonable price. I will prove to them that low prices are disadvantageous, and that, if they did not have sufficient to satisfy their hunger when bread cost three and a half cents, they will starve when it costs only two; for if they demand any article for less than its worth, that article is withdrawn from the market, and they must do without it altogether. I will tell them, and you must let me do so with your permission, M. Commandant, that bread can only become cheap and good by means of the assembly of the Estates in Paris, and that the people must leave this, as well as all other matters, in the hands of representatives, whom they themselves freely elect. Do you think that this will do good?"

M. de Caraman shrugged his shoulders, and said, after a pause: "We must try every means, and we have placed our hopes on you, Count Mirabeau. What you do here to restore peace will be rightly valued at Paris. I may tell you in confidence that I have received orders to watch all your steps in this province, but I am not quite the man for such a commission. If, however, you had refused to act as mediator, for which you are well qualified by your relations with the people, I would have had some suspicion of your intentions; but now I thank you, count, from the bottom of my heart."

Mirabeau repressed his indignation at the words of the commandant, yet he felt it keenly that the request he had received was intended as a test of his sincerity. He considered it more worthy of his dignity not to be shaken by any expression of distrust, but to act for the people's reconciliation, as if he had the confidence of his equals. He hastened away, therefore, promising to send in reports as to what transpired, if he could not bring them himself. He turned his horse into the shortest route, for he knew well the windings of the small streets near the harbor, where the seafaring population dwelt; and the dashing of the old waves upon the strand was a familiar sound—recalling to him the sports of his childhood!

On arriving at the shore, he noticed but few persons. Soon he was attracted by low voices proceeding from various points, and occasionally loud and angry ejaculations. Suddenly the moon broke through the clouds, and he was surprised at the vast concourse surrounding him, boldly demanding his business.

"We have made no great catch this time!" cried a rough voice. "He appears neither like a mounted policeman, nor a lost member of the honorable citizen patrol. He looks more like a runaway courtier from Paris who has come to cast himself into the moonlit Mediterranean, to escape the ruin of the court!"

These words were received with applause. Mirabeau, however, thought he recognized the voice thus preparing an unfavorable reception for him, and he looked toward the speaker, calling in a tone not likely to be unheard: "Laurent, come to me!"

The man bearing that name uttered a cry of joy, and rushed toward the horse, clambering up and peering into the countenance of the rider, when he exclaimed: "Yes, that voice has not deceived me. Comrades, this is Count Mirabeau! He is a friend of the people, and is one of us. Now we shall triumph!"

The short, insignificant figure of the man who had spoken glided away like a lizard. He whispered a few words, which soon passed through the crowd. Covered with coal-dust, he showed that his occupation was among coal-barges. His influence, however, far exceeded his position, as could easily be perceived, since he was obeyed with exultation, and a resounding "Long live Count Mirabeau!" mingled with the noise of the waves.

Mirabeau lifted his hat, and raising himself in his stirrups, said in a voice to be understood far beyond the multitude: "My friends—for so I call you with all my heart, since I find myself so heartily welcomed by you!—whenever I come to Marseilles, I am drawn to this place to exchange opinions on the state of public affairs with the gentlemen laboring in the harbor. You can easily find a better leader than myself, when the time comes to confront your enemies (which are also mine) in the open field. But that time is not now, and I am not here to put myself at your head, but to dissuade you from what you probably have in view. I am deeply grieved to find you in the wrong in all you have done for several days past, and in what, it seems to me, you intend to do. People are often deceived as to their true interests, but I, who am continually occupied with yours, know that you have been led astray by false ideas as to the price of food. And to this you add acts of violence, threatening the safety of your city, by which articles of necessity become dearer than before!"

The first answer to this address was a murmuring dissatisfaction. Then arose threatening voices: "Who has given you the right to blame us? If you wish to mingle in our affairs, you ought at least to share our feelings. A count knows nothing of how much bread and meat cost a poor man!"

"Silence!" commanded Laurent, in his loudest tone. "This is not one of the nobles who know nothing of the condition of the poor! It is Count Mirabeau, who, notwithstanding his descent, gladly eats at the same table with the people, and will explain to you exactly how much food ought to cost. Listen to him attentively; for he is the friend of all the laborers on the piers of Marseilles, and can tell us what we most need and how we can best obtain it."

Mirabeau was about to speak again, when wild cries were heard from the adjoining streets, announcing the approach of another disorderly company. Those among whom the count stood made demonstrations of joy, and met the others, who were evidently returning from a successful raid upon some of the citizens.

The count called his friend Laurent, to question him as to the new-comers. The lighterman said that these people had been sent to destroy several of the stores on the Rue Vive Neuve, as well as to assault the house of the tax-gatherer Rebuffet. The most daring had been chosen for this purpose, and they were returning with the news that they had executed their commission; that the windows of the hated Rebuffet's house were broken by a volley of stones, his furniture destroyed, and his whole dwelling dismantled; and that the residence of M. de la Tour was served in the same way. Mirabeau saw with vexation that the mob were beyond his control—that the reins he thought he already had in his hands had slipped from him. Dejectedly he spurred his horse into the midst of the crowd, who were going nearer to the wharf buildings.

Suddenly he was surprised to see torches above the heads of the rioters, throwing an ominous glare over the whole neighborhood. The lights increased rapidly, one kindling another, and apparently distributed according to preconcerted arrangement. Then a whistling was heard, which Mirabeau comprehended as the signal for Laurent, who was their acknowledged leader, and who was still holding the bridle of his friend's charger. This man seemed attached to the count, through some former kindness, and he would not leave his patron, although the impatient calls of his comrades increased.

"I suppose you have something bad in view, you dangerous fellows?" asked the count of his companion, who stood silently and thoughtfully at his side.

"Certainly," replied Laurent, "our object is to set this part of the city on fire—that is the meaning of those torches. It will be pleasant to illuminate the waves of the Mediterranean. Wealthy citizens, who will do nothing for our relief, will be rather alarmed when they see that we are resolved to do the worst. It is possible that this may be a wild sort of night, count; for, in the confusion, we intend to open the prisons, and to set free many honest persons."

"What madness, Laurent!" cried Mirabeau, with alarm. "Go and try to dissuade your comrades from an undertaking both useless and criminal, bringing more trouble upon you all. You are a sensible man, with whom I had many conversations about the state and society, when you accompanied me in my bathing excursions; and you always took good care of the boat. Now I ask you to use your influence, and restore those men to sanity—if not, they will endanger many innocent lives, besides destroying property to their own injury."

"I can do nothing," replied Laurent, in a disheartened manner. "But if you speak to them again, do not forget that we are really suffering, and that we must at least have some hope for the future; such a strain might prevent our resistance now against those who oppress and defraud us!"

The count rode into the midst of the rioters, who were holding a final consultation as to their operations for the night. "Extinguish your torches, my dear friends!" he cried, springing to the ground, and handing the reins to one of the most reckless-looking in the crowd, who in his surprise quietly took them. Mirabeau went about among the men, looking into their countenances and talking to those who seemed to be the more intelligent, offering his hand, and conjuring them not to begin the sacred conflict for right by acts of violence and wrong. "And, my friends, let me explain to you why you cannot have food cheaper than you have it now," he continued, standing on a rock near the shore, and looking down upon the mob, who, with their torches, seemed to be in earnest. They quietly waited for his words, although the night was becoming inclement. A storm was brooding on the sea, for the waves were rising, and flung their spray over the orator's stand.

"As to this matter of food, my dear friends," Mirabeau resumed, "there are two obvious considerations: bread must be plenty and cheap."

Shouts of approval were heard: "Bravo!" "Count Mirabeau is right! That is the truth!".

The count could not refrain from smiling at the readiness with which the starving multitude accepted his propositions. He continued gravely and solemnly: "Well, my friends, you agree with me in these two points. Now you will also see the truth of this doctrine, that nothing ought to be expected by the consumer for less than it costs the seller. And let me tell you another thing, that if bread is to be cheap, wheat must be cheap!"

"Yes, wheat ought to be cheap!" they repeated while they pressed closer around the speaker. "Long live Count Mirabeau! He is a true friend of the people!"

"But, my friends, wheat is very high at present!" resumed the count. "You are just and reasonable men; let us talk a little on that point. If wheat is dear everywhere, how can you expect it to be cheap at Marseilles? The harvests have been at best very indifferent; it was God's will that they should be so, and in another year He will give us abundance as a compensation. That is a law of the Supreme Wisdom in Nature. And again, the wars waged in distant regions of the world are partly the cause of the high prices prevailing. You know, my worthy countrymen, that the wheat you consume does not grow here. Some comes from other districts of France, but by far the larger part from America and Africa. The grain grown in Africa is bought by the Turks, who are engaged in war, and the hostilities existing between the United States and Algiers also obstruct this commerce. As wheat, however, in

other places is even dearer than in Marseilles, many merchants that would otherwise trade here, as formerly, do not come at all, but go where they can realize most money. How, then, can you expect your fellow-citizens, who have to purchase at high rates, to sell to you at low ones? They will cease to purchase at all, and you must starve. What do you think, my friends?"

Renewed applause followed. Laurent jumped upon Mirabeau's horse, and standing on the saddle, cried in a screaming voice: "Wheat is dear because the Turks make it so, and we in Marseilles cannot help it. Hurrah for Count Mirabeau, who has made us understand this!" Scarcely had he spoken these words, which had great influence with the crowd, when, the horse making a movement, he was thrown from the saddle, and, with a groan, fell into the arms of one of his friends. This accident excited laughter, plainly indicating that the violent measures the rioters had in view, and which Mirabeau was trying to prevent, were already half forgotten.

After silence was restored, the count began again: "Every laborer is worthy of his hire. Bakers must also be paid for their trouble, for bread is not made without hands. You are all workers, and I consider myself as one of you—there can be no higher dignity than that of labor, each doing according to his strength and skill. And are we to exclude bakers from their privileges by forcing them to receive less than they earn? Some one will have to bear the loss if you insist on buying for two cents what is worth three and a half. You may reply that the community should pay the difference; and I ask, who constitute the community? It is not a fabulous dragon, living in a cave, guarding a mine of gold. You yourselves are a portion of society, and if any among you have hitherto not been so considered, they shall be in future, and rightfully. I vouch for this. As soon as the new Estates of the kingdom assemble in Paris, I will speak for you—for your bread and meat, and for all your rights. Will you not have patience and believe me when I say that better times will soon come? Wait until the king and the whole nation have been born again to a life of liberty. Then all the necessaries of life will be as cheap as you desire them. To-night, then, throw your torches and pitch-hoops into the sea. I know you will have patience; your manly features do not deceive me; you will again pay the customary prices, to which the authorities will have to return, if you are not resolved on anarchy and starvation. Give me your word that you will be honest in your poverty, and great and good in your determination!"

Mirabeau seized a torch, held by one of the men nearest to him, and hurled it into the waves. The man who first followed this example was Laurent, and soon the rest emulated each other in their efforts to throw in as skilful a manner as possible, amid laughter and jests. In a few minutes the count could scarcely recognize the faces that a moment before were so distinctly before him in the glare of hundreds of torches now extinguished in the sea. As he hastily vaulted into the saddle, he fancied that the crowd had already dispersed, but departing he heard behind him persons uttering his name, and blessing him for the wise thoughts that had destroyed their purposes.

Mirabeau rode back into the interior of the city to make a report to Count de Caraman of what had transpired. The commandant was asleep, and Mirabeau would not have the old gentleman awakened, as he himself could now undertake to guarantee the tranquillity of Marseilles. Then he went to the prefecture, to inform himself of the amount of wheat in the city. After much trouble he managed to assemble the officials, but his exertions were well repaid by the favorable results of the examination. It was ascertained that sufficient provisions were on hand to last more than three months.

The count returned to his hotel, not, however, to rest, but to write an appeal in his own name to the people of Marseilles. He rode to a printer's office, to have the paper printed and posted at all the street corners before daybreak. His ardor was unwearied, for, after having made all his arrangements, he returned to the harbor to greet the rising sun by the seaside. Passing up and down, he noticed that the laborers were again at their work, having been idle for many days, and that they were quiet and orderly. Several reminded him of the repulsive faces he had seen during the night, and by their abashed greetings he saw that he was not deceived. Others stood in apparent wonder, not comprehending how the rider of the black horse could still be in the same place. He was pleased that at his approach the men whom he had disarmed but a few hours before were desirous of showing their willingness to work. Riding past one of the street corners the count noticed that his appeal was already published, and that the passing laborers were aware of the fact that it contained special information for them.* They were reading it and making favorable comments. His presence was soon observed, and one of the group, respectfully approaching him, said: "You have done well, count, and we thank you, particularly now that you have had your words printed, that we may remember them."

Mirabeau recognized his friend Laurent, who was expressing his gratitude. But when the count, after uttering a few hearty words to the men, was about to continue his route, the lighterman seized the reins of the horse, begging a word of explanation for himself and his comrades. "Are you in earnest in your published address on the wall yonder, as to what you say of the king, asking us not to grieve so good a man? and when you say, 'remember his love and kindness for us, and shed tears of joy for the pleasure our good order and obedience will cause him?' During the night you mentioned the king several times, at which many of us were greatly surprised."

"How could that surprise you?" asked Mirabeau, gravely. "The king is the head of the nation. During the past stormy night, when I saw you around me tossing your torches, I became a little monarchical; that is to say (do not misunderstand me, my children), when sovereign and subjects love one another, there must be a very

---

* "Avis de Mirabeau au Peuple de Marseilles," by Montigny, vol. v., p. 411.

happy state of affairs. If the people bring their king near their hearts, they have a friend in him often more to be relied on than themselves. Have we not sometimes considered it a benefit to have our irregular inclinations restrained by the firm will of a friend—one who has an interest in us, and whose will may easily be our own. Therefore I repeat to you: Love the king, and call on him in your troubles, for he must love you as himself, and his welfare is indissolubly yours." *

This was listened to in silence, and the count continued his way, politely greeted by the people. Exclamations of "Long live the king!" resounded as he passed. He rode to the résidence of Count de Caraman, who he hoped would now be accessible. The commandant met him with an anxious countenance, while Mirabeau expected some expression of joy and gratitude:

"Do you not know how tranquil your Marseilles is?" asked the latter, in rather an irritated tone.

"I know it," replied Caraman. "You have effected wonders, count, and we are indebted to you for restoring order in our city. And the manner in which you have acted will be favorably remembered and recognized at Paris, for you have improved the opportunity to strengthen the love of the people for our good king. I shall not fail to report all to the ministry. But news has arrived that really alarms me. Similar disturbances have broken out in Aix, and things are in no better condition there than they were at Marseilles. At the same time I have received reports from Toulon, where the people have ill-treated the royal troops. I am afraid we are approaching evil times."

"No," replied Mirabeau, confidently, "the future will not be so—it is the past that may be so designated. The shadows that frighten you belong not to what is coming, but to what is departing. I must hasten to Aix immediately, for I have many good friends there. I have not taken a moment's rest since I left, and have lived on horseback from the moment of my arrival, but I

* Mirabeau's proclamation to the people of Marseilles.

will reëstablish order there to-day, rest assured of that, M. Commandant."

"But you are said to be the cause of the commotion in Aix," said Caraman, casting a distrustful side-glance at Mirabeau. "I am told that your association with the populace there has excited them, and that you have aroused their passions to gain your own purposes."

"You have received these fine reports from the landed proprietors of the vicinity, I think!" said Mirabeau, laughing. "Those blind men forced me to assume the role of tribune of the people, and if I act against them, it is for the preservation of truth and order. Farewell, M. Commandant; I shall have the honor of sending you a very satisfactory account this evening, or, at the latest, to-morrow morning."

He hastened to his hotel, and, quickly mounting his horse, was in a few moments on the road to Aix, moving at the speed of a racer. It was market-day, and the sale of provisions was about to begin as Mirabeau entered the town. His keen eye soon perceived that a popular tumult was intended, in order to resist the high prices, which had excited as much dissatisfaction at Aix as at other places. Troops were in different parts of the streets, stationed to preserve order. Visiting the commandant of the town, he urged with eloquence the withdrawal of the soldiers. His success at Marseilles was remembered, and he was intrusted with the security of the market at Aix, being permitted to organize a body of militia, which he accomplished in a very short time. He went to the houses of several of the principal citizens with whom he was well acquainted, and engaged their aid in forming citizen picket-guards, having power to elect their own officers. He distributed his men at the gates and at various points of the town, so that he soon had it under his control. Disturbances, however, arose in several districts, because the rioters intended to prevent the wagons loaded with wheat from having access to the market, so that they might obtain food by force. He went on foot to those scenes of violence, and, mingling with the crowd, talked to the most sensible among them, obtaining a promise that they would be just and reasonable. In addressing them, he asked for their word of honor (which they felt to be highly flattering) that they would not attempt to break the peace. Passing from post to post he was successful in allaying the passions of the people. On receiving notice that large numbers of citizens from the vicinity had armed themselves, and were approaching to the assistance of the inhabitants of Aix, he rushed out of the gate and induced them to return home without delay.

It was as much the irresistible oratory of Mirabeau as the impression of his personal self-sacrifice and enthusiastic devotion, that influenced the minds of the people, and attached them to him and his doctrines. After all fear of outbreak was removed in the town and its vicinity, he was surrounded on the market square by a vast crowd, who only wished to hear and see the "friend of the people"—their "father," as many of the laborers called him. Men, women, and children, pressed around, following him everywhere, calling him their protector, who, if he would only remain with them, would point out to them the right way, and defend them from oppression and starvation.*

Meanwhile, several of the aristocracy arrived armed, and noisily inveighed against those who had formed military organizations without making the nobles their officers. It was considered due their rank and dignity that they should command, and their appointment was insisted upon. The Marquis de Marignane and others, who had shown themselves particularly active in expelling Mirabeau from the assembly, made themselves equally conspicuous on this occasion. The count deputed his friend and partner Le Tellier to advise them to return to their cellars, where they had passed the hours of danger, hiding their treasures and persons in fancied security.

When he considered his labors ended, the count returned to the hotel to greet Henriette, whom he had not seen since his return from Marseilles. She met him with joy, and covered his hands with kisses. "Rumor has informed me of the good deeds you have done," she said, "and I was about to enter the street among the people, who thank and admire you. But now you are here, I almost feel inclined to kneel to you."

"No, my love," he replied, embracing her, "a day approaches when one human being may not kneel to another, because all will then be equals. Now that I have finished my duty in this place, I shall start immediately for Paris with you. Perhaps my conduct here may aid me in more rapidly arranging my affairs."

"What!" exclaimed Henriette, "for thirty-six hours you have had no rest, and perhaps no refreshment!"

"It is true," said Mirabeau, "I have been on horseback nearly all that time, and I have taken but a glass of Bordeaux wine and a small roll, But I feel as strong as a young god, and I do not see why I am to waste my time in sleep, while my enemies in Paris are endeavoring to prevent my presence in the National Assembly. On the contrary, we ought to be in the greatest haste to depart. The travelling-carriage must be here in half an hour."

"Indeed, no!" replied Henriette, firmly, and in a manner which was sometimes successfully assumed. "You will remain here, my friend, and to-morrow morning, at a reasonable hour, the coach will be at the door. Your strength is exhausted, say what you will, and if you are not more careful of yourself you will be forced to keep your room while the National Assembly is in session. In a word, I cannot let you depart today."

"You are charming in your refractory mood, as in every thing else," said the count, looking at her tenderly, "and simply to please you, I will remain another night. To make up for lost time, let us order a good supper. I have had some trouble, during the past two days, about the people's food, and I think I deserve a little myself."

* From a description of this scene by Mirabeau himself.—Montigny, vol. v., p. 305.

CHAPTER XXVIII.

THE DEPUTY OF THE THIRD ESTATE.

MIRABEAU remained but a few weeks in the capital. He soon succeeded in coming to terms with the ministry through the influence of his friends. The book on the secret history of the court at Berlin was condemned by the Parliament of Paris to be publicly burned, but the author was entirely passed over; the count could leave the city without fearing prosecution, and return to Provence, where he hoped to be elected deputy to the National Assembly. Henriette saw her friend depart with pain and uneasiness, for she was obliged to remain with Coco and await Mirabeau's return. He travelled with extraordinary speed; the election day was at hand, and he considered it necessary to speak once more to the voters of the Third Estate, in order to destroy any influence acting against him during his absence.

In a small village, about five post-stations from Aix, where the count changed horses, he was delayed by the sudden illness of his valet de chambre Boyer. He loved his servant too well to leave him in such a helpless condition, especially as the disease seemed to be increasing. While trying to obtain assistance for the sufferer, who was ill of cholera, in the small post-house, the count was standing in a despairing mood before the door, and heard part of a conversation between the postmaster and his wife.

"The courier has gone to Aix," said Louis Martin, "to announce the arrival here of Count Mirabeau. They intend to show him great honor, and will carry him into the town in triumph. I am in a quandary as to what I am to do. I have been ordered to detain the count by some pretext, that time may be gained to finish the preparations for his reception. What can I do to keep him here?"

"You are a fool and will ever remain one," replied the wife, with an ardor not at all complimentary to her lord and master. "Do you not see that the illness of the servant is sufficient to detain the count? What need have you to torment yourself?"

"The illness of the valet may retard the master, but I do not. I have been expressly ordered by the department at Aix to detain him at least six hours. It is an official affair, and I must obey unconditionally. Now I am undecided whether I shall make a pretext of want of horses to the poor count, who seems to be concerned for the illness of his servant. They are about to elect him a deputy of the Third Estate, and I am selected to vex such a man!"

"You surpass yourself to-day, Louis," replied Mrs. Martin, in a contemptuous tone. "On looking at others, like Count Mirabeau, for instance, I discover what a man is. And I, who was certainly born for something better, have married such a blockhead!"

Mirabeau thought he had heard enough, and returned hastily to his valet. "Be of good cheer, Boyer," he cried to the poor fellow, "I shall remain with you until you are better. My election in Aix is sure. I have just heard it by a singular accident."

The faithful servant nodded with a joyful expression. In the mean time the physician of the neighborhood made his appearance, who began to occupy himself with the patient, giving, however, no hope of his recovery. He declared that he had no remedy for a disease which had lately carried off so many. In a few hours Boyer died in frightful convulsions.

"My poor valet!" moaned Mirabeau, contemplating the body, "no more magic lanterns, or Chinese comedies! Oh, what a terrible scourge is this cholera! Does it teach me of the moral and civil disorders of society, assuming at last its most fearful form of evil? Is it the forerunner of new terrors? I feel sad indeed when I think that this malady may arrest me also on my journey to-day." *

The count now prepared to leave. On approaching Lambesc, he was greeted outside the gates by a deputation, consisting of the principal

---

* Vide Montigny, "Mémoires de Mirabeau," vol. v., p. 274.

officials, who waited to receive him in the name of the community. He was led into the town, in the streets of which thousands cried: "Long live Count Mirabeau! Long live the father of his country." [*] The exclamations were accompanied with the ringing of bells, and the firing of cannon. Tears glittered in Mirabeau's eyes. "I see now," he said to himself, while his carriage was slowly moving along, "what abject slaves men are! When tyrants lose all hope of governing, they may still rely on a feeling of gratitude!"

Arrived in the centre of the market square, the people wished to unharness his horses and draw the carriage themselves. "My friends," he said, gravely and in a distressed tone, "men were not made to carry their fellows. You have already enough to bear, and I intend to lighten your load, not increase it!"

The count next changed horses at the village of St. Cannat, a league from Lambesc. In this place also the people assembled to greet him, and with shouts of honor and personal good-will were mingled those of "Long live the king!" As he was leaving St. Cannat he noticed a travelling-carriage approach from the opposite direction, in which he recognized his sister, the Marchioness de Saillant, who came to surprise him. He left his own conveyance in charge of his servants, and entered that of his sister.

"You do not appear cheerful, my brother," said Caroline, looking at him more attentively after welcoming him. "I hoped at least to see you smile, having gained the height of your wishes, and become the favorite of the people!"

"I cannot forget the death of my best servant, who was suddenly called away from me during my journey," replied Mirabeau, sadly. "But it cheers me that you have come, Caroline; for I must confess to you that these rejoicings really make my heart ache. From the moment that I felt myself elevated by the popular favor, I have almost regretted that I have attained my object. I love the people, as I would a fellow-creature in distress, but now that I have associated myself

with their destiny, I feel how momentous this is. Suppose that nothing good can ever be instilled into them—that on account of an original perversity they are excluded from happiness and liberty? I almost wish that I had not succeeded in reconciling the ministry in Paris; and that M. Necker had persevered in his intention of a criminal process, and thus driven me from the elections."

"I see you are satisfied in reference to your personal affairs in the capital," replied Madame de Saillant, smiling at his melancholy. "And in Aix you have been unanimously elected deputy of the Third Estate. As soon as we approach the town, you will have evidence enough. But I wished to be the first to inform you. I know you have set your heart on this matter, and although I still half belong to the other party, I came to share your pleasure, as I did when we were children."

"You are right," said Mirabeau, pressing her hand; "I am sometimes glad the decision is drawing nigh, for which I have so long waited. The people are probably better than they appear, and the question will be, to make them a power in the government. M. Necker did not behave so badly toward me as I had been led to expect. I really did attack him violently for his unfortunate introduction of paper money, by which conjurer's trick he thought to sustain the treasury of France; and yet he complied with the petitions of my friend the Abbé Cerutti, and allows me to do as I like, although I am his opponent, and will continue so in the National Assembly. Truly, I repeat it, men are better than they appear, and I will not let this thought leave me to-day. If there be such a disease as a melancholy from success, I should say I suffer from it while the people are making these grand preparations for my reception."

They were about two leagues from Aix when they beheld a procession coming to meet them. Mirabeau recognized by their different standards the committees of the various wards of the town approaching to pay him homage. They expressed their joy in shouts of welcome, and wreaths of

[*] So described by Mirabeau's sister, the Marchioness de Saillant.—Montigny, vol v., p. 274.

flowers were thrown into the carriage. Arranging themselves in order, they formed an escort for their favorite deputy. Having reached the mountains, he beheld the town before them filled with people from the surrounding country awaiting to greet him. Stopping the carriage, they would not be satisfied without seeing and hearing their chosen delegate, who immediately addressed them, expressing thanks for his election, and their determination to send him fully authorized to the National Assembly in Paris. "And I bring you," he continued, "many greetings from your friends in the capital. For in the clubs I attended, those of the same mind with yourselves inquired about you, and I answered, that the people whose hearts are warmed by a southern sun, will give strength to the liberty of France. They sent you by me the greeting of free fraternity, which will be heard through the whole land. But I must tell you, my friends, that in many respects my sojourn did not agree with me, and I thank God that I am in the fair vales of Provence, where I inhale again the breath of your sweet flowers. Shall I tell you what it is that so displeased me in Paris, and what you must suffer no longer to exist? It is the new ministry, to which we certainly owe the convocation of the Estates-General, but which, when well examined, is not worthy of confidence.

"Many well-meaning people think it a good sign that Minister Necker has been replaced at the head of our finances; others consider him but as a foreboding gull that belongs to the approaching tempest. God created the world out of nothing, it is true; but it does not follow that the financial minister could bring it into existence out of paper-money. Now Necker expects to reëstablish the credit of France and insure its happiness by issuing such currency, which is worse than nothing, for it is a delusion, dispersed by the first ray of returning reason. I warn you against this sham of tyranny. It is the origin of all falsehood, leading to dissipation and violence.* This state policy is a conjurer's device, such as you have often seen at fairs. You remember the trick with the gob-

lets, where all the magic consists in rapidity of motion? Suddenly something turns up that was not expected; so you need not be alarmed at results of which you do not dream.

"All free nations have a dislike to paper-money, which is more or less based on dishonesty, and is obnoxious to a government of real liberty. The Americans endured every hardship to rid themselves of their oppressors, but the necessary issue of such money was soon redeemed. France requires new credit, if she is to outlive the unexampled prodigality of her own citizens in high places; but this credit itself would be another swindle, and cannot be entertained. National confidence must first be created, and this is the reason why your king (and he is good to you all) now convokes a National Assembly.

"We will take the government at its word, and call upon the representatives of the people to institute what taxes are necessary. Directed by the popular will, we shall demand a new constitution for France. Our country must be remodelled, my friends, so that the freedom and rights of the masses may be recognized, and financial fraud abolished. Because you think me worthy of representing you, I feel courage to undertake and hope to succeed in what is best for our common interests. Long live the king and liberty!" *

This cry was taken up by a thousand voices, and reëchoed among the hills. The count ordered the horses to be driven rapidly, as he was anxious to reach Aix. The people ran alongside the carriage to the residence of the Marchioness de Saillant, where the count was to stay. Her house was situated at the Place des Prêcheurs, in front of a square which was soon crowded with citizens, shouting for the friend of the people. He was finally forced to appear, and as he descended was seized and carried away in the arms of the populace. They brought a sedan-chair, decorated with garlands, and upon the strong shoulders of his admirers he was borne through the town.

As they were returning, the count noticed that another no less excited crowd came from an op-

---

* "Correspondance entre M. C. (Cerutti) et le Comte de Mirabeau" (1789), p. 39.

* "Correspondance entre Cerutti et le Comte de Mirabeau," p. 23.

posite direction, having an open carriage in their midst, which they escorted with unusual acclamations. The lady seated within it was soon recognized by the count, to his great consternation, and he endeavored to persuade the friends by whom he was carried to turn down a side-street. His words, spoken in a low voice, were either not understood or were intentionally misinterpreted, for he was soon brought face to face with his former wife. Emilie stretched her arms toward him with a cry of anguish, and fell back pale and fainting.

The people in their strange excitement had resolved to reunite the long-separated husband and wife. A formal deputation having been sent to Castle Marignane, the countess was requested to return with them, and offer her hand to Mirabeau in token of reconciliation, as they could not suffer an enemy of their favorite to dwell in Provence! [*] Emilie was almost alone at the castle, as her father, the Marquis de Marignane, and the rest of the aristocracy, preferred to leave the neighborhood on this day, so as not to be witnesses of what was most hateful to them. The poor countess, seldom timid or vacillating, could not resist. Perhaps the secret wishes of her heart made it difficult for her to meet the people with her natural decision. She suffered them to lead her away to meet the man she still loved.

Mirabeau, in great surprise, sprang from his seat. His steps turned toward the carriage, in which Emilie was still reclining in a state of unconsciousness. Her pale countenance, bearing all the traces of her former extraordinary beauty, reminded him of the troubled days of his youth. He was about to enter the coach, when he perceived his partner Le Tellier upon the box, nodding to him in a sly and approving manner, giving him to understand that this expedition to Castle Marignane was the work of the cloth-merchant. Mirabeau suddenly felt his heart chilled. He remembered that his sister had had many communications with Le Tellier, who could be made serviceable in this way, and he suspected that Madame de Saillant was the originator of this strange meet-

* Montigny, vol. III., p. 425.

ing, for the purpose of accomplishing her wishes as to a reconciliation.

Mirabeau's first emotion at the generous activity of the people vanished. He ordered Le Tellier to go to the Marchioness de Saillant, and ask her presence; but this lady had observed every thing from her window, and was already running to the assistance of her friend. Many hands were offered to aid in carrying the countess into the house, and the triumphal chair, with all its decorations, was used for that purpose. The people were deeply interested in this scene. The homage paid to Mirabeau ceased for a moment, for all were occupied, from curiosity and sympathy, with the sufferings of the beautiful lady, led away by her sister-in-law with tears and kisses.

The count took occasion to withdraw from any further demonstrations of his friends and electors, passing unperceived into another street, to the dwelling of the lawyer Jaubert, where he was expected at dinner. The invitation had been sent to Paris, and the count gladly accepted it, as he would meet there the leaders of the popular party.

"Poor Emilie, we are separated and must remain so forever," he said to himself, as he passed to his friend's. "I have always done justice to your amiable qualities, although we did not render each other happy. Beautiful, sensible, and courteous, as you were, you could not give peace to my heart. While you lay before me pale and helpless, I remembered that I even once threatened to raise my hand against you, accusing you of infidelity to our vows. Shame overwhelmed me, and to-day I had an opportunity to make amends for the past; but as you were once too weak to resist your father's hatred toward me, and rendered your divorce from me as public as possible, so my proud heart rejected you now in the presence of the people. I scarcely wished it, but I could not act otherwise. Society and morals have their laws of compensation—more than men generally imagine." Revolving such thoughts, he arrived at the residence of M. Jaubert. As he was about to enter, he noticed a man approaching on a horse, covered with perspiration and dust.

"A dispatch from the electors of the Third

Estate of Marseilles to Count Mirabeau!" said the courier, drawing forth a letter and handing it.

The count quickly opened the paper, and read the announcement of his election. "You rode well, my good man," replied Mirabeau, smiling, "nevertheless you come a little too late. I am proud of having been elected representative of the men of Aix, though I express my gratitude to the gentlemen of the Third Estate of Marseilles. I love one of these cities as well as the other, and would gladly be a resident of both, if I could. But Aix first demanded my services, and I must give them. Return this answer, for the present, to the commissioners. I will shortly visit Marseilles myself, and express to the people my sincere thanks!"

After dismissing the messenger, he entered the house of his friend, where the company were waiting him.

CHAPTER XXIX.

THE PROCESSION OF THE THREE ESTATES.

ON the 4th of May, 1789, a bright, balmy day, Chamfort was seated in front of a café at Versailles, engaged in a game of chess with the Abbé Cerutti, with whom he had come from Paris a few days before.

The two friends were absorbed in their play, although the place was by no means favorable for profound study. It was so crowded that little room was left for the players; but they maintained their position at the small table, and made their moves undisturbed by the commotion around them.

The people, finding that the expected display in the streets was retarded, amused themselves by watching Chamfort and Cerutti. The former looked up several times at the persons nearest him, nodding to them, although he was only acquainted with their faces, having frequently seen them at the Palais-Royal in Paris, when he played chess at the newly-organized "Club Politique."

Those thronging the usually silent streets of the royal city belonged mostly to Paris. They had come to witness the solemn ceremonies preceding the opening of the sessions of the Estates, announced to take place on the 5th of May. The sensation this event produced in the capital of France, caused nearly the whole population to visit Versailles. Many of the savage-looking figures moving about since the elections, were among them. They so suddenly appeared in Paris, and so unexpectedly, that one might almost suppose them to have come from the barbaric ages. The capital for some time had been turbulent and dangerous; nor was there full confidence of order at Versailles, which suggested to the stranger good-feeling and courtesy. The more sober-minded remembered those roving bands that had terrified Paris a few days before, and for whose restraint the commandant, M. de Besenval, had summoned two regiments of the guard. This old city of the French kings, however, presented a more cheerful aspect than ever before. The thoroughfares were ornamented with crown tapestries, and the balconies of the houses variously decorated, while at the windows stood spectators of all classes, among them groups of ladies in gay toilets. All eyes were turned toward the place where the procession could first be seen.

The French as well as the Swiss guards were already stationed along the streets from the church of Notre Dame to that of St. Louis, passing through the principal portions of the city. It was intended to solemnize the occasion by religious exercises, to be held the day previous to the opening of the assembly, as a fit preparation for the important labors before them. The deputies had met in the cathedral of Notre Dame, and every ear was listening for the first sound of the bells announcing that the procession had moved for the church of St. Louis.

"At the moment our representatives pass, your king will be checkmated," said Chamfort to the Abbé Cerutti, suddenly checking the king of the latter.

"It certainly looks like it," replied the abbé, smiling. "But I place my queen before him, and the situation is different, which will give you some trouble, my dear friend."

"That is the worse thing you can do," said Chamfort, with a comic gesture. "It is what has nearly caused the ruin of our land, and you expect to succeed by such a move, Cerutti? The queen ought never to become more prominent than her consort, because she then appears to reign conjointly with him, and meddles with politics, which is no work for ladies. How much better would be the condition of Louis XVI. if Marie Antoinette, vain of her superior mind, and supposing that state affairs are best in her hands, had not interfered between the sovereign and his subjects! Pay attention now; my rook advances, protected by two pawns, which I always fancy resemble a popular party in their strength and energy. My pieces place themselves immediately before your queen, and threaten both her and his majesty." Several of those looking on expressed their approbation by cries of "Bravo!" which seemed to amuse Chamfort.

"The case is not so bad as it looks," replied the abbé. "My bishop relieves both my royal personages."

"The bishop cannot save their majesties." said Chamfort, impressively. "They are faithful courtiers, brought up with kings and queens, and move obliquely. They are lost as soon as a knight bestirs himself."

"The knight," replied Cerutti, in a tone of vexation, "certainly interferes with my plans. It is a very democratic piece—one of the 'philosophic nobles of the epoch.' His insidious movement reminds me of certain sophisms in reference to the king. However, I attack him with a pawn, for you must not suppose the field is quite abandoned by the peasants."

"I care nothing about that, but take your bishop with my knight." "Your queen is now face to face with the 'philosophic nobleman,' and she may bite her Hapsburg under-lip, if she pleases. For if she tries to take her disagreeable neighbor, she falls into the hands of the rook. I see, M. Cerutti, that we do not yet think quite alike, and, even on the day before the opening of

the National Assembly, it seems that we cannot agree."

"I must always be more conservative than you, my friend," said Cerutti. "For I find that your knight, who has so boldly attacked my queen, protects the royal position; I can now remove her, and say check to your king!"

"The tables are turned," replied Chamfort, laughing. "Very well, my reactionary abbé, I see that your friendship with the present financial minister, M. Necker, has been of advantage to you, who have learned how to retire by a *coup de théâtre*. Your royal lady is lost, sir, for you must cover your king; and my rook, a democratic gentleman, protected by the knight, approaches and again cries check."

"I see you are a dangerous opponent," exclaimed the abbé, in an irritated tone. "I can do nothing but surrender. It may be that your manner of attack is the right one, and I might be converted to the democratic side, if your partisans were less tumultuous, and did not talk so much of blood."

"Do you allude to the sanguinary scenes a few days ago in Paris?" asked Chamfort, his eyes beginning to sparkle. "Believe me, the poor laborers of the Faubourgs Saint Antoine and Saint Marceau, who burned down the house of the manufacturer Réveillon, were merely the instruments of a certain plot. Whether this man is an aristocrat or not, the populace would scarcely have cared about him, if they had not been instigated by the agents of the Duke d'Orleans."

"What!" replied Cerutti, quickly. "Do you really think that the duke could have had any interest in such disturbances in the capital?"

"I not only think it—I know it," said Chamfort. "I have seen the creatures of the duke distribute money among those laborers, and they did not conceal the name of him who commissioned them, because he wishes to have adherents among the people. You know how anxious he was, who has suddenly curried the popular favor, to be elected deputy of the Estates. He merely wished to frighten the court by forsaking them. And he has really succeeded in being chosen delegate by the aristocracy of Crespy, who fancy themselves well represented by a royal prince who can command the working masses."

"Réveillon is said to have excited the laborers by mere arrogance," replied the abbé. "He told them that a workingman ought to be able to live on fifteen cents a day. This so greatly inflamed the populace, who are ready for any commotion, that they burned his property. The bands that have suddenly appeared in Paris are a dangerous sign of the times, my friend. I met them rushing through the streets with terrific cries, stopping the carriages, and forcing those they took for aristocrats to descend and walk through the mud. They demanded money from any one to drink the health of the Third Estate. My good sir, I fancy your eulogized Third Estate, for which so much enthusiasm is expended, comes into the world in rather a scandalous manner."

"Many things are not very elegant, or even apparently favorable, at their beginning," said Chamfort. "But in due time they declare themselves as they were intended by nature. I think our game of chess, played while waiting for the procession, has ended in not the best humor. The politics of the day have disturbed us, or perhaps my friend the abbé has engaged me in this conversation with clerical cunning, to prevent me from enjoying my triumph. The popular party is victorious, Cerutti!"

"At all events, I acknowledge a defeat," replied the abbé. "But whether the popular party will really win the day, who can tell?"

The bells were ringing the signal that the delegates were moving from Notre Dame. Chamfort stepped upon the table to see over the heads of the people; the tall abbé stood near him on a chair, remarking that he already saw the first rank of the line of march.

"They are the bells of 1789 that we hear!" said Chamfort. "They will sound in the ears of all nations. They announce to you, Cerutti, that the popular party is victorious, whose will is the same as their action. These bells ring not only for all nations, but for all times!"

The bands, placed at certain distances from each other, played solemn airs. At the same time the military tramp was heard, with the sound of drums and trumpets, and the hymns of the priests. The procession approached. — First came the clergy of Versailles, and in their midst the choir of the royal chapel. Then the deputies of the Third Estate, or of the commoners, as more prudent persons called them. They were all dressed in black suits, with small black silk mantles, and white cambric cravats—six hundred men, thus forming a large part of the spectacle, and by their appearance making a peculiarly grave impression on the spectators. But they walked with such a quiet, determined demeanor that they suggested their importance, as the élite of the people. The assembled populace burst into shouts of applause, clapping their hands, throwing their hats into the air, and expressing their joy in various exclamations. The ladies waved their handkerchiefs from the balconies and windows; all countenances expressed hope, and many eyes shed tears.

"This is the Third Estate!" said Chamfort. "At every step my heart beats like that of a bridegroom. They are not the representatives of only one class, but of the whole nation. Mark me, they are the true defenders of liberty!"

"You will fall from your chess-table if you do not take care, friend Chamfort!" cried Cerutti, holding his friend to steady him. "I love the Commons as much as you do, although I cannot consider them as the whole nation. But tell me, why are they habited in such a costume, on their day of honor? I understand that many of the delegates felt hurt that the regulation required them so to clothe themselves."

"They are not the best men who feel annoyed on that account," replied Chamfort, warmly. "The delegates prove themselves to be the nation because they wear no badges and superfluous ornaments distinguishing them as belonging to a separate rank. See the aristocracy! how they glitter in their gold embroideries and waving plumes! They are nothing but a class! The regulation as to dress seems to me to have resulted in what is most becoming for the Third

Estate. The people's condition is not the brightest, and they have assuredly suffered enough to mourn for a government that has oppressed them so badly. But this is the dress also of the lawyers and state councillors of the Middle Ages—a very shrewd idea. For they have been called to give counsel to the state, and decide between the king and the nation—the past and the future."

"Ah, at last I see our friend Mirabeau in the midst of his colleagues!" cried Cerutti. "But why is he not dressed like the rest? Why does he wear his cavalier costume among the black cloaks?"

"The black habit has been prescribed only to the citizens," replied Chamfort, "and Mirabeau does not like to change his toilet. But to make up for this, he is walking arm in arm with that strong peasant, Gérard, from Brittany, who is the apostle of liberty in his region, and is a power in himself, with his sunburnt brow and gigantic form. Our friend celebrates to-day a triumph. How the crowds throng around to catch a glimpse of him! They notice him from afar and whisper his name. Bravo, Mirabeau! You have attained the summit on which we long desired to see you! You have suffered much, but you had a noble companion in your misery—the people, and they will make a hero of their comrade!"

"His name is decidedly the most popular in France!" said the abbé, looking after the count. "The people know his history by heart, and relate it to each other as they would an old story of some knight—the personal events of his youth, his conflicts with his tyrannical father, his incarcerations, and the tortures he suffered in prison, as well as his love-adventures. He has become distinguished—we hardly know how—and the greatest deeds of this century will be associated with his name."

"So much depends in the world on a name," replied Chamfort, thoughtfully. "Mirabeau has been a loved and a hated one, and this fact will aid in making him an historical character. The day before yesterday, he aroused again the ill-will of the aristocracy. When the three Estates presented themselves before the king at the palace,

Mirabeau was the first to give expression to the dissatisfaction of his colleagues, because the distinction of rank was made in a manner very insulting to the people. The nobility and clergy were received by his majesty in his cabinet, but the commons in a separate hall, and before being admitted into it they had to wait a long time. This so excited the indignation of our friend that he proposed to write a remonstrance and lay it at the foot of the throne. When Louis XVI. appeared, and covered his head during his address, Mirabeau also put on his hat, his significant example being, of course, followed by the rest of the delegates, announcing in this manner the new era of liberty and equality. Hitherto none but the aristocracy and clergy had a right to be covered in the presence of the king." *

"I have heard it," said Cerutti. "The instructions of the deputies of the Commons, received from their electors, certainly require them to give no preference to the others as to ceremony or etiquette; however, it required a Mirabeau to make the beginning. But, see! the nobles are approaching! Quite a democratic line is drawn between the black of the commoners and the tinsel of the aristocracy."

The one hundred and fifty delegates of the nobility now appeared, while the cries of the people, "Long live the Third Estate!" had not yet ceased. As soon, however, as the next section of the procession came up, an ominous silence ensued. They also wore black coats with vests of gilt cloth, laces, and costly embroideries, colored silk mantles, and brilliant badges. What most characterized them was the turned-up hat, à la Henri IV., with white plumes, and which they fancied made a profound impression.

"What a swarm of marquises, counts, viscounts, barons, marshals, generals, and presidents!" said Chamfort, glancing along the shining ranks. "And whom do we see at the head of the aristocracy in all his glory? Louis Philippe Joseph de Bourbon, Duke d'Orleans, the delegate from Crespy in Valois, the first imitator of the British, who has

---

* Toulongeon, "Histoire de France depuis la Révolution de 1789," vol. i., p. 22.

studied liberty in the London clubs, and become suspected at court. He prefers to appear in the midst of his colleagues, although his proper place is among the princes, who come last. This conduct of the former Duke de Chartres surprises me —it is one of the wonders of the times."

These words were almost inaudible in the shouts of the people. "Long live Orleans!" resounded on all sides, at which the prince smiled.

"The duke seems as pleased with popular liberty as if it were a new vice he had discovered in his Palais-Royal!" said Chamfort. "I really shudder at the experiment of this prince of orgies. I become suspicious when I think of him as a convert to the freedom of France. And the populace rejoice over him! Well, let them; if they believe in him, he may be made useful; the people, after all, have true instincts."

"They have already been benefited by him," replied Cerutti. "The Duke d'Orleans is the cause of the double representation of the Third Estate. I can assure you that this is the principal article of the secret union between the duke and Necker. Besides, can you name any other man, either at court or among the nobility, who has been as active as this prince in alleviating the sufferings of the poor? He has not confined his good deeds to Paris, where whole parishes live and are clothed by him—he cares as a father for all those who are unfortunate on his property. Through the hands of his officials he distributes among them wheat, wood, and wine, and all who address him find him accessible. He yielded to the importunities of Necker in becoming a deputy for the aristocracy. I am quite surprised, my friend, at such narrow-minded judgment of your neighbor in the Palais-Royal. How does it happen that the philosopher Chamfort measures with a common rule a man who, drawn into dissipation by the influence of the times and his rank, suddenly feels himself born for something higher, and endeavors to release himself from his degradation?"

"This is the first time that any one ever intimated to me that I am a fool on account of my austere virtue," said Chamfort, with a good-natured smile. "Both the duke and Necker are enemies

of the queen. My dear abbé, if a revolution take place in France, it will be to his wife's enemies that the good Louis XVI. will owe it. But if Orleans and Necker are secretly allied, what follows?"

"That you would deserve the thanks of the whole nation," replied Cerutti, "if you would induce Mirabeau to join these two. They would receive him with open arms; this you may consider, by the way, as an authentic invitation."

"I think I understand you," said the philosopher, "but you must know that I am too indolent for a mediator. But now comes your Estate, abbé, the clergy, with their decorations."

The ecclesiastical members appeared, bearing at their head the host. They were arranged according to rank: the bishops in their violet-colored robes of ceremony, separated from the inferior clergy in their large cloaks and four-cornered caps. The king and queen accompanied the consecrated wafer, borne by the Archbishop of Paris under a splendid canopy, the cords being held by the Counts de Provence and d'Artois, on one side, and on the other by the Dukes d'Angoulême and Berri.

The king, walking pale but calm, was hailed with renewed shouts of applause, which seemed to make an unexpected impression on him. But no voice was heard for the queen—no word of love or admiration, such as Marie Antoinette was formerly accustomed to on her public appearance. She felt the meaning of this silence, and determining not to receive what she considered a personal attack without some sort of resentment, she suppressed her emotion, and acted as she had done before on similar occasions—she stared at her enemies in a contemptuous manner, and, so far as she could, manifested her hatred and defiance of them. Suddenly, however, she grew pale, and seemed to be fainting. The Princess de Lamballe, who was nearest the queen, endeavored to sustain her mistress. For a moment there was danger that the procession would be interrupted, but Marie Antoinette regained her self-control and walked on.

The queen's trouble on this occasion originated

chiefly from the conduct of several women, who tried to have themselves noticed by her. They made grimaces at her and uttered the most hateful expressions, crying, with gestures that could not be misunderstood: " Long live the Duke d'Orleans! The family d'Orleans forever!" The queen's eyes chanced to meet those of the Duchess d'Orleans, and she felt deeply wounded by the triumphant malice that shone in them.

All the members of the court closed this remarkable procession, dazzling the spectators by their costumes, radiant with gold and precious stones.

Chamfort sprang from his chess-table, saying to the Abbé Cerutti: "Now, my friend, let us follow quickly, that we may arrive early at the church of St. Louis, and take the seats reserved for us. If we go through yonder street, we shall be in advance of the king and the Estates."

The friends attempted to push their way through the crowds, which they found at first rather difficult. At the cross-street they intended to take, they were forced to stop, being pressed against a balcony, on which many well-dressed ladies were seated.

"We are fortunate," said Chamfort, glancing at the ladies. "Is not that the daughter of Necker, Madame de Staël-Holstein; and the one near her, Madame de Montmorin? They are engaged in rather loud conversation, and if we can excuse ourselves for becoming eavesdroppers we can hear every word."

"I know no day of my life on which I have been so happy," said the daughter of Necker, her eyes sparkling with enthusiasm. "It is a sublime spectacle! The people and the king have embraced, and are about to pray together—to take an oath of union for the regeneration of the fatherland—is not that a scene for tears of joy?"

"She always expresses herself in that manner," whispered Chamfort to his friend. "In her book on Jean Jacques Rousseau I find too many ejaculations, that make me half smile and half frown, and I am not sure whether the fair authoress deserves a kiss or a reprimand. M. Necker's opening address to-morrow is sure to contain a few

ideas from his intellectual and adored daughter. He is said to be entirely under her control."

"Let us listen to Madame de Montmorin," replied the abbé, silencing him. "She is reproaching Madame de Staël for her too great exultation."

"I pray you," said Madame de Montmorin, "how can you attach such joyful expectations to this day? You are wrong, for the greatest misery to France and ourselves will be the consequence." * Madame de Staël trembled at these words. She seized the hands of her friend, and burst into tears.

Chamfort and Cerutti were driven farther on by the crowd, and heard no more. The music of the procession sounded in the distance; and the friends, anxious to reach the church, increased their speed.

The three Estates were seated on the benches in the nave of the church. The king and queen, surrounded by their suites, took their places under a violet velvet canopy, strewed with golden lilies. Marie Antoinette looked pale and disturbed; and Louis XVI., who was otherwise unembarrassed, seemed concerned for his consort, and turned constantly toward her.

Chamfort and Cerutti were on one of the platforms, where seats had been reserved for spectators. "We shall see every thing plainly from here," said the former," and I begin to appreciate the value of connections in this world, for without your intercourse with Minister Necker we would not have had such good places. I am anxious to see all the solemnities, for I have promised a report of them to our friend Mirabeau, which he intends to make use of in the journal he is editing about the sessions of the Estates of the kingdom. He thinks that the hero of our age must also wield the pen, in order to reach the heart of this century. I can look directly into the queen's fair countenance, and read the traces of a secret grief, which belongs to history."

---

* Madame de Montmorin was afterward involved in the events of the revolution, and ended her life on the scaffold.—Vide Madame de Staël, "Considérations sur la Révolution française," p. 187.

"She really looks as if she suffered," replied the abbé. "She has long feared this day, and struggled against it. Her misunderstanding with France showed itself to-day; and, I apprehend, sadly against her. If her opinion had been followed by the state council, the assembling of the Estates would have taken place sixty miles distant from the capital, and she would scarcely have been aware of that which has cast such gloom over her heart. But Necker's idea prevailed, and I think it is creditable in the minister to have this parade here at Versailles, demonstrating that he does not wish to avoid seeing the delegates of all classes brought into the presence of the people, and having some notion of their life and hopes. This confidence will redound to M. Necker's favor."

"But you cannot deny the accurate foreboding of the queen," replied Chamfort. "Great storms are coming, and her fair locks will be tossed into some disorder."

The aisles of the old cathedral now resounded with the hymn *O salutaris hostia*. Soon after, the Bishop de Nancy, M. de la Farre, ascended the pulpit, to deliver the sermon, which many waited for with great expectation. The courtiers scarcely trusted their ears when the pious ecclesiastic, in a noble address, spoke of the luxury and despotism of courts, the duties of monarchs, and the rights of the people. The congregation were so moved that they could not restrain their applause —a gross infringement of propriety, which disturbed especially the attendants of their majesties; for even at the theatre the presence of the king suppressed all such noisy demonstrations.*

Louis XVI. remained unmoved. His eyes did not turn from the countenance of the queen, which changed from a marble pallor to a deep red. As soon, however, as the concluding ceremony was performed, the royal party disappeared. The congregation then assumed a different appearance. The delegates left their places, where each class was separated from the other. The members of one rank greeted those of another;

the deputies of the aristocracy, however, in many instances, endeavored to leave at the same time with their majesties, only few of them remaining to converse with the clergy and the Third Estate.

In the centre of the edifice were several groups holding animated conversations. Chamfort and Cerutti approached to greet Mirabeau. He received them in a hearty manner, but was soon withdrawn from them by others. He was talking warmly with the clergy, among whom were several personally known to him, and whose acquaintance he wished to renew. This was especially his object in reference to Talleyrand-Périgord, who had lately been raised to the dignity of Bishop of Autun, from which city he was delegated. While this admirable man was an abbé, Mirabeau lived in intimacy with him. Subsequently they met almost as strangers; Talleyrand did not care to meet his former friend, and was evidently shunning him now.

Mirabeau had noticed the bishop's manœuvres for some time, and without further ceremony approached him, shaking his hand in a hearty manner, regardless of his reluctance, and saying: "On a day such as this, when the nation is reborn, let us renew our friendship, Talleyrand-Périgord! Is it possible that that miserable book on the Prussian court, for the publication of which I am in no wise to blame, should really have separated us?"

Talleyrand, with a grace that always characterized him, scarcely returned the count's salutation, and yet, with a polite smile on his grave countenance, he replied: "Is this a time to think of books? Books may be forgotten, but true friends never. And now we all need the assistance we can get, as the convocation of the Estates of the kingdom proves. The government calls upon us to aid it, and we must stand by each other as well as by the state. Thus you see we are reconciled, Count Mirabeau!"

"If you really mean what you say, it signifies success to the assembly," replied the count. "The Third Estate, which I represent, would gladly unite with the clergy to effect certain objects. The excellent sermon of the Bishop of Nancy

---

* Mirabeau, "Journal des États-Généraux," no. 1.

gave us hopes for such a union. What M. de la Farre said from the pulpit about the wickedness of courts and the rights of the people, challenges the commoners to form a defensive and offensive alliance with the ecclesiastics. I see you still believe that I had that unfortunate book printed against your advice and express desire."

"Why, my dear count," said Talleyrand, in a satirical tone, "it is a very pretty book, and you have eulogized me as one of the most hopeful men of the period. However, it appeared at a very unfavorable moment for the government, for Prince Henry of Prussia was in Paris, whom you criticised in so offensive a manner. Because I am acquainted with the prince, and it was believed by many that I suggested your mission to Prussia, the work appeared to me contemptible at the time.* However, now we are standing together on the floor of the new assembly, my old friend! The Third Estate and the clergy will certainly have to unite, although I am not in such ecstasy as you are about the discourse of my venerable colleague the Bishop of Nancy! But you were always favorable to those of my cloth in spite of your vagaries. I will tell you what did not please me in his address. It was intended to act in exciting the applause of the auditors, which was a grave violation of etiquette, and I was sorry to see it originating from a distinguished member of the clerical order. What is etiquette? You smile, count. I think I can read your thoughts. You mean to say that the first attack at the forms of ceremony came from the queen, and that therefore we must not be surprised if the fire she kindled burn below as well as above."

The countenance of the Bishop of Autun betrayed his irony, which he usually concealed by an appearance of thoughtful gravity, seldom permitting himself to look as he felt. He expected to provoke a smile from Mirabeau also; but to Talleyrand's surprise, the count remained very serious, and remarked: "I confess that the queen made me sympathize with her to-day, and I have asked myself whether the most lovely woman in France was destined to become the most miserable? Perhaps I was affected by her beauty, that never before seemed to me so pure and perfect. You know I have a democratic head, but an aristocratic heart. With you, it is the contrary: you are a democrat at heart, while your intellect bows to the lords of the earth. That is why we were inclined to quarrel in our former political debates. We were alike only in one thing—in having creditors."

"We begin a new life, if it is God's will, with the General Assembly," said the Bishop of Autun, piously folding his hands. "It is often good to have creditors—we gain believers thereby; for one who trusts and runs after us, we can soon lead to what is good. But I notice here are other good friends, with whom I should like to gossip a little."

The approaching group constituted Chamfort, Cerutti, and a third gentleman in clerical dress, recognized by Mirabeau as the Abbé Sièyes, who was a small, compact man, having a strong will impressed on every feature; but his manner was reserved. Mirabeau met this gentleman with lively greetings, exclaiming: "All honor to the Paris elections, which send us such a man as Count Sièyes! You are the only ecclesiastic representing the Third Estate, and that is a good omen."

Sièyes returned the compliment in a friendly manner, adding: "Can there be a better representative of the commoners than a clergyman? If he is not a man of the people, he is a hypocrite. There can be neither state nor church without him."

"And our Sièyes has become the oracle of the commoners," said the Abbé Cerutti, tapping the other on the shoulder. "His pamphlet 'What is the Third Estate?' is the oriflamme of the present movement in France. It has pointed out the right way. It has given the people self-knowledge, which is as a sort of sacrament."

"That is not so bad, Cerutti," said Sièyes, in his laconic way. "But if you speak of my tract, here is the man to whom I owe every thing—not

---

* "Correspondance entre le Comte de Mirabeau et le Comte de la Marck," vol. i., p. 344.

only the general idea, but many of the most important passages." He looked at Chamfort, standing near, who started when he heard himself thus referred to.

"Our friend blushes like a young maiden," said Mirabeau, laughing. "I once said of him that he somehow provides serpents' eggs, and gets eagles to hatch them."

"I find that you are all too generous," replied Chamfort. "You give more credit than is due me.'

"No," said Mirabeau; "you are a little lazy, it is true, or you might have been elected to the General Assembly—and I do not indeed see how we can get along without your correct judgment."

"The spectators' seats must also be filled, if good acting is to be on the stage," replied Chamfort. "With the pamphlet of the Abbé Sièyes I only played the part of a good audience, nothing more. He explained his ideas to me, and I gave them a good dress, which he mistakes for new thought and information. A hero becomes such chiefly through the acclamations of the people, and I, my dear friends, wish to remain one of them—I may be useful in that way; certainly, in no other!"

All laughed at the modesty of Chamfort, but Sièyes said, while his dark eyes brightened: "He is right. I was thinking of the same thing to-day. Perhaps I do not belong here either, and ought to have remained at home in my quiet .study, talking to my books or composing music; for nothing, except Mirabeau's eloquence, can be of avail."

"Do you still compose music?" asked Talleyrand, who had been conversing with General Lafayette. "Your pamphlet, Sièyes, on the Third Estate, is a sort of opera, in which wind instruments play a considerable part. But you belong to the cloth, abbé, why not compose a few peace hymns?"

"I am not a general composer, bishop," replied Sièyes, dryly.

The bells of St. Louis, which had been ringing since the close of the ceremonies, ceased with a sound like a sigh, and the deputies departed to the carriages awaiting them at the gates.

THE NATIONAL ASSEMBLY.

CHAPTER XXX.

THE FIFTH OF MAY.

The opening of the General Assembly was to be at the palace of Versailles, on the 5th of May. Mirabeau had hired, contrary to his custom, very plain apartments in the house of a citizen of the place, a dyer by trade, and a very excitable politician. They stood together in the small garden, where breakfast had been served. The dyer himself waited on his high-born lodger, who, in addition, appeared to him in all the glory of a representative of the people. The host very naturally took this opportunity of entering into conversation with his guest, and endeavored to gain some information on the important questions of the day. The count, however, showed little patience with this inquisitive citizen, often looking at his watch, to see how near the hour was which would call him to the castle. It was only six o'clock, and the carriage was ordered to be at the door half an hour after.

"You have asked me enough about liberty, equality, human rights, and popular sovereignty, Master Camille," said Mirabeau, "Let us look a little at your roses. You know how to cultivate them; they are arrayed in a beautiful morning toilet, and the dew from heaven shines upon them as diamonds."

"No, count, I have other things in my head than foolish flowers," replied the burgher, walking restlessly up and down, and then standing as if lost in anxious thought. "Every one is talking of popular sovereignty—some even speak of a 'revolution'—a curious word lately come into fashion, we hardly know how. I went not long ago to Paris, and took a cup of coffee in the Rue St. Nicaise, where the diligence starts for Versailles. All the people there were so well informed that I was quite ashamed of my ignorance. One man spoke of a 'Contrat Social,' and looked as solemn as a priest administering the sacrament, so that I edged myself shyly into a corner, and listened with great attention. Another read some paragraphs from a periodical, the title of which was very cheering; for it was said to be printed at the house of the 'Widow Liberty,' and could be procured at the store of 'the revolution.' Now, tell me, count, what is the meaning of the word 'revolution,' and what kind of business the widow carries on."

"You are a dyer as well as a florist, Master Camille," said Mirabeau, smiling. "If the color of a stuff fades, and the material is still good, would you despair of giving it another shade? No, you begin to work. You first wash it thoroughly, beat, rub, and shake it, and then you immerse it in the new dye, which gives the piece a fresh appearance. Well, you have made a 'revolution,' for you have turned gray into black, yellow into green, white into red, and I know not what other changes you may have wrought. With your sweet roses you manifest yourself even more like a creator. You infuse life into a sickly species from the strength contained in another, or you mix the several kinds of seed, and a new and beautiful blossom is the result, probably different from any you may have seen before. Here again you have made a 'revolution.' As you do with your flowers, we shall have to do with the different ranks and classes of men. The question of new and living forms of life from a degenerate or dead past in society will probably be debated to-day, or at farthest to-morrow. For both the court and the ministry are mistaken if they think that at our meetings we intend to recognize social grades. The Three Estates must be united as the essential elements of the nation; the commoners will see to that, and Mirabeau will lead the way! Such action you may denominate as you please— in your horticulture you are engaged in it every day, accepting the hints given you, employing your reason, as it is so meant to be exercised; and, while gratifying your own intelligence, you are permitted to clothe nature with new beauty."

Camille clapped his hands at this explanation, while the count paced the little garden with impatient steps, and then sent his servant to hasten the carriage.

"When I am restless about any thing, some obstacle usually occurs," said Mirabeau to himself. "I ought to have brought Henriette and Coco with me; their faces always have a tranquillizing influence on me. Well, this is a great day, and we shall see what are its results!" The coach at last arrived.

An early hour had been appointed for the assembling of the Estates, so as to have time for all the forms of ceremony, which the ministry wished particularly to be observed. It was intended also to prepare a humiliation for the deputies of the Commons.

A large and beautiful hall in the palace of Versailles had been considered as proper to receive the twelve hundred, as well as a numerous audience, and it was accordingly fitted up for that purpose. Louis XVI., who was an amateur in such things, engaged himself in the decorations. It had long been a cherished fancy of his to adorn in the most brilliant manner the place where he was to meet the General Assembly. He had selected the tapestries and curtains, and superintended all the arrangements.

When Mirabeau arrived, he was not admitted as the gentlemen belonging to the aristocracy and clergy, who came at the same time. The latter entered by the principal gate, but the deputies of the commoners were taken to a back-door leading through a coach-house—then through a dark corridor, where they waited until allowed to pass in.

"This is a worthy antechamber for the delegates of the nation!" said Mirabeau to his neighbor the Abbé Siòyes, whom he recognized, after they had knocked against each other in the closely-packed crowd. The government desires us first to loosen our teeth before we appear before them. The question: 'What is the Third Estate?' our Siòyes answered by: 'It is every thing!' but the ministry replies to-day: 'It is a certain something that is permitted to enter, by a back-door and through a carriage-house, into an Egyptian darkness, reminding it of its obscurity.' But no, gentlemen, we shall hold up our heads notwithstanding, and confound our opponents by the good order in which we march to the attack!"

"I think we are treated like children who are shut up in the dark at Christmas before they get the presents intended for them," said Siòyes. "It is therefore better to receive no gifts; for the liberty that comes as such is hardly considered a right. I propose that we accept nothing, after we have entered (which I hope will be soon), but that we take what belongs to us. All that we obtain must be the trophies of right over wrong— else they are of little value."

"Gentlemen, we may almost fancy that the government are playing hide-and-seek with us!" cried a shrill voice, belonging to a young lawyer from Arras, named Maximilian Robespierre. "They hope to find us in this corner where they have driven us, but that game will not do—we shall soon be everywhere, and the ministry may not so easily lay their hands on us. They think they have caged a mouse, but when the doors open they will see a lion."

"But they shall not recognize us as traders, at least, with whom a bargain may be made," said Mirabeau. "This is like one of the passages of the Exchange, where people throng to await the opening of business.* In these swindling days the government folks expect perhaps a loan from us; but it must be well paid for—so many francs for you, so many rights for the people, is my motto."

In such conversations the deputies sought to pass the time. It was two hours before they were released from their prison by a sign from the head master of ceremonies, Marquis de Brézé, and permitted to enter the hall.

Mirabeau was at first charmed with the display before him. The *Salle des Menus*, which had been prepared for the reception of the deputies, contained two rows of Ionic columns, giving it a sort of cathedral appearance. The light fell from above through an immense oval window, under which was an expanse of white silk to dim the sun's rays. At one end was the throne, the arm-chair for the queen, the tabourets for the princesses, and the rest of the royal family, and above all was spread a canopy adorned with fringes of gold. Below was the estrade for the ministers and state secretaries. On the right of the throne the clergy were to be seated; on the left, the aristocracy, and, in front, the deputies of the Third Estate.

The Marquis de Brézé aided by two other masters of ceremonies, marshalled the delegates to their seats according to their districts. When the Duke d'Orleans appeared among the representatives from Crespy, there was great commotion among the spectators, occupying places arranged in the style of an amphitheatre; their applause was not suppressed, but even joined in by many of the deputies, when they saw the prince invite a fat ecclesiastic, who was walking behind, to take precedence. Among the state ministers taking their places, only one appeared in plain citizen's dress, appearing as if the event about to take place were but some every-day business

affair or a drawing-room entertainment. As soon as he was seen there were indications of respect from all sides. Necker expressed his appreciation with a smile, that brightened for a moment his grave and furrowed face.

The deputation from Provence now passed; in their midst arose the tall and powerful form of Count Mirabeau. Several persons, in a distant portion of the hall, began to clap their hands, to show their admiration for a man whose name was becoming a household word in France, and of whom such impossible things were said. He was raising his head more proudly, as if conscious of his popularity, when he started as if stung by a serpent; for he heard loud cries of disapprobation, silencing those who would show themselves his friends. Mirabeau, conscious of his strength, folded his arms, and cast a lightning glance in the direction whence the sounds of displeasure came. Silence ensued, while he took his place with commanding dignity.*

Soon after, the king entered, followed by the queen, the princes and princesses. The whole assembly rose with exclamations of joy. Mirabeau gave the signal to the Third Estate, but they did not bend the knee, as it had been their duty when the Estates last met. On the present occasion, any demonstration of that kind would have been ridiculous in view of the change which had taken place in public opinion, and the new condition of affairs.

Louis XVI. wore the large royal ermine mantle, and a plumed hat, the bow of which was radiant with diamonds of extraordinary value. He seemed at first to be pleased, and deeply moved at his reception; but, when he had opportunity to contemplate the stern and manly faces of the commons opposite, he trembled. Mirabeau noticing his confusion, and, smiling at his costly decorations, said in a voice heard by many beyond those near him: "*Voilà la victime!*"†

---

* Mirabeau, "Journal des États-Généraux," no. 11.

* Madame de Staël, "Considérations sur la Révolution française," vol. i., p. 172; Montigny, vol. vi., p. 35.
† "Behold the victim!" Weber, who was present, reports this expression of Mirabeau.—"Mémoires," vol. i., p. 335.

The person sitting beside the count was Barnave, a young landed proprietor from Dauphiny, who was especially remarkable by his manner at the appearance of the court. He replied: "Until now the people were the victim, and were not so well adorned. The sacrifice in the ermine will be more acceptable than that in a blouse! But how simple is the queen's toilet! Never has she been seen in so plain and modest a costume. She will have to be more sumptuously dressed on the day when crowned heads fall, and she seems to feel something of this in anticipation, for she is pale as death!"

"She looks more beautiful than ever!" said Mirabeau, in a lower voice, as she took her place near the throne.

Louis XVI., taking off his hat, began his well-conned address. His voice was clearer and more melodious than it usually was when excited. His style, always natural and unstudied, could not but make a favorable impression on all unprejudiced hearers. Yet the temper of the assembly was rather irritated, because the king spoke first of finances, wishing to have it understood that the representatives of the nation were convoked for no other purpose than to secure the state revenues. In concluding he called himself the best friend of his subjects, and reiterated his love for France.

The speech was succeeded by applause, as the king resumed his seat, and put on his hat. All the members of the aristocracy did the same, and Mirabeau also covered his head, several of those nearest him following his example, while others were not pleased with this violation of etiquette. Soon loud cries were heard. "Put on your hats!" "Take off your hats!" Scarcely, however, had Louis XVI. understood the cause of the commotion than he removed his hat, all in the assembly imitating him.[*]

"The discourse of the king," said Mirabeau to the gentleman sitting at his right (the Abbé Sièyes), "sounded to me as a love-poem, and I have no doubt he has a great regard for the peo-

ple; but it must be disagreeable to the object of his adoration when a lover begins to talk of his debts, and how they are to be paid—his affection looks like avarice—he is a heartless speculator, debasing all tender sentiment. He ought at least to have left us to the illusion of political liberty, and avoided money matters altogether."

"The Estates have been convoked to discover the sincerity of the king's love for the nation," replied Sièyes, sternly. "The seal-keeper, M. de Barentin, and M. Necker, will soon change the royal lyric into matters of hard fact."

M. Barentin began his speech in a weak voice, and an utterance that could hardly be understood, although he was bold in his assertions, insisting that his majesty desired the universal happiness of the nation, which he wished to reconstruct on the basis of popular liberty. Then he referred to the treasury and the taxes, but embodied his remarks so skilfully with political reform, that if he had been better heard, he would have made a considerable impression on his audience.

Necker rose to explain the state of the finances. Great attention was paid him, amid an almost breathless silence. All expected to hear of the regeneration of France in terms clear and decisive. He commenced with much dignity, using noble language, but his hearers were astonished when, instead of comprehensive ideas, such as they expected, the information given consisted of dry statistics, artfully arranged in the most favorable light possible. He dissected the gigantic subject of the national deficit with the self-possession of a surgeon, lightly remarking that it was only fifty-six millions, and decidedly rejected the idea of state bankruptcy, enumerating the resources whence the government could obtain means, and become reëstablished in its credit. It was well understood what he meant when he said that the king might have forborne to convoke the representatives of the nation, and easily have obviated every difficulty without them, if he had chosen to do so. Necker treated all embarrassments in this department as trifling matters, promising to remove them in a short time, and in such a manner, that payments would be easily made, loans refused, interest

---

* Duchez, "Histoire de l'Assemblée constituente," p. 262.

reduced, and capital, now lying useless, brought into the treasury, thus increasing the wealth of the nation. At length, he touched a question the most interesting to the minds of the assembly, and in which lay the inflammable ideas of revolution. Continuing with artful ease and apparent indifference, he reminded the assembly that they consisted of the aristocracy, clergy, and commons, as estates; that they probably would not remain thus separated, but unite as one in their deliberations for the general good.

The court and the ministry had hitherto avoided this point. It was Necker only who referred to it, adding, in careful words, that occasions might arise when it would be preferable to take counsel separately, as, again, in some cases, a union of all might be considered desirable. He touched this dangerous matter very timidly, but unwilling or unable to retain it, he threw it into the midst of the assembly, expecting, from the generosity of the first two Estates, that their discussion would render the subject harmless, and to secure their favor he closed by overwhelming the aristocracy and clergy with flattery.

When Necker had spoken almost two hours, the assembly adjourned in great excitement, confusion, and ill-feeling. The nobles expressed themselves very unfavorably of the ministry. They were displeased at their own presence, because Necker had just told them that, so far as the financial affairs of the state were concerned, it was by no means necessary to convoke the Estates. Since he promised to restore the revenues in the space of eight months, they asked each other, in surprise and irritation, why they had been drawn into this position, and why the scandal of such an assembly had not rather been avoided?

Mirabeau and Lafayette met at the door of the hall, and greeted each other with more friendliness than was usual, considering their mutual dislike. "Well, count," asked the general, shaking his hands, "how did you like the benches of the Third Estates?"

"Very well," replied Mirabeau, "we were at least safe from the eulogies inflicted on your class by such a man as Necker. And you, my American hero of liberty, how do you like your election as representative of the aristocracy?"

"We were not much hurt by Necker's attack," said Lafayette; "his praises are harmless."

"It was a worthless and deceitful speech, to my mind, designed as an ensnaring one," cried Mirabeau, in anger. "If he wished to speak of finances only, he ought to have remembered the inalienable right of such an assembly to vote the amount and kind of taxes, particularly as the king has awarded this right to his subjects for more than a year! He must hold this first step toward liberty, or we stumble at the beginning. And not a word was said about a constitution for France! In place of it a wretched coquetry with the privileged classes. He ought to have taken it as a matter of course that we are a single national body—a unit that cannot be separated, but, instead of that, he aimed at producing contention in the most offensive manner. If we all act as the court desire us, I suppose M. Necker will pat us on the shoulder, and call us his dear provincial assembly. He is a wise man, and yet he does not perceive that old things are passing away, that the people can no longer be ruled by means of cabals and intrigues, and that he who would swim against the stream of public opinion must inevitably be carried off!" *

"The wisest people are often obtuse, and many do not discern that they now live in a new epoch," said Lafayette. "Farewell, Count Mirabeau! I see that you still have too good an opinion of a royal minister. I think the future looks gloomy. Affairs have come to such a pass, that what we call evil, will be the best thing that can happen. We shall see what turn matters will take to-morrow. We shall have to try the validity of the elections, and then know whether the privileged classes will permit that in full session, or insist on their right of separate deliberation. To-morrow, count!"

They separated. Mirabeau was sad and hast-

* Mirabeau, "Journal des États-Généraux," no. xiii. This number was the first that was entitled "Lettres du Comte de Mirabeau à ses commettans," because the Court of Censure disputed his right to edit a journal.

ened to his carriage. He met several friends awaiting him, whom he had not seen for some time, and in their merry mood he felt some surprise that they did not share his own painful and irritated feelings.

"Welcome, Etienne Clavière!" said the count; "and Dumont and Duroveray! I recognized the trio of Genevans among the spectators in the hall. But tell me why you are all laughing? Is there any thing about me ridiculous, or are you in good humor at the opening session of our assembly? Perhaps you were pleased to see that I was almost turned out again, before I had made my entrance? I suppose you heard the hisses?"

"They added to the comicality of the assembly," said Clavière. "Was it not amusing to see such a flock of vultures perch with so much solemnity on the dying body of the monarchy. Instead of beginning their banquet they seemed as if bandying compliments with the king, courtiers, and ministers, who will certainly become their prey? Among them all you are the only earnest and lion-hearted man, and yet you have been insulted, only because you are not like them! Well, how do affairs look, since you have entered the Estates of his most Christian majesty, the King of France?"

"You know, Clavière, that our paths are not quite the same, since this movement commenced! You are steering in a dangerous vessel toward republicanism, and madly invoking the tempest, while I adore the star of a constitutional monarchy. You cannot interfere with me, however, and I do not the less regard you and your compatriots, and wish not to lose your friendship."

It was proposed to take a walk to Trianon, as the dinner-hour had not yet come, and in the park at that place they would have opportunity for confidential conversation, which the Genevans seemed greatly to desire. The sunny May day persuaded the count to accompany them.

CHAPTER XXXI.

THE WALK TO TRIANON.

MIRABEAU and his friends passed through the park of Versailles on their way to Trianon. The populace moved in crowds through the paths and groves of the garden, looking at the marble statues, and making bolder remarks than formerly on the fountains, gods, tritons, and dolphins, sporting with the water in various fantastic shapes, in celebration of the Estates of the kingdom. Among the people were many of the deputies, especially from the Commons, who, with provincial inquisitiveness, never were wearied with the curiosities about them, and the world-renowned magnificence of the palace. Mirabeau and his party left the principal avenue, as the presence of the multitude did not agree with his irritable mind.

"You are amused at the inauguration of the session; but you are wrong, if you think meanly of it!" began the count, after a pause, during which the friends walked silently side by side. "Do you know what influence it has exerted on me? I feel already as if the park and castle of Versailles and all belonging to them were old-fashioned. Has the new era really dawned? Yes, I believe so! And all these ornaments—these fountains with their gods; the verdant couches; the vases with their garlands; the marbled fancies of Proserpine and Pluto, of Apollo and Venus, and all these splendid memories of a once actual life in love and war, in poetry and science—seem to me to lose their value, as a worn-out wardrobe of the old French monarchy. Henceforth there will be an *ancien régime* in France. I feel it in every step I take! But the crown of France will survive!"

"You are and always were an enthusiast, count," said Etienne Dumont. "We practical men cannot quite follow you, for we are not apt to deceive ourselves about the questions of the day. A decayed monarchy can never be restored—certainly not by a National Assembly. We are anxious about the action of the deputies, and on that account we intend to remain a few months in this city; we hope that the result of your deliberations will not be a new royal government, but new institutions for all Europe."

Dumont was a man of middle age, of insignificant appearance, but who, on better acquaintance, made known his decision and energy. He was formerly a clergyman in Geneva, having been forced to leave his home in consequence of the revolution of 1782, when the aristocracy prevailed: against this party he had been one of the most zealous opponents. He had since lived in London among people of influence, and came to Paris to make Mirabeau's acquaintance, the latter having a great reputation among the refugees in the British capital.

"What a terrible republican my gentle Dumont is!" said the count, placing his arm in that of his friend. "At first sight one might fancy you still the peaceful pastor; for your ecclesiastic appearance is I think as inalienable as the French monarchy—even your revolutionary freaks partake of the solemnity of your profession. It is sad that at this moment so many intimate friends part. Chamfort, who, it is true, is not a countryman of yours, for several weeks has been so excited that he imbibes nothing but the strong drink of republicanism, and my principle of royalty appears to him like buttermilk. I am ready to fight like a gladiator in order to change your opinions."

Duroveray was amusing himself in knocking with his walking-cane the mythological statues they passed on the way. He struck a Jupiter so hard a blow that the image sounded. "Old Jove does not seem to like such a salutation," said Duroveray, a tall man, of quite imposing presence. He was formerly general-procurator of the Republic of Geneva, and forced to leave in 1782. Mirabeau had made his acquaintance in London, and was pleased with his quiet conduct, characterized as it was by great efficiency in the interests of the democracy.

"Do you think of attacking Jupiter Olympus with only a walking-cane, Duroveray?" asked Mirabeau, smiling.

"Yes," replied Duroveray, "all that is necessary is a very common stick to make sad work with the follies of the past. The gods will assuredly fall from their pedestals; Etienne Clavière will become financial minister of France, and Count Riquetti de Mirabeau may assume the office of minister of foreign affairs, or be sent as ambassador to Constantinople, where he may have a harem, and study the best forms of monarchy."

"How did you know my favorite wish?" asked the count, laughing aloud. "The position of ambassador to Constantinople is really what I most desire. You may say more on that subject, for if you give me either of those enviable places, I will desert the National Assembly, Versailles, Jupiter, Louis XVI., Venus, and Marie Antoinette."

"But I must ask you to be silent about my future dignity," said Clavière, placing his finger on his lips. "For the present incumbent M. Necker might hear of it, and we require his assistance for our cause in Geneva, at which we are laboring under his superintendence. Dumont and Duroveray have daily audiences with the minister, and owe their presence in France to this political intrigue."

"Can any thing be done with a Necker?" asked Mirabeau, with a contemptuous gesture.

"You know," replied Clavière, ardently, while they stood a moment, "that in this blessed year 1789, in which liberty began to make her claims in your land, our beautiful Geneva commenced a new revolution, but it is not satisfactory—there is too much hurry. The popular party were satisfied in regaining some of the privileges they lost in 1782, but the aristocracy have secured too much, and will obtain possession of all. Besides, the little republic can only have real liberty when released from the chains cast around it by France and the other guaranteeing powers, without whose consent and approval there can be no new constitutional laws. Our friends hope to be so relieved by Necker's aid, and we shall soon see whether he is that friend of the people which he is said to be."

"Dumont has worked out a new constitution

for Geneva, aided by his fellow-refugees in England. You see, Mirabeau, the watch-making republic intends to profit by you Frenchmen; but, on the other hand, she will be enabled to advise and be useful to you during your coming revolution; for if men like Dumont and Duroveray are only spectators of the Estates of this kingdom, their presence is a gain for all." *

The count and his friends continued their walk, and reached the extremity of the park of Versailles, beholding in the distance the palace of Great Trianon, which Louis XIV. built for Madame de Maintenon, with its colonnade of green and red marble. Mirabeau looked grave and sad.

"You owe us a confession," said Dumont, in his usual quiet manner. "It seems to me that in your heart you are much of our opinion, believing the assembly contains not the best material, and that you will find it a difficult place for the exercise of your genius."

"You say that, because they hissed me on my entrance!" said Mirabeau, anger and sorrow rising in his countenance. "That could only have originated with a few wretches who fear my strength, and are endeavoring early to undermine my position. I have no doubt, when I have once spoken, that they will follow my path; but envy and jealousy are already active against any one that might distinguish himself, and this makes me sorrowful. It is a foolish malignity against talent that brought out those serpent voices today. What have I done? My enemies among the aristocracy pretend to find me objectionable on account of my past life! Those privileged gentlemen intend to excuse their hatred in the fact that I was obliged to struggle with my own father for liberty and honor; that I abducted several women; that I made many debts; that I have been an inmate of innumerable dungeons; that I have produced much scandal, as in truth almost every man of the world does. Are they better than I? The difference between us is, that they successfully hid their immorality, and, by an unmanly obsequiousness, remained at court,

while I rushed unthinkingly into vice, because its publicity did not for a moment concern me.

"Those men would wish to eject me from an assembly into which they have entered unwillingly, and to which they add no glory, either in name or morals, while my honor shall become that of the nation. They intend to attack the validity of my elections at Aix and Marseilles, contending that I exerted undue influence. O the fools, who are so hardened in their selfishness that they cannot understand how a man can be devoted to the people for their own sake!" His voice indicated emotion, and his friends saw that his eyes were tearful.*

"I do not comprehend how you can be so surprised and excited by this, Mirabeau," said Dumont, in his straightforward manner. "A man who has acted independently, as you have, giving his thought freedom wherever he found it right or agreeable, may expect umbrage from some quarter; how can he hope for sympathy from his enemies? Do you think that your *Journal des États-Généraux*, which you are publishing, and in which you censure the assembly collectively and individually, will propitiate the aristocracy? You sprinkle pepper into the wounds you formerly gave them, and you are astonished that they do not consider it a balsam! You may be angry, but not sad.

"If you had always lived in a republic, you would know how to let each party have its way; so much the sooner comes the hour when you can break it down, because it has developed itself, and you have facts to work with. Have patience! Those men, shallow in genius and morality, who are now resisting you, will creep into the shade and the dust, as soon as you have given your own strength fair play. At the same time you must remember that you can only rise by means of the assembly; you cannot enter a career of fame, but by them—that is certain, Mirabeau!

"You are now acting in the most considerable theatre in the world—you may be its master-spirit; but you must not stand in your own light.

---

* Etienne Dumont (de Genève), "Souvenirs sur Mirabeau" (Paris), pp. 3, 4.

* Dumont, "Souvenirs sur Mirabeau," p. 48.

What, then, are the little annoyances of to-day in view of the great future? But we think you must work on a new plan! First of all, you must not be precipitate, but wait for a special and important occasion, where only you can say what is just and decisive, and where you will carry all before you! Then you must avoid a too bitter tone in your journal, and even condescend to praise some of the deputies, representing the assembly as a dignified body. We, the Genevan republicans, thus advise you; if you follow our counsel you work for us all, and may the glory of the just shine for ever on your brow!" *

"Very good!" exclaimed Clavière, while Mirabeau and Dumont shook hands. "Our friend has spoken well and truly, but he could not avoid his old clerical custom of evoking Heaven's blessing, and I cannot help saying, Amen!"

The count was consoled, and said: "I may have but few virtues, but that I have a heart formed for friendship, no one can dispute. Your words, Dumont, are as morning dew, and you may be certain that I will follow your advice."

"Shall we go to Great Trianon or Little Trianon?" asked Clavière, as they were standing where the road separated, leading to the two celebrated palaces.

"I think we intended to visit the latter," said Mirabeau, taking the direction of that beautiful pavilion, and followed by the rest.

"Ah," said Clavière, "our friend longs to lose himself in the pastoral dwelling of the lovely queen. Yes, we noticed how your eyes, during the entire session, were turned toward Marie Antoinette, who sat opposite you like a pale Magdalen. What is to become of you? If you should really fall in love with the queen, the revolution may rest, so far as you are concerned. You will probably play the part of Rinaldo in the enchanted garden of Armida."

"This enchanted garden," said the count, pointing toward the one surrounding the little palace, "is very prettily laid out in the English style, according to the taste of Marie Antoinette, in-

dicating thus an amiable and natural mind, but no romance. I am aware that you Genevans are prejudiced against this princess, and are everywhere exciting the minds of people against her. Is it a part of your system to make the first attack against the most charming woman in the world?" *

"Mirabeau," said Clavière, raising his finger in a playfully-threatening manner, "it is evident that you are ensnared in these walks! You are surprised because we act against the queen. Well, she is the most vulnerable point of attack in the French monarchy. A good general moves against that fortress least able to resist. Marie Antoinette places herself before the throne of France, and contemptuously looks down upon the people, so that whatever hurts her must disturb the security of her husband. And how is it possible for you to think her so beautiful? The Roman nose and the Austrian lip struggle for preëminence; her eyes are humid, and her beauty is undeniably that of an insipid and proud woman, having hardly any intellect whatever. Her complexion is good, to be sure, but that does not constitute beauty."

"You are always an ill-natured scoffer," replied Mirabeau. "You wish to induce me to deny beauty itself where it really exists. If you allow the British ministry to pay you for entering the field against a woman, our roads must soon part!" †

"Mirabeau is angry!" laughed Clavière, turning to Dumont and Duroveray, who had each taken an arm of the count, and sought to pacify him.

The friends approached the palace, with its Corinthian pillars. They went into the garden, thrown open to the public on this day, as the queen remained at Versailles. In the different paths they met many of the deputies. The count

* Dumont, "Souvenirs," p. 49.

† It was well known that Clavière, Dumont, and Duroveray, were paid by the British government to assist in overthrowing the French monarchy. This conduct was thus sanctioned on account of the influence of France during the American struggle for liberty.—Soulavie, vol. v., p. 296.

and his friends could not entirely avoid conversation with some of them, answering their questions, particularly addressed to Mirabeau, and which demanded much explanation, as the inquirers were generally from the most distant provinces of France, and were ignorant of almost all they saw and heard around them. Among these people were the wine-merchant Bernard Valentin, from Bordeaux, and the farmer Choisy, from Châlons-sur-Marne, who, like most of the delegates, had taken up their quarters in the houses of small citizens at Versailles, and heard incredible things about the court, the royal family, and the various palaces.

"Where are the notorious *petits appartements*, Count Mirabeau?" asked Bernard Valentin, looking back at Little Trianon with uneasy glances. "Is it true that traces are still found of the banquets given there by Louis XV.? Is there really a cabinet where spots of blood are yet seen that could never be erased?"

"And Queen Marie Antoinette, does she do such wicked things here as we have heard?" asked Choisy, not less excitedly, looking anxiously around. "I was told that she sleeps in the same bed in which Madame Dubarry slept, and that is scarcely proper for an honorable queen." *

"And is it true," again began Valentin, with much solicitude, "that the queen walks about at night on the terrace of Trianon, while her husband retires at eleven, and knows nothing of his rambling wife? She is said to associate freely with all sorts of persons, and lately sat half the night with a young clerk under a tree. Is this true?"

"And is the queen really so extravagant," asked Choisy, "that she knows nothing of housekeeping, and wears diamond buttons on her nightgowns? How can we be surprised that the finances of France are in a bad condition?—and I hope we shall speak on that subject at our next session."

"I have heard," said the wine-merchant, "that this palace is also called 'Little Vienna' or 'Little Schönbrunn,' and that an Austrian bureau is concealed in a cellar of the castle, where the object of the business conducted is to sell France to the house of Hapsburg."

Clavière and his friends rubbed their hands and laughed, while Mirabeau stood a moment gravely shaking his head. Then he said: "My dear colleagues! What we hear from our hosts at Versailles we must be careful not to carry into politics. We have been elected as representatives of the people, that we may act freely and intelligently. I am lodging with a very worthy dyer, who wishes to make me believe that our good king is a drunkard, and consumes daily enormous quantities of wine.* But every one ought to know that Louis XVI. is the most abstemious man in his kingdom. If all your customers were as sober, M. Bernard Valentin, you would soon close your store.

"It is the same with the suspicions against the queen. Does this innocent Trianon look like a place for orgies? Can you imagine any lewd secrecy about it? This English garden, with its sweet flowers, is her favorite resort. Here she often walks with her children without ostentation, and in the plainest dress; or seats herself on some bank, sewing or embroidering, as one of your own wives might do. The domestic life Marie Antoinette leads here ought to prove to you that she has lost all taste for the extravagances of Versailles, preferring simple pastoral pleasures to the splendors of a court. It is impossible for any one to live in a purer or more undisguised manner than the king and queen in this place.

"Marie Antoinette is not only beautiful, but benevolent, my friends and colleagues. Those twelve cottages, distributed so picturesquely on the heights behind the park, indicate that. They were built by her order for poor and unfortunate families, who there find all that is necessary for them. This palace is an asylum for misery and a temple of mercy; and yet the queen's enemies wish to make it appear as a theatre of vice, such as shocks the imagination. It may be that the queen is not highly intellectual, and that her edu-

---

* Campan, vol. i., p. 110.

* Campan, vol. ii., p. 4.

cation in some respects has been neglected; it is also probable that she knows little of literature, aside from a few romances; but she is a true woman, and when we have improved the monarchy (which I believe to be the real object of our assembly) you will see her in her glory!"

The two deputies cordially shook hands with Mirabeau, thanking him for his satisfactory information, and continued their pilgrimage of discovery through the park. The count proposed to his friends that they return, as the dinner-hour was near.

"You have well instructed your colleagues, Mirabeau," said Clavière, as they were taking the shortest route back to Versailles. "But what is to become of Louis XVI, if you infuse your love for the queen into all the rest of the deputies from the Commons? The king is said to have again become very jealous, and will repent having doubled the number of representatives of the Third Estate, if they are destined to become six hundred lovers of his fair wife. That would be the most dangerous side of the revolution, and his majesty would rather send you all to Africa, while he made a constitution to his own taste, or gave you a fragment of the English one, which you so much admire!"

"Listen to me!" said Mirabeau, impressively. "I always acknowledge your merit, and what we owe you and your friends for your activity in introducing the present state of affairs. Your country-seat in Surène, where we passed so many important hours, will always be called the cradle of the revolution. The double representation of the Commons, the manner of their election, the decisions by the number of voters, and not according to rank, the abolition of privileges,—all these points were thoroughly debated at your villa, and referred with a strong will to the people.[*]

"The secret meetings at your house, as well as those at the mansion of the noble Duke de Rochefoucauld, were so efficient that that history would be unjust which would omit to mention them, or impress their value on the public mind. I have

most cause to remember Surène, because there I saw for the last time our unforgotten Holbach.[*] You, Clavière, knew how to bring those men over to your own opinion, but perhaps you may lose me. Let us make a resolution that we remain friends, even if we are the antipodes of each other in some political views. For such I am afraid will be the case! I must adhere to the task I have set myself. I desire democracy, but restrained by the monarchy! I fear, dear Genevans, that we shall soon be separated. You have become members of the ' Club des Enragés' at the Palais-Royal, and there I cannot enter. I shall without doubt become excited, be assured of that, and when I have broken the assembly to my will, I will use it as my Pegasus of the revolution. The only difference between us is, that I know what my object is, and you do not. Let us shake hands as a sign of our superiority to any grovelling feeling of malice or anger."

"Our friend Mirabeau is in a sentimental humor to-day!" exclaimed Clavière. "Come, let us assure him by our strong republican support, and hope that he may regain his former daring!" They surrounded the count in a laughing and jesting humor.

"He is a man around whom we can take a walk," continued Clavière. "It is easy to see that he was intended for the Hercules of the revolution. On his broad back he could carry an entire state, if he would only take it up.—Mirabeau, without you, we cannot advance; we must therefore associate ourselves with your destiny, come what may!"

Amid such conversation the friends reached Versailles. In front of the Hotel Charost, the count noticed a travelling-carriage, from which descended a tall, slender lady, followed by a maid and a footman. He looked after her with surprise. Her face was not seen, but he recognized her well-known walk, and it instantly occurred to him that she was his former wife. For a moment he stood gazing in perplexity, and then came to a decision, knowing he could not be mistaken as to

---

* Dumont, "Souvenirs," p. 32.

* Holbach died on the 21st of January, 1789.

the identity of the lady who had entered the hotel, and could not doubt as to the motives that induced her now to take up her residence at Versailles. He also remembered that his sister, from whom he had received a letter a few days before, had plainly intimated to him the intention of the countess, which was nothing less than if possible to force herself upon him, in order to plead for a reunion; or, if unsuccessful, at least to be near him, and admire his conduct in the important business to be transacted by the assembly.

The count had forgotten the information sent him by his sister, thinking it frivolous and beneath his notice; but he saw now how Emilie, contrary to her usual temper, was importunate in her desire to reconcile the difficulties between them, and that more than ordinary caution would be necessary to elude her.

" You seem to be in doubt about our dinner, Mirabeau!" said Clavière, shaking the count, as if to rouse him from sleep. " Every thing in the Hotel Charost is good, and you need have no fear in that respect. The proprietor keeps the best table in this city, or we would not have honored him with our patronage."

" I am really hesitating whether I am to accompany you or not," said Mirabeau. " The pleasure of being in your society made me quite forget a promise I made yesterday to my honorable host, the dyer in the Avenue of St. Cloud. I must dine with him to-day, and I believe he has cooked a whole ox to entertain me and some other deputies, cousins of his. Such invitations must be honored nowadays, according to your own principles. Excuse me, therefore, and I wish you a good appetite. Adieu!" He left in great haste, while his friends looked after him, surprised to see him turn the nearest corner so precipitately that it might almost be termed a flight.

CHAPTER XXXII.

THE MARQUIS VICTOR RIQUETTI DE MIRABEAU.

A FEW leagues from Paris is situated the village of Argenteuil, with its pretty residences, always sought after during the summer months by the Parisians, as well as by many foreigners of rank. In one of these the Marquis de Mirabeau had lately established himself, drawn by the events of the day from the solitude of his estates, where he had lived for many years. Bowed by age and disease, he would not take up his abode in the capital itself, where, since the opening of the National Assembly, threatening commotions became daily more frequent. The peaceful villa at Argenteuil, on a pleasant hill near the public road, afforded him the double advantage of hearing the news immediately, and of promoting his health in the quiet of country life.

The marquis sat in an easy-chair at an open window, giving him a view for a great distance of the highway, for this was his favorite place during most of the day. His eyes wandered in the direction of Paris with an expression of restlessness. It could not be that he was expecting the newsman, who brought the journals from the capital; for the grand-daughter of the marquis, the fair Marchioness d'Arragon, had already read every item to him; but he still sat at the window with the same look of anticipation, apparently waiting for some person whose name never passed his lips.

Helena d'Arragon, the oldest daughter of the Marchioness de Saillant, had always been the favorite of her grandfather, who induced her to make his house her home after the early death of her husband, whom she had married in her sixteenth year. This was contrary to the wishes of Madame de Pailly, who ruled the family of the marquis since his separation from his consort, and who was the cause of the misunderstanding between husband and wife. The childlike amiability of Helena was however such, that she soon conquered the jealousy of the elderly lady, and the household arrangements of the marquis were greatly improved by the presence of this lovely young woman, who took her share in amusing the old gentleman.

Madame de Pailly attended to the physical condition of the sufferer. She knew that her services could not be dispensed with, as the marquis, who had reached his seventy-second year a few days before, suffered greatly from gout, and latterly from a violent catarrh that at times completely prostrated him. His tall and once powerful frame was daily more bent and shrunken, and had almost lost the carriage that formerly characterized him, giving place to the tremor and weakness of age. On the other hand, his pale and grave countenance, which betrayed the indefatigable thinker, bore traces of that beauty which was his in the bloom of manhood.

The cheerful Helena undertook the task of participating in her grandfather's occupations, and was the companion of his thoughts on the exciting topics of the times. She had become so necessary to him, on account of her sound and appropriate ideas, her good-humor, and her art of brightening the future, that he would undertake nothing without her. He could not make up his mind as to any question, if she did not sit opposite him on her little tabouret, or stand at his side, and point with her small white hand to a passage she had just read, and which she thought of sufficient importance to recite to him. The marquis was accustomed to speak frankly to his grand-daughter, revealing almost all his mind, but he obstinately persisted in concealing from her whom he was hoping to see on the road from Paris to Argenteuil, and for whom he anxiously waited from day to day.

"Is he not coming yet, grandfather?" asked Helena, one day, after she had read the leading articles in several journals, and, finding them uninteresting, thrown them on the table in the middle of the drawing-room.

"Whom are we expecting, my child?" said the marquis, startled, and withdrawing his head from the window.

"I mean the news concerning the two parties in Paris," replied Helena, looking down with an arch smile. "Will the decision about them never arrive, dear grandpapa?"

"The question is whether an accommodation between the conflicting factions is desirable," said the marquis. "The papers of to-day show that the great struggle between the king and the National Assembly has not advanced one step since the opening session. The Three Estates neither deliberate separately nor unite in one body, and it appears as if the court and ministry aid in this inactivity, the sooner and easier to break the web the assembly has woven around the royalists."

"But that would be extremely wrong, grandpapa!" replied Helena, warmly. "You and I are much interested in the sessions. You have two sons there, who are of course both my uncles; and as we women take every thing personally, I call the aristocratic party 'Uncle Boniface,' and the national party 'Uncle Gabriel.' But I have no doubt you still incline to the former, and are expecting to see Viscount Mirabeau every day riding up the road, for he has not been to visit you for several weeks."

"I am not looking for the viscount," said the marquis, with sudden impetuosity. "You know he sent me lately a speech he intended to deliver in the assembly, and I returned it with a marginal remark, which no doubt vexed the vain boy, for since then he has not made his appearance at Argenteuil. Besides, I must confess, that I do not care much whether he comes or not. His discourse against the union of the Three Estates contained foolish words, and wholly unsuitable to a thinking nobleman of the present day."

"Yes, I remember, your criticism was not very gracious, grandfather!" exclaimed Helena, laughing. "You wrote very laconically: 'If I were you, and had a brother among the deputies such as yours, I would hold my tongue, and let that brother speak.'" *

"Did I really write that, Helena?" asked the marquis, some irritation marking his stern countenance. "You repeat those words as if you thought I had suddenly taken a fancy to my elder

---

* Montigny, vol. viii., p. 85.

son, Count Mirabeau. But such is not the case, although I wish to do him justice, and—I think I have always been just toward him, even when obliged to prove it by my severity."

"Oh no, grandpapa," said Helena, with the confidence of a favorite. "According to what I have heard in our own family, and, in fact, what is said in all France, you have been very unjust to your son Gabriel. I was quite a child, scarcely six years old, when you imprisoned him in the Château d'If; if I had been a little older, I would have lectured you well for maltreating a son like that—a man of such greatness of will and genius. I would have told you that only an Attila in private life would have acted so unnaturally."

The marquis trembled, but not in anger, for a shadow of melancholy and remorse passed over his features. He leaned his silvered head upon his hand, and was silent. Presently he looked out again upon the road, where a cloud of dust announced the approach of a horseman.

"It is not he!" exclaimed Helena, half banteringly, half sadly, approaching the window.

"Of whom are you talking?" replied the old gentleman, somewhat moved.

"I do not know, dear grandpapa," she answered, with indifference, standing behind his chair, and placing her soft hands upon his shoulders. "But if just now I ventured to say harsh things, it was only in reference to what happened long ago, and we have less and less to do with the past, as we are told in the papers every day, and as we hear from the orators. Grandpapa, the sun is shining on your head—and there is one whom you never loved who returns to you the glory of your name. He is yet worthy of your affection. Let me kiss the light beaming on your brow." She bent over the old man, pressing a long and tender kiss on his forehead.

"How do you know that I have changed my mind?" asked the marquis, after a pause, resuming his haughty dignity.

"Ah, my dear grandfather," cried Helena, triumphantly, "I can bring you many proofs. I might remind you of last month—the 24th of June, after the session at Versailles, when M.

Comps, secretary to Count Mirabeau, arrived here with a report of the proceedings from your son. After I read it to you, and some passages two or three times, you sent for young Comps, to give him your message to his master; but you could no longer restrain yourself, and burst into tears. 'Young man,' you said, seizing his arm, 'tell the count, "this is true renown!"' and then you motioned him to leave, for you were so agitated that you could speak no more." [*]

"Oh," said the marquis, raising his head proudly, "those words had no reference to my son Gabriel; though I cannot deny that his heroic manner in the assembly really pleased me. I have always been impartial to him, and will remain so. At the opening of the sessions he showed himself as the man for the exigency, when the interests of rank and an ambiguous ministry resisted what the representatives were attempting to do. I should like to have heard his thunder against the separation of the deputies of the different Estates, to try the validity of the elections. It was a just idea, for he immediately excluded the subtlety of Necker's ministry by reference to his mercenary duties. The financial minister thinks he can reform the country by giving it a pinch of snuff, but Count Mirabeau soon showed him his mistake. Indeed, I wish I had heard his utterance of the words, '*Va, banque!*' He must have shaken the marrow in Necker's bones.

"My lion-hearted son also exerted his influence that the Third Estate, holding themselves aloof from the aristocracy and clergy, should constitute themselves the real assembly of national representatives. It is true, that shrewd Abbé Sièyes, whom I greatly esteem, first proposed this, but it is owing to the count that the measure was carried through. It was my son again who presented for consideration that the delegates in session should be called the representatives of the French nation, saying, with a courage spurning all concealment, that the only object of the convocation was the organization of a government of the people and the throne.

----

* Montigny, vol. iv., p. 130.

MIRABEAU IN THE NATIONAL ASSEMBLY. p. 209.

'The Third Estate took the title of National Assembly during the memorable session on the 16th of June, and all France rejoiced. Count Mirabeau, by his indefatigable activity, had won to his side almost a majority of the ecclesiastics, when Louis XVI., urged by the intriguers of his court, held that unfortunate royal session in which he dared to command the Estates to meet separately, and not as a whole, wherein the nation might see its own unity. On the previous day, however, the deputies of the Third Estate, at the instigation of my son, assembled in the ballroom, and took an oath, not to adjourn the assembly, or permit others to do so, until they completed a new constitution for France; the next day they renewed this oath at the altar in the church of St. Louis.

"After the foolish king had issued his declaration, and, with the aristocracy and a portion of the clergy, left the hall, the rest remained as a firmly-united body. And were there ever grander words than those from the lips of Count Mirabeau, hurling defiance into the teeth of the Marquis de Brézé, who was sent by the ministers to remind the members of the royal wish, and request them to adjourn? Read that passage to me once more, Helena. I find those immortal words reported differently in the various newspapers—the *Monitour*, for example, reports them with an omission. Bring my son's letter, for I cannot hear it often enough!"

Helena listened to him, and her eyes sparkled with joy, when she saw how the marquis was absorbed in the fame of his son. She hastened to the desk, and brought the letter to her grandfather.

"Here it is," she said, "for it always lies at the top. These are the words which Count Mirabeau uttered in a tranquil tone to the frightened Marquis de Brézé: 'The Commons of France have resolved to meet. We have heard of the intentions introduced into the king's mind; and you, sir—who cannot even be his organ in the National Assembly, as you have here neither a seat nor a vote, nor a right to speak—you are not qualified to call to our remembrance his majesty's speech.

Go, and tell your master that we are here by the will of the people, and that we can be removed only by the bayonet!'"

"Excellent!" exclaimed the old man, rubbing his hands, and a slight color suffusing his sickly face. "Yes, he was always remarkable! He was born ugly as a son of the night—he had two fully-developed back-teeth, so that we were all astounded—and he seemed as if he had the strength of Hercules even in his cradle. He fought every day with his nurse, and she, being a passionate woman, would return the blow; but she did not always have the advantage, for he gave her many a bite." *

The marquis began to laugh so heartily at these reminiscences that his grand-daughter was alarmed, and her apprehensions were soon realized, for he began to cough violently.

After he recovered, Helena said, in an insinuating voice: "If he was so ugly and unbearable as a child, that was no reason why you should hate and persecute him as a man. Your other son, Uncle Boniface, is said to have been so handsome formerly that all who saw him were charmed; and now he is so stout and awkward, that he can scarcely move with any grace, and has received the nickname of *Mirabeau-tonneau*. He is also addicted to wine, and is among the worst foes of his brother. You see now what has become of your former favorite, while your 'Son of Night,' as you called him, has become the pride of France, and will add to the honor of your name."

"Nevertheless, I think I have been just toward him!" said the marquis, in a trembling voice. "He had no reverence for authority, and that soon estranged us. A man like myself, who, until my fifty-fourth year, never retired at night before I had knelt to my old mother to receive her blessing, could never become a friend of such a lawless enthusiast. I certainly used a stout whip, but what would have become of him if my chastising arm had not restrained him from the abysses into which he was ready to fall? The prisons in which

---

* Montigny, vol. i., p. 238.

I confined him preserved him from far greater shame, and from a miserable death. But now he has entered a career that I must honor.

"If I rightly understand Gabriel's views, he wishes to remedy the wrongs in the state and society, and these have been growing for a long time—all men, even of opposite opinions, must agree to that. Every thing in France is worn out—the soil must be renewed, and the marshes drained, before the seeds of happiness can be planted. To effect such a revolution, a strong nature like Count Mirabeau's is required. With all his power and passion, however, he is temperate in his demands; and, while his eloquence is overwhelming, his reason is right and lawful. He is a daring man; he has moved the nation, but he will establish it upon a sure foundation—a tribune of the people, he struggles for royalty as well as for them. He is acknowledging that some authority is necessary, although in his youth he spurned it, while I was obliged to act despotically toward him. Should I not love him now, Helena?"

"You must, you do love him!" exclaimed the young marchioness. "And, since you confess it, I will tell you whom you are so anxiously expecting, when you sit at your window looking out upon the road to Paris. You daily hope to see your son Gabriel—you think he must come and throw himself into your arms. You love him now, and therefore cannot comprehend his absence."

"And why will he not come?" asked the old man, sadly. "He writes to me sometimes, but avoids my presence."

"He will come!" said Helena, smiling confidently. She again approached the window, and long watched the highway. Suddenly turning to her grandfather, she said: "Yonder, dust rises on the road. A horseman is moving rapidly. Can it be my uncle the count?—It is he!" cried Helena, clasping her hands. The marquis hastily closed the window, as if to prepare for this meeting with a persecuted son whom he had not seen for many a year.

The rider entered the court-yard, and in a few minutes stood upon the porch. The Marchioness d'Arragon went joyfully to meet him, and led him to her grandfather, who, sinking back into his easy-chair, was greatly agitated in his surprise and excitement.

"Are you very ill, my father?" asked Mirabeau, rushing toward the marquis to embrace him.

The old man rose quickly, and looked at his son with an indescribable expression. The count beheld the tall and reverend form with feelings of mingled fear and delight; for he remembered the awe with which in his youth he regarded this stern parent, expecting to see the same merciless glance which had so often condemned him; but, to his astonishment, a tender affection was beaming in the eye of the marquis, such as he had never seen before. He took his father's hand and pressed it to his lips.

"You look as if you suffered, my father!" said the count. "I heard you were ill, and hastened to see you to-day, because great movements may soon occur in Paris that may prevent me from leaving again. But I am not told what is the nature of your disease."

Mirabeau met the eyes of his niece, the Marchioness d'Arragon, who, standing behind her grandfather, gave her uncle to understand that he must not betray that she had secretly written to him.

"You certainly do not find me in a very good condition, my son!" said the marquis, resuming his seat with a sigh, and motioning Mirabeau to take a chair opposite. "A man who has the gout and a cough is worse off than even France, threatened with revolution; for if you, brave gentlemen of the Third Estate, disturb the country, it is for the purpose of giving it future health. With me it is otherwise—my time is past. It is wrong of Boniface, who knows well enough how we are here, not to give you more exact information; for, since the union of the Three Estates has taken place, according to the wish expressed by the frightened king, I suppose you hostile brothers now see and speak to each other every day?"

"Yes, we see one another," said the count, evasively. A rather awkward pause ensued, which Helena, however, knew how to employ by asking questions on various topics. Among others, why her uncle was dressed in such a strange costume, in which she had never seen him before.

"It is the uniform of the Third Estate, which I represent," replied Mirabeau. "I suppose that my lovely niece does not find this black coat and mantle very fascinating? At first, from mere indifference, I did not wear it; but since the Commons are fighting for the nation, I adopted this dress, that I might be recognized as a soldier of the century."

"You have acted well, my son," said the marquis, approvingly, casting a searching glance on the count. "Though you may not suspect it, I have become a sincere friend of the Third Estate. Besides, Gabriel, I think our opinions do not differ so much as perhaps you imagine."

"Your approbation will be a triumph for our cause!" exclaimed Mirabeau, ardently. "The *Ami de l'homme*, as your great philanthropic work is entitled, could not but become our friend; and it renders me happy, because you must also, as a natural consequence, be the friend of your son."

"The friend of my son!" repeated the marquis, in a gentler voice than usual. His hands trembled, and his whole frame was convulsed. Helena arose to conceal her tears.

"My dear son," resumed the marquis, "it is a satisfaction to us both, that we can be reconciled by the events of the present! Take my hand, if only for a farewell; but consider it as a promise for the future, to which, I hope, you are looking cheerfully and confidently!"

"Oh," replied Mirabeau, holding the hand of his father, "the future is a dark and stormy night for France! The worst must occur, and only by that means do I hope for good. The king and the queen seem to desire evil results; they despise the signs of the times, and the presentiment of their fate, and no advice can reach their reason."

"Is the situation of affairs bad in Paris?" asked the marquis.

"The court trust to the regiments they have marched to the environs of Versailles and the capital," replied the count. "In the error that

the National Assembly is the cause of mischief, troops have been stationed around it, so as to prevent the people from having access to the debates. Not satisfied with that measure, the ministry have increased the military by the presence of foreign soldiers, principally Germans and Poles, thus intimating what we may expect in certain contingencies.

"The number of troops and the resources of war daily increase between Versailles and Paris; thirty-five thousand men are there already, and twenty thousand more are expected, as well as heavy parks of artillery; places have been chosen for batteries; the roads, thoroughfares, and bridges, are garrisoned; the promenades have been turned into military posts. The king surrounds himself with this power of a despot, opposing the assembly as the camp of a foe, while his strongest protection lies in the free debates of that body.

"In this crisis, we resolved to hand an address to Louis XVI., which I was commissioned to write. We conjured the king respectfully, yet firmly, to withdraw the troops, and, as neither the person nor dignity of his majesty is endangered, to discontinue these warlike preparations, which are only calculated to destroy confidence. I was one of the deputation sent to present this petition; but the king was too infatuated to listen to us: he went so far, by the advice of his ministers, as to propose that the assembly should retire to some small city, such as Soissons or Noyou. The only laughable circumstance in this affair is, that Necker has been exiled. The ex-minister seems to have acted honorably in this instance; for he counselled the king against conduct that would alienate every mind. And so the financial minister was obliged to return to Switzerland in such a hurry that he hardly had time to pack up his clothes."

"He is no loss," said the marquis, who listened with great attention. "I always found him an opponent of my opinions. I was told you had a secret interview with him, to endeavor to come to an understanding. How did you succeed?"

"My friends Cerutti and Mallouet arranged this

conference several months ago," said Mirabeau, laughing. "We met. I had never spoken to Necker, and was curious to know his style and behavior. He was stiff and dumb as a board— of course, that made me proud and reserved. Expecting me to make propositions, he did not speak, nor did I; and so we separated after a few frigid phrases. However, I think he is not an evil-minded man, any more than he is profound or original."

"Will you thoroughly take up the cause of the working-classes?" asked the marquis, after a short pause, during which he seemed to have been struggling with physical pain. "I think the time will soon arrive when you will find that we old advocates of an agricultural system have long since discovered what is best. Attend, my son! No state can be free, secure, and happy, that is not based on landed possessions, labor, and free trade. Make prominent these principles in your assembly, and you will deserve the gratitude not only of France but of the world." The venerable man would have said more, but his strength was exhausted. He sank back pale and faint, and his cough began again. His situation appeared so critical, that Mirabeau anxiously inquired who was the family physician; but the marquis refused medical attendance, and all medicine, save that which Helena administered. When he partially recovered, the count approached to take leave, repeatedly and reverently kissing his father's hand.

"I must return to Paris and Versailles to-day," said Mirabeau, in a low voice. "The threatening appearance of affairs will not permit any longer stay. I will see you soon again, my father!"

The marquis slowly shook his head, dismissing his son silently, but with a look full of meaning. The count departed quickly. Helena accompanied her uncle to the adjoining apartment, and weepingly whispered her fears. He endeavored to cheer her, and exacted from her the promise to send him a report of her grandfather's health on the following day.

CHAPTER XXXIII.

THE FIRST REPUBLICANS.

MIRABEAU mounted his horse, and rapidly passed over the short distance between Argenteuil and Paris, whose gates he reached a little after mid-day. As he approached he found his progress obstructed by an army camping on the plain before the capital, only permitting him to continue his way slowly and with many interruptions. Among the noisy troops, he observed many of the citizens, moving busily about, and conversing with the soldiers in a lively and familiar manner. They were exchanging pledges of friendship in full glasses, and the people were assured that they would not be fired upon by the military. Mirabeau understood that the Parisians had not been unsuccessful in shaking the allegiance of the king's regiments.

Entering the streets, the count saw to his astonishment that the excitement reigning among the inhabitants was taking a decided and practical form. In several of the thoroughfares barricades were building, armed crowds ran about shouting, while bitter abuse of the court, mingled with applause for Necker and the Duke d'Orleans, was heard on every side. The farther he went the more he became aware that nearly the whole population were in the streets. The theatres were closed, according to the custom during periods of public mourning. From the northern portions of the city the report had come that the barrières were in ashes. A furious mob, gratifying their propensities for outrage and destruction, and whose ragged and starved figures marked them as from the lowest depths of wretchedness, passed by with howling threats, on their way to other scenes of violence.

Mirabeau wished to go to the Palais-Royal, where he expected to discover the origin and the leaders of the riots, as well as to see Chamfort, and inquire about the fate of Henriette and Coco. While riding down the Rue de Richelieu, there passed several divisions of the dragoon regiment called the *Royal-Allemand*, headed by their commander, Prince de Lambesc, on a white charger, and preceded by a band of music. Mirabeau was obliged to stand at the corner of a small street while the soldiers marched by. On both sides the crowd expressed themselves very insultingly against the dragoons and their leader.

This regiment of cavalry was composed almost wholly of Germans, ignorant of French, who neither comprehended the curses hurled at them, nor the friendly words by which the citizens at first attempted to win them to the popular side. A volley of stones was at length discharged upon the troops, when, obeying their commander, they drew their swords, and charged the mob, who, with some loss of life, were driven down the street: but, though dispersed, they called to each other to reunite for vengeance. This was the first time the military acted against the people, and throughout Paris the cry resounded that the residents must arm themselves, and form a citizen guard!

Mirabeau left his horse at a friend's house, and went on foot to the Palais-Royal, the avenues to which were besieged by angry men, rushing hither and thither, and uttering threats against the king and court. The count, however, succeeded in forcing his way through, and reaching Chamfort's dwelling in the Arcades. No one was at home, and he again found himself in the midst of the heaving masses, who bore him into the first court-yard of the palace itself, to take possession of which seemed to be their object.

Several times Mirabeau fancied he saw well-known faces about him, such as those of Clavière, Duroveray, Dumont, and even Chamfort, in that great tumult; but, tossed about in every direction, they did not recognize him. At last the count managed to seize the skirt of Chamfort's coat, and thus make his presence known.

"There is much to do now, friend Mirabeau," said Chamfort, in a tranquil and good-natured voice, very different from that in which he had but a moment before aided in the commotion.

"But tell me what is the matter?" asked the count. "Is it all on account of Necker, whom the king sent away in such haste? Have the people been inflamed by his disgrace? If so, I am also one of his partisans, and cry long life to the ex-minister as fervently as this little Savoyard, who in his enthusiasm has almost broken my ribs."

"The revolution to-day loves the name of Necker, and therefore let us reiterate it in the ears of the populace!" replied Chamfort. "Even the name of the Duke d'Orleans sounds well. Our friends have resolved, you hear, to ring the bells, and they give the first alarm of fire at the court."

"And who are our friends?" asked Mirabeau, taking Chamfort's arm, and allowing himself to be dragged into the middle of the crowd.

"You must not be proud to-day, Mirabeau," replied Chamfort. "Our friends are all those going the same road with us. We are walking in darkness, but toward a light in which we shall recognize each other."

"And is that also one of our friends—that puppet-like fellow, stepping out of the Café de Foy, followed by numerous admirers?" asked the count, pointing to a young man, at the head of a separate crowd, gesticulating in a very excited manner.

"That is Camille Desmoulins, a lawyer; he possesses great art in influencing the lower classes," replied Chamfort. "He is a good fellow, as it seems to me, perhaps a little too inflammatory, but he has a ready tongue. He has no education whatever, supplying its place by natural oratory, persuading the people that if they follow his advice, they will gain the treasures of India. Besides, he is supposed to be an agent of the Duke d'Orleans.—See, he is going to speak! A table is brought, and he is preparing to mount it, with a dignity peculiarly his own."

Camille Desmoulins was a man of twenty-seven years, whose complexion was almost as dark as a negro's. His appearance was extremely vulgar, and a nervous activity trembled in all his limbs. His black eyes rested on the mob until they gradually became quiet, when he said, in a melodious, distinct voice: "Citizens! I have just returned from Versailles, and I assure you not a moment is to be lost! Necker is dismissed, and that is the signal for another St. Bartholomew's night for all patriots! This evening all the Swiss and German battalions will march from the Champ de Mars to massacre us. We have but one resource —to take up arms in self-defence!"

These words were echoed with loud applause, but accompanied with murmurs. Desmoulins, standing on the table, waited the effect of his address, and then he anxiously turned his eyes in a certain direction. Presently, he cried in a loud voice: "Behold the spies of the police looking in my face; but I shall not fall alive into their hands!" He drew two pistols from his pocket, and, leaping down, placed himself at the head of his friends awaiting him. "Follow my example, citizens!" he said. "Come, defend your lives, as well as those of your wives and children!"

With a fearful cry the multitude followed him, soon, however, separating into groups, rushing along the different streets with shouts of vengeance, and demanding arms.

At the outlet from the Palais-Royal, Mirabeau and Chamfort met Desmoulins, who, as soon as he saw the count, approached him with an air of great respect. "The people express their esteem for Count Mirabeau through me!" cried the orator, swinging his pistols in the air, and pointing to the deputy. "Long live Mirabeau, the hero of the National Assembly and the friend of the people!"

The count thanked him smilingly, in a few friendly words, and only adding in a lower voice: "It is well to give an impetus to the people, but save them from bloody deeds!"

"Such deeds are necessary, perhaps to-night!" replied Desmoulins, with a mysterious air. "And if the people cannot shoot, they can hang their foes. The king has cannon; and we, lamp-posts. I have long reflected on the best means of arming ourselves, and have come to the conclusion that the lamp-post is our most effective weapon. Long live the lamp-post!—May I visit you at Versailles, Citizen Mirabeau?"

The count nodded, but found no time to re-

ply, for Desmoulins rushed away with his followers.

"Do you not think that such men are very serviceable?" asked Chamfort, looking searchingly at his friend.

"They are petrels, telling of the coming storm, and rejoicing in its terrors," replied Mirabeau, thoughtfully. "But when the danger is upon us, we require experienced helmsmen, and we must find them."

"And do you think we approach a revolution?" asked Chamfort, with a flashing look.

"Do you not see the clouds gathering over our heads?" said the count, softly.

A loud report was heard in the vicinity. The people were astonished, for a cannon had been fired, and some minutes elapsed before they could investigate the reason. It happened that during the day the sky was dark and lowering, when suddenly the July sun burst forth in all his splendor, and was so reflected, from a mirror at the Palais-Royal, as to fall upon the priming of the cannon, and discharge it in this surprising manner.[*]

"The sun is giving the signal for the revolution!" said Chamfort, after he and his friend had satisfied themselves of the cause.

"But did not Camille Desmoulins say that the cannon was the weapon of kings?" asked Mirabeau.

"But the sun is the weapon of the people," replied Chamfort, enthusiastically. "Wherever light appears, it originates with them."

The count and his friend passed to another outlet of the Palais-Royal, leading to the Rue St. Honoré; they wished to go toward the Tuileries, most of the crowd appearing to move in that direction. In the first court-yard stood a carriage ready harnessed. Multitudes surrounded the porch, awaiting, with joyful emotion, the appearance of the Duke d'Orleans. Just as Mirabeau and Chamfort were about to proceed, the duke issued from his palace in haste and apparent consternation. He was received with exclamations

---

[*] Louis Blanc, "Histoire de la Révolution Française," vol. ii., p. 296.

of delight, all pressing around him as if seeking protection, and at this crisis confiding their well-being to his care. He wished to speak to them, but could find no suitable words, and it was evident that he was violently agitated. When he entered his carriage, he said, in a hoarse voice: "My friends, no other remedy is left but to take up arms!" And he drove off with a rapidity that looked like flight.

"The people entreat his assistance, but the prince lacks just one trifle to become head of the revolution—courage!" said Chamfort. "He is going to Versailles, as I have learned from his valet de chambre; and yet, if he had nerve enough, he could this day be proclaimed king in Paris. But fear is his postilion; and the revolution, after all, does not agree with him."

"He is a coward, with whom we must have no intercourse!" exclaimed Mirabeau, indignantly. "And I am suspected of having a secret understanding with such a wretch! If heaven itself descended to the earth, I would never be found in the same region with the Duke d'Orleans!"

The crowd disappeared gradually, and the friends could easily find egress. In the Rue St. Honoré they met a procession, headed by a Savoyard and a young man costumed as a person of rank. The former carried a bust of the Duke d'Orleans, which he raised on high, to show it to the multitude, at the same time swinging his black cap triumphantly. The young man near him, dressed in a coat of striped silk, and wearing two watches, besides other articles of jewelry, carried a bust of Necker. Both these images were covered with black crape, intimating that those they represented were in disgrace at court. Various banners waved above their heads, inscribed with words of defiance and victory. What was singular, this throng consisted not altogether of the lower classes, for many persons of rank were to be seen among them.

"What can the people care about Orleans or Necker?" asked Mirabeau of Chamfort. "The masses always need idols, and will have them, even if they steal them from a plaster-cast store. I recently saw those busts in the studio of Curtius,

on the Boulevard du Temple. Let us go with them. It is instructive to see in what manner ignorance creates its divinities—it must have something to worship, though it would destroy what intelligence offers as most worthy of adoration."

The crowd continued on their way toward the boulevards, passing the most populous streets, and becoming more numerous. They met a detachment of French guards, and, inducing them to make common cause with the people, swelled the triumphal march—an incident which gave to the whole proceeding great weight in the estimation of the multitude. On arriving at the Place Vendôme, one of the cavalry stationed there fired among the citizens, and the young man carrying Necker's bust fell with a shriek. He was mortally wounded, and died in a moment. He was carried into a house, while another picked up the image and took his place in the procession. The cavalry were ordered to retreat, but, vacating the square, reappeared from a side-street behind the people, who had reached the Place Louis XV. Confusion ensued, the order of the procession was broken, another shot fired, and the Savoyard wounded. He received also a sabre-stroke in his breast, and fell a corpse to the ground. Borne upon the shoulders of his friends, he was taken into the Palais-Royal, to be exhibited in state to all Paris.

When this Orleans and Necker parade closed, the populace separated to different parts of the city, intent on mischief. The French guards, occupying the barracks in the Rue Verte, were becoming restless, demanding to be led against the foreign regiments that had acted so inimically toward the citizens. A man named Gonchon, who had lately caused much of the excitement in the faubourgs, appeared among the guards, and stirred the soldiers by his rude eloquence, such as had seldom been heard from one of his class. He insisted that the French troops should challenge the foreigners to mortal conflict; and so successful was he, that, as Mirabeau and Chamfort approached the Rue Verte, the armed troops were rushing from the garrison after him, who, in his coarse blouse, ran at their head.

"There is Gonchon," said Chamfort. "Look at him well, Mirabeau; he is one of those hideous figures lately visible in Paris, as if suddenly risen of a dark night from a cavern deep hidden from the day. He is ugly as sin, and his red-speckled skin seems to mark him as the former inhabitant of some other abode than man's. Nothing equals his haughtiness, and in speaking of himself his pompous gravity makes him say, ' Gonchon will do so and so.' "

"Is that the Gonchon who is called the Mirabeau of the faubourgs?" asked the count, regarding the man in the blouse with smiling surprise.

"Yes, my friend," replied Chamfort, "the Mirabeau of the National Assembly has a companion. You will have to work into each other's hands. You have become the hero of the deputies, although at first received with hisses, and your colleagues kicked and reared like a charger that does not know its rider; but they know better since your first matchless speech against the separation according to rank—both horse and rider have become renowned. But you, gentlemen of the Salle des Menus at Versailles, must not think that the Parisian street-vagrants have not also their Mirabeau. You must not despise Gonchon, for you see he has his work to do, and knows how to do it."

"Perhaps he has fewer enemies than I," said the count. "You are well aware that I hate commotion on the street. However, our National Assembly are a weak and pitiful set, as I told you from the beginning. All the good I can see in them is, that the revolution may develop its lungs by their means, much in the same way as the crying of children is a healthful exercise."

"I am surprised that you are not present at the debates to-day," said Chamfort, as the party followed in the direction of the guards to the Place Louis XV. "An important session is held. It is intended to deliver a declaration to the king, informing him that the new ministry have not the confidence of the nation and its representatives, and that the immediate recall of Necker is necessary for the public good."

"I heard the preparatory debates this morning,

before I left Versailles," replied Mirabeau. "But a report of the ill-health of my father, called me to Argenteuil. I wished to see him, as he is said to be in a critical condition. We are reconciled, and all the woe that was associated with that name for me, has been turned to love."

When arrived at the Place Louis XV., it was rumored that at the approach of the French guards, the foreign troops under the command of M. de Besenval, were ordered to retire. Assurances were given that bloody collisions would be avoided, and the military withdrawn from the interior of the capital. Soon none were seen except the guards, who were on intimate terms with the citizens.

In the mean time the alarm-bells rang in all the steeples and towers. The insurrection was developing itself in different parts of the city; the stores containing weapons were plundered, to equip the multitudes eager for them; and soon armed crowds roamed about the streets vociferating their intention to attack any one obnoxious to them. The number demanding arms seemed to increase, and a furious crowd rushed toward the Hôtel de Ville, and entered the large hall, where a few electors and officials of Paris were holding a meeting, to deliberate about the order and security of the capital. A promise was made that the guns and swords in the building would be delivered to them; but the depository of weapons was soon discovered, and the doors broken open, when each person seized what first came to his hand. The sentinels before the city-hall had left; their place being suddenly occupied by a strange figure who seemed to have assumed this position of his own accord. He was a gigantic man, whom no one knew, or whence he came. He had on nothing but a shirt—not even shoes. On his shoulder he carried a gun, and paced before the Hôtel de Ville.[*]

Mirabeau and Chamfort gazed at this apparition with the greatest astonishment. "Here is another of those frightful creatures, hatched by the insurrection, who never before had a visible existence among us!" said Chamfort, looking with awe upon

* "Procès-verbal de l'Assemblée des Électeurs," vol. 1., p. 189.

the unknown sentinel. "See with what ease and determination that almost naked man shoulders his arms. He must be Rousseau's natural man, who, the offspring of the philosophers, is on guard before the temple of the revolution. Would you take it amiss should I kneel before this herald monster, and worship it?"

"It would not be the first time that the maker kneels before his own work," replied Mirabeau. "But, believe me, you can do nothing with such people. National hunger, assuming the shape of an armed spectre, is a messenger of blood, if it thus paces in front of the vestibule of the future. I have learned much these days, and, among other things, that we must accept nothing from a republic. It will not be a commonwealth of heroes, but of ragamuffins. What else is your divinity, before whom you would bow?—And I must tell you that the articles you are now writing for the *Mercure* do not please me. You are building an air-castle, and with infernal subtlety; here you see one of its lords before you. He is nearly naked, and, careless of the future, he has probably now even loaded his gun."

"Is it true then that our path separates?" asked Chamfort, in a melancholy tone. "On this day, the 12th of July, there are perhaps but ten republicans in Paris; and they tell you how small is our beginning;* but this party will grow. Do not abuse that poor fellow on account of his costume. Nature gave him his well-developed limbs, the revolution will make a god of him, after hunger has given him the look of a saint. When the ancient deities reigned on Olympus they had no tailor, and that was the golden age. Farewell, Mirabeau! A toilet question estranges us; for I know you will employ your influence in endeavoring to have a new lining for the rent ermine."

Chamfort suddenly disappeared. The last crowd that passed seemed to have engulfed him. Mirabeau looked a long time in the direction where his friend had disappeared, and stood as if lost in painful reflection.

The evening approached, and the disturbances in the streets were more to be dreaded. The passers-by were forced to contribute money for the purchase of powder and ball. Many ran with torches, asking all they met whether they belonged to the Third Estate. Some were reading periodicals or placards by the dismal light, expressing their misery with bitter irony, and sometimes with wit. Others again passed, who, from their exclamations, revealed their purposes of firing the principal buildings in the city.

The count continued his way, having resolved to remain in Paris during the night, as he would have difficulty in reaching Versailles on account of the troops surrounding the capital. He hastened to find the small dwelling of Henriette and Coco in the Rue Montmartre, which was his home whenever he was in the city.

All Paris was in fear of approaching evil. The bells of the Hôtel de Ville and Notre Dame rang incessantly. Divisions of the citizen guard, just organized, were seen marching the streets. Here and there windows were illuminated, for the night was dark. The French guards united with the armed inhabitants for the protection of the capital; and from time to time reports of fire-arms were heard, followed by cries of alarm. Paris was like a man dangerously ill and tormented by fearful apprehensions.*

Mirabeau reached the Rue Montmartre about midnight. Henriette had not yet retired, and met him with joyful surprise. She saw him now but seldom, and she kissed his hands with a sort of reverential love. Coco also came running into the room, and was heartily greeted. The boy complained that Henriette would not permit him to go out and assist in raising a barricade at the corner of the street.

"Why do you wish to build fortifications against the king, my friend?" asked Mirabeau. "What in the world has Louis XVI. done to you? Have you not grown as tall as any lad of seven years, during his reign? You will be much better and stronger if you love your king, my boy!"

Henriette smiled and asked pardon for her little

---

* "Fragment de l'Histoire Secrète de la Révolution," par Camille Desmoulins, p. 11.

* Buchez, p. 376.

protégé. The count was at last aware that she suffered more than her letters led him to suppose. Her lungs appeared to be dangerously affected, and her beautiful form, once so fresh and strong, was clearly under the dominion of an incurable disease. As he took her in his arms she seemed to him as a fading flower, and he scarcely dared to press her to his heart. Sorrow overwhelmed him when he looked on her hollow and fevered cheeks, and remembered the love she bore him. Begging her to go to rest with Coco, he assured her that nothing more need be feared for that night in the capital.

When Madame de Nehra and the child had left Mirabeau alone, he found some relief at his desk, describing the events of which he had been an eye-witness, and intended for his journal. It was a pleasure and a duty for him to express himself freely, and he warned the people not to sacrifice their rights to a blind desire for destruction and the unhallowed gratification of revenge.

CHAPTER XXXIV.

A COFFIN.

AFTER a short rest, Mirabeau arose to make preparations for his speedy return to Versailles. He wished, however, to ascertain the situation of affairs in Paris, in order to make propositions in the National Assembly, whose object was the calming of the public mind, and the removal of danger. As he was about to depart, having silently taken leave of Henriette and Coco, who were asleep, he was met by a courier on the threshold, who had orders to follow the count to Versailles if he should not be found in Paris. Mirabeau opened with anxiety the letter handed him, for he recognized in the address the handwriting of his niece the Marchioness d'Arragon. He glanced at the contents, and the paper fell from his hand, as he went into an adjoining apartment. Helena announced to him in this letter that his his father had died suddenly, a few hours after his interview with the long-neglected son. On his departure at the last visit, the marquis appeared to rally rapidly. His grand-daughter read to him an article from Mirabeau's new journal, while the old gentleman was in his favorite seat near the window. He listened attentively, and noticed an omission, requesting Helena to read the paragraph again; scarcely had she excused herself for her oversight, and recommenced the passage, when she observed that her grandfather closed his eyes. She hastened toward him, but his head drooped, and, as if happy in the last remembrances of his son, and with a smiling face, he ceased to breathe.[*] According to the expressed wishes of the marquis, his remains were immediately to be taken to Castle Mirabeau, and placed in the family vault. Helena had written the count to procure a leaden coffin in Paris, to be sent as soon as possible to Argenteuil, and, awaiting the arrival of the body at the capital, undertake the further execution of his father's will.

As Mirabeau passed into the street to attend to this sorrowful duty, he beheld the people again in motion, having been but little interfered with during the night. The thoroughfares were crowded with armed men. Several groups, headed by soldiers of the French guard, marched with drums and trumpets, inducing those they met to join them, in order to assault St. Lazare in the Rue St. Denis, and make themselves masters of the flour depositories. Others went from house to house, alarming the inhabitants, and threatening with fire and death those who would not follow them. Many were hastening toward the Hôtel de Ville to enroll themselves for the organization of a citizen guard.

The count was informed on the way that early the same morning the electors of Paris had assembled at the city hall, and formed a permanent committee, who were endeavoring to reëstablish order, by calling for forty-eight thousand citizens to constitute the Parisian militia. The royal troops were resting in the Champ de Mars, at St. Denis, Sèvres, and St. Cloud, and the opinion

---

* Montigny, vol. vi., p. 129.

prevailed that the new ministers, especially Messrs. De Breteuil et de la Galaisière, who had hostile intentions toward the people, preferred to let the insurrection reach a certain point, so as to justify them in the adoption of the severest measures.

Mirabeau found the store he was seeking locked, as but few shopkeepers could be induced to trade on such a day. After some difficulty he gained an entrance into the warehouse, and, examining the ready-made coffins, selected the largest for the remains of his father; then, turning to the proprietor, who regarded him doubtfully, he said: "You are surprised that I make such a purchase to-day. Do you expect so little business that you lock up such indispensable articles? However, I suppose you think that the permanent committee at the Hôtel de Ville will make peace?"

"Peace?" replied the man, shaking his head. "This citizen militia can do no good, even if they disarm the mob, and I am concealing myself that I may not be forced into this new service. The city cannot be protected, but will be divided, in this way, forming two separate camps, of which the court will take advantage."

"You are right," said Mirabeau, after a pause, "and I find that there is much wisdom where I did not expect it. The idea of a citizen guard is a reaction; it is the same as arming a popular movement against itself; it insures the death of liberty. I must go to the Hôtel de Ville and request a guard to accompany my father's coffin, and preserve it from attack."

"You must apply to M. de la Salle; he has been appointed commander of the citizen guards," replied the merchant. "They will no doubt gladly accommodate you, for you look like a man of rank. The true friends of the people have no confidence in the new committee at the city hall, and, least of all, M. de Flesselles, who has been chosen president!"

The count hastened away, meeting other crowds tending to the prison of La Force, to set free those within its walls—for the most part victims of malice or poverty. At another point he met the rioters returning from St. Lazare, and rejoicing over fifty-two wagon-loads of flour, guarded by men of apparent respectability, but oppressed by hunger and distress of every kind. They had expended their fury upon the convent, well supplied with all the necessaries of life; but, when money was offered them, they disdainfully refused it, taking only what would relieve to some extent the terrible want among the lower classes in Paris.

At the same time a number of country people entered the city. Taking advantage of the burning down of the barrières, they brought in a great quantity of provisions, which satisfied the starving mob, and in some measure allayed their passions. Persons who had never seen one another embraced in the open street, vowing fraternal affection, while in other places cries for arms and ammunition were still heard. Some rushed toward the Hôtel des Invalides, entering it by climbing over the walls and ditches, and ransacked it of all its armament, bearing it to the Palais-Royal. Cannon were mounted in different parts of the city—at the entrance of all the faubourgs, at the Tuileries, and upon the quays and bridges of the Seine.

When Mirabeau arrived at the city hall, he was immediately recognized, and received with loud cheers. He was conducted to the apartment in which the committee held their meetings; the members believed that he came from Versailles, bringing them a communication from the National Assembly, and surrounded him in great excitement; for one of the first movements of the permanent committee was to attempt a union between themselves and the representatives of the nation, and thus effect more than by separate action. The count assured them that he came as a private citizen, to request a protective force for the remains of his father. Flesselles, the president, obligingly promised to make all the necessary arrangements.

On regaining the street, Mirabeau met a strange procession. Those composing it were holding each other by the hand, and shedding tears that could flow only from a sense of victory in the cause of freedom. They were the debtors imprisoned in La Force, just liberated by the populace. Some had been there from their early youth, and had passed the allotted life of man within dungeon walls; while others, still young, had grown gray before their time.

Another crowd was on the Place Grève, whither they had dragged the carriage of the Prince de Lambesc, intending to burn it; but first sending all the articles found in it to the Hôtel de Ville, that they might be returned to their owner. In another quarter, several laborers were hurrying one of their comrades into the garden of the Abbey de Montmartre, to hang him on a tree for having stolen a chicken.

The people decorated themselves with badges, expressive of their opinions, and the women gave their ribbons to ornament the guns. There was a rivalry in the display of various colors. At first every weapon had something green fastened to it, telling of hope that national and social life would be regenerated; but this color was not long a favorite, as it was remembered to be that of the Count d'Artois. Then some one appeared with a cockade of white, blue, and red, which was adopted by all anxious to run to extremes, and end in a radical revolution.

"White, blue, and red!" said Mirabeau. "That is the livery of the Duke d'Orleans.* When a people seek liberty, it seems they merely exchange one master for another; and, in this instance, they choose the most cowardly among men! His agents understand their business. The badge of the revolution bears the colors of a royal livery! And are we of the National Assembly to be behind? The king alone can make the best and happiest change in the government! Royalty should be an institution leading the march of all salutary ideas, and Louis XVI. is its best representative. He knows what ought to be; he need but consult his heart to feel what is best for his subjects. And who prevents him from giving practical form to his impulses? Is it Marie Antoinette? No, fair lady, you are falsely accused of being a foe of your people!"

* Ferrières, vol. ii., p. 121.

Thus meditating, the count made his way back to the coffin-store, and concluded his sad business. As he passed to the house of one of his friends, he met multitudes on the road hastening to leave the city. The wagons were filled with articles of value, and among them were seated women and children, with countenances full of fear, believing that there was no safety but far away from Paris. Families of high rank, and some of them relatives of the count, were fleeing in dismay from the terrors of an enraged populace.

An order was issued from the Hôtel de Ville that none must leave the capital; those already on their way were forced to return, and detained as hostages.

CHAPTER XXXV.

THE CONFLICT AROUND THE BASTILE

THE remains of the Marquis de Mirabeau arrived in Paris on the following morning, the 14th of July, solemnly escorted by twelve of the citizen guards. The coffin was placed in the entry of the house where the count was residing, until its further destination could be decided. He was waiting for his brother the viscount, who had promised to come from Versailles, that the two sons might follow their father to his last resting-place.

The capital presented a more gloomy appearance than on the preceding day; at sunrise the masses seemed to be bent on mischief, but their movements were better organized, and as if in reference to some definite object, which made them only the more dangerous. Mirabeau sat by the coffin, leaning sorrowfully against it, while the guards were walking up and down before the door, their guns rattling, and demanding from time to time whether the funeral would not soon move. Their impatience arose from the anticipated events of the day. An attack from the troops was expected, and the committee at the Hôtel de Ville were busy all night, arranging measures by which Paris could make a brave and victorious resistance. They resolved to make the people master of the Bastile, thus obtaining a base for the protection of all parts of the city against the advancing soldiers of Marshal de Broglie.

At last the viscount came. Entering the dwelling quickly, he stepped back confounded, for the first object that he beheld was the coffin. Mirabeau did not rise at his brother's approach, merely pointing toward the remains of their father. The fat and ungainly form of the viscount shuddered, and he sank upon a chair standing at the head, while the count remained at the feet. The brothers were silent for several minutes, not even exchanging a glance. Suddenly a trumpet sounded as a signal for the militia to repair to their appointed rendezvous, and the alarm-bell of the city hall was again rung.

Mirabeau sprang from his seat, and hastened to the street door, where he saw the last of his escort disappearing in the distance. "They have all left their posts of honor here," he said sadly, returning and offering his hand to his brother. "We must bury our own dead, for our guards have rushed into the fight at the side of their comrades. We are all alone; this street is far distant from the tumult."

The viscount arose, slightly touching his brother's hand. "This will be a terrible day in Paris, but perhaps also a good one!" he said. "As I was driving hither, every thing appeared ready for a street combat. The people swarmed in excited crowds toward the square before the Bastile, and I was informed that brave Delaunay, the governor of the fortress, had refused to deliver it into the hands of the city. The committee at the Hôtel de Ville have sent several detachments of this miserable militia, and three companies of our faithless guards, to attack the Bastile from the side of the Porte St. Antoine."

"Let us dismiss politics to-day, my brother!" exclaimed Mirabeau. "I am thinking how we can bear our dear dead from out this confusion, and get our burden safe to the public road. The carriage is ready, and we must not delay, for soon it will be impossible to pass through the streets without endangering our lives. Can you take hold at one end, Boniface, and assist me in lifting the coffin upon the vehicle? For, with the exception of the driver, we are abandoned by all."

The viscount looked at himself with embarrassment mingled with his usual sarcasm. Then he said, pointing to the uniform of a colonel of a Toulouse regiment which he wore, and the many orders on his breast: "I have been in many a battle, my dear brother, while you rode your goose-quill, with which you sought to make the people happy, but to carry a coffin I have neither courage nor skill. It is shocking to ask such a service of a cavalier, and I propose that we quietly leave the marquis our father here, until order has been restored. We can lock up the house, and I will go to the Champ de Mars, and request an escort from Marshal de Broglie. My brother, the count, the high-born friend of the mob, may go to the city hall and see his friends."

"No, neither the one nor the other shall be done!" exclaimed Mirabeau, indignantly. "It was the express desire of our father that his mortal remains be at once conducted to Castle Mirabeau. We must honor his will; who knows whether Paris will not be in flames before night?"

"Have you, friends of the people, such evil intentions?" asked the viscount, ironically.

The count did not reply. He beckoned to the driver, and, with his assistance, carried out the coffin. The viscount affected indifference, and looked on, saying, with a smile: "Our father was always proud that kings and princes honored him during his lifetime, and that he carried on a familiar correspondence about his *Ami des Hommes* with Stanislaus Augustus, King of Poland, and Gustavus III., King of Sweden. Now he may be even more exalted, for the hero of the Third Estate is carrying him on his broad shoulders, who is no other than his lost son."

"Yes," replied Mirabeau, aiding the man in fastening down the pall, "the hero of the Third Estate is his lost son, but found again; and his former favorite, the well-fed pupil of the aristocracy, rubs his hands and indulges in untimely wit. Now enter your carriage, M. Viscount, I shall follow on foot."

"Had we not better wait?" asked the younger brother, in great agitation. "They seem to be fighting yonder; I hear the sound of arms, and we may perhaps be dragged into this fearful conflict."

As some armed men ran by, Mirabeau stopped them, and was informed that the people had commenced the attack on the Bastile, assisted by three companies of French guards with their cannon. The first drawbridge was already in the hands of the assailants. A report was spreading that Delaunay intended to blow up the fortress with all the garrison, and great consternation seized the inhabitants in that vicinity..

"We may be perfectly tranquil," said Mirabeau to his brother. "Our father is beyond the reach of harm, and we are taking no part in the battle. On the contrary, according to our best ideas of prudence, we are in an advantageous position. If the people are victorious, I am able to protect you; should the court gain the upper hand, then I hope that you will at least not forsake me; for I may yet do good."

"You are in error," replied the viscount, spitefully; "you have already done too much for me to save you from the gallows. On my side, I do not even expect to be spared the lamp-post!" *

"The moment appears all-important," said the count, thoughtfully. "The lion-hunt of 1789 begins to-day."

"The assembly at Versailles have made matters worse," rejoined the younger brother. "Perhaps you do not know that they addressed a declaration to the king yesterday? In it they make the councillors of his majesty personally responsible for all this mischief and bloodshed, and announce that their sessions are henceforth permanent. At the same time they elected Marquis de Lafayette vice-president, because the Archbishop of Vienne was incapable of his duties as president."

---

* Condorcet, "Mémoires," vol. ii., p. 150.

"These are great deeds in conjunction with the destruction of the old prison of tyranny in the Rue St. Antoine!" replied Mirabeau. "Our father was at one time an inmate of the Bastile, because one of his works gave umbrage to those in authority. Now the thunder of its ruin echoes over his corpse; truly, the brothers Mirabeau could not find a time more suitable to bury their father. Let us then hasten—even the dead must lose no time." He motioned the viscount to enter the carriage, refusing the seat offered him, and slowly followed on foot. They passed through several of the principal streets in order to reach the gate of the city, and suddenly found themselves in the midst of a multitude whose faces expressed joy and terror. Mirabeau learned that the fortress had fallen. It could not long withstand the attack, being inefficiently defended by the invalids and the Swiss guards. After a murderous fire upon the besiegers, they crossed the bridges and court-yards, and began a butchery of the garrison. Delaunay, the governor, who had not the courage to kill himself, was in a cruel manner dragged outside the gate, dashed upon the steps, and his head cut off. Smoking in its hot blood, it was fastened on a pike, and, high above the howling multitude, carried through the streets of Paris.

The same fate overtook the major of the Bastile, Desolmes-Salibrai, although he was as greatly esteemed and beloved by the prisoners as Delaunay was execrated. His clotted head was the second trophy borne with songs of triumph to the Palais-Royal. Two other officers of the garrison were drawn as dogs to the Place Grève, but the thirst for blood was too impatient, and they were massacred on the way.

On passing through another street, Mirabeau and his funeral cortége met others quarrelling over their victims. There were left of the garrison of the Bastile twenty-two invalids and eleven Swiss soldiers of the Salis regiment who had fired on the citizens, and they were to expiate their crime by being hanged on the lamp-posts; but the French guards, who had assisted in taking the fortress, favored their former comrades, and demanded their pardon. At the slow approach of the black hearse, silence ensued, the loudest declaimers ceased, and all stepped back respectfully to give a passage to the dead marquis. Some regarded the incident with superstition, and faces that were swollen and red with passion now suddenly paled with fear.

Mirabeau was soon recognized, and greeted in a silent and considerate manner, for they understood his feelings and his place. It was soon generally known that the count was burying his father, and, as if by preconcerted arrangement, the people formed a guard of honor, accompanying him through many of the streets. While the tumult raged on all sides, and its sounds were heard like the roaring of the stormy sea, all was calm and silent wherever Mirabeau appeared. Thousands followed, as if some new standard had been raised, but so quietly that the count could scarcely refrain from an outburst of gratitude when he looked round at the impromptu escort, at whose head he was walking in his costume of the Third Estate. He was now aware that the carriage of his brother must either have turned back or into a side-street. The viscount could no longer endure the mob, and ceased, as soon as practicable, to accompany the remains of his father to the grave.

A letter from Flesselles, the president of the permanent committee, was found in the pocket of the governor of the Bastile. The former had long been considered a traitor to the people, and did not belie his reputation, for he thus wrote to Delaunay, whose streaming head at this moment was passing on a pikestaff through the thoroughfares of the capital: "I am amusing the Parisians with cockades and promises; hold out till the evening, and you shall have reënforcements." Thus it appeared that there was truth in the reports that he had a secret understanding with the court. He was known as a gay and dissipated man, forcing himself into higher circles, and contemning the lower classes. He now paid for it with his life. He was hurled from the Hôtel de Ville, and the mob rushed upon him, beating him until he died. His dissevered head, like the others, went the rounds of Paris, to be afterward added to those already in the Palais-Royal.

A new direction was now given to the popular movement. The insurgents thought that they might deduce from the letter of the unfortunate Flesselles an attack upon the city before night by the whole military force. All felt the danger, and hastened to make active preparations for defence. The committee sent divisions of the citizen guards for the protection of the most exposed places. The streets resounded with the hammering of workmen and the rattle of arms; all classes were engaged—men, women, children. Even the priests were busy. Barricades like mountains arose as by a sorcerer's wand. The paving-stones were carried to the roofs of the houses, to be cast down upon the heads of the soldiers. Valuable furniture, statues, bronze ornaments, and ponderous books, were collected for the same purpose. Before the barrières deep pits were dug to check the approach of cavalry. On the steeples and towers sentinels were stationed to give the alarm as soon as they saw the first advance of the troops.

Mirabeau beheld these preparations with profound regret. He heard the passwords expressive of liberty given in the different districts, and sometimes remembering Washington as the defender of American independence. In a blacksmith's shop he noticed the men forging lances; and in other workshops casting balls and making instruments for the construction of barricades. In the streets and squares were impatient crowds swearing that they would have liberty or die in the attempt.

The count followed his father's remains beyond the Barrière du Trône. The country was so peaceful, that he almost believed the fears prevailing in the city were exaggerated. Yet he felt undecided whether he ought to take advantage of his duty in one respect to neglect it in another, and he hesitated to turn his back upon the great events transpiring. The driver was a trustworthy man, and no doubt was felt that he would safely lay the body intrusted to his care in its last abode.

Mirabeau at length halted the carriage, and, in a voice choked with grief, said: "Farewell, my father! My duty to you is cancelled by that I owe my country. The occurrences of to-day bid me enter the strife, and necessity forces me to repeat, 'Let the dead bury their dead!'" Stretching his hand over the coffin in a last adieu, he quickly returned to the tumult of Paris, which seemed like a vast factory of unceasing labor, and yet in all this busy preparation for resistance there was manifested a calm and dignified resolution, which deeply affected the count. He determined to remain in the capital until the evening, and then ride to Versailles, where he designed to report what had happened to the National Assembly. On the square, before the Hôtel de Ville, he met Camille Desmoulins, pale and weary, staggering beneath the huge gun on his shoulder, and his clothes spotted with human gore. He recognized the count, and saluted him familiarly.

"You have been at sad work to-day, Desmoulins," said Mirabeau. "Do you think more will be done to-night?"

"Certainly; to-night we shall have the pitched battle of the revolution!" replied Desmoulins, with flaming eyes. "The first thing necessary in the destruction of a government is plenty of blood. That is the reason we have just brought to the lamp-post two more of the invalids belonging to the garrison of the Bastile."

The count looked toward the place indicated, and beheld the bodies struggling in death, while the mob howled around them. "You have not kept your word to me," said Mirabeau, turning away in disgust. "You promised to promote the excitement, but to avoid such orgies as these."

"He who brings home the bride should kiss her," replied Desmoulins, laughing, and disappearing among his comrades.

Mirabeau was about to proceed, when he found himself accosted by Clavière, Dumont, and Duroveray.

"I was surprised in not having seen the three Genevans in this awful work," said the count, shaking hands with them. "You appear to me like the three Parcæ, spinning the thread of the destiny of France."

"We have just arrived from Versailles," replied Clavière, in great excitement. "People are merrier there than they are here. The court give banquets, while the inhabitants of Paris are gathering their heart's blood to fling it into the face of tyranny."

"What kind of enjoyment can they have?" asked Mirabeau, in surprise.

"Well, on the terrace of the orangery at Versailles," rejoined Clavière, "you may see what royalty is. The two regiments Royal-Allemand and Royal-Étranger, appointed to massacre the populace, are in the mean time enjoying the music of the dance. The German soldiers are waltzing with that grace of which they are capable. Wine flows plentifully, for drunken troops are always the most useful in a civil war. The voice of merriment resounds through the city. The most beautiful ladies are there, and wave their delicate hands in applause. You may see the queen, the Count d'Artois, the princes and princesses, the Polignacs, and the swarm of courtiers, present as spectators of those amusements, which are considered a sort of prologue to a victory over the people. The court intend an attack very soon; if I am not deceived, about midnight an assault of the capital may be expected."

"And did the king appear?" asked the count.

"Louis XVI. sits in his cabinet, brooding over his misfortunes," replied Clavière. "For he is sensitive and noble enough to realize his own misery in the anarchy of his country. Your dear National Assembly have dispatched one deputation after another to him, but he replies evasively, thus revealing his anxiety. When requested to withdraw the troops, he answers briefly that the regiments stationed in the Champ de Mars were ordered to remain there. As we were leaving Versailles, the storming of the Bastile and the death of Delaunay and Flesselles became known. I cannot deny that the representatives of the people maintain a dignified demeanor; their fate depends on that of the capital; the attack on Paris will be the signal for arresting the members of the assembly. The latter are well aware that the hussars and body-guards, standing all day before the castle, are ready to surround the hall of the deputies at any moment, and arrest those obnoxious on account of their patriotism."

"There is also a proscription-list, Count Mirabeau," Dumont now began. "Your name is not omitted; the ministry have put you in good company. At the commencement of the struggle, you, Sièyes, Chapelier, Lafayette, Lameth, and others, are to be seized.* These gentlemen have not slept in their dwellings for some time, passing the nights in the hall where the sessions are held, as they are safer there, among the crowds that continually surround it, waiting only a word from the representatives to massacre the troops, and who would scarcely spare even the king or the royal family. You see what you may expect from the court, in spite of your advocacy of their principles!"

"Oh," exclaimed Mirabeau, with flashing eyes, "if I am monarchical it is on the side of liberty, not otherwise! After such a night as the one threatening us, the king becomes guilty, and the people innocent, of the misery and bloodshed that ensue. A new order of things will arise from the conflict, and who can tell by what name it will be designated?"

Clavière proposed to go to the club of the Palais-Royal, where they would meet those engaged in guiding the revolution, and where they might find something in the way of refreshment at the Café de Foy. As they proceeded they met the former inmates of the cells of the Bastile, accompanied by their liberators, returning to their homes and families. Among them were many sad-looking figures, thin and sallow, from the prison damps in which they had languished for many years; they seemed to have lost control over mind and body, and tottered like aged men. A youth named Whyte particularly attracted attention. He walked with a vacant smile, replying to no questions; none knew of what crime he had been accused—he himself could not tell. Mira-

beau entered into conversation with him, and discovered that the poor fellow had indeed lost his mind. Another, named Tavernier, fought with his deliverers, whom, on their entrance into the cell, he had mistaken for executioners. His resistance was at last conquered by the compassionate assurances of his friends.*

The crowd stopped before a house, and at first the meaning of this delay was not understood by those at a distance. Clavière, however, succeeded in forcing himself to the door, soon returning with the intelligence that it was the paternal mansion of Count de Solages, whose irreconcilable father had incarcerated him in the Bastile ten years before, from motives that were utterly unknown.

"And did not his father receive him with open arms?" asked Mirabeau, in a trembling voice. "The time ought to have passed for unnatural enmity between parent and son."

"M. de Solages has just heard that his father is dead," continued Clavière. "His relatives will not recognize him, his fortune being in the hands of a collateral branch of the family.—See, the count reappears, turned away from his own home, and the tears are on his cheeks. The people are throwing stones, and smashing the windows!"

The friends walked on, arriving at the Palais-Royal, where the public passion was at its height. At this hot-bed of the insurrection a kind of market was opened, which greatly increased the agitation. The objects found in the Bastile were arranged and sold to the highest bidder. The money thus obtained was put by a national guardsman into a large box, on which was a placard with these words: "For the wounded of the people." Among the things regarded with superstitious awe, were weapons and instruments of curious form, and machines the use of which no one seemed to know. The respite that took place toward evening in the preparations for defence, was occupied in disputes as to the application of these articles for torture. An old iron corselet, that prevented him who had worn it from voluntary moving, was found specially interesting.

---

* Dumont, "Souvenirs sur Mirabeau," p. 118.

* Louis Blanc, vol. i., ch. vi.

Many handcuffs and chains were lying about that seemed to have been in use for many years.

"Behold, my friends, the people are forging new chains in this struggle," said Mirabeau, pointing to the multitude in the court-yard, as he entered the Café de Foy. "And they are in fact the old ones from which they have freed themselves by such violence and bloodshed."

When the evening approached, the count with his friends again passed through the streets of the capital. The position of affairs was the same, and nothing indicated that greater danger was to be feared. On the other hand, all the measures for defence were completed. Lamps shone in every window, to illuminate the thoroughfares. At the corners stood sentinels, crying: "Attend to your lights, for to-night we must see well!"

Mirabeau, wherever recognized, was received with shouts, to which he sometimes replied in short addresses. He congratulated the people, who were called upon to enter into so great and just a combat for liberty, never omitting to add that their honor consisted not so much in courage as in temperance. Clavière, however, made furious speeches, speaking of nothing but revenge, and invoking shame and sorrow upon the privileged classes.

From time to time, certain persons stepped forth from the masses, and moved about, examining the different posts, and encouraging the populace by words that promised every thing. They seemed to have some secret power of control, and an authority to which all bowed. At the Pont Neuf, a detachment of hussars made their appearance, but were soon surrounded, and their progress stayed, while the officer declared that he and his men came to make common cause with the citizens. At this moment one of those active and mysterious men hastily approached, placing himself under a lamp and watching the proceedings for some time. His countenance was naturally repulsive, and the occasion had wrought in it a most ferocious expression.

"That is a remarkable man," said Mirabeau, who chanced to be in the vicinity with his friends. "I have never seen in a human face such signs of cruelty and bloodthirstiness. His limbs are like those of a tiger, and I am wondering upon whom he will presently spring."

"That is young Marat," said Clavière, smiling. "He is a physician, and this night he will gain the highest honors of the revolution. You are right as to his tiger look and nature. I know him well; his family are from Switzerland."

Suddenly Marat leaped into the midst of the multitude. He stood before the commander of hussars, and said, in a piercing voice: "If you are in earnest, surrender your arms!" The officer stared and then refused. Marat turned to the people, and, addressing them in passionate words, invited them to follow him, and take the hussars to the Hôtel de Ville, whence they should be conducted beyond the gates by a citizen guard. The proposition was received with applause, and Marat placed himself at the head of the escort.

"The citizen guards are used for all possible purposes," said Mirabeau, continuing his way. "I am almost sorry that I originated the idea, and induced the people to adopt it. I am laughing at myself, for all my theories go wrong in practice. It was in Prussia where I first thought of national guards; I am now disgusted with them, for you hear nothing but 'national guards'—they are introduced into all conversation, and ready for any movement."

"And yet for several weeks you have done nothing but clamor for them, my friend!" exclaimed Clavière. "But what harm is there in these virtuous citizens? If they and the lower classes are separated by this organization, it is a very important affair. At last nothing will remain but the poor populace, with whom one can do any thing, because all has been taken from them!"

Mirabeau silently shook his head. He thought he saw Chamfort at that moment in the crowd, with a sword and a gun, and soon recognized the thoughtful features of his friend, now glowing with fanatical ardor. Their eyes met for an instant, and the count, raising his arm, was about to say that he must not be angry at what occurred the day before but he disappeared, casting a stern glance on his former friend.

Midnight came, and no attack was yet made on Paris. Fearful reports, however, were disseminated by the emissaries of the leaders of the revolution. At one time, it was said that the city would be bombarded from the Montmartre, where it was affirmed cannon and mortars were placed; but as all remained quiet, Mirabeau was convinced that nothing would be done, and he resolved to start for Versailles, where he fancied other measures had been urged, and the assault postponed. He left his friends, and, rapidly riding along the public road, passed unhindered through the camps. The tranquil sleep of the royal soldiers assured him that the anxiety in Paris had no foundation. Approaching the palace of Versailles he found the regiments stationed there rioting near daybreak, reminding him of what he had heard of the banquet on the terrace. Their revelry resounded in the morning air; and toasts, by no means suggestive of the happiness of France, were responded to in the orgies of wine and lust.

Entering the city, Mirabeau met several deputies going to the session-hall, who informed him that an early meeting was to be held, to deliberate about another address to the king, in which the assembly would utter their final words to his majesty.

The count soon after hastened to the apartment of the delegates, which presented a singular appearance. The session of the previous evening had been adjourned but for a short time, that the members might have a few hours' rest. Clermont Tonnerre had uttered these remarkable words, when the assembly were on the point of sending a third deputation to the king: "No, let us give them the night to take counsel; monarchs as well as other men must buy experience in a dear market!" Many delegates passed the night in the hall; for some of the older gentlemen, tapestries were spread upon the table, but no one slept—all in fear awaited the coming day.

As Mirabeau entered, the members were taking their seats. Lafayette opened the session in his capacity of vice-president. Several deputies read their sketches of the address to Louis XVI, but the count listened in sorrow, for they were unsatisfactory at such a crisis.

CHAPTER XXXVI.

LOUIS XVI. AND MARIE ANTOINETTE.

IN the palace of Versailles all was quiet on the evening of the 14th of July; the greatest anxiety had reigned during the day in the apartments of the king and queen, and various resolutions were taken and abandoned. Marie Antoinette remained awake; for many a night, indeed, terrible presentiments agonized her mind. She passed the long hours in an arm-chair, revolving thoughts she could not banish.

The queen dismissed Julie de Polignac about eleven o'clock in the evening; until then the duchess endeavored to divert the sorrow of her mistress by her cheerful conversation, but became wearied in mind and body from her efforts to entertain the queen, and to repress her own sadness. While she was relating a laughable story, she burst into tears, and Marie Antoinette, who herself felt very much like weeping, permitted her favorite friend to depart. The queen sat sad and thoughtful, and put herself into the hands of her lady-in-waiting, Madame Campan. On the toilet-table four tapers were burning, shedding a bright light in the quiet cabinet. The queen began to speak of the events of the day.

The residents of the palace of Versailles had but a very imperfect knowledge of what happened in Paris. Although many reports came of the storming of the Bastile, they were kept secret in the circles of the National Assembly, and the few persons at court that knew of it had not sufficient resolution to inform their majesties of the occurrence. The royal couple, however, knew well that, in the present excited state of the capital, the worst was to be expected.

The queen was giving expression to this fear in trembling words, when one of the four lights upon the table went out, without apparent cause. Marie Antoinette noticed it with a sort of ominous dread; and, while Madame Campan hastened to rekindle it, the second ceased to burn, and immediately after the third. The queen seized the hand of her waiting-woman, saying: "Misfortune makes me superstitious, dear Campan. If the fourth candle also goes out, I shall consider it as an evil presage." Scarcely had she ceased, before the fourth light was extinguished, leaving them in darkness! * At the same time the door opened, and the voice of the king was heard asking permission to enter; he was surprised at the obscurity, for Madame Campan did not succeed in relighting the candles until after he gained the middle of the apartment, where he was accosted by his consort with her pale cheeks wet with tears. Louis XVI. smiled when he was told the cause of Marie Antoinette's emotion, and invited her to take a seat beside him on the sofa.

"It is contrary to the habits of your majesty to be awake at this hour," said the queen, in an almost complaining accent. "I hope nothing evil has happened to disturb your usual sleep?"

"No," replied the king. "I feel better than ever after this terrible day. The inducement was great to do evil, but I resisted the clamor of my own anger and the advice of my ministers. They demanded orders for the troops to move against my revolted capital. One thought alone obtained the victory. It was this, my dearest queen: that my hand must not shed French blood. That must henceforth be the first law of all my actions; it will lead me aright. My love for France is at stake, and that is paramount to all other interests. My predecessors permitted themselves to be made an object of idolatry to the French; I will reverse this relation. I will make them the objects of my fervent love. Can they resist that, do you think? And can we not be happy then, Marie?"

The king took her hand, tenderly pressing it to his lips. Marie Antoinette started at the question directed to her; sighing, she said: "No, my husband! we cannot be happy. To love the French

is unfortunate; we sacrifice all, cheerfulness, confidence, and youth. Such love has made me old, and it will cost us our lives. Why can we not try hatred? Let us return distrust with distrust, violence with violence!"

"I know that is your opinion," replied Louis, suddenly growing very grave and melancholy. "You coincide with my ministers; but I am obliged to follow my own ideas of prudence, although opposed to yours. We may yet agree; for who knows to what we may soon be driven by foolish and thankless men? However, let us for a moment forget our cares. Conscious that I have performed my duty, I came to get a goodnight glance from the beautiful eyes of my queen. That is why I disturbed you."

"Perhaps all may yet be well, my husband," said Marie Antoinette, smiling sorrowfully. "But a weapon is used against us which all the power of the world cannot resist—slander! Whence can you get courage to be yourself, to let your heart—your best thoughts guide you, when you are represented as a monster? That is the reason we must be unhappy."

"Yes, it is true, we are the objects of calumny!" exclaimed the king, springing up, and pacing the room heavily and awkwardly, as was usual with him when excited. "A false partyspirit rumors many absurdities about me," he continued, in a rough voice. "They say, for instance, that I have had the hall of the National Assembly undermined, intending to blow them up at the earliest opportunity!"

"Pardon me, your majesty, if I ask permission to make a remark!" said Madame Campan, who, since the entrance of the king, was standing at the door. He kindly nodded to her, and she continued: "I wished only to say that I supped last night with a deputy from Havre, M. Bégouin. He is one of the delegates of the Third Estate, but a man of honor, as I can assure your majesties. He told me that many estimable persons believe it was done against the knowledge and desire of the king." *

---

* "Mémoires de Madame Campan," vol. ii., p. 88.

* "Mémoires de Madame Campan," vol. ii., ch. xiv.

"But he believed such a foolish and wicked deed, your honorable M. Bégouin?" exclaimed Louis XVI. "Very well, if your virtuous provincials give credence to such fables, I shall have to do something for my justification. To-morrow, at dawn, I will have the floor taken up, and let slander see that this time it has missed its aim."

The king slowly regained his composure. He looked at the queen, who, though veiled in sorrow, was not the less lovely. He approached, and, taking her hand, said jestingly: "And how does it happen that persons in the suite of your majesty sup with deputies of the Third Estate? If that is the case, these delegates cannot be so badly off, and I need not repent having permitted a double representation to the Commons."

Marie Antoinette smiled, and concealed her tears. Then she said: "How happy I was, when I did not even know that there was a Third Estate! I hate the name National Assembly, that has cost me so much happiness. It appears that the Commons have been organized to irritate us? Conflicts have begun, showing a daring spirit, and whose aim is the crown of France!"

"These struggles certainly come very near us," replied Louis. "But their origin is natural and honorable. The aristocracy have abused their privileges, and have not been examples of virtue to the people; they have corrupted public morality, and brought monarchy to shame by their licentiousness. The nation suffers as well as royalty; and the latter need not fear the people—it calls them rather to its assistance. The Third Estate will become the firm pillar of the throne, while maintaining their own rights. We avoid civil war, if the nobility and the citizens meet for deliberation; and the clergy, if they carry out their mission, must also join the Commons. We have an opportunity of coming to a good understanding by means of the assembly. And why can we not succeed? Why must poisonous weeds grow with the blossoming fruit?"

"Your heart is great, my husband!" said Marie Antoinette, gently. "But if you give way to sentiment in these times, we perish. Your majesty would govern as they do in Great Britain, and that is magnanimous on your part, but I fear that the English constitution does not suit the French. I am glad on that account that we have dismissed Necker, for he was always endeavoring more or less to introduce that system into your councils. My opinion is different. My first principle is, that we must make no alliance with our natural enemies. You know I was always a friend of liberty. Did I not plead for the banished Parliaments? But at this crisis more is at stake than merely the rights of the Commons. The foes of the throne have assumed the mask of the Third Estate, and have reached our persons. An open warfare must be waged, and we must resist, unless we consent to be dragged from our position!"

"The Third Estate are not enemies of royalty," said the king, after a pause. "I know them; formerly I had some intercourse with them, and observed them well. Labor is the blessing of those classes; it gives them a consciousness of their power, united with respect for the rights of others."

"Your majesty has not forgotten that you learned the trade of a locksmith while dauphin," said the queen, smiling, "and you have an amiable prejudice in favor of the working-classes, discovering good traits in them that are invisible to me."

"I think of those days with regret," said the king, dreamily. "Yes, I had confidence in the tradesmen and laborers working in the palace and gardens, and whom I studied for days. How happy I was, when I could assist them in raising a stone or a beam!* And when I was apprenticed to the smith Gamin, he treated me with great severity. I think, however, it was good for me; I wished to be in my turn austere, to realize the desires of my youth for order and virtue, and to be designated 'the severe;' to resist vigorously the dissipation of the court was my most cherished object."

"Your trade did your majesty some harm," said Marie Antoinette, "for it spoiled your hands,

---

* Soulavie, vol. ii., p. 41.

which became so blackened as never to have recovered their whiteness. I often called you 'my god Vulcan.'"

"Do you think I can ever forget it?" asked the king, with a smile. "Oh, in those days we were very hopeful, and, because we loved one another, we confided in all, sincerely thinking that they were in harmony with us. Since then, it has become more difficult to believe in our good star."

"In what are we to believe, if that becomes extinguished, as my lights did a little while ago?" replied the queen. "But now, good-night, my best friend. It is past midnight, and you require sleep. Who knows what storms may awaken you before to-morrow's sun?"

"If to-morrow I find you as now, there can be no storms for me," replied the king, tenderly embracing his wife. They quickly separated, retiring to their different chambers.

The monarch had slept but a few hours, when he heard a noise near his bed. He recognized his valet de chambre, who in great consternation announced the Duke de Liancourt, grand master of the wardrobe to his majesty. The duke was in the antechamber, and urgently desired an immediate audience. The king was startled, and mused a moment; then he rose, ordering the valet to proceed with his toilet; Liancourt was told to await him in the adjoining apartment, where his majesty wished to receive him. On entering, it was at once noticed that the duke was pale, and trembling with apprehension. He was well known as a devoted servant of his royal master.

"What has happened, my friend?" asked the king, hastily.

"Sire," replied Liancourt, in a low voice," by virtue of my position, which gives me access to your majesty, I have undertaken to inform you of what has been fully confirmed, and is so shocking that it would be criminal longer to keep you in ignorance of it."

"Are you speaking of events that have taken place in the capital?"

"I was told that your majesty had as yet received no reports," continued the duke. And yet what occurred yesterday in Paris is awful. The people have stormed and destroyed the Bastile. This was known here as a rumor yesterday before nightfall. I have, however, just received a courier declaring that it is true. I consider it my duty as a faithful subject to inform you. The taking of the prison-fortress in the capital is only an item of the dreadful deeds accompanying the assault. The gory heads of Delaunay and Flesselles were paraded on pikes by the maddened mob; some of the garrison of the Bastile have been massacred; the venerable invalids hanged on lamp-posts; the French guards have deserted the colors of their lord and king; among the rest of the troops, disloyalty is rampant; the armed inhabitants of Paris, camping in the streets, are supposed to number two hundred thousand men. We fear a universal insurrection to-night!"

The monarch listened sadly. His countenance was pale, but his demeanor calm. "So this is a revolt!" he said, after a pause, as if awaking from his abstraction.

"No, sire," replied the duke, "it is a revolution!" *

"The queen was right," said Louis XVI. to himself. "I have allowed the time for action to pass. A vast loss of life would be necessary to avenge the mischief done. But my mind is resolved; the blood of the French shall not be shed."

"Sire," exclaimed Liancourt, solemnly, "the weal or woe of France and the royal family depends on the decision of your majesty. I must be frank. The greatest danger threatens if you follow the faithless counsels of your ministers. I bless the moment that gives me an opportunity to see your majesty alone, and to appeal to your own judgment and heart. The spirit of insurrection developed in Paris will gain ground. I conjure you to make your appearance at once in the National Assembly, and speak the word of peace. Your presence will almost work miracles—it will disarm parties, and make the deputies the best friends of the crown."

---

* Weber, "Mémoires," vol. i., p. 385.

The king looked at the duke searchingly; he seemed touched by the youthful enthusiasm of Liancourt, and said, gently: "You are one of the most influential members of the National Assembly. Can you give me your word that my personal appearance will be regarded, as I intend it, for the interests of the crown and the well-being of France?"

"We long day after day for a word from your majesty," exclaimed Liancourt. "The doubts and disunions among the delegates are growing every hour, and can only be allayed by your gracious countenance. Let it shine on us to-day! The morning session will commence in a few hours; its deliberations will take an unhappy direction unless you present yourself."

The door opened, and the Counts de Provence and d'Artois entered; they seemed highly excited, and from their demeanor it was evident that the news Liancourt came to announce to the king was already known to them. The duke approached the Count d'Artois, saying in a very decided tone: "Prince! the people have outlawed you! I read the placard announcing the fact!"

The prince started and moved perplexed into the middle of the room. "It is well, that they do this!" he said, composing himself. "I declare open war against them, as they do against me. They desire my head, and I theirs. Why do we not shoot them down? A firm policy—no concessions to their fantasies about liberty, and well-served cannon, alone can save us!"

"His majesty has come to different conclusions!" said Liancourt, bowing low to the king, who stood with folded arms, in a dignified attitude.

"I request my brothers to accompany me this morning to the Assembly of Estates!" said Louis, firmly. "I intend to announce to the members that the troops shall be withdrawn. This will prove to them that they may terminate their deliberations in peace; for I have no higher aim than to discover through them the will of the nation."

The Count d'Artois stepped back in astonishment. His countenance, generally expressive of levity, was full of disappointment and sarcasm.

The Count de Provence received the words of the king in a very different manner. He approached his brother quickly, pressing his hand in friendly approval: "This step of your majesty," he said, "has become necessary from the pressure of circumstances, and may effect a reconciliation. You know that, although from principle a partisan of the absolute power of the throne, I pronounced myself in favor of the double representation of the Third Estate. We live in extraordinary times. History seems to be trying old experiments again, and we must apparently grant every thing to the people; they will the sooner advance so far and no farther, where they of their own accord will be likely to return to obedience."

A commotion took place in the anteroom—quick steps and many voices could be heard. The door opened, and Marie Antoinette entered with some of her immediate attendants. "Does your majesty know what has occurred?" she asked, seizing the king's hand with tearful eyes.

"All will soon again be well," said her husband. "We have nothing with which to reproach ourselves—that is in our favor. I am going to the National Assembly, and will give them evidence of my personal confidence, by ordering the removal of the soldiery from Paris and Versailles."

The queen looked at her husband in amazement; then, dropping his hand, she stood with bowed head, and a profound and painful expression on her countenance. "Your majesty makes an irretrievable fact of the revolution by this action," she said, slowly raising her eyes. "And I am sorry, sire, that you again place your foot in an assembly among whose members are so many captious and inimical men. The resolution you made last month, of dissolving the sessions, ought to have been executed."

"Are there really so many bad members among the deputies?" asked the king, smiling. "I see two of the delegates here, who indeed are very amiable men, and whose presence inspires me with courage—I mean my old and faithful friend the Duke de Liancourt; and, in your majesty's own suite, the brave Count de la Marck, whom I welcome heartily." The king approached a cavalier who was distinguished as much by his tall and slender figure as by his attractive and polite manners.

Count de la Marck, Prince d'Arenberg, was about thirty-six years old, maintaining a prominent position in court society. He belonged to a noble family, originally from Brussels, who had performed signal services for the Austrian imperial house. After passing through a military career, the Empress Maria Theresa gave him special letters of recommendation, and he arrived in France at the same time that Marie Antoinette became dauphiness.

"May I not expect some favor from your colleagues, M. de la Marck?" asked the king, kindly.

"Sire," replied the count, courteously, "I know no one in that incongruous assembly who would close his heart against the appeal of his sovereign. The aristocracy, on whose side I sit, will be confirmed in their loyalty, the clergy will thank God for an interposition that will bring peace, and the Third Estate will have to own that every thing good proceeds from their king."

"But there are evil-minded men at the head of the Commons, like Count Mirabeau," said the queen, hastily.

"Count Mirabeau is not that," replied La Marck, smiling. "I look upon him, in fact, as the future prop of royalty in France."

"I have always felt an unutterable horror in reference to that man, whenever his name is mentioned," said Marie Antoinette. "Why did not your majesty send him away as ambassador to Constantinople, or any other city—a position he would gladly have accepted?"

"I may not treat personally with my opponents," replied Louis. "That would be like a duel which the crown fights with individuals.—But I think it is time to attend the session. Their royal highnesses the Counts de Provence and d'Artois will accompany me. I charge the Duke de Liancourt with the commission to announce to the assembly that I shall be present at to-day's meeting in person." He dismissed the company, taking a tender leave of his consort, who had never seen the king so decided and confident. She almost felt at ease, but her doubts and cares soon returned, and she left in agitation and sorrow.

At the session of the National Assembly, violent debates arose as to the order and importance of the proceedings. After the reading of several outlines as a base for another address to the king, Mirabeau suddenly interrupted the useless business of the members, and denounced the style and meaning of their remarks to his majesty with an irresistible eloquence. His flashing eyes showed his excitement. The hall which until now was the scene of angry commotion, suddenly became so still that a breath could be heard. Even a whisper in some corner was silenced by a call to order.

Mirabeau regarded his audience for a moment, and then began in a sonorous voice: "M. President, let us say nothing to the king, except that the foreign hordes by which we are surrounded received yesterday a visit from the princes and princesses, and all the courtiers, as well as their caresses, exhortations, and presents!—that these executioners, flushed with wine and their pockets filled with gold, all night long sang of the subjugation of France, and in the coarsest language demanded the dissolution of this assembly—that the inmates of his own palace danced to their outlandish music, and supposed that the bloody orgies were at hand of another St. Bartholomew's night. Tell him that Henry IV. (whose memory we all bless, and whom Louis XVI. intended to make his model) once sent provisions into Paris while the city was in insurrection, and he himself besieging it; but that the present king's advisers adopt a contrary policy, and forbid the entrance of the necessaries of life into the starved and faithful capital!" *

Great sensation ensued, which was still increased; for scarcely had Mirabeau concluded, amid loud applause, when the Duke de Liancourt entered the hall. Ascending the steps of the tribune, he announced the king's intention to be present at the session then in progress.

---

* Mirabeau's speech in the session of the National Assembly, July 15th, 1789.

There was as much astonishment as uneasiness at this news. The members left their seats, standing in groups to exchange opinions at this unexpected turn of affairs, and arrange their proceedings in advance. Very few seemed to be really glad, and they expressed themselves grateful to his majesty for acceding to the wishes of the nation. The democratic party were nearly all discontented. The Duke d'Orleans stood in one corner with Sièyes and Latouche, who showed by gloomy faces and expressive gestures their vexation and embarrassment. They appeared to be reproaching each other that they had not by some decided act prevented any possibility of a reconciliation of the people with the king. The aristocracy and court party appeared even more disconcerted. They considered this movement of his majesty momentous, because it indicated that he would abandon his friends.

Among the deputies, as usual, many members from the clubs at Paris and Versailles were seen, who latterly found their way into the sessions. The Club Breton was at that time beginning to exert an influence upon the assembly, and had appointed a committee from among themselves as constant visitors, who aided not a little in promoting irresolution and disorder. It was believed that this club made use of the aspirations of the Duke d'Orleans, as to the throne of France, for their own purposes, and at this time the men sent by the club were making themselves very busy around him, as he stood deliberating with his partisans how they should receive the king.

This question was the subject of conversation, when Mirabeau again ascended the tribune, saying in a voice that commanded attention: "Let us receive his majesty with silent respect. At a moment of universal grief, silence is the best rebuke a people can offer a king!"

These words were received with a storm of applause. The noise had not ceased when Louis XVI. entered, accompanied by his brothers, and without other attendants. His appearance made such an impression that, in spite of all previous calculations of the different parties, the oft-repeated cry, "Long live the king!" resounded on all sides. He stood in the midst of the assembly, in an unembarrassed attitude, and with uncovered head. An easy-chair was placed for him upon the estrade, but he did not seat himself, unceremoniously beginning to speak in a truly paternal style.

The king called himself the chief of the nation, coming to the representatives to express his sorrow for what had occurred, and asking them to find means for the reëstablishment of order. Almost all faces expressed satisfaction at this. In a melancholy voice he referred to the reports current as to the personal security of the deputies; reminding them of his "well-known character," he said that it was unnecessary for him to refute such criminal suspicion. "Ah!" he exclaimed, "it is I who have to confide in you! Assist me, in these difficult circumstances, to confirm the well-being of the state! I expect this from the National Assembly." Then he added, in a tone of touching sadness: "Relying on the love and fidelity of my subjects, I have given orders that the troops be withdrawn from Paris and Versailles; and I request and empower you to make this known in the capital."

The king's speech was interrupted by many exclamations of joy and enthusiasm, and at the end applauded in a rapturous manner. After the Archbishop of Vienne expressed the thanks of the delegates in a few words, his majesty prepared to leave. All present arose to follow him; in silence they arranged themselves, so as to form an escort for their sovereign, who intended to return on foot to the palace.

The excitement of the moment seemed to have conquered even the most stubborn. A vast multitude outside, awaiting the result of this unexampled incident, and beholding the king emerge from the hall, surrounded by the National Assembly, joined the procession, incessantly crying: "Long live the king!" "Long live the nation!" On the Place d'Armes stood the body-guards and the Swiss and French regiments, who, when they saw the strange cortége, caught the general enthusiasm, and celebrated with drum and trumpet the reconciliation of the king with his subjects.

On the large balcony of the palace of Versailles stood the queen, awaiting her husband's return. She was drawn from her cabinet, where she sat in sad foreboding, by the exclamations which seemed so cheering to her. She held the dauphin in her arms, and little madame by the hand. Marie Antoinette's eyes sparkled with joy when she saw the king at the head of the procession. She had not looked so happy for many a day.

"Her majesty looks well!" said Mirabeau to the Abbé Sièyes, at whose side he was walking. "She is showing her dauphin to the people, and the smile of a Madonna transfigures her beautiful countenance."

"But the people cease their rejoicings as soon as they behold the queen," replied Sièyes. "The picture on the balcony is filling up—there are the two younger princes, raising their arms to the little dauphin to kiss him. The masses, however, are not touched by such scenes—there is no sign of respect or love from them. It is evident that she has lost favor."

"No!" said Mirabeau, impetuously. "The queen must be supported, whatever may happen! I see you are the real woman-hater you are said to be. But look at her majesty! Her tears are falling, and the people are obdurate Frenchmen; the most gallant and sensitive community on the globe, are silent when a woman and a queen appeals to them!" The count was so intent in his adoration of Marie Antoinette, that he did not hear the reply of Sièyes.

The crowd disappeared, having it understood to the last moment that their devotion was exclusively given to the king. Toward evening the square before the palace was deserted. Only the sentinels paced before the principal gates, and Versailles seemed to have regained all its former quiet and solemnity.

Later in the evening, several closed travelling-carriages, loaded with trunks, left the inner court-yards of the palace as fast and noiselessly as possible, taking the highway leading in the opposite direction from the capital. In them were the Count d'Artois, the Dukes d'Angoulême, de Berry, de Bourbon, and d'Enghein, and the Prince de Condé, who were preparing to leave the kingdom secretly. Louis XVI. himself advised his brother to pass some time in foreign lands until happier and more quiet days again blessed France. The other princes, although not threatened in the same way (the head of the Count d'Artois being demanded by the populace of Paris), were so overwhelmed by fear that, with the exception of the Count de Provence, all joined in the flight. The new minister followed them on the next day. The latter handed in their resignations, in accordance with the wishes of the National Assembly, but they did not consider themselves safe until far beyond the walls of the capital, filled as it was with material that might involve it in destruction at any moment.

The king resolved to recall Necker, desiring to prove in this way to the people that he would make every reasonable concession. But all was done in great haste—the sovereign would gladly have impoverished himself for his subjects, if thereby he could have assured their happiness. While in this frame of mind, he concluded to go to the capital, and endeavor by his presence to allay the revolution. All day he took counsel with the queen concerning the prudence of this step. At night, while taking leave of the Duchess de Polignac, he could not refrain from tears. Marie Antoinette entreated her dear friend to withdraw from France, with her sister and husband. Both the sovereigns perceived that with the new era that had commenced they must part with all they formerly loved.

On the same day, the deputation from the National Assembly, headed by Lafayette, and accompanied by many inhabitants from Versailles, departed to announce the good intentions of the king at Paris. They were received in triumph by the people, but had to climb over the barricades that obstructed the streets. Arrived at the Hôtel de Ville, after numerous hinderances, Lafayette reported the royal speech with his usual eloquence. He was answered by *vivats* for Louis XVI. and the National Assembly. No better man than Lafayette could at that moment have been sent to Paris, for he had the confidence of all—the lower classes considered him as best fitted to be intrusted with their affairs, and to obtain for them the rights for which they appealed to arms. The president of the Paris electors, Moreau de Saint-Méry, pointed to a bust of the general, in the great hall of the Hôtel de Ville, which the American State of Virginia had presented to the city of Paris, in 1784. Shouts resounded in every direction, and Lafayette was chosen by acclamation commanding general of the Paris citizen militia, an organization which was to be enlarged and designated the National Guards. Lafayette drew his sword, and, returning thanks, took an oath to devote his life to the defence of liberty.*

The second important nomination, made on the same day, was that of the deputy Bailly as mayor of Paris. He had been president of that decisive session in the ballroom when the delegates of the Third Estate swore not to dissolve until they had attained their object. Mirabeau had been invited to become a candidate for the office of mayor, but he neglected to make his appearance at the city hall, although he was assured that there was no doubt of his election.

The king left for the capital the 17th of July, after having partaken of the sacrament. He took a painful and tender leave of the queen, who remained at Versailles. A small detachment of his body-guards accompanied, who very suddenly abandoned him on his arrival at the Barrière de la Conférence, when he found himself surrounded by his other rebellious soldiers. The cannon taken from the Bastile moved before his carriage, with their muzzles toward him. Louis XVI. sat with woeful feelings in the midst of these trophies of the revolution. He could not deny in his own mind that a strange and adverse condition of affairs existed, and that he entered Paris as a prisoner brought before his judge.

The people, however, did homage to their sovereign, on his arrival at the Hôtel de Ville, in their usual riotous exclamations. He uttered no word, but his silence and princely bearing were eloquent, and his glances responded to every cry that came from the multitude. All acted as if a treaty of peace had been concluded between the king and his subjects, and Louis was well content to permit this apparent explanation to remain. It was not until evening that he could return to Versailles.

"Sire, you have become the King of the Commons," said Marie Antoinette, with a smile both sarcastic and sad, as she received her husband, after anxiously awaiting him all day.

"Let them call me what they please," said Louis, "if France is only happy!"

---

* Lafayette, "Mémoires," vol. ii., p. 259.

THE LAST DAYS OF MIRABEAU.

CHAPTER XXXVII.

THE ARISTOCRATS.

MIRABEAU accepted an invitation to dinner at the house of Count de la Marck, with whom he had lately become rather intimate, although they belonged to opposite parties; but this seemed to have a peculiar charm, attracting them only the more toward each other.

"It is strange, count, that you have asked me to dine here to-day," said Mirabeau, entering the brilliant drawing-room, in which several other guests had already gathered, mostly members of the National Assembly. "And it is still more wonderful that I accepted it, as we have such an important session on this 4th of August!" he added, smiling.

"We are taking a holiday, gentlemen!" said La Marck, quietly. "We cannot be so unselfish as our colleagues, who are throwing away the rights and privileges of a thousand years' inheritance; let us at least eat in peace. Who knows how long the *enragés* on both sides, this night attacking all property, will leave us any thing to enjoy? It will soon be considered a feudal privilege if you call a good appetite your own!"

"A man who has never suffered from indigestion will, in that sense, always fight for feudal privileges," said Mirabeau, lightly. "It is a fact, however, that I would have remained at home in painful solitude, if I had not the pleasure of being in the present company; for on no account would I have attended to-day's session."

"Bravo, Count Mirabeau!" exclaimed the Duke de Lauzun, shaking the count's hand in a very friendly manner.

"I do not deserve your approbation," replied Mirabeau, with a ceremonious bow. "I am certainly an opponent of those who decree the abolition of feudal rights and certain privileges of rank—for they have been well earned. I have not attended, because it is distressing to me to see the National Assembly attempting such dangerous business; for it is not safe to undermine a foundation where you intend to raise a new edifice. If I resist this measure, it would hurt me in the eyes of the people, who consider me their friend, and to whom I yet hope to be useful. The deputies are perpetrating their first political blunder, but I shall endeavor to drag them from the abyss on whose brink they are tottering. I spare myself, therefore, on this occasion.—And what may be the cause of your absence, gentlemen?"

"We only wish to have the pleasure of dining with Count Mirabeau in the capacity of fellow-sufferers," said La Marck, taking the count's arm and conducting him to the dining-room. "We do not agree with the right, you do not with the left; is not that a cause for mutual affliction?"

The company seated themselves at the table. The banquet was intended only for a few select friends, but it did not detract from the reputation of the host, who was famous for his parliamentary dinners. The guests comprised, besides the Duke de Lauzun and Mirabeau, the Duke d'Arenberg, an elder brother of Count de la Marck, the Count d'Escars, one of the gentlemen of honor of the Count d'Artois, General-Lieutenant Count de Grammont, the Marquis Foucault de Lardimalie, the Prince de Poix, and a few others, all aristocratic members of the National Assembly.

"I was expecting the Abbé Sièyes," said the host, pointing to a vacant chair. "He did not intend to be present at to-day's session, but I suppose the sense of his duty to the Third Estate drove him to his bench. Or maybe he will come late to contribute his intellectual silence, for this man's taciturnity accelerates and controls conversation, you hardly know how."

"I am aware that some one will be very miserable at Count Mirabeau's absence from the National Assembly," said the Duke de Lauzun, always ready for a jest—"the lady in black, who never fails to be among the spectators, and when the count casts his thunderbolts among us, her eyes flash as the lightning. Who in the world is this interesting incoguita, count? I met her yesterday at the warehouse of the statuary Palloy, who has worked such fine busts from pieces of the ruined Bastile.* She was buying a Mirabeau hewn from a gray stone of that former prison fortress."

"That lady in black was my wife, from whom I am divorced, gentlemen," replied Mirabeau, quietly. "I do not think she goes to the debates in the Salle des Menus on my account. She always took an interest in politics."

"No," rejoined Lauzun, "a lady does not purchase the bust of a man unless she adores him. Besides, these things are exceedingly expensive. It seems the revolution values very highly the destruction it has caused. Although I am an old aristocratic sinner, I wished to have one of those pieces of art chiselled from some fragment of the 'tyrant's stronghold,' as it is now called. I fancied I could best associate the reverence I feel for my ancestors with a Voltaire, and so I bought the old

joker, from whom came originally all this trouble now surrounding us. But I had to pay three hundred francs for the author of 'Candide,' though the material is not worth a sou."

"Not a sou?" asked Mirabeau, smiling. "It has cost France much more. I purchased a Rousseau, manufactured from the same material, and placed him near my inkstand, on my desk at the session-hall. It is strange that the busts of Necker find no ready sale. The people received him on his recall in great triumph, but they seem to have cooled suddenly toward him. The commotion is beyond that minister now, and he will probably soon be pensioned off, as he is no longer of any use."

"On this day another Bastile is stormed, gentlemen—the feudal rights," said the Marquis Foucault de Lardimalie, with an expression of solemnity. "But I think they cannot be as easily razed and carried away as the fortress in the Rue St. Antoine. Feudal rights are the bone and sinew of the state, for without vassalage, ground-rents, tithes, rights of jurisdiction and of the chase, exemption from taxation, and unrestrained personal liberties, the monarchy cannot live. And all this, which it has taken centuries to establish, the men in the Salle des Menus expect to destroy in one night. Any nobleman giving his consent to such a crime, ought to be branded as a sacrilegious wretch."

"And yet two noblemen are the originators of the parliamentary folly of this night," said Mirabeau. "Those propositions did not come from the left side; but your party, gentlemen, has evoked them against yourselves. I am almost sorry that the division of right and left was made. Thence sprang the confusion now reigning; for there are democrats on your side as there are aristocrats on mine. The Viscount de Noailles and the Duke d'Aiguillon, who made the motion for the abolition of the customs of the feudal system, both sit on the right, while Sièyes and myself sit as opponents on the other side."

"The real incendiary is the Viscount de Noailles," said the host. "He is a young and lightheaded officer, possessing nothing, and of course

* Condorcet, "Mémoires," vol. ii., p. 74.

having nothing to lose, who was more attracted by the idea of popularity than the costly wines he drank at the table of the Duke d'Aiguillon, whose companion he is. The duke is the richest feudal lord of the French monarchy, and would surrender much in the way of privileges and income, if the 'altar of his country,' as he calls it, demands the sacrifice. But Noailles is the chief fanatic, who would rush into destruction and drag others with him."

"Noailles is a brother-in-law of the Marquis de Lafayette," said the Prince de Poix. "And he has been misled by the example of the latter to court popular favor. The poor viscount will not fill his empty pockets in that way. These fools suppose they can deprive us even of our right of the chase, the most coveted privilege of the aristocracy. If a nobleman cannot shoot a deer when he has a chance, all knightly virtues are at an end, and the mere mob become confounded with the nobility. The chase has its advantages, not only in preserving the character of the aristocracy, but benefiting that of the lower classes. If the hunt leads, for example, through the ripening field of a peasant, less bread is the result, and this, in view of hunger, renders him more obedient and faithful. But let no one suppose that starvation has caused this revolution. The well-fed *canaille* are by far the more dangerous. When the people are satisfied, they desire to dance; when they are permitted to dance, they desire to crown themselves."

There was some merriment at the comic remarks of the captain of the body-guards and governor of Versailles, who was at the same time busily engaged in carving a capon.

"We ought not to laugh, for the case is very serious," said Count d'Escars. "Just before the departure of Count d'Artois I had a philosophical conversation with his royal highness on this matter. We agreed that it was not a conflict about privileges that was raging in France as well as in other parts of the world. No, gentlemen, it is a war of races that has broken out among us—two distinct races are disputing for sovereignty. And are we not different from the lower classes? Our

faces, noses, hands, and feet, are not like theirs; our whole structure is of another pattern, and why cannot we have exclusive pretensions and rights?"

"All depends on family," said Count de Grammont, in a low voice. "I have no doubt that a chemical analysis would prove that the blood of the aristocracy is composed of different ingredients from that of the people—that it is of a deeper color and a higher temperature. A man who has a vital fluid like that of a fish, cannot be considered or treated as a lion. It is easily comprehended, therefore, that vassalage is a law of Nature that demands respect!"

"Gentlemen," said Mirabeau, "we should not draw too strong inferences from what we merely owe to the accident of birth. I own that I would rather be a count than a day-laborer; for a nobleman is necessarily a man of honor, having a character which he is obliged to maintain in society. We ought to renew our titles from the people, whose protectors and leaders we are. We would be greater after having aided in founding a natural liberty for the nation, but we shall remain aristocrats!"

"Your view contains as much prudence as good-nature," said La Marck. "We ought to rejoice at the labor suggested to us by Count Mirabeau. But would it not be rather dangerous to bestow privileges on the lower classes? I am afraid we would not gain much by it. While we looked on to see how they enjoyed them, we might very possibly starve!"

"We know you mean well, Count Mirabeau," said the Prince de Poix, "but you have already exposed yourself to the worst suspicions. You are said to be the instigator of the incendiarism now raging in the provinces. You are accused of secretly inciting the peasants in all parts of France to rise against their landlords, to destroy their obligations to duty, and burn down the castles of those to whom they owe service. You may despise this calumny, but you see how hazardous it is to become a leader of the people. They do not become ennobled simply because they are under the guidance of a count, but he is very likely to deteriorate."

"You are witty, prince," replied Mirabeau, gravely, "but you may soon know from sad experience that these things are not matters of jest. You do not suppose me to be an incendiary; and you see I prefer to dine here rather than help to overthrow in the National Assembly the privileges of landed proprietors. I think that the relations of proprietor and tenant, when they are burdensome, can only be ameliorated by a free constitution; but that a *coup de théâtre* scattering honest possessions and destroying inherited rights should not be made. You will, however, have to make some sacrifices, whenever the right time comes, gentlemen! The Prince de Poix has a very slender and aristocratic neck, and it would be a pity if it should ever make the acquaintance of a lamp-post!"

"That would be unpleasant, particularly as I am rather sensitive in that region under such circumstances," said the prince, rubbing his neck with both hands. The conversation took a less serious turn, and midnight approached.

Suddenly the door opened and the Abbé Sièyes entered, in ill-concealed excitement, giving to his generally calm and stern air a very strange appearance. He refused to take the place reserved for him at the table, excusing himself while he took a seat on a corner sofa.

"I ask pardon for coming so late," said the abbé to La Marck. "I was present as a spectator at the hall of the National Assembly. I wished to witness the battle for a moment, although I neither would nor could take a part in it. The sight, however, so overpowered me that I was not able to leave in time to accept your invitation. At length I crept away in the confusion—wounded, though not one of the combatants. They are still hard at work in the direction of all rights of property; one resolution after another is passed amid the utmost confusion, and the hall resounds with noisy passion."

The company left their seats and surrounded the alarmed and exhausted abbé, many questions being asked at the same time. He could but imperfectly reply, as he was not only fatigued, but irritable on account of what had occurred.

"Their conduct, in some respects, was really touching," resumed Sièyes, in a voice gentler than was customary with him. "It was remarkable how one influenced another, in sacrificing well-founded rights, showing himself magnanimous at the expense of his neighbor. A contagious fever raged among them, and it was difficult to escape. After the abolition of feudal rights, tithes, and all provincial privileges, were decreed in extraordinary haste, many of the deputies embraced and wept with joy. Other questions were brought up in the midst of this enthusiasm, involving matters declared burdensome to the people, and in a moment disposed of without consideration or understanding. As soon as one was decided, another was ready; and so it will continue until daybreak, when probably regret for what was done during the night will make many a delegate ill!"

"We can very well understand that the abbé must have felt sadly the abolition of tithes," said the Prince de Poix. "However, as he is the liberator of the Third Estate, he should be willing to sacrifice a little filthy lucre for such an honor!"

"Do you think that it is pecuniary interest that makes me an opponent of such measures?" exclaimed Sièyes, rising impulsively. "No, gentlemen, it is my hatred of landed proprietors; for to abolish tithes without indemnification is robbing the clergy and enriching the landlords. But what has that to do with the Commons? These men are driven by a political spirit. Ah, they desire to be free, and know not how to be just!" *

"Believe me, this night session is nothing but an intrigue of the Duke d'Orleans!" exclaimed Mirabeau. "Messrs. de Noailles and d'Aiguillon, I know, dined every day at his house during the past week, and the whole plan was arranged at his table. That was one of my principal reasons for remaining away from the debates. The duke failed in his ambition of being proclaimed lieu-

---

* "Ils veulent être libres, et ils ne savent pas être justes."—With these words Sièyes closed his speech against the abolition of tithes, held at the special session on the 4th of August.—Vide Dumont, "Souvenirs," p. 147.

tenant-general of the kingdom and successor to the throne, because the king went to Paris on the 17th of July, and confided himself to the generosity of his subjects. Now the duke operates with the abolition of aristocratic privileges, in order to cause endless confusion, and perhaps in the dark stumble upon a diadem. We must warn the people against him."

Count de la Marck became uneasy, begging Mirabeau in a low voice to be careful, as the duke might enter at any moment, having promised to come after the session was ended; adding that his object was to make Mirabeau's acquaintance. The latter was surprised, and glanced inquiringly at his host, who avoided making any reply. The Abbé Sièyes soon departed, followed by the rest of the guests, as it was past midnight, and Mirabeau remained alone with La Marck. They were both glad of this opportunity to exchange opinions on many subjects.

Count de la Marck was one of the most benevolent and self-sacrificing of men, who, although a devoted friend of the royal family, loved to have intercourse with persons of all parties, particularly the leaders of the left in the National Assembly; politically they were his opponents, socially his friends. He acted with a tact and sincerity that apparently came from his heart; however, it could not be denied that his principal object was to gain partisans for the king and queen.

The servants were dismissed. La Marck took a seat near Mirabeau, who was impatiently awaiting whatever revelations his host had to make. "My dear count," began La Marck, after a pause, "we must speak of an affair that, believe me, I have at heart even more than you have. I sent an intimation to the queen, concerning her interests, by the Countess d'Ossun, as I have already told you. This lady was commissioned to say to her majesty, in my name, that my relation with Count Mirabeau, about which singular reports were current, must not make her distrustful of my devotion to the royal cause. I have two things in view: to arrest your revolutionary degeneracy, and to make your talent useful to the king and

the monarchy, to which you are already greatly inclined. I believe the ministers would soon be obliged to come to an understanding with you, if they wished to maintain their position."

"Excellent, my dear friend!" exclaimed Mirabeau. "And what did the queen reply?"

"Not very favorably," replied La Marck. "She gave me credit that what I did was with the best intentions, but that she did not believe I could really influence you. Nor was the opinion entertained that the ministers of the king would ever need your assistance. 'I hope,' her majesty added, 'we shall never be so wretched as to take refuge with Mirabeau.'"[*]

Mirabeau looked disconcerted. "Is it possible that Marie Antoinette has such an unconquerable dislike of me?" he asked, in a low voice. "I wished her to know that she had a devoted friend on whom she could rely in the National Assembly. I have become a sincere supporter of the royalty, as I have before told you: for I see no other way out of our present difficulties, than to connect liberty with monarchy—to unite firmly the interests of the throne and the nation. However, I would have followed my own path without troubling myself about any of the persons at court, if I had not been affected by the deeply-afflicted countenance of the queen, not gladdened by a single ray of joy from the crown she wears. No other reason induced me to ask you to become a sort of mediator between their majesties and myself, informing them that they ought to regard me as a friend rather than a foe; but if Marie Antoinette cannot understand me, the position of affairs remains the same as before."

"We must have patience," said La Marck, quietly. "The king and queen will soon feel nothing but gratitude toward you. Only your Titanic strength, united as it is with prudence, can turn the present ideas of freedom in a monarchical direction. That is the problem of our age, and you alone can solve it. I never would have dared to say a word to you on that subject, if I had not perceived that you were laboring in our

---

* "Correspondance entre le Comte de Mirabeau et le Comte de la Marck," vol. i., p. 107.

favor. Her majesty has become timid and distrustful, but, believe me, as soon as your aims are clearly seen, her heart will be softened. The court will owe you their salvation, and your reward will not fail."

"What reward do I demand?" exclaimed Mirabeau, in excitement. "You know I only speak in public as I feel; in no other way could I utter a sentence. If I desired advantages of any kind, I never would have been concerned to remove the difficulties existing between the royal family and myself. I would have accepted the propositions of the Duke d'Orleans. Then I need only have gone down into the revolutionary mud, until we had decided on a king, and proclaimed the duke Regent of France. His money has been almost forced into my pocket, but I would not have it, although my debts press me. You know all about that, count, for I have lately made many inroads on your purse."

"My dearest friend," said La Marck, shaking Mirabeau's hand, "we owe such little services to each other, just as in riding we would hold each other's stirrup, or strike the dust off a friend's shoulder."

"What a cloud of dust would arise if my debts were cast off my back!" said Mirabeau, with a tragi-comic sigh. "But I shall never forget your kindness, and especially the manner in which you have obliged me. The last fifty louis d'or I have not yet returned, and at present I cannot say when they will be."

"You desire to make me blush," replied La Marck. "You must pardon me that I had not more at my disposal the last time. I am afraid there will be some delay before you gain possession of your inheritance. You have suffered enough by your relatives, and of what use is friendship, if it is not in some measure to compensate injustice?"

"My family affairs are again a source of annoyance to me," said Mirabeau. "My father has left me a yearly income of fifty thousand francs, but to be drawn from our landed property, and this has brought me into collision with my brothers and sisters. They have commenced a lawsuit against

16

me. In the mean time, I am penniless, though many persons think that I am growing rich by bribery, but my pockets are those of an anchorite. I am not ashamed to confess that I am in want every day, and that often I cannot pay even my servant. The allowance I receive as a deputy sorrowfully reminds me that there is such a thing on earth as money."

"A good idea occurs to me," rejoined La Marck, thoughtfully. "You will have to make me a promise, count, to apply to no one but myself in any of your pecuniary embarrassments. In that case, I will take pleasure in lending you fifty louis d'or every month. I would then know how to make my own arrangements accordingly, and this sum, together with your allowance, will probably cover current expenses. As to your debts, I would advise you to leave their settlement until you receive the inheritance of your father; that will be a sufficient guaranty to your creditors. Will you permit me to serve you in that way?" *

"There are few friends like you," said Mirabeau. "I accept your offer, and make myself a vassal of your friendship."

"Vassalage is one of the things I am willing to have abolished," replied La Marck, smiling. "However, they may resolve on what they please in the National Assembly, we shall only the more energetically follow our own plans. Let us support the king and the monarchy; if you wish it, on the broadest foundation of liberty. Even if I, as an old aristocrat, cannot love some of these measures, I am willing to suffer them, if royalty has the control."

"We can only reach this quickly and certainly by a new constitution; and I am urging this truth with all my might. Why not a government like that of Great Britain? I find in it every guaranty for a true, natural, and rational freedom. The equilibrium of the throne and the people can be maintained by an aristocracy. What more can we desire to make the state worthy of being inhabited by human beings? We noblemen may therein find our honor preserved. But I do not

* "Correspondance entre Mirabeau et La Marck," vol. i., p. 95.

see what is to be done with our wretched assembly. At one time they spell, like children, for months at a single political syllable; and again, they put on seven-league boots, endeavoring to reach an object at one step—to overturn in a day institutions of a thousand years' growth. I have been elected one of the committee on the rights of man, about which we are to debate in a few days."

"Yes, the rights of man!" repeated La Marck, shaking his head. "Are they not an American invention, now to be inscribed in a separate codicil? I must confess that, until that insane motion was made at the sessions, I did not know that human rights could be registered just as my inspector registers the sheep on my farms."

"What a ridiculous idea that was!" exclaimed Mirabeau. "I lately talked this affair over with my Geneva friends, and even those radical gentlemen agreed that the declaration of the rights of man, separate from a political constitution, is but child's play, and would become a mere farce.* I will endeavor to move the Convention, first to attend to the construction of a free government, and then consider human rights; the latter can be defined, or considered at all, only where there are laws.

"Is it not a silly falsehood to declare: 'All men are born free and equal?' They are very far from it—they come into the world more dependent than any other creatures, and in ever-varied differences of constitution, mind, and temper, and in vastly dissimilar outward relations, inseparable from their very existence! The most gifted are sometimes obliged by the force of circumstances to become slaves, while the meanest ascend to places of wealth and authority. We are born with very few rights. My features are naturally my own, but that I may freely express my thoughts, worship the Creator in any way I please, are privileges I can obtain only in a well-ordered, law-abiding community. Let the assembly first build up the state, and then furnish it with all the rights they choose."

* Dumont, "Souvenirs de Mirabeau," p. 138.

La Marck pressed the hand of his guest, as a token of unanimity of opinion, saying: "You delight me, dear count! Would I could always hear you speak as temperately in public! Promise me that you will make use of such thoughts in the heat of debate. When you speak you are often under the power of a revolutionary passion, and it carries you away. I have felt pained, and it is only while privately conversing with you that I understand what you might be."

"It is true," replied Mirabeau, gravely, "when I speak publicly, I feel as if my words would burn all that is useless in the world, and I am perfectly aware when I go too far. To be frank, I purposely promoted the commotion among the people; for if quiet ensues too soon, the ravenous birds will consider themselves safe, and return to new objects of prey. It will soon be no longer necessary to make a murderers' den of my heart. I will offer my hand to all my opponents, if they desire nothing but a free and strong monarchy."

"Your extraordinary talents will be appreciated, count!" said the host. "And you will have a position in France more powerful than any other man ever enjoyed. You shall be our minister, as soon as we have put Necker aside. You are still looked upon with suspicion at court, on account of your past life. I will, however, direct the eyes of the queen toward you. She will soon understand that there is but one who can save her in her necessity, and he is our Mirabeau!"

"You have access at all times to her majesty!" exclaimed the guest. "Marie Antoinette feels true friendship for you, for your father was an Austrian field-marshal! She will be guided by you. Tell her that on my knees I pray for the opportunity to be of service to her. Let her but say the word, and I would descend to any service in order to assist in erecting a temple according to her wishes!" He seized his hat, adding, as he was about to take leave: "Pardon me for not awaiting the Duke d'Orleans. No friendship can ever exist between us, and it is better if he does not make my acquaintance. There are already reports that I belong to his party; you know that such is not the case, and I must say that I would not employ the duke even as my valet de chambre." * Count de la Marck laughed, and dismissed his friend with renewed assurances of regard.

———♦———

CHAPTER XXXVIII.

MADAME LE JAY AND THE VETO.

ON a bright September day, Mirabeau left Versailles to attend to some business at Paris that had rendered him uneasy for several weeks. He had undertaken to edit a journal, together with Dumont and Duroveray, which was printed in the capital under the title of *Le Courrier de Provence*, containing very able articles on the politics of the day. The paper, however, was so irregularly served by the bookseller, Le Jay, its publisher, that the subscribers were continually complaining, and urging Mirabeau to make a change.

Dumont and Duroveray, his co-editors, importuned the count to get another publisher, at the same time making it understood that they suspected the reason of his leniency—a liaison with Madame Le Jay. Rather than offend her he was willing to ruin a journal so important that during the first few days it had more than three thousand subscribers.

Madame Le Jay was the real principal of the bookseller's establishment, submissively assisted by her husband, whom she ruled with a rod of iron. A suspicion arose that the irregularity in the publishing of the journal was not only the result of bad business conduct, but that the subscriptions were diverted from the rightful parties. Besides, Le Jay was always complaining that he had no money to pay the postage expenses—that the printer would not work, as he was not paid; and so the issue of the *Courrier de Provence* was interrupted until Mirabeau made new advances.

The count had so far avoided any definite reply

to the urgency of his friends, but now they managed to influence him against his will to go to Paris in order to make a thorough investigation. He sat in the carriage in ill-humor, until Clavière, who had joined the party, ventured some remarks.

"Our Mirabeau fears to enter into explanations with his fair friend Madame Le Jay," said Clavière, jestingly. "Why was the publication of the journal given to a man with such a seductive wife? It is true, she is no longer young, but she represents the brilliant woman of thirty-six. Who can think of settling accounts or talking of business-matters, when looking into her black eyes? I am convinced she keeps no books at all, for it is impossible to owe her any thing. And now we are carrying this gigantic man to Paris, almost like a prisoner, to demand her receipts."

"You are a fool, Clavière," replied Mirabeau, violently. "You understand my acquaintance with Madame Le Jay perfectly, and, of course, this kind of business is not at all pleasant. I have given her all my share of the profits, and would continue to advance money, if you would only exempt me from investigating this paltry affair; and I consider it a token of friendship that I have consented. You are aware that I do not wish to leave Versailles at present even for half a day. The debates about the veto and the union of the two chambers have commenced, and these questions are so important that I do not like to lose a single word in the Convention."

"Why, you made a powerful speech in favor of the king yesterday," rejoined Clavière. "The popular hero has broken a lance for the veto of his majesty, and I can tell you that certain clubs have sworn to be revenged on you. You wish to give to Louis XVI., who ought to be rejoiced that he has gained you, the right to say to all the acts of the legislature, 'I forbid!' You have proved yourself more monarchical than the king himself and his ministers; for Necker only demanded the privilege for the crown, to postpone the execution of the resolutions, and appeal to a newly-elected assembly, who would decide for or against it. But you, my friend, intend to put the constitution entirely into the hands of the king; and, after your

---

* The well-known expression of Mirabeau in reference to his alleged relation with the Duke d'Orleans.—La Marck, vol. i., p. 128.

exertions yesterday, I think you may allow yourself a little rest, and visit the charming Madame Le Jay. Let the others read off their addresses, they will not influence the deputies."

"I know that I will never agree on these subjects with you Genevans," said Mirabeau, looking dreamily out of the carriage. "I assure you, however, that if the king is not to have the veto in the new form of government, I would rather live in Turkey than in France. No nation can exist without a chief who is responsible in his will and actions. I believe in monarchy because I desire order! but the throne must have the authority that is natural to it. I fear the encroachments of a sovereign much less than those of an assembly." *

No reply was made, Dumont and Duroveray urging forward the postilion. "We must hasten," said the former, "for I hear the fair lady goes so far as to arrogate to herself the proprietorship of the *Courrier*. Lately, when I attempted a few slight reproaches, she became furious, assuring me that she would soon dismiss us altogether, and employ other editors, who would be more reasonable and accommodating."

Mirabeau could not refrain from laughing, but said, in a conciliatory tone: "We shall manage to come to an understanding with her. I do not think it advisable to have any difficulty, for her tongue rules the whole Boulevard Poissonnière, where her store is; that is a very populous part of the city, and I must be very careful lest she paint me too black. It is possible that she has learned many expressions and adventures of mine, as I breakfasted with her nearly every morning while she had the small store on the boulevard, where the newspapers and pamphlets of the day could be read."

"I was told," said Clavière, laughing, "that her establishment was often closed, and all knew that the revolution was having a respite, while you took Madame Le Jay to a restaurant. Did she influence you for the king's veto? She is a zealous royalist, and many of the courtiers read her tracts."

"Her reading-room exists no more," said Dumont. "I was surprised yesterday when I found it transformed into a splendid bookstore, where Madame Le Jay, surrounded by all the literature of the day, was enthroned before a counter of marble and gold. She has made good use of our subscription-list, while she not only withholds from us our own, but ruins our journal by her neglect and indifference."

Mirabeau changed the conversation, which was becoming very disagreeable. Soon the carriage reached Paris, where was universal tumult. Brawling crowds were rushing through all the streets; on the squares, meetings were held and addresses delivered of a very inflammatory nature.

"I hear nothing but words about the veto," said the count, listening to what was passing around him. "The people really have made great progress. I could not have believed that such an interest would be taken in ideas of a constitution; and where not long ago stood barricades, they are holding disputes!"

"The people did not at first know very well what the veto was," replied Clavière, smiling, "but our friends have made them comprehend it in an odd way. Yesterday a man in a blouse, with whom I had a long talk, asked me confidentially in what district M. Veto resided, and whether it would not be better to hang him on some lamp-post."

The postilion found it difficult to push his way through the masses to the small street near the Boulevard Poissonnière. The public soon recognized Mirabeau, pressing round his carriage with exclamations of love and devotion, mingled with disapproving cries concerning the veto; in the background there were signs of dissatisfaction, intimating that since Mirabeau was in favor of the king, he was not a friend of the people. Clavière drew the count's attention to this popular discontent.

The party approached the house of Madame Le Jay, and Mirabeau noticed that the throngs who had followed now gathered around him as he descended from the coach. He recognized several of the lower classes with whom he formerly had

---

* From Mirabeau's speech for the veto of the king.

some familiarity, and who were supposed to exert great influence in the various clubs and on the streets. Their countenances expressed great emotion, and they seemed desirous of speaking to him. An old laborer seized Mirabeau's hand, saying: "Count, you are the father of the people, and must save us. If you do not defend us against those who would deliver us bound hand and foot to despotism, we are lost. If the king exercises the right of a veto, of what use is the National Assembly? We are slaves as much as we ever were."

Mirabeau looked at the man, and saw that he was in sincere grief. After being pacified by a few words he disappeared. Others approached, conjuring the count not to permit the king to have an absolute veto, and he promised to do all he could for them. "You exaggerate the importance of this matter, my friends," he said. "But you may rely on me. Believe me that I have your true interests at heart, and will advance them at all times and in all places."

Great applause succeeded these words, and the people seemed ready almost to worship their friend; but he was not deceived—hisses were heard in the distance. He looked in the direction whence they came, and recognized many whom he had seen at the clubs, looking threateningly toward him. Presently a stentorian voice was heard above the tumult. A man had sprung upon a lamp-post, to deliver an address.

"The veto is a monster, that will devour us!" said the speaker, violently gesticulating. "It has claws like a tiger, with which it tears the sovereignty of the nation; it has a poisonous tooth; it has a upas breath, and drops a venom on the life of our young liberty which will wither all our hopes before they have a chance to be realized."

"Let us slip into the store under cover of this man's speech!" said Mirabeau.

Madame Le Jay was aware of the arrival of the gentlemen, and at once opened the door of her establishment. They saluted her rather gravely— a style she was not accustomed to, particularly from Mirabeau; and as she knew with what intentions they had come, she began to assume a

position of defence. Crossing her arms, she stood in the centre of the apartment, awaiting the onset in a defiant attitude.

The count appeared absent-minded, pacing the store, and examining the books on the shelves. "You are well provided with literature, Madame Le Jay!" he said, taking down a book and turning toward her. "This is a very pretty edition of the *Liaisons Dangereuses*. Tell me the price, and enter it to my account, for I intend to purchase the volume for the sake of the copperplates. And you may as well take this opportunity of letting me see our business-books, that I may know how the credit of the *Courrier de Provence* stands. Otherwise, I can only make purchases from your store by paying cash."

"See how carefully he goes to work!" whispered Clavière, who had withdrawn to the background with the others. "And what an ingenious transition from the *Liaisons Dangereuses* to our own affairs! That work was written by the wretched La Clos, and is a special favorite of Mirabeau. He has, I fear, dangerous connections everywhere! I do not speak of that which will very likely ruin our journal, but there are others which will ruin him. He is talking softly to her, squeezing her white hands, but she looks as angry as a hyena, shaking her head, and rejecting his propositions."

"Madame Le Jay," said Mirabeau, in a voice intended to be heard by the rest, "if honesty did not exist in the world, we ought to invent it, as the only means of enriching ourselves." *

The lady, however, seemed to lose all control over herself. Trembling with anger, she stepped forward, and, raising her clinched hands, cried in a piercing voice: "Count, and you other gentlemen, you have so degraded the *Courrier* by your blasphemous articles, that I do not consider it good enough to clean the window-panes of my store—and you wish to see my books, in order to accuse me of swindling! I have no books for you, my gentlemen; for I am an honest woman; and, if you say another word, I shall have to dis-

---

* Mirabeau's expression on this occasion.—Dumont, p. 122.

charge you, and employ two other editors, who have already made application. You have not all the talent in the world. There are other writers besides you. Paris is a city where you can find hosts of people able and ready to labor for money. For example, there is M. Guiraudez, who, by the way, is still a very young man, but of such ability that you are not fit to hold a light to him. I intend that henceforth he shall be one of my editors. And now go, or your presence will make me angry. I will use my rights of proprietor, lacking neither the will nor the power. March! all of you; my hands are itching to try their effect on your pretty faces, and it will not be my fault if you do not soon discover it, if you stay many minutes longer!"

The fury of the woman so excited the risibility of the Genevans that they could not refrain from expressing it, while they acted as if they were really afraid of her. Mirabeau, who was inclined to return her compliments, was almost restored to good-humor by the merriment of his friends. "Let us depart, for it is rather stormy here," he said, taking leave in a very prompt manner. "I must come to some satisfactory agreement, rely on it, and all causes of complaint shall be removed."

Dumont and Duroveray declared that they would withdraw from the editorial management of the journal. "Then M. Guiraudez will fill your places!" exclaimed Madame Le Jay, with triumphant eyes.

"Poor fellow!" said Clavière. "He will be tied to her apron-string, and have the labor of a Sisyphus! I believe it is better to sell one's self to the court. What do you say, count?" Mirabeau pretended not to hear the question, requesting his friends to leave.

The multitude in the street had dispersed, and all was silent. The Genevans separated from Mirabeau, as they had business to attend to in Paris, and would not immediately return to Versailles.

"Well," said Clavière, before he went his way, "is that all we have accomplished to-day? It is a pity that your assembly, among their seventeen rights of man, did not decree the following: 'Every citizen has the right of loving Madame Le Jay and imagining her to be the queen.' "

"Adieu!" said Mirabeau, laughing, though the jest appeared to irritate him. "I wish you better success than that we have just had. I must, however, say, for my justification, that the madame is generally very amiable. Olympus, you know, had divinities of all tempers!"

Before night the count was again at Versailles. His servant delivered him a letter which had come during his master's absence. The black seal made a melancholy impression on Mirabeau. Hastily opening the envelope, addressed in a writing unknown to him, he read the announcement of a death that grieved him. It was one of the solemn voices of the past, bringing the memory of days which he little thought of in the turmoil of later life. The time of youth and hope revived in his mind, and his wild love seemed as a dream when his tears fell upon the lines conveying to him the intelligence of the decease of Sophie de Monnier.

Sophie had breathed her last in her small villa of Gien, where she had dwelt since leaving the convent, and whence no information of her ever reached Mirabeau. One morning she did not appear at the usual hour, and, when her room was entered, she was found in her easy-chair, with a charcoal fire on each side of it. Thus, in her thirty-sixth year, with the charms of her youth still undecayed, she ended her life by suicide. Her physician, Dr. Ysabeau, sent the news of her death to her former lover, considering it proper, in view of the relations once existing between them. The doctor added some explanation why she sought death. She had become attached to a M. de Poterat, and their affection was sincere. Since death robbed her of this friend, she determined to outlive no other.

"Sophie de Monnier dead!" sighed Mirabeau, with profound melancholy, stepping to the open window and looking out into the silent night. "Ah, she was gentle and yet passionate—but when I loved her was I happy? I was a youth without a future; and, without thought or honor,

revelled in the follies of the present. Sophie and
Henriette! stars ever shining in my memory!

"When I loved you, Henriette, it was a happy
union of hearts! You were young and pure, and
our affection was founded in our mutual happiness. Our regard for liberty was the same, and
we looked with hopefulness to the well-being of
the people—we were both enthusiastic in our
ideal of the future of France. Often you looked
at me with those innocent eyes, asking me
whether real love, liberty, and popular happiness,
would ever dwell on the earth, changing it into a
paradise. My poor Nehra, this sad death reminds me of your illness—consumption is fast
wasting away your beauty and your life, and I
know not the hour I may be called upon to mourn
your death. I seldom see you in these days of
national sorrow, and, I confess, I fear to behold
your pallid cheeks and hollow eyes! My friend,
I am about to engage in those measures of which
we often talked; but you are ill, and my success
can be of little importance to you. It would seem
as if I were guilty of neglect, but it is the tumult
of the day that bears me from you. But what
you so enthusiastically desired cannot be wholly
executed! The people's heart is like a woman's
—it must have and feel a master to be truly happy! Left to itself, its temporary boast is empti-
ness—its strength becomes weakness—its tenderness, coarseness.—But see! the sun is rising in
adorable splendor, and the stars that once shone
so bright to my outward view are now fading
away. Who art thou, whom I behold throned
as in light? Thine eyes are like the eyes of a
queen, and thine apparel as the glory of the
morning. I worship thee—the last ideal of my
life! The monarchy shall remain—the destructive hands of men shall no more reach it than
they can the firmament above them—it shall hal-
low all our dreams and realize our hopes of happiness. O Marie Antoinette, reach forth your
hand, and avert the tempest that threatens you
and those committed to your sovereignty."

————+————

CHAPTER XXXIX.

THE OCTOBER DAYS.

On the 5th of October, while the National Assembly held an early session, disquieting and
gloomy reports reached the benches of the deputies, and also the president Mounier, who for a
short time was at the head of the Convention.
The deliberations ceased. All arose to leave the
hall for the streets, where the angry populace
had already gathered. Mirabeau walked arm in
arm with La Marck toward the gate opening on
the high road leading to Paris.

"I think I see a cloud of dust yonder!" said
Mirabeau to his friend. "Do you really believe
that a revolutionary procession is coming to Versailles to offer violence to the king? My friends
in the capital have failed to apprise me of it."

"I can add some strange news to the rumors
already current," whispered La Marck. "About
ten o'clock this morning Vanvilliers, the president of the Paris city council, arrived at the palace, bringing information which has completely
frightened the ministers. At dawn about a thousand women assembled on the Place Grève, who,
making their starved condition a pretext, abused
the king and all in authority, and endeavored to
enter the Hôtel de Ville, amid furious cries for
bread, and threats of revenge. They rang the
alarm-bells and brought together a vast number
of people, who sympathized with them. The
French guards became their friends, demanding
vengeance on account of the late officers' banquet held at Versailles, where the royal bodyguard tore the three-colored cockades from their
hats and trod them under foot. Those women,
the outcasts of Paris, have formed themselves
into a procession, attended by multitudes of citizens, an artillery-train, as well as several thousand of the National Guards, and are on their
way hither. Vauvilliers has preceded them and
announced their demands. They will not only
ask for bread, and an apology for the insult to the
tricolor, but will force the king to go with them

to the capital, and take up his dwelling in the midst of the revolution." *

"The women did not act so of their own accord," said Mirabeau, thoughtfully. "The Orleanists may have originated this new farce; but, as far as I know, the duke would rather not have the king in Paris. He fears the attachment of the Parisians for their sovereign. It would suit him better if Louis XVI. left the kingdom or even the world. Can the commander of the National Guards, Marquis de Lafayette, be at the bottom of the affair? He fancies that he could influence the king better when in the capital, and is dreaming of a ministry of which he will be the head. He would at all events be better than Necker. And what did his majesty say to the news from Vauvilliers?"

"He had already left for the hunt near Meudon," replied La Marck. "Messengers have been sent after him in all directions. He is really a wonderful character; for in the midst of the most dangerous commotions, he is not disturbed in his habits—nothing interrupts the regular occupations and pleasures of the day. He himself maintains his calmness, almost the same as indifference, and is as unconscious and dignified as if the nation had nothing to complain of, and were perfectly happy."

"And did you think the answer read this morning in the assembly was dignified?" asked Mirabeau. "I am afraid it will increase the discontent at such a time as this. The king is too frank, and that is a great disadvantage. He openly declares his opinion of the first articles of the constitution and the rights of man. He does not say that he accepts, nor does he oppose them, adding that on one condition he will accede, but on no other consideration can he be induced to do so; that the deliberations of the Convention shall have no other object than to confirm the executive power in the hands of the sovereign! You know that I desire this earnestly, and am continually laboring for such a purpose. Messrs. Necker and St. Priest, if they

had any political tact, ought never to have let the king say any thing that puts him in an ambiguous position; for this declaration betrays half a boaster and half a coward, making the monarch dependent on the National Assembly."

"Only have patience, my friend, we shall soon have a better ministry," said La Marck, significantly. "When your name stands at the head of the cabinet, we shall have a steady light to guide the decisions of his majesty.—But, hear the noise! It is like the sound of a river rushing nearer and nearer!"

"I believe that was thunder," rejoined Mirabeau, scanning the horizon, which was darkly clouded, and looked like a vast range of dark mountains. "I scarcely remember such a hot October—it is a fit day, for the sky above us is looking very tempestuous." They went farther out upon the public road.

"The cause of this social storm will soon appear!" said La Marck. "The fish-women of Paris are infecting the atmosphere. You may scent them as they approach. The hesitation of the king is at the bottom of this new disturbance. Perhaps it may be considered a good sign that the people are so crazy about their rights. The philosophers of the Palais-Royal have made out a list of the men who voted against those rights in the National Assembly—a long proscriptive roll, count!"

"Our names cannot be there," said Mirabeau, "for we were not present when the votes were taken."

"That was good advice you gave me, and a proof of your political genius!" replied La Marck.

"I only wished to let the people see that I was willing to please them," said Mirabeau, smiling. "They almost knelt to me in the streets of the capital, conjuring me not to give my voice against the rights of man. I never was disobliging, and I thought they might perform some service for me at a future time."

The shouts of the procession were now plainly heard, and, as soon as the dust permitted, the first soiled and oddly-dressed figures made their

---

* Sybel, "History of the Revolution from 1789 to 1795," vol. i., p. 66.

appearance, all running and threatening to annihilate every thing that obstructed their way.

At the head were two gigantic men, the chosen leaders, bearing rods tipped with iron as the signal of their office. They were two of the *Forts de la Halle* (as the male members of the fish-market of Paris were called), followed by several drummers incessantly beating. Then came the women of the *Halle*, in their peculiar costume and masculine stride, with pale faces, expressive of hunger and boundless fury. There were more than a thousand of them, and from their vile lips foamed curses of every kind. In their midst and following them were several of those frightful-looking men who always appeared on such occasions, but vanished as soon as all was quiet again, as if, having accomplished their mission, they had returned to some infernal abode. They wore high, pointed caps, surmounting long hair; dirty and untrimmed beards added to their ferocious look; and, armed with pikes, iron-pointed sticks, and other weapons, they seemed to be the *élite* in a crowd preëminent for cruelty and vice of every kind. As they rushed by with heavy pieces of cannon, and displayed their vast strength by handling them as toys, one involuntarily shuddered, and asked, Whence came they?

"There you may see the *generatio æquivoca* of the revolution!" whispered Mirabeau. "It is difficult to know from what quarter these persons come; and how mysteriously they disappear!"

The procession was closed by some National Guards, who voluntarily joined the rioters. The noise of the women was fearful—one howling cry of complaint and vengeance began in front, and was reëchoed by those in the rear.

"These demands for bread are dreadful!" said Mirabeau, taking the arm of his friend to return to the city, where they wished to arrive as soon as possible.

"It is certain that great want reigns in Paris," said La Marck, in a pitying voice. "Yet I think it is not the natural result of affairs. France has had a good harvest, and bread has not risen higher than three cents a pound—the market-price for years in the capital. Now suddenly no food is to be had. The ministry ought to discover the originator of all this misery. Whispers are heard here and there of an enemy of the king, buying up all provisions by his agents. Oh, I could weep for our good Louis; for where such intriguers are at work, the noblest man that ever ascended a throne will perish!"

"Yes, you are right; he is an intriguer, this Duke d'Orleans, ambitious of usurping the throne!" exclaimed Mirabeau, with a violent gesture.

"For Heaven's sake, do not speak that name so loud!" said La Marck, looking carefully around. "It is time, however, for us to be at our post. The session was to reopen at three o'clock, and the president desires us to be punctual. Whatever may happen to-day, the National Assembly must be ready to promote law and order."

"Then let us be in time to announce the ladies and their train," said Mirabeau, laughing. "I have been informed that their first visit will be to the Convention; and there they are, following us. I am of opinion that the deputies receive them with all the politeness due the fair sex. Let us hasten!"

When Mirabeau and La Marck entered the hall, Mounier had just taken the chair. A desultory debate, having no connection with the exciting question of the times, was commenced; but the delegates were absent-minded, and occupied with the extraordinary intelligence they had just received. All were looking toward the doors, expecting to have notice given them of the arrival of their strange visitors.

An usher entered, with signs of perturbation on his countenance, and whispered something to the president, who arose, gravely informing the members of the National Assembly that the *Dames de la Halle* from Paris were about to pay them a visit. By a large majority it was decided to admit them. Immediately after, a number of women appeared, and with some confusion and noise seated themselves wherever they could on the benches of the deputies, and in close proximity to them. The same men who led them in the street were still at the head of the crowd. One of them boldly took his stand near the president's chair, and began to speak. He said they had come to Versailles to obtain bread and money, and to have the royal body-guards punished for insulting the patriotic cockade !

The women then began to scream that food must be given to the city of Paris.

The president tried to make them understand that the National Assembly had already done much in forwarding provisions to the capital, and that still other relief would be given ; but that it would be better for the "citizenesses," as he politely called them, to return peaceably to Paris.

"That does not satisfy us !" cried several apparently masculine voices, but they belonged to the fish-women.

"Why do you not speak, deputy !" said a tall and stout *poissarde* to her neighbor, addressing him in the familiar style to which she was accustomed.

"Hold your tongue, deputy !" said another, drawing down to his seat by the skirts of his coat an unpopular delegate, who was about to make an address. Just then loud reports were heard in rapid succession from the cannon brought by the multitude; for those of them who could find no room in the session-hall went to the avenues of the palace, and amused themselves in the practice of artillery.

The countenances of many of the members of the Convention turned pale, and indicated great fear. When Mirabeau rose, at the sound of his voice all was instantly hushed. He asked in a commanding manner, "by what right the lady citizens had come to prescribe laws to the National Assembly, and influence the deputies? The women of the fish-market, however well they may deserve of the fatherland, were bound to hold their peace in the Convention, and show respect to the legislators elected by the people !" The women burst into boisterous applause, and showed their appreciation of this energetic appeal. *

---

* "Mémoires de Rivarol," p. 273; Ferrières, vol. i., p. 323.

"What a splendid fellow is this Count Mirabeau !" cried several of the *poissardes*.

"Bravo, my son !" said another, making a courtesy, and smilingly shaking his hand.

Mirabeau turned to the president, asking him to nominate a deputation, at the head of which should be Mounier himself, in order to demand an immediate declaration from the king that he would accept those articles of the constitution already laid before him ; they were then to request assistance for Paris, so that food might be distributed and order restored.

The female part of the audience again testified their gratification at Mirabeau's words. The deputation was quickly named, and Mounier was about to depart with them, when the market-women rose tumultuously, expressing their intention of accompanying the members to the king. Nothing could induce them to desist from their undertaking, and finally an arrangement was made that no more than six of them should appear before his majesty ; but they all left the hall, some in anger, and others in merriment.

The rain fell in torrents. The deputation wished to lose no time in procuring carriages, and therefore went on foot to the palace, followed by a crowd of women. They found all the avenues to the castle surrounded by vast multitudes. The *poissardes* arranged themselves in a kind of battle array near the outer railing ; the body-guards, who were stationed there, not permitting any nearer approach, though they seemed to have been commanded to make no use of their arms, however insolent the conduct of those who attempted to pass.

As soon as the members of the National Assembly were recognized, a way was speedily opened, and an escort, consisting of ragged and repulsive-looking men, surrounded the deputation. Thus they arrived in the inner court-yard, and had themselves announced to the king. The female portion of the embassy, however, was more than doubled on the way, and by Parisiennes of such robust constitution and determined demeanor, that few men would have contended with them.

Louis XVI. quickly returned from the hunt,

after having been overtaken by his master of the horse, the Marquis de Cubières, whom the queen in anxiety sent after her husband. As he approached, several small-arms were fired, exchanged between the body-guards and the people; some of the balls rebounded against the hall where the Convention held its sessions. The king's first order was that the troops should return no fire. When the captain of the Gardes du Corps asked for further instructions, the king asked, smilingly: "What! instructions against fish-women? I think you must be jesting!"

The royal anterooms were in the mean time filled with many persons, among them Necker, and the minister of the interior, M. de St. Priest. Conversations were held in a low voice, and several began to dispute whether the king should leave or not, and whether it were not better for the safety of the throne if he withdrew for a while to some distant province.[*] Mounier and his companions stood some time in the midst of this company before they were admitted to his majesty.

Louis XVI. received the deputation with his usual simple and touching kindness, proceeding from the consciousness of his good intentions, and in this instance containing more of the strength than the weakness of his character. Mounier first made known the requests of the National Assembly, then diverging into an eloquent and impressive description of the misery existing among the population of the capital. The king replied that no means should be left unused to remedy the evil, and spoke in so sympathetic a voice that tears stood in the eyes of the women.[†] Mounier then demanded to know at what hour his majesty would give an answer concerning his acceptance of the articles of the constitution. Nine o'clock on the same evening was the time appointed. It was now about six. The king, after a very friendly farewell, retired to his cabinet, followed by his ministers.

While this was passing in the interior of the palace, the position of affairs was taking an un-

favorable turn in the court-yards, owing to the continued wordy collision between the masses and the body-guards. Some of the people tried to gain a forcible entrance, and one of the National Guards of Versailles, who had united with the Paris rioters, shot down a captain of one of the companies belonging to the guard around the palace. This was the signal for a terrible massacre, in which the Gardes du Corps, to whom the officer belonged, had the worst, as they endeavored as much as possible to obey the king's command, and not fire upon the multitude. The latter, however, opened a murderous discharge of small-arms upon the soldiers, who attempted to aim a cannon at the crowd, stationed before the barracks of the old French guards.

The monarch ordered the military to retreat to quarters, hoping thus to pacify the people. The cavalry formed themselves in line and left the Place d'Armes; but the mob, having reloaded their guns, followed up the departing regiments and sent a shower of balls after them. They were thus received along the streets and from the houses they had to pass, so that many fell dead from their horses; but the larger number retired in good order, and refrained from attack.

This outrage caused the greatest uneasiness to the inmates of the palace. In the council held, the ministers spoke openly of the prudence of the king's flight, but he gravely refused to entertain any such idea. Then a proposition was made to send the queen and the dauphin to some place of safety; but when the carriages came to the door, the mob cut the traces, broke the wheels, and ran through the thoroughfares of Versailles, crying that the king's departure for Metz must be prevented!

Marie Antoinette never intended to leave. She went to her husband's apartments, declaring in a courageous voice that she would stay, and, if necessary, die with him! The king regarded his consort in confidence and joy. Her countenance beamed with heroism, and her fear had vanished. Her eyes were no longer sad, but flashed with a fire that cheered and encouraged her husband.

---

[*] Madame de Staël, "Mémoires et Considérations sur la Révolution française," vol. i., ch. xi.
[†] Rivarol, p. 278.

It was about ten o'clock at night, when the queen noticed a paper in the king's hands, and asked the meaning of it. She was told it was the written declaration he was about to deliver to the National Assembly, assenting to their demands. Marie Antoinette trembled for a moment, but soon recovered herself. Louis XVI. then sent for Mounier, who had been waiting an hour for this reply in the antechamber. The king transmitted the paper to the president, with a smile, though it was said that the latter was seen among the soldiers of the Flanders regiment, endeavoring to induce them to desert the royal cause. Accordingly they refused to take up arms, or to be stationed in any of the palace court-yards, when the king sent for them an hour before, having become alarmed at the position of affairs. He also recalled his faithful body-guards. Many of them immediately obeyed, though on repassing the streets they were again fired upon, some of them being killed and others dangerously wounded.

An adjutant of the Marquis de Lafayette arrived after ten, announcing that the marquis was on his way to Versailles at the head of the National Guards. The confusion of the ministerial council was greatly heightened by this information; for it was accompanied by the further intelligence that Lafayette was authorized in this act by the committee of the Paris Commons, and it was certain that he brought new demands. The king said that the arrival of the general must be awaited quietly and without distrust, adding, as he turned to the queen, that there still remained something to oppose to the marquis—the sword of his ancestors!

As night advanced, the monarch felt himself more and more influenced by a desire to which he finally gave expression. He thought it advisable at this dangerous hour, to call to his safety the inviolability of the representatives of the nation, and sent word to Mounier that he would be glad to see at the palace the president and as many deputies of the assembly as he could collect. As the crowding of the people into the hall had long interrupted the session, Mounier dispatched a drummer through all the thoroughfares to bring together as many of the delegates as possible. At last the president appeared with the most prominent members of the Convention, among whom were Mirabeau, La Marck, Volney, Robespierre, Guillotin, and others. Several of them were armed, thus greatly increasing the disquietude. Mirabeau wore a sword in a shoulder-belt. It was the first time he added a weapon to the costume of the Third Estate.

About midnight, Lafayette reached Versailles at the head of twenty thousand of the Paris National Guards. His drums first aroused the fish-women, who formed themselves on the Place d'Armes, in quite a martial array, sending out patrols to investigate the cause of this new movement. The marquis halted his troops before the palace, disposing them at all the avenues to the castle, the square before it, and the adjoining streets. Dismounting and accompanied by the commissaries assigned him by the Paris Commons, he went into the king's presence. In a short address the general said that he had come to re-establish order, and make peace between his majesty and his subjects. The demands of the Paris Commons were, that the service of the palace should be performed by the National Guards only; the Commons must understand from the beginning all the acts passed in reference to Paris; the enumerated rights of man must be accepted, and the king make the capital his usual place of residence.*

Louis XVI. replied that he granted the first demand; that the second and third were already conceded; that the fourth was not contrary to his inclination, but he would come to a decision at some future time.

Lafayette hastened to execute the object of his embassy. He ordered divisions of the National Guards to occupy the palace; the rest were quartered in the churches and other buildings of the city, or encamped in the streets. Their bivouac-fires were centres of attraction to the masses, who seemed to have made up their minds to pass the night out of doors. Gradually all the women and

* Sybel, "History of the Revolution," vol. i., p. 69.

MIRABEAU DEFENDING THE QUEEN'S BED.

P. 253.

their attendants settled around them, adding to the excitement, and encouraging the tendency to daring deeds. It was soon determined to storm the barracks of the Gardes du Corps and exterminate that hated regiment.

These threatening symptoms of violence were announced to General Lafayette, but he left the palace, being exhausted by need of rest, taking up his abode in the Hôtel Noailles. The members of the assembly also departed for their temporary homes. Quiet seemed to have returned for the inhabitants of the royal abode, and the king and queen retired to their chambers to seek forgetfulness in sleep. For a few hours the clamor of the day contrasted with the silence of the night.

In the streets, however, there was a new and terrible tumult, beginning at the barracks of the Gardes du Corps. The edifice could not resist the furious attacks of the populace, who destroyed all that came in their way. But few of the soldiers were there, and they sought safety by fleeing toward the palace, but most of them were killed or wounded on the way.

As the morning dawned, the people, by a silent agreement, turned toward the castle. One entrance was found deserted by the sentinel, and through this the raging crowd penetrated, filling all the court-yards and corridors, and approaching the royal apartments. Suddenly a voice was heard: "The head of the queen!" and the fearful words resounded through the palace. The invaders passed farther into the interior, killed some of the guards who resisted them, and fought their way with the soldiers posted at the very threshold of Marie Antoinette's chamber. Defending it to the last, the faithful guards fell beneath the blows of pikes and clubs.

The uproar awakened the queen, while at the same moment her lady-in-waiting rushed in, informing her of the dangers threatening her life, and from which it would be difficult to escape. The queen sprang up, and, without giving herself time to dress, ran as she was to a side-door, leading to a corridor, and by a long and narrow passage thence to the rotunda, connecting with the king's apartments. To her terror she found the door at the end of the corridor locked; but her husband coming to meet her, she cast herself into his arms.[*]

The assassins broke open the door of the queen's chamber, entering with shouts, declaring their murderous intentions, and demanding their prey. They rushed to her couch, and a notorious criminal drew aside with a laugh the curtaining silk. When it was discovered that the queen was absent, the fiends expended their fury on the pillows and bolsters, tearing them to atoms, and piercing the bed with daggers and pikes.

Mirabeau appeared during this scene. He was overwhelmed with horror when he thought of what might have taken place. During the night he was aroused by the rumor of what was passing at the palace, and, with other members of the National Assembly, forced his way through the crowded corridors. Hearing that the life of the queen was threatened, he entered her room, animated by an ardent desire to save her. With burning eyes he drew his sword, and, placing himself before the bed where so lately Marie Antoinette had slumbered, drove the ruffians away. He forgot his own danger in his noble impulses to save a defenceless woman. Being recognized, it was not believed that he was in earnest in preventing them from sacrificing the queen wherever they could find her, and they hurried away to discover her hiding-place.

When Mirabeau awoke from his thoughts, as from a hideous dream, he was almost alone in the chamber of Marie Antoinette. Near the door, however, some persons still lingered, walking up and down, but keeping away from him. Suddenly he felt a strong hand rest upon his shoulder, and turning, he saw the grinning and merciless face of the deputy Pétion.

"A captivating scene for the men of the left," said the delegate, with a savage laugh. "Our colleague Mirabeau appears to be enchanted by the perfumes of the royal cabinet. Have we again caught you betraying the cause of the people?"

---

[*] Weber, vol. i., p. 446.

Mirabeau replied in a few sharp words, when he noticed that quite a number of deputies surrounded him, among whom were Robespierre, Barnave, and Dr. Guillotin. The former looked at the count distrustfully; but the doctor, with his invariably gentle and attractive smile, offered his hand to Mirabeau, remarking in a bantering manner that he must excuse them, if they recalled him from his pleasant visions to the dreary realities of the day.

The count silently crossed his arms, and contemplated these gentlemen, whose revolutionary zeal he had lately been forced to combat in the public debates, and whose hatred he believed he had incurred.

"It was really affecting to see how Count Mirabeau protected the queen's bed against the brave men of the people!" exclaimed Robespierre, contemptuously. "He stands there like the high-priest of the reaction? But why are you a belated royalist?"

"It would be desirable even to die here!" said the gentle Barnave.

"Our Dr. Guillotin will furnish you with an agreeable mode of dying!" said Robespierre. "He has invented a wonderful beheading-machine, of which I saw the plan at his house. It cuts off heads in so swift and merciful a manner that it ought to be considered a blessing to humanity. I hope it will soon be practically adopted."

"Is the instrument really completed, doctor?" asked Barnave, inquisitively.

"I cannot positively say that," replied Guillotin. "Our friend Robespierre seems to be in haste. I will not be able to hand in my report on capital punishment until the end of the year, and I will propose the employment of my machine at the same time. If I succeed, it will really be a triumph over other methods in the infliction of capital punishment."

"Well, then, in the mean time we must find other things to dispose of the enemies of the people!" exclaimed Robespierre, spitefully. His eyes met the questioning glance of Mirabeau, who felt strange apprehensions.

Robespierre turned quickly and left, followed by Pétion, Barnave, and Guillotin, so that the count was again alone. The lamp had burned low, and was flickering in the gloomy apartment, when Mirabeau hastened with a shudder into the lighted corridor, where numerous persons were still passing from one end to the other, uttering dreadful curses. Some of them wore masks, or had chosen whimsical costumes to disguise themselves. Through one of the passages the Duke d'Orleans glided, and his pale face was presently again seen in a corner, where he was whispering with his confidant, the Duke d'Aiguillon and his secretary, La Clos, the author of the *Liaisons Dangereuses.* The duke was apparently giving instructions as to the progress of the sedition. Marat and the colossal Danton, in all his deformity, were also present.

The report that Lafayette had arrived spread rapidly through all the halls of the palace. He had quietly slept, but, when aroused to be informed of the proceedings of the night, he at once mounted his horse and hastened to the royal residence, followed by strong detachments of the National Guards, whom he ordered to be stationed at all the passages. The mob were speedily ejected into the court-yards, where they continued their riotous conduct, filling the air with howlings for the royal blood.

As the autumn day was dawning, Lafayette stood before the king, and endeavored to give him confidence in his subjects, but intimating that for the future his majesty would have to dwell in Paris. Louis was listless and careworn. While every consideration was urged to induce him to transfer his residence to the capital, the queen moved aside, and avoided the glances of her husband. Finally, he consented to start for Paris about noon—news which soon passed to the ears of the multitude outside, who signified their pleasure in deafening shouts.

The troubled king stepped out upon the balcony at the side of the general, to confirm his promise. They were received with enthusiasm, but, when the cheers and firing of musketry ceased for a moment, execrations were heard against the queen.

Lafayette then led forth Marie Antoinette into the full presence of her enemies. She went unhesitatingly, with the dauphin on one side, and the little princess on the other. A loud voice came from below: "No children!" The queen quietly sent them back into the drawing-room, and remained alone with the marquis. In dignified silence she seemed to await death, but when Lafayette took her hand and kissed it, cries of "Long live the queen!" resounded from all sides. A few hours later the royal carriage drove with their majesties toward Paris.

The National Assembly followed a fortnight after, to hold their sessions in the capital; and Mirabeau, accompanying them, reasserted that the Convention was inseparably allied with the sovereign!

CHAPTER XL.

MIRABEAU'S JOURNEY TO THE QUEEN.

On the 3d of July, 1790, the count and La Marck entered a carriage to drive to Saint-Cloud, where the court was sojourning since the commencement of the summer, watching in retirement the course of events, which were neither better nor worse for the well-being of the king and his consort. Each morning brought a fresh feeling of insecurity, which the evening relieved, because what was favorably doubtful was accepted as true, and became a source of consolation.

Mirabeau believed and urged that the king ought to take decisive measures one way or the other. For days he prayed Count de la Marck to obtain for him an interview with Marie Antoinette, expecting from it the most happy results. He fancied that by a few words he could change her convictions, and direct her in what was necessary to be done. La Marck had hitherto resisted such requests, knowing the dislike with which the queen continued to regard his friend, whom he never dared to mention in her presence. The Austrian ambassador, Count de Mercy, who had a

high place in her confidence and esteem, undertook, however, to conquer her aversion, after he himself had several conversations with Mirabeau as to some scheme for the salvation of the monarchy.

When informed that Marie Antoinette would grant an audience at Saint-Cloud, Mirabeau was so interested in the prospect of a reality of which he had so long hopelessly dreamed, that he sat silent by the side of La Marck. His talkative companion, however, could not endure this a long time, and thought it necessary to give a few well-meaning hints and some plain advice, in order to warn his friend against any error into which he might fall from imprudence; adding, with characteristic politeness, that Count Mirabeau was a true aristocrat, maintaining his self-possession in the most difficult circumstances, and well taught as to what he should do, where to begin, and where to end.

"You are very generous, my dear friend," replied Mirabeau, "because you still consider my birth, when our National Assembly abolished the whole aristocracy a few weeks ago, and I am nothing but plain M. Riquetti, while you are good M. Marck!" The latter laughed, but seemed to have something on his mind.

"I know you entertain great and beneficent projects for France," said La Marck, after a pause. "But you must be careful about making any proposition to her majesty that bears too hard on the finances; there are no funds to undertake any thing extensive. It was impossible to procure money on Necker's last loan, in spite of the consent of the representatives of the nation, and no banker would advance one sou on it, so that the royal family find themselves greatly straitened at present."

"What I intend to propose will cost little, and bring in much," said Mirabeau, smiling. "I will save the king at any expense, if he will promise to divide with me the great income that must necessarily accrue to him in future, or at least pay my debts."

"He will do more than that," replied La Marck. "You know, I have undertaken to be your busi

ness man, and I will not rest until I have settled your affairs in the most advantageous manner."   •

"You are right," said Mirabeau, carelessly;
"a man must have money. If the monarchy is
out of pocket, that is no reason its savior should
be in the same condition. But do not trouble
yourself so much about it, my dear count! Your
truly kind care concerning my finances I appreciate highly, but you know me well enough to be
aware that I care very little about money in itself. So much of it has slipped through my fingers that it is indifferent to me whence it comes,
or whither it goes; and I have found that somehow I have generally had it in my pocket when
I least expected it. Did I ever tell you that Lafayette, about the close of last year, offered me
fifty thousand francs? My embarrassment was
so great at the time, that probably something of
it became publicly known; but this money was to
be charged to the civil list of the king, of which
the marquis had the control as commander of the
National Guards. I did not like the arrangement,
and spoke of it in such a way that the subject
was dropped." *

"It is however important, count, that your pecuniary affairs should be well managed," said La
Marck, gravely. "I think and act about them
every day. You promised to give me a complete
list of your debts, and I now repeat my request."

"I did undertake that miserable business," replied Mirabeau. "But I am not very clear in
such reminiscences. I have calculated that the
total must be about two hundred and eight thousand francs, but the details have been very trou-
blesome. Just imagine that among my unpaid
bills I found that for the wedding-dress of my
former wife.† I am certain if Emilie de Marignane knew it, she would give up all thoughts of a
reunion with me. I feel very much inclined to
inform her of it in an anonymous letter. Now I
think of it, I have not lately observed her in the
National Assembly."

---

* La Marck, vol. i., p. 180.
† Ibid., vol. i., p. 159.

"Because you attend so rarely yourself," said
La Marck.

"I speak on special occasions only, and that is
quite sufficient for my audience, becoming daily
more stupid, and unworthy of any thing like oratory," replied Mirabeau, with a haughty gesture.

"Do not let us wander from the point of our
conversation," resumed La Marck. "Not long
since I had an opportunity to speak confidentially
to the king. He acknowledged that you were
the man to reconstruct the monarchy, shattered
as it is to its foundation, and he would be willing to make any sacrifice to secure your services."

"Do with me as you will, my dear friend," replied Mirabeau. "If you really desire it, I will
even condescend to be bribed; but on one condition—that I defend royalty as I have hitherto defended it; it is the only way to save it! But do
not let me consider the favors bestowed in a
very serious light; let them fall into my pocket
without my exactly knowing how, and without
saying much about them."

"So it shall be," said La Marck.

The travellers reached Auteuil, where they were
to separate. According to previous agreement,
La Marck was to proceed to Saint-Cloud to announce his friend's arrival, as the latter was to be
introduced to the queen in a sort of private manner, so that even those most intimate with her
should not be aware of it. The count was to
come quietly, without any attendant, to a certain
designated gate of the park.

The niece of Mirabeau, the Marchioness d'Arragon, resided in Auteuil since the death of her
grandfather, and had lately seen very little of her
Uncle Gabriel, but it was at her house that the
count intended to stay until the proper hour to
visit Saint-Cloud. In a short time he was ready
to finish his journey on horseback. His toilet
was the costume of the Third Estate, which he
now always wore; he had, however, made a few
alterations, such as a lace cravat and colored vest.
On his way he was careful to keep as free from
dust as a ride on the high-road permitted.

It was a clear summer-day. Mirabeau's complexion, which lately had changed into a pale-yellow color, in consequence of some strange action that seemed to disturb his health, glowed in an apparently healthful hue. His figure resumed its youthful elasticity, and in a sort of rapture he fancied the queen beckoning to him, away in the bright distance; spurring his horse to its utmost speed, he was obeying the summons.

CHAPTER XLI.

THE SAVIOR OF THE MONARCHY.

WHEN Mirabeau approached the appointed gate of the park of Saint-Cloud, he was received by a confidential valet de chambre of her majesty, who took the horse and led it to a stable. Returning, he pointed, with a gesture recommending silence and prudence, to one of the darkest alleys of the garden, where the trees above intertwined their foliage. They went, so quietly that the crumpling of a leaf could not be heard, through this path toward the private gardens of the queen. Upon a hill stood a pavilion, shaded by acacias and plantains, which the guide indicated as the place where Marie Antoinette was awaiting her visitor, who passed on with quick and confident steps.*

The queen met Mirabeau as he advanced, though she was hesitating and uncertain, being alone. All was silent, and the evening shades were fast gathering around them. She replied to the respectful greeting of the count with all the grace and dignity natural to her, and which she never lost even when her heart was agitated by unseen conflict. Her visitor was too acute not to discern the struggle of her feelings on beholding him, and he himself was pained in the realization of this long-desired meeting. He saw what was taking place in her mind by the momentary pallor on her countenance, and her anxious and wandering eyes.

Mirabeau remembered that Marie Antoinette associated him with the events of the night of the 5th of October at Versailles. Nine months had scarcely elapsed when the terrible deputy of the National Assembly was depicted to her as a monster, who had penetrated her chamber, the chief of robbers and assassins! The Convention had indeed absolved him from all suspicion of having participated in that outrage, but he believed that the queen had not altogether changed her opinions, notwithstanding the representations of his friends.* A smile of innocence, and devotion to his sovereign, beautified his features, and the queen was embarrassed. She, however, approached him, and felt it no difficult task to utter words of kindness. Again lifting her eyes to the count, she said, in a voice at first constrained, but soon regaining its natural tone: "The measure I am now taking would be interpreted in an evil sense by an enemy—some man who had sworn the destruction of the monarchy, and who could not appreciate its worth for the well-being of a great nation; but, while speaking to a Mirabeau, all cowardly scruples vanish, and I may hope to come to an understanding with you about the little of good that yet remains!"† The queen paused and smiled, appearing pleased with her own introductory speech. She had uttered the words "a Mirabeau" with peculiar stress, so that he seemed ready to kneel before her.

"Madame, I must accuse myself as being one of the principal causes of your sufferings!" he began, expressing his emotion in a gentle voice.

"Indeed, count, you were not always friendly toward us!" said Marie Antoinette, gravely. "And may we now call you one of the few faithful to the throne of France? Then, we heartily welcome you. But is it not too late to save the crown?"

"No, madame," exclaimed Mirabeau, enthusiastically. "The fountain of the life of a monarchy is liberty!"

"Liberty?" repeated her majesty, startled; but she endeavored to recover her composure, and

---

* La Marck says (vol. i., p. 189), that the queen received Mirabeau in her apartments at the palace; this must be a mistake of memory. All other authorities mention the pavilion as the place of the interview.—Vide Madame Campan, vol. ii., p. 125.

* La Marck, vol. i., p. 190.
† The queen's words.—Campan, vol. ii., p. 125.

looked at the count, expecting further explanations.

"The monarchy can only be so maintained, and national liberty can live but through the monarchy!" continued Mirabeau. "Formerly I wished the nation to be independent, and I forgot the throne; in that I was guilty of crime! I have been the originator of misery, and have forced eyes to weep that should never be dimmed by tears! But my knowledge has increased in the presence of this suffering, and I feel the strength of an Atlas to carry the monarchy on my shoulders, but only at the bidding of national liberty."

"You speak of our distress," said the queen; "have you not also suffered in our cause? The king and myself have noticed with great pleasure your exertions in the National Assembly for the right of the crown to make peace or war. Your words were resistless. Yes, Count Mirabeau, our foes have become yours, and that fact should inspire us with confidence. But the Jacobins are wicked. They made the people of the streets attack you, and, I hear, they even attempted your life—and you are a member of their society, meeting in the old church of the Jacobin monks, in the Rue St. Honoré! Will you be kind enough to explain this contradiction to me?"

"I think the Jacobins will soon desire my connection with them to cease, madame," replied Mirabeau, quietly. "However, so long as they do not forcibly dismiss me, I shall remain among them. I attend their meetings seldom, but if we wish successful navigation and a prosperous voyage, we must study the winds and tides, and have some experience of the ocean-storms. To elevate the monarchy from the depth into which it has fallen, we must endeavor to gain an insight into the purposes of those Jacobin gentlemen, for they seem to be trifling with the throne. If we undertake to oppose the popular movement, and without any concession, we are lost; we must learn in which direction that movement tends, and then act accordingly. We shall afterward find that it is the best we could do, whatever may be our opinions now. Tempests purify the atmosphere; and my relation with that club, madame, is simply

to know how and why they originate, and what may allay them when they become too destructive."

The queen could not refrain from shuddering at this explanation, but silently awaited further disclosures.

"It is said that the Jacobins are endeavoring to take my life," Mirabeau resumed, after a rather painful pause. "Papers written against me are hawked about the streets, in which I am represented as a traitor to the people's cause. While I was publicly speaking for the veto, or the right of the king to decide on peace or war with foreign nations, the populace were led to the Champs Elysées to select a tree on which to hang me. However, I allowed nothing to divert me from my purpose, and gained the victory. I have conquered a right without which every constitution is but a shadow—a body without life; for, at the head of a free monarchy, a free sovereign must exist—a living person, not a dead formula. The king loses his individuality if he has not this privilege of the veto, and the whole state loses it with him. That is my idea of constitutional royalty. Let us do justice to all, and the throne is secure!"

The count cast a searching glance upon the queen, endeavoring to read her inmost thoughts. He noticed that she was greatly excited, and in danger of losing her presence of mind. She drooped her head, musingly, then suddenly rising she said: "You are right, count, we can only be saved by a constitution. And you may rest assured that as soon as the king and myself see that our dignity is not threatened, we shall adopt it with sincerity, never thinking of undoing any thing intended for the good of the nation. But how can we gain our object? Will not many dangers threaten the best of kings?"

Mirabeau fancied he saw tears in Marie Antoinette's eyes; his love for her almost gained the upper hand, and came near betraying him, but, laying his hand on his burning brow, he soon regained his composure, and said, gravely and urgently: "I think his majesty should withdraw from the perils that menace him in Paris. I do not mean that he should leave France, or separate himself from the revolution and the people or use foreign arms against his country. That would be imprudent, and destroy the belief entertained of the paternal and magnanimous views of the sovereign. I think he ought to retire temporarily to Normandy—a province devoted to him, and adjoining Brittany and Anjou, in both which districts many hearts yet beat for his welfare. Let his majesty there recall the people to obedience by pacifying proclamations, reminding them that, from the first days of his reign, he has proved himself an enemy to despotism, and all abuses and dissipation; that he will never cease to use every means for the amelioration of the condition of his subjects, and that he will give an example of yielding to their political rights, as no king of his dynasty ever did before. Then we shall have a new order of things, instead of that which can no longer be defended, not even by myself!"

Marie Antoinette listened calmly, and with an affecting assent; but soon all her firmness returned, and she said, with a proud smile: "I thank you, count! I feel that some confidence still dwells in my heart. I think all will yet be well, and the future compensate for the present. I never could believe that the purposes of my enemies were wholly bad. I beg you, let this not be the last time, as it is the first, that you communicate your ideas to us. Write down every thing you may think useful, giving your advice, which will be received with gratitude, and send your remarks to the king; thus you will greatly oblige him."

Mirabeau felt himself dismissed. He looked at the queen with a glowing eye, and, approaching her, said, in a voice trembling with emotion and audacity: "Madame, when the Empress Maria Theresa, your august mother, granted the honor of an audience to one of her subjects, she never permitted him to depart without allowing him to kiss her hand." *

Marie Antoinette offered him her hand gracefully and cheerfully. "This kiss saves the monarchy!" exclaimed the count, overwhelmed in his enthusiasm, while he pressed his lips upon the white hand of the queen, and then hastened into the garden, where the birds were at rest, and the flowers scattering the perfume that he so much loved. As he was walking down from the height on which the pavilion was built, he thought he saw some one hastily hiding in the bushes, wearing the uniform of a national guardsman. Mirabeau pursued him to assure himself that his conversation with her majesty had not been overheard by a traitor, but his efforts were vain. He approached the gate with sad foreboding, where he found the attendant with his horse, and rode slowly away. Suddenly he heard his name called, and, turning, saw the carriage of La Marck, who had overtaken his friend, to ask for information as to what had occurred.

"The queen has been taken ill," said La Marck. "It seems the interview excited and fatigued her greatly. Madame Campan has just told me that her majesty was obliged to retire immediately after your departure.* About what very stirring topics did you converse?"

"I think Marie Antoinette was disquieted by the mere appearance of my person," replied Mirabeau, riding at the side of the coach, and telling all that passed between him and his sovereign.

<hr>

CHAPTER XLII.

MIRABEAU AND THE JACOBINS.

It was about six o'clock in the evening when an unusually large assembly met at the church of the Jacobin monks in the Rue St. Honoré—so great was the concourse that they scarcely found room to stand. The old edifice had been turned into a regular session-hall. It was of oblong figure, where seats for the members of the club rose as in an amphitheatre. At each end were two platforms, with benches ascending in the same way, and intended for the public, who

* Weber, vol. ii., p. 33.

* Madame Campan.

could only gain entrance by means of tickets of admission. In the most conspicuous places was painted in large red letters: "*Vivre libre ou mourir !*"

The old church, with its dark corners and arches, had a singularly odd and confused appearance, now that it had become a modern parliamentary house, showing so little taste and art in its arrangement. Yet something picturesque could be discovered. Behind the chair of the president was an altar, around which gathered the gray memories of a far-distant worship—the same altar at which the monks of former generations bowed in their religious adoration. In the centre was a tablet, on which was engraved a list of the rights of man, surrounded with decorations, arabesques, and symbols of various kinds. In the once sacred places themselves stood the busts of Jean Jacques Rousseau and Helvetius. Above these philosophers drooped the standards of liberty, and in their midst a bundle of pikes, surmounted with a civic crown. One of the pikes, more prominent than the rest, was tipped with the red cap. Pictures hung upon the walls, telling the story of the Bastile and the procession of the fish-mongers to Versailles, with other illustrations of the events of the times.

The object of the meeting was to elect a new president, and to pass judgment upon Mirabeau. He had determined unreservedly to oppose the secret machinations of his enemies; and had offered to be present at a session when all accusations against him would be openly published, that he might have an opportunity to refute them, designating the proceedings against him in his absence as cowardice. He demanded a bold judiciary action, such as became the men of the people and the advocates of truth and liberty.

Mirabeau insisted the more urgently for a public and manly decision, because the republicans were beginning to associate the name of the queen with his own, intimating that his visit to Saint-Cloud had a dishonorable purpose. On the day following that interview, an account of it was published in the *Orateur du Peuple*, edited by the remorseless Fréron, giving particulars, which, although purposely distorted, had some probability. The count could only come to the conclusion that the conversation had been overheard, as he had from the first feared, and this was another inducement to force his adversaries to an undisguised battle, where he had no fear of his successful defence.

The count generally came late, and this evening he did not make his appearance until some time after the president had opened the meeting. Dupont, one of the most violent members, occupied the speakers' stand, giving a picture of the situation of France since the decision of the National Assembly concerning the veto. The transition to Mirabeau was easy, for it was imputed to his parliamentary eloquence and perseverance that this measure (supposed to be inimical to the people) passed, in spite of the exertions of Barnave, Robespierre, and Pétion. At the moment when the obnoxious member's name was about to be pronounced, and all present were waiting for it, Mirabeau entered. He made a great sensation, for his presence was not anticipated. He was received with frowns, exclamations of rebuke, and anger, and even threats; but he was not moved to change his calm demeanor. Proudly, but with a good-natured smile, he walked to a vacant seat, turning attentively toward the orator. All were silent, and Dupont, who almost lost his self-control at the entrance of the count, resumed the thread of his discourse with greater impetuosity.

The name of Mirabeau fell from the speaker's lips, characterizing him as a man who had usurped a parliamentary dictatorship in the National Assembly, and whose despotism was highly detrimental to liberty; "and it is with a melancholy feeling of duty," he said, "that I fulfil the oath every Jacobin has taken, to designate those who are dangerous. If, however, Mirabeau can honorably justify himself, I will be the first to offer him the hand of friendship."

When Dupont had concluded, the accused walked calmly toward the speakers' stand, asking permission to say a few words. His remarks expressed sorrow that he was persecuted so relentlessly here and elsewhere, while in the National

Assembly (the rightful place for such conflicts), no one dared to attack him, and that general charges as well as secret whisperings proved nothing against any man's conduct or character. He demanded specific accusations, being certain that he could disprove them to the satisfaction of all unbiassed minds.

This simple management of his position, plainly bearing evidences of contempt, made an impression—but such as deepened the hatred of Mirabeau's adversaries, who on this day meant to annihilate him at a single blow. Alexander de Lameth hurried to the tribune, stumbling against the count, who was descending the steps. Lameth's eyes flashed an intense hate, and vengeance played in all his distorted features. He was a man of low and slight stature, of a serpent-like motion; one who was now so much under the dominion of passion, that his manner conveyed even a more decided challenge than his words.

He began by lauding the Jacobin Club, regretting that they should have provided a refuge for those who, to act against the cause of the people, had put on a mask of patriotism to conceal a despotic face; for only as a member of that society could Mirabeau, assuming a false friendship for the nation, move the lever of public opinion. "That man found it to his advantage," he said, "to remain a member of the club, because as such only could he maintain his position, and serve his secret masters. If he would leave us, much would be better understood in the situation of France. But," the orator concluded, "the man will presently address you again, and tell you that he is the best friend the people have; that he never voted against their interests; never spoke in favor of the absolute veto and the assumed rights of the king. He will again tell you that he is enthusiastic only for your good, and cares nothing for the caresses of those who are enthroned above the people!"

This speech had various effects. Applause followed in some parts of the hall, and in others were heard words any thing but inimical to Mirabeau. He turned his head in all directions, as if to read the countenances of the members, and

discover his friends. Several men in blouses sat near, whose demonstrations were satisfactory to him; for the charm of his personal influence on people of their class did not now belie itself. While his enemies fancied that sentence would be passed on him, these men respectfully took their short pipes from their mouths, and bending toward him shook his hand as a sign and seal of their confidence and friendship. One of them, with his head bound up in a blood-stained rag, patted the count familiarly on the shoulder, and, in a stuttering voice, said: "Speak, Mirabeau; speak, and all is well again."

"Speak, Mirabeau!" was soon repeated by many others.

The count, standing in his place, said: "Citizens, I may not yet speak, for the triumvirate have not fully declared themselves. They consist, as you know, of those great friends of the people, Messrs. Dupont, Alexandre Lameth, and Barnave. We have heard the first and the second, and are waiting now to hear what the generous Barnave has to say. He knows, no doubt, much that is evil of me. And then I will tell you at once what my opinion of them is—whether or not they are just and magnanimous!"

"Bravo, Mirabeau! Let Barnave speak, and then we must have no more accusations!" said many voices in no gentle tones.

Barnave rose to say, in his usual solemn and half-sentimental style: "I decline to speak; but I unite in all the charges brought by my friends Dupont and Lameth!"

"And I accuse Mirabeau of a bungling national constitution—actual high-treason against the people," cried the piercing voice of Robespierre. "He has united himself with the opponents of liberty by his continual demand for a constitution, involving in it, in order to destroy them, as in a trap, all the rights of a nation!"

Mirabeau now ascended the tribune, and began to address the club, in the midst of a profound silence. "Citizens!" he said, shaking his locks, as if he felt at home. "Excuse me from disproving what my colleague Robespierre (who is certainly a friend of the nation) has just asserted.

It is not a pleasant business to dispute with men who are useful to France. If the National Assembly has become a mere constitution-making machine, it is not my fault, for I have but one vote there. I would rather that our great people had framed in a primary assembly a form of government worthy of themselves: they are competent—they have their prophet and lawgiver among themselves. As the affair, however, has been placed in our hands, we must work at it, just as our honorable friends, the bricklayers and joiners, in building a house. Now, as you permit me not to refute a man of honor like Robespierre, I ask you, do you seriously wish me to say anything about the charges of Messrs. Dupont and Lameth? Before you answer, allow me to read a few words to you from a paper I have here."

Mirabeau drew forth his pocket-book, and taking from it a paper, read in a low and almost timid voice as follows: "'Action before the Criminal Court concerning the accusation made by Citizen Riquetti against a pamphlet entitled "Great and fully-discovered Treason of Count Mirabeau." The Criminal Court, Commissioner Defresne presiding, declare: first, that the author of this pamphlet has been discovered to be a certain Lacroix, the son of a royal procurator, at Châlons-sur-Marne, who admits the fact. Second, that this youth, as yet a minor, and exceedingly fanatical, was incited to write the work by Alexandre Lameth, Dupont, and Barnave, who promised him protection against any suit. Third, that six thousand copies of the libel were printed, and gratuitously distributed in the streets. Fourth, that Citizen Riquetti may institute a suit against said Lameth, Dupont, and Barnave.'" *

Mirabeau gave the paper officially sealed to the person nearest him, to have it passed around to the members of the club, who were all in the wildest excitement.

"I have desisted from making any charge!" added Mirabeau, quickly, in his tremendous voice. "I am united with these gentlemen by a sacred bond. I will never rend it. We are here as one

man, in the name of the people, and I offend them if I accuse my brethren. I forgive Messrs. Lameth, Dupont, and Barnave; and I beg you, my friends, to follow my example."

Boisterous applause followed these words. All pressed around Mirabeau, but he motioned them to return to their seats. Lameth and Dupont sat silently with pale and angry faces, while Barnave's expressed pity. Lameth wished to speak, but he was roughly ordered to keep his place until Count Mirabeau had ceased. Notwithstanding the abolition of titles, the people would call him "their count."

"I have many faults," resumed Mirabeau, "but not that of treason to my friends, for such I consider this truly patriotic society. I love the Jacobins, and I wish them to enter the ministry of the king. I have drawn up a paper on this subject, after consultation with the Count de Provence. I am sure you take no offence at my having spoken to him? Even friends may sometimes differ, though in important matters they are likely to agree. The Count de Provence is an enlightened man, and the king listens to his advice. We must have a new ministry, for the present one is faithless and corrupt! I have made propositions to have you share in the public service, for thus alone can France enjoy a guaranty for the future. Long live the Jacobin ministry!" All responded in a shout, which shook the old church of the Jacobin monks.

"Is not that selling us to the court?" exclaimed Robespierre. "Rather let us begin a universal conflagration and massacre to-day, than have this hollow reconciliation with our enemies!"

Many members of the club were again of Robespierre's opinion, and manifested their approbation, but the majority were in favor of Mirabeau, who stood calmly waiting the moment to continue his address.

"Even liberty must have organization, government, and order," resumed the count. "There is no pleasure in assuming the duties of a royal minister, and I am glad of that decision of the National Assembly which excludes any one of its members from an office of that kind. The thirty votes on the left, which carried this question, thought they were embarrassing me. No, gentlemen, you are deceived! I shall continue to work; my energy is not derived from nor dependent on a portfolio, but rather on the applause and happiness of the people, which I am endeavoring to secure! I wish no deputy to become a minister; but there are honest laborers and tradesmen here whom I would be glad to see as chiefs of the national bureaus. But every thing should be done according to the understanding and will of the people, in order to be useful to them. The people above all!"

Mirabeau descended amid loud applause. He was congratulated on every side; many seized his hands and clothes, showing him how he was beloved. In fact, it was with difficulty that he could escape from the crowd of admirers, as he passed from the heated hall to breathe the fresh air. Excusing himself on account of indisposition, he left the meeting while the chairman was calling to order for the transaction of other business—the election of a new president.

The count walked up and down an adjoining corridor, as if waiting for some one, and with a smile listened to the shuffling made by the members in depositing their votes. The dark passage-way led to a small enclosure outside, and thence to a side-street, near which Mirabeau long waited in impatience. As he lingered in the twilight leaning against an old stone cross that had long stood there, he heard footsteps, and soon a figure approached whom he recognized as La Marck.

"I bring you good tidings," whispered the new-comer. "The king consents to every thing. He will find it to his interest in accepting your services. You are to write notes, memorials, and reports of all kinds about what is important or remarkable, and your advice and judgment will have great weight in the decisions of his majesty. He also expects you to maintain your influence in the National Assembly, where you have already done such good service to the monarchy. The king begs you to accept a monthly allowance of six thousand francs. Your debts, according to our recent calculation, amounting to two hundred and

eight thousand francs, will be paid from his majesty's purse. The Archbishop of Toulouse, M. de Fontanges, whose devotion to the royal cause you are aware of, has received orders to attend to these affairs. You must send your reports to him. The archbishop will also pay three hundred francs monthly to your copyist, M. de Comps; and as he will have to be in the secret, we must secure his silence. Besides, the king intrusted to me four checks, signed by his own hand, each for two hundred and fifty thousand francs, saying: 'If Count Mirabeau serves me well and faithfully, as he has promised, you will deliver these to him at the end of the session, which together make a million!'* Here are the bills!" added La Marck, in a lower voice, opening his pocket-book.

"Well, let it go!" said Mirabeau, looking at the signature of Louis XVI. with a smile. "The court have always had money enough for traitors; it is right that they should expend some on a true friend!" Suddenly becoming excited in his happiness, he struck his hand by way of emphasis on the weather-beaten cross, and added: "Let life begin again! Let us build up the new monarchy, and enjoy its auspices! Let the golden goblet again foam with pleasure! We can best fulfil our ideas when free from pecuniary pressure. The king has shown himself appreciative, wise, and prudent: but I do not think I can serve him better than by writing just as I feel. I cannot lie—no, not for millions; and, besides, falsehoods would ruin him. I hope, however, to keep him alive, as every honest man in France does. The times are indeed evil; and, if we do not act right, the dead bodies of their majesties will yet be dragged over the flag-stones.† But let us have confidence. Let us often celebrate in a sparkling cup the union of the monarchy and liberty!"

"Farewell, my friend!" said La Marck, pressing the hand of Mirabeau. "I do not think it advisable to stay longer so near the Jacobins. You are to dine with me to-morrow, you know." He hastened away, while Mirabeau looked dream-

---

* La Marck, vol. i., p. 163.
† An exclamation of Mirabeau, often repeated during the latter part of his life.—La Marck, vol. i.

ily after him. Then, returning to the hall, and finding that the tedious election was not yet over, he remained in the anteroom. In an adjoining apartment was a sideboard, where the count noticed his secretary Comps, whom he had taken with him to the meeting. Calling the young man, he requested him to bring a glass of lemonade. When Comps returned, Mirabeau thought it strange that he emerged from a side-door leading to a small cabinet, in which might have been seen the gloomy Lameth, looking more than ordinarily repulsive, and exchanging a few words with the secretary.

Shouts of joy issued from the hall, mingled with hisses. The chairman had read the result of the votes, and it was Mirabeau's name that stood foremost. The members rushed out to conduct him in triumph to the presidential chair. He quickly drank the lemonade, and then returned to the church, to receive the congratulations of his friends. "Mirabeau is president of the Jacobin Club!" was heard on every side.

"Who could have anticipated that I would on this day become King of the Jacobins!" said the count to himself, as he again ascended the tribune to express his thanks.

CHAPTER XLIII.

HENRIETTE.

MIRABEAU took up his residence in a palace in the Chausée d'Antin, the most beautiful quarter of Paris; he had bought this property at an extravagant price. He disposed of most of the articles of his former vagrant life, and the costly style now adopted indicated a permanent settlement. He displayed a taste for luxury such as he was little suspected to possess. His suites of apartments, in which art found a place for all that was beautiful, and the expensively-provided table, at which his numerous friends were daily feasted, asserted the position the count intended to hold in Paris. Nor did he neglect more intellectual

enjoyments, for he bought the large library of Buffon—a treasure which he hoped to enjoy in more quiet times. He had, however, lost something by this change in his circumstances—the society of his friends Yet-Lee and Coco, who until then were indispensable.

These companions were still dear to Mirabeau's heart, but he had to domicile them in a quiet street near the Luxembourg; the retirement and the salubrious walks in the neighboring gardens being the chief reasons for their removal. Madame de Nehra's illness had increased, and she was rapidly failing. An unusually brilliant light beamed in her eyes; her slender form was shattered by an incessant cough; her complexion became daily more transparent, and a fevered glow upon her cheeks too often heralded the rapid approach of death. Her association with Mirabeau resulted thus, for he did not sufficiently consider her delicate constitution, and, like a true and loving woman, she had sacrificed her comfort and health in accompanying him in all his wanderings and poverty.

Poor Henriette, at the time of the count's improved fortune, had withdrawn to the farthest corner of his sumptuous residence, in order not to disturb others; but she soon saw that her disease interrupted the happiness of all. This was the more painful to her, as Mirabeau was very irritable when disturbed in his few hours of sleep, and was often in no gentle mood with his suffering friend.

One morning Madame de Nehra entered the apartment where the count was dressing for breakfast. She appeared fresh and buoyant, while her manner indicated some firm purpose as well as an unbounded love. Mirabeau, who himself was beginning to suffer from nervous attacks, never before noticed in him, was startled by her appearance, but he kindly awaited her communication.

"Listen, Mirabeau," said Henriette, in a cheerful voice, but not wholly free from melancholy, "I have come to you with a petition—I wish you would dismiss me; for I am only a burden to you, giving you no rest night or day."

"What nonsense, Henriette!" replied the count, angrily. "I am not the man so to forsake a friend, especially on account of illness. Besides, what will become of me, if you leave me? What in the world has put such an idea into your head?"

"But hear me," resumed Madame de Nehra. "I know not what to do with my cough—I am not now fit to be seen in your beautiful apartments, and I know, my friend, that I greatly disturb you during the hours of the night. The great public movement you are controlling consumes your strength. If you do not take care of yourself, we lose you before your time—a loss that can never be supplied for the friends of liberty. And am I to be the unfortunate creature to deprive you of your necessary sleep? I ask you therefore to let me go. You will not be separated from me; my thoughts will turn continually to you, entreating you not to forget your Yet-Lee. And perhaps I may soon recover; my enemy may be conquered, and then I shall appeal to you for my old place in your heart and at your feet, and you will not reject me?" She ceased, and clung to him as she used to do in the first days of their love.

Looking at her musingly, and kissing her, the count said, "And whither will you go, if you leave me?"

"I should like to remain on your property," replied Henriette. "I have been thinking of the pretty little sunny dwelling opposite the garden of the Luxembourg, which you leased some time ago, but did not occupy because you were enabled to purchase this magnificent residence. As you are still paying rent for that small house, and I am as usual economical, I thought you might permit me to live there until I cease to cough. The sweet tranquillity of the neighborhood attracts me, and, as I can be of little more advantage to you, let me pass my few remaining days there. I shall not want much—the service of an old waiting-woman will be all I need."

Mirabeau silently paced the room several times. He looked pale and anxious, for a change had recently taken place in his whole appearance.

Then he said, with profound sadness: "Your words, though loving, awaken a melancholy sentiment within me that I cannot express, because I feel it too deeply. However, you must be conscious that my affection for you has never changed, even if I appeared to neglect you. I am borne on the waves of popular commotion, and who knows whither? One thing is certain: I cannot tell where I may live—whether I shall have a home or not, or whether I am to be the object of love or hate. We have started a revolution, and are continually occupied with it; and yet treason will be an accusation against many on both sides. We who mean honestly are driven by the force of circumstances, and must blindly obey. Such a man as myself, in my present circumstances, is no worthy object of love, and utterly unable to promote comfort or peace around him in his domestic relations.

"You are ill, poor Yet-Lee, and I cannot be of service, or minister to you as I would, with the tenderness of a father. I am even irritated with you when your cough disturbs my rest. Besides, I live in such a whirl of excitement, that no one can expect consideration where I am. The different factions hold their meetings here, and devour my time, my patience, and energies. I am constantly sent for; councils at all hours are held in my apartments; I am required to give breakfasts and dinners; I am dragged against my will to the hotels, and obliged to manœuvre from morning till evening to come to some result on the question of a republic or a monarchy, or both together. It is not hard to imagine, therefore, that the presence of yourself and Coco makes me feel sad. You are so out of your element, that I have often reflected what would become of you, until we could again live tranquilly together, away from the turmoil, the follies, and wickedness of political life. I have indeed sometimes thought that perhaps it would be better if we did temporarily separate; that you might take care of yourselves in retirement, until I could claim you again —you who are the happiness and glory of my life!"

Henriette pressed his hand to her lips, and

bathed it in her tears. "Ah," she exclaimed, "do our wishes again agree, dear friend?"

"Yes," he replied, looking embarrassed; "our hearts and minds were always in union, and we can never forsake each other. I will arrange the dwelling near the Luxembourg as comfortably as possible for you, and take charge of your household expenses; you need have no fear of want—you will be better off than myself in these uncertain and troubled days. You will have to take Coco with you, my good friend, for I know of no place where he could be safer: he loves you, and you have always devoted yourself to him with a mother's tenderness. With me, the boy would be ruined; and who knows what will become of me, in the conflicts growing daily more dangerous? With you is deposited forever the poetry of my life, and you will keep me in your memory. I consent to your removal, but on condition that I often see you. I must be permitted daily to pay my respects to the Countess Yet-Lee."

Henriette regained her cheerfulness, continuing the levity with which Mirabeau had skilfully concluded, but her sad smile betrayed the wounded heart. Coco came running from an adjoining room, and was highly delighted when told that he was henceforth to live with Madame de Nehra, near the beautiful garden of the Luxembourg, in which he was fond of playing. He was so happy that the count reminded him with some sensitiveness that he would then no longer remain with his father in the palace of the Chaussée d'Antin; but the boy did not seem disturbed in his pleasure at the contemplated change.

Several members of the National Assembly were announced, interrupting the conversation. Important matters were to come under discussion, both in the Convention and the Jacobin Club, and for a time the debates into which Mirabeau immediately entered buried in forgetfulness his domestic cares.

Henriette observed that the count busied himself on the following day with her removal, without being reminded of it, giving his orders to his secretary, M. Comps, and manifesting the greatest care for his two loved ones by noticing every detail for their comfort. He asked Cabanis to take charge of Madame de Nehra. The doctor had latterly renewed his relations with Mirabeau, particularly since the health of the latter began to fail in a very mysterious manner. Cabanis differed widely in his political views from the count, for the former was a radical republican, like Chamfort.

The hour approached when Henriette was to bid farewell to her friend. He would not admit by any means that it was a separation, and, with many humorous remarks and caresses, led her and Coco to the carriage, accompanying them himself to their new quarters. But Madame de Nehra could not consider her removal in any other light than that of a delicate breaking up of their former relations; and several times she stopped on the staircase to embrace the count with ejaculations of regret, looking at him tenderly and anxiously.

"My friend, if your opponents only refrain from doing you harm!" she whispered, repeatedly. "I am tortured by gloomy presentiments, as I leave your side, resigning my duty of watching over you, and discovering from your appearance whether you were well, and had escaped the snares of your enemies. I leave you with a heavy heart. I feel as if I ought to mourn more on your account than my own. What will they do to you? What will be the nature of their assault? How will they strike you?"

Mirabeau was about to reply jocosely, kissing her brow, when he shuddered, grew pale, and stumbled on the steps. "I fear that some evil has already befallen me, Henriette!" he said, placing his hand on his heart.

During the first few days, the count visited Madame de Nehra and Coco several times; but soon his attentions ceased altogether, and she would have heard little of him, if Dr. Cabanis and the faithful Chamfort had not brought her information.

CHAPTER XLIV.

THE POISON.

MIRABEAU'S vast physical strength seemed to have gradually been destroyed—a fact at last so plain as to lead to suspicion of foul play. His suffering commenced with violent attacks of fever and inflammation of the eyes, renewed from time to time, with intense pain. He was anxious chiefly on account of the swelling of his feet, and the spasms in his chest and arms. He was also tormented by an affection in the regions of the stomach, which made him despair of life. His muscular system, formerly of such power, became so weak that he often asked, with a sad smile, whether any one could tell him how he was so strangely transformed, as if into a nervous and hysterical woman. The most surprising change had taken place in his hair. Formerly his locks, as if instinct with life, waved around his ponderous head, but now they were spotted and torn, like leaves dead in the autumn winds.*

It was singular that he did not consent to receive the visits of Henriette and Coco. He felt himself so weak that, at the thought of again seeing them, the perspiration stood in drops on his forehead. Madame de Nehra, though herself on the brink of the grave, came every morning with the boy to the palace in the Chausée d'Antin, but always departed with a bowed head, and the little Coco did not repress expressions of disappointment and anger.

The daily habits of Mirabeau were of course changed by this unexplained illness, whose origin he vainly endeavored to discover. He was obliged to renounce all exercise—the practice of fencing, in which he indulged in his leisure moments, as well as the rides on his swift courser. Even the short distance from his residence to the session-hall of the National Assembly he could only pass over in a carriage, which was always surrounded by the people, with whom he was more popular than ever. He had been elected president of the Assembly by the votes of all parties, except those of the well-known thirty of the extreme left.

The count felt somewhat better one morning, and arose to finish a memorial intended for the king and queen; he was interrupted in the middle of a sentence by something like a sudden blow in his chest, and his eyes again became inflamed. With a sigh he tied on the bandage that prevented the bright daylight from increasing his sufferings, hoping to be able to continue his labors after a short rest. He toyed with the inkstand, representing some antique figure, and set with precious stones; but at last he pushed it from him in despair. His pains became intolerable, and, tearing the bandage off, he walked up and down, as if haunted by the Furies.

Count de la Marck was announced; he entered softly, and made kind inquiries. Mirabeau sank into an easy-chair, pointing to a seat beside him for his friend, who always had some word of consolation that the disease was but a natural consequence of over-exertion.

"I am of opinion," said La Marck, "that your intense labor, as president of the National Assembly, has affected your health. And, permit me to say, it is conceded on all sides that such position has never been filled in so distinguished a manner, either in France or England, and you have added additional lustre to your name. You satisfy all parties by your dignity, grace, and justice, throwing light upon every question; and you establish order, where no other man could succeed; one word calms all tumult. And, moreover, you take part in the debates. Yesterday, notwithstanding your evident physical pain, you spoke five times on one subject. My dear friend, this will not do; you exact too much from yourself, and I have come to propose that you ask a few weeks' leave of absence from the Convention. It is our great object to keep you alive! We have no other man on whose shoulders we could lay the welfare of France and of the monarchy!"

"It is not that, my friend," replied Mirabeau. "Work is mere play to me, always increasing in-

---

* Cabanis, "Journal de la Maladie et de la Mort de H. G. Riquetti de Mirabeau," p. 238. (At the end of the work: "Du Degré de Certitude de la Médecine.")

stead of weakening my power; but something is tormenting my chest and stomach. If I could believe such a thing possible, I would declare that a slow poison had been administered to me. I feel that I am fast dying—as if placed over a fire increasing in intensity every day. " *

"For Heaven's sake, how can you have such thoughts!" exclaimed La Marck, seizing his friend's hands. "I am as sure of it as I am of my existence, that no one in France has either the courage or the motive to injure in any way the best man in the country!"

"I do not know that," rejoined Mirabeau. "But some enemy, it is certain, is within me, drying up the fountains of my life."

"This is a fine March day," resumed La Marck, in a soft voice. "We have seldom had so warm a spring. My equipage is below—let us drive to the Marais, the property you bought near Argenteuil. A few hours in the fresh air among your fields will do you good. I am sure the time you pass in our new session-hall is deleterious to your health: since we began to assemble in the small, damp Salle de Manège, we are nearly all ill; some of the most robust members of the assembly are suffering with inflammation of the eyes and fever, in the same manner as yourself."

"You are amiable, Count de la Marck!" replied Mirabeau, smiling sorrowfully. "But I can undertake nothing to-day; and I have a thorough dislike to the Marais. I had an attack of colic while there, during which I expected to die. If I regain my strength at all, I mean to finish these notes to the king; they will probably be the last he receives from me. I confess to you that I become daily more dissatisfied with the demeanor of the monarch, and I shall be glad when my engagement with him ends. He has not acted on my advice in a single instance, however necessary I represented it. That Necker has been dismissed we owe to the urgency of the National Assembly. May he slumber at his Coppet as a deceased financier!

"But what is to become of the monarchy, if Louis XVI. continues in this indecision, so unworthy of a true man? Indignant at his conduct, I have sent him no reports for several days; as soon as I feel a little better, I will speak my mind for the last time! Truly with a strong arm the king ought to oppose this assembly, that already wears the red cap over one ear. If the Convention cannot bridle its vain and overbearing passion, it must be dissolved; and the electors so influenced that they send other deputies, with sound views concerning the monarchy and the regulation of state affairs. If this cannot soon be done, all is lost. I again repeat, that both their majesties will be dragged dead through the streets! It is true, life is not worth much: am I not one of the first that falls beneath the sickle of Fate?" *

Mirabeau was so exhausted that La Marck asked to be dismissed, and his friend sank into slumber. The door was hastily opened, and Mirabeau's sister, the Marchioness de Saillant, entered with her two younger daughters. She had heard of her brother's ill-health, and hastened to Paris. The count awoke surprised, but when he saw who it was he became quite cheerful.

Madame de Saillant, embracing him tenderly but with anxiety, said: "My brother, we must keep a stricter watch upon your servants. Another present of wines and liquors from unknown persons has arrived; and notwithstanding my orders that they should be poured out of the window, your steward has kept them. Lately a cup of coffee was sent to you from the neighborhood, ostensibly from a poor woman, who wished to show her sympathy for the great Mirabeau. One of the inmates of your house tasted the beverage, and was seized with vomiting. We have a legion of enemies to combat, and we must guard your precious life!"

"I know you are troubled on my account," replied her brother, smiling. "But calm yourself, I pray you. I am already mortally wounded, or I am invulnerable. I am informed that you have ordered your son to sleep armed in the room adjoining my cabinet. It is true, I have many

---

* Mirabeau's words.—Dumont, "Souvenirs," p. 226.

* La Marck, vol. i., pp. 218, 224.

foes. The extreme party, who are nothing now, and hope to become every thing after my death, are interested in shortening my life; they have even attacked me in the street; but every ball does not reach its object—all may yet be well with me.*—And now go, children," he added, softly. "Permit me, however, to press one farewell kiss on the blooming cheeks of my nieces."

The two young ladies approached him, and, as the count bent over them, he said, with a tremor: "Thus death embraces life!"

Dumont and Clavière were now announced. Madame de Saillant permitted this visit on condition that the gentlemen came only to see and not to converse with her brother. With this understanding they entered, manifesting a profound sympathy. Dumont wished to take leave, intending to return to Geneva. Mirabeau shook his friend's hand, saying; "I have not yet been able to do any thing for your native city. The time given me has been shortened, and now I am about to seek a new fatherland, of whose constitution and government I am ignorant." Dumont's eyes were filled with tears. "And you, my strong Clavière, who seem to be made of iron, do you still think that the assignats we drew on the confiscated church property will assist in making every one partisans of the revolution?"

"My dear friend," replied Clavière, with a trembling voice, and an unusual softness of manner, "at present I am concerned about you only, for without you I care nothing for the subversion of governments. I have often been your opponent, secretly and openly, but your powerful influence, restraining the court and the Jacobins at the same time, has become a necessity! You are our guiding-star; when you expire, we stumble. Preserve your life to us, Mirabeau!"

The count made a motion with his hand; he could not endure longer the presence of his friends, and both Genevans silently left the apartment. Other visitors afterward appeared, and among them his old friend Cabanis, whom he longed to see. He seemed to be infused with new life when Cabanis was announced, and immediately rose to meet his beloved physician, who, although of a different political creed, had never seriously come into collision with the count, keeping himself in comparative retirement from the troubles convulsing the country. The doctor was in company with Chamfort and Condorcet, whose presence greatly excited Mirabeau, for he had not seen them for a long time, and he might have supposed them maliciously inclined. They looked as kindly upon him as if he had but lately conversed with them in the old familiar style. The unforgotten past saluted him in Chamfort's eyes; and from his lips he fancied he heard again the misanthropic jests, and the humanity-loving philosophy of other days. Mirabeau would have embraced him, but Chamfort, overwhelmed by the change in the count's appearance, did not appear to notice the movement toward him. Mirabeau ardently saluted the calm Condorcet, whose usual stoicism of manner gave way to sympathy, from the moment of his entrance.

Cabanis inquired anxiously about his friend's health, asking what effect his medicines had. Observing no improvement, the physician lost himself in melancholy musing.

Mirabeau essayed to relieve the unpleasant silence by commencing a conversation. "Do we really at last have a revival of our former friendly intercourse, belonging as we do to different camps?" he asked. "I know you desire a republic. Even Cabanis inclines to that; and, after my death, I have no doubt he will become a sturdy partisan of the extremists. However, you do not belong to those who think it necessary to hate me. I desire a monarchy, but one that cannot conflict with the interests of honor or of liberty. Only yesterday I declared to an influential friend that, if the king follows the advice of certain persons at court, and betakes himself to flight, I shall declare the throne vacant, and the republic inaugurated!" *

"Only remain, Mirabeau!" said Chamfort, in a

low voice. "Your exertions alone can satisfactorily settle the question about a royal or a free government. You must not die, for, after your departure, men from whom we turn with abhorrence will fancy themselves heroes, and then indeed all is ruined."

"Yes!" exclaimed the count, shuddering. "When I go I take with me sorrow for the destruction of the monarchy—the parties will fight for its remains."* A solemn pause succeeded these words. "My friends," resumed Mirabeau, almost cheerfully, "I feel as if we were still enjoying the same intimacy as when we used to meet in the drawing-rooms of Madame Helvetius at Auteuil, frankly exchanging our opinions. How is that dear old intellectual lady? Why does she not send me a pigeon-post from her aviary, to bring me her regards?"

"She will visit you herself," replied Chamfort.

A deputation of the National Guards were announced. When Madame de Saillant declared it impossible to admit them, they sent in a message to the effect that Mirabeau was elected their chief of battalion. He smilingly contemplated the sash sent him as a sign of his new office, placing it beside the other evidences of honor which were of late frequently presented him.

The report of a cannon was heard. "Are they already beginning the funeral ceremonies of Achilles?" asked Mirabeau, breathing heavily. His friends soon after took leave of him, for he needed solitude and rest.

CHAPTER XLV.

THE DEATH OF MIRABEAU.

THE morning of the 1st of April, 1791, dawned bright and balmy, bringing with it the voice of birds, and the flowery promises of spring. Mirabeau had passed the night under the watchful care of Cabanis, who had a temporary bed near

that of his dying friend; but the doctor could not sleep, for sometimes violent convulsions weakened his patient, and again came a sudden suspension of breath, followed by a rattling in his throat and intense suffering. On the preceding day the count's consent was at length obtained, in accordance with Cabanis's wishes, to consult Dr. Le Petit. Henriette, languishing on her sickbed, sent letters, urging Mirabeau to engage that skilful physician, having herself been greatly assisted by his skill, since Cabanis was wholly occupied with his old companion. Coco had delivered her communications, and by his tears showed how well he understood the condition of his great father.

Both physicians agreed that Mirabeau's system had somehow absorbed poison, but the manner in which he ought to be treated was by no means clear. When the count asked Dr. Le Petit to tell him frankly what his prospect of life was, the doctor replied that no hopes could be reasonably entertained of recovery. Mirabeau immediately made his will in presence of La Marck, who requested him to mention the legacies he desired at once paid, and that, if the testator's fortune did not suffice, he himself would advance what was needed. This offer was recognized with a grateful glance. The largest bequests were for Madame de Nehra and Coco, but the former could scarcely hope to outlive the count.

On this sunny spring morning, Mirabeau arose with surprising alacrity, and Cabanis, silently wondering, followed him to the window, which the dying man opened, so that the sun might shine in the chamber. His movements seemed like those in the days of his strength and activity; but his face had for days given signs of speedy death. "My friend," he said, with a firm voice, "I die to-day! When one comes so near his transition, he need only be lulled by sweet music, and have his couch sprinkled with flowers, to pass away as in a pleasant dream to that slumber from which he never awakes!"*

Cabanis endeavored to prevent the count from

---

* "J'emporte dans mon cœur le deuil de la monarchie dont les débris vont être la proie des factieux."

* Cabanis, "Journal de la Maladie de Mirabeau," p. 306.

exposure to the cool breeze. "Oh," he replied, "you are a great physician, but there is one greater than you—the Creator of the wind, that plays with the rose and uproots the pine; of the water, that penetrates and fructifies; of the fire, that quickens and destroys. Call Him by what name you please —but this morning He decides my destiny, and makes me happy!"

Seated in his easy-chair, the count looked smilingly out into his garden, where the sun in its splendor was beaming upon the trees bursting into leaf and flower. "See, Cabanis," he said, "if that is not God Himself, it is certainly a good representative."

Mirabeau then sent for his valet de chambre, and ordered him to array his master in the richest toilet, such as he had not worn for a long time. When he was dressed his countenance seemed to say that he had fulfilled a duty and was satisfied, but death had placed his seal upon his brow and there was no escape. He had a singular yearning to behold the human countenance, and begged Cabanis to admit all who came to see him.

The first announcement was the royal messenger. The king had sent regularly every morning to inquire after the count's health, and on this day did not fail. When once more alone with his physician, he said: "I pity Louis XVI. from my heart. It pains me to think of him—he is abandoned and betrayed; among all those who surround him there is but one brave friend, and that is his wife!" [*]

A deputation from the Jacobin Club came next, to express their sympathy. The count hesitated a moment, but requested their admission. At their head was Barnave, who was so moved that he could not suppress his grief. Mirabeau felt that he had perhaps not always done justice to this opponent in the heat of debate and party passion; he held out his hand, and Barnave could utter but few words.

"Ah," said Mirabeau, "I am almost sorry to leave life, since I find a friend so unexpectedly!" [†] Then he looked searchingly at the rest of the dep-

uties. "I am sure you all came with a willing heart," he said, saluting them. Presently he noticed that Alexandre Lameth was not among them, who was always considered his most violent enemy. "I know not why it is, but I should like to have seen my honorable opponent Lameth here," he said, looking anxiously around. "Did he refuse to come?"

"He felt a disinclination that we could not remove," replied Pétion. "The club selected him to visit you, but he refused."

"Well," said Mirabeau, "I knew he was a strong party man, but I now discover that he is also a fool." The feeling that thus overcame his mind in his last moments cast a dark and vengeful shadow on his face.

The next visitor surprised him. It was Talleyrand, the Bishop of Autun, who was acting as president of the National Assembly, and who came on their behalf as well as from his own personal regard.

"Three times daily I have tried to gain access to you, my dear friend!" said Talleyrand, taking Mirabeau's hand, with a graceful expression of sorrow. "But it was impossible in my carriage to reach you through the crowds around your house, so I was forced to be contented with the reports in the street respecting your health. The people are publishing printed bulletins about you; they are found at all public places in Paris.[*] It is dreadful to think that you are so ill; but if it is any consolation to be 'an event,' you may enjoy it to the utmost. It is of vast importance to all France that your health suffers. I notice that the citizens have barricaded the streets near your residence, that you might not be disturbed by the passage of vehicles."

"I am sorry you had to walk a part of the way," said Mirabeau, smiling. "But I thank you for your visit, and wish to be at peace with you before my departure; for I hurt your feelings once unintentionally. I am glad that the people throng around my house until my last breath. Ah, Talleyrand, they have deep feeling—they are

---

* "Le roi n'a qu'un homme, c'est sa femme."
† Fissot, vol. ii., p. 284.

* Montigny, vol. viii., p. 435.

worthy of our service, and that we do all in our power to make them free and happy It was my boast that I was useful to them during my life, and I feel how sweet it is to die in the midst of their loving sympathy." *

"You have no time to die," replied the bishop. "The weal of France depends on you!"

"You will live longer than I," said Mirabeau, calmly. "You will have much to perform in the world, and all material will be plastic in your hands. If ever you think of me, let it be your earnest endeavor to effect a close alliance between our country and England; in this union lies the only guaranty for the liberty and civilization of the nations of the present day. This is my political testament, and I appoint you executor of it, as I have taken the liberty to do in other respects." †

Talleyrand kissed the dying count three times on the cheek, saying that his emotion would not permit him to remain, and, promising to return on the following day, he quickly departed.

Soon after Count de la Marck entered, requesting a private interview. Cabanis retired into an adjoining room, and La Marck began about a matter which had been spoken of a few days before. Mirabeau knew what it was, and was ready with his answer: "Your solicitude is well founded. I have a number of papers by whose publication many persons would be most dangerously compromised, particularly those whom I would gladly save from any embarrassment. The wisest plan would be to destroy all those letters, but I cannot find courage for that, for they must justify my actions to posterity. I deliver them therefore to you, that you may disappoint our enemies, who are already waiting for them. You must promise me, however, that, if necessary, you will publish them in future; for it is reserved to your friendship thus to defend my memory!" ‡

La Marck solemnly gave his hand to Mirabeau, receiving a key from him which opened a secret drawer of a closet, where were found the papers

referred to, carefully arranged and bound up, which he put into his pocket.

While the two friends were still engaged in their confidential conversation, Mirabeau did not observe that near the door of his apartment were several men and women, grouping themselves silently, not venturing to approach until he should request them. When he became aware of their presence, he rose and looked at them with surprise, while some were moving toward him.

"Who are you?" he said. "Oh, I know you —those dearest to me during life. Are you there, Yet-Lee, my sweet friend? How pale you are! You have left your sick-bed to bring me the last greeting of your eyes. And that is Coco, whom you are leading by the hand. Ah, you are Mirabeau's 'tribe!' Farewell to both of you, farewell!" Henriette stretched her arm toward him with an agonizing cry, but he motioned her away.

"And there are Chamfort and Condorcet! and yonder the Abbé Cerutti, who has a good heart with an eloquent tongue!" continued Mirabeau, looking at each as he named him. "You must preach my funeral sermon, Cerutti. Will you do so?" The abbé replied by a grave and sorrowful gesture.

"Ah, and there is my old faithful friend, Madame Helvetius!" he resumed, bowing to the lady, who was standing in tears in a corner of the room, holding the arm of Cabanis.

"And who is that page?" he asked again. La Marck whispered that the queen had sent the boy to inform herself of the count's health and express her sympathy. "Oh, the queen!" he repeated. "I would gladly lose my life to save hers!"

The dying man's eye rested upon Madame de Saillant, who now entered with another lady, clothed in black. "There is my sister!" he exclaimed. "We always loved each other with great fidelity. And who is that with you?" He recognized his former wife, who saluted him from a distance in a reverential manner. He motioned his hand toward her, expressing his reconciliation.

Mirabeau began now to totter; Cabanis and Chamfort assisted him back to his seat. "And

---

* Cabanis, p. 297.
† Montigny, vol. viii., p. 459.
‡ La Marck, vol. i., p. 956.

have you all come to crown me with the wreath of death?" he said, after a pause, in a very changed voice. "When I arose this morning I asked for music and flowers, and now you come to adorn me with the garland of love, and your farewell is sweet though sad music to my ears! Receive my thanks!" He was seized with spasms, complained of a strong pulsation, as of blows, in his head, and requested his physicians to give him opium. He spoke no more. Mirabeau was dead!

An incident occurring in Mirabeau's house on the day of his death confirmed the suspicions awakened in reference to his illness and its fatal result. The count's secretary was found in the garret, where he had made an attempt to hang himself. Some persons saw him ascend the stairs crying in great agony: "Poison! poison! What a crime!" He was recalled to life, but pretended insanity, so as to avoid giving further information; but his secret connection with the Jacobins, and particularly with Alexandre Lameth, made him suspected.

The reports increasing, and for the most part believed, induced the state attorney to insist on a post-mortem examination of the body. Four of the physicians decided that poison was found in the system; four others were as certain that no trace of any thing of the kind was present; but these considered it their duty to reconcile all parties, or at least not to render them more bitter against each other. Mirabeau's family never had the least doubt that he was poisoned.

The funeral procession gathered all ranks and parties—the members of the assembly, the royal troops, the citizen guards, and the people generally. The coffin, decorated with military insignia and a civic crown, and preceded by priests chanting hymns of sorrow, was borne by twelve of the National Guards and four members of the Convention. Next, was carried the heart of the beloved patriot. The National Assembly and the whole Jacobin Club followed, with the exception of one or two. The Abbé Cerutti delivered the funeral sermon in the church of St. Geneviève, where his remains were at first deposited.

On the old monk's altar, in the session-hall of the Jacobins, might have been long seen the bust of Mirabeau by the side of that of Rousseau and Helvetius; and, at the request of the department of Paris, his body, soon after disinterred, was the first entombed within the walls of the Pantheon.

THE END.